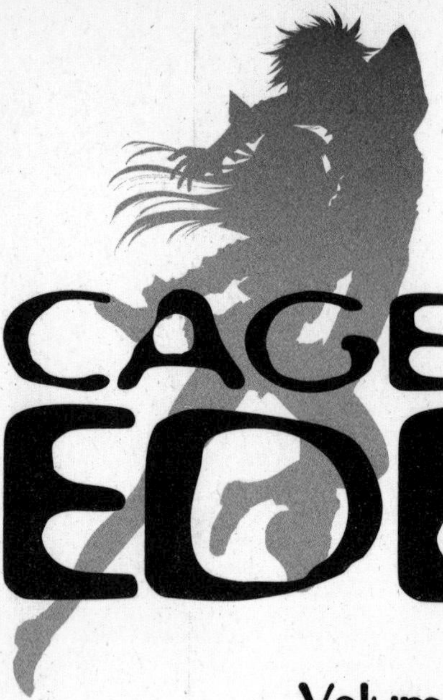

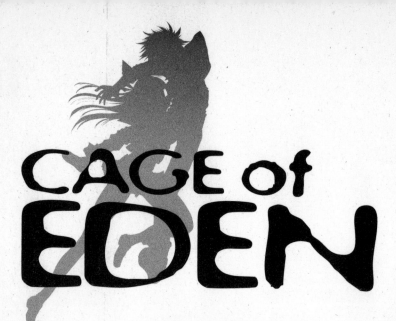

CAGE of EDEN

Volume 1

Yoshinobu Yamada

Translation by
Mari Morimoto

Lettered by
North Market Street Graphics

KC
KODANSHA COMICS

Cage of Eden volume 1 is a work of fiction. Names, characters, places, and incidents are the products of the author's imagination or are used fictitiously. Any resemblance to actual events, locales, or persons, living or dead, is entirely coincidental.

A Kodansha Comics Trade Paperback Original

Cage of Eden volume 1 copyright © 2009 Yoshinobu Yamada

English translation copyright © 2011 Yoshinobu Yamada

All rights reserved.

Published in the United States by Kodansha Comics, an imprint of Kodansha USA Publishing, LLC, New York.

Publication rights for this English edition arranged through Kodansha Ltd., Tokyo.

First published in Japan in 2009 by Kodansha Ltd., Tokyo as *Eden no Ori*, volume 1.

ISBN 978-1-935429-25-8

Printed in the United States of America

www.kodanshacomics.com

9 8 7 6 5 4 3 2 1

Translator: Mari Morimoto
Lettering: North Market Street Graphics

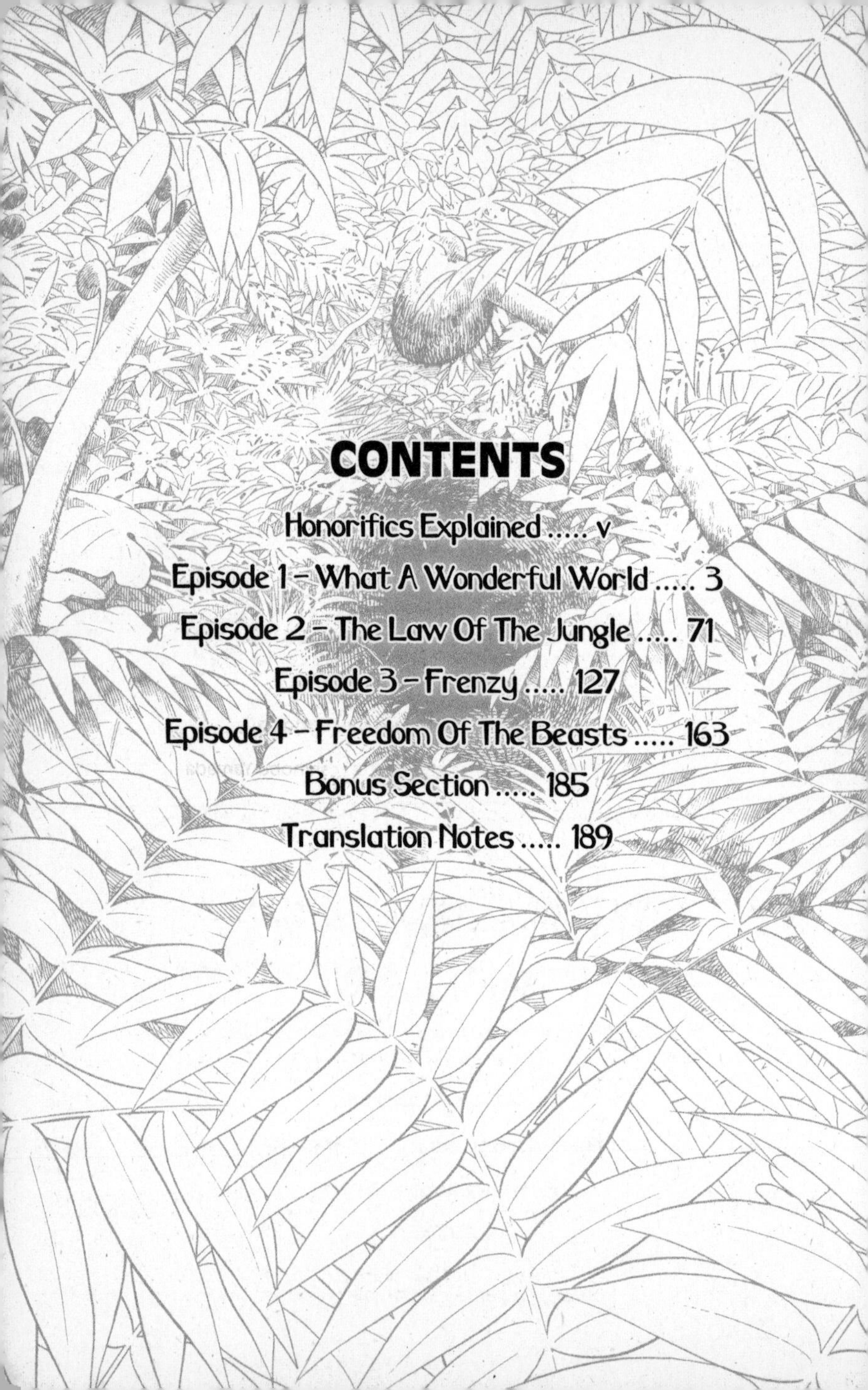

CONTENTS

HONORIFICS EXPLAINED

Throughout the Kodansha Comics books, you will find Japanese honorifics left intact in the translations. For those not familiar with how the Japanese use honorifics and, more important, how they differ from American honorifics, we present this brief overview.

Politeness has always been a critical facet of Japanese culture. Ever since the feudal era, when Japan was a highly stratified society, use of honorifics—which can be defined as polite speech that indicates relationship or status—has played an essential role in the Japanese language. When addressing someone in Japanese, an honorific usually takes the form of a suffix attached to one's name (example: "Asuna-san"), is used as a title at the end of one's name, or appears in place of the name itself (example: "Negi-sensei," or simply "Sensei!").

Honorifics can be expressions of respect or endearment. In the context of manga and anime, honorifics give insight into the nature of the relationship between characters. Many English translations leave out these important honorifics and therefore distort the feel of the original Japanese. Because Japanese honorifics contain nuances that English honorifics lack, it is our policy at Kodansha Comics not to translate them. Here, instead, is a guide to some of the honorifics you may encounter in Kodansha Comics books.

-san: This is the most common honorific and is equivalent to Mr., Miss, Ms., or Mrs. It is the all-purpose honorific and can be used in any situation where politeness is required.

-sama: This is one level higher than "-san" and is used to confer great respect.

-dono: This comes from the word "tono," which means "lord." It is an even higher level than "-sama" and confers utmost respect.

-kun: This suffix is used at the end of boys' names to express familiarity or endearment. It is also sometimes used by men among friends, or when addressing someone younger or of a lower station.

-chan: This is used to express endearment, mostly toward girls. It is also used for little boys, pets, and even among lovers. It gives a sense of childish cuteness.

Bozu: This is an informal way to refer to a boy, similar to the English terms "kid" and "squirt."

Sempai/ Senpai:	This title suggests that the addressee is one's senior in a group or organization. It is most often used in a school setting, where underclassmen refer to their upperclassmen as "sempai." It can also be used in the workplace, such as when a newer employee addresses an employee who has seniority in the company.
Kohai:	This is the opposite of "sempai" and is used toward underclassmen in school or newcomers in the workplace. It connotes that the addressee is of a lower station.
Sensei:	Literally meaning "one who has come before," this title is used for teachers, doctors, or masters of any profession or art.
-[blank]:	This is usually forgotten in these lists, but it is perhaps the most significant difference between Japanese and English. The lack of honorific means that the speaker has permission to address the person in a very intimate way. Usually, only family, spouses, or very close friends have this kind of permission. Known as *yobisute*, it can be gratifying when someone who has earned the intimacy starts to call one by one's name without an honorific. But when that intimacy hasn't been earned, it can be very insulting.

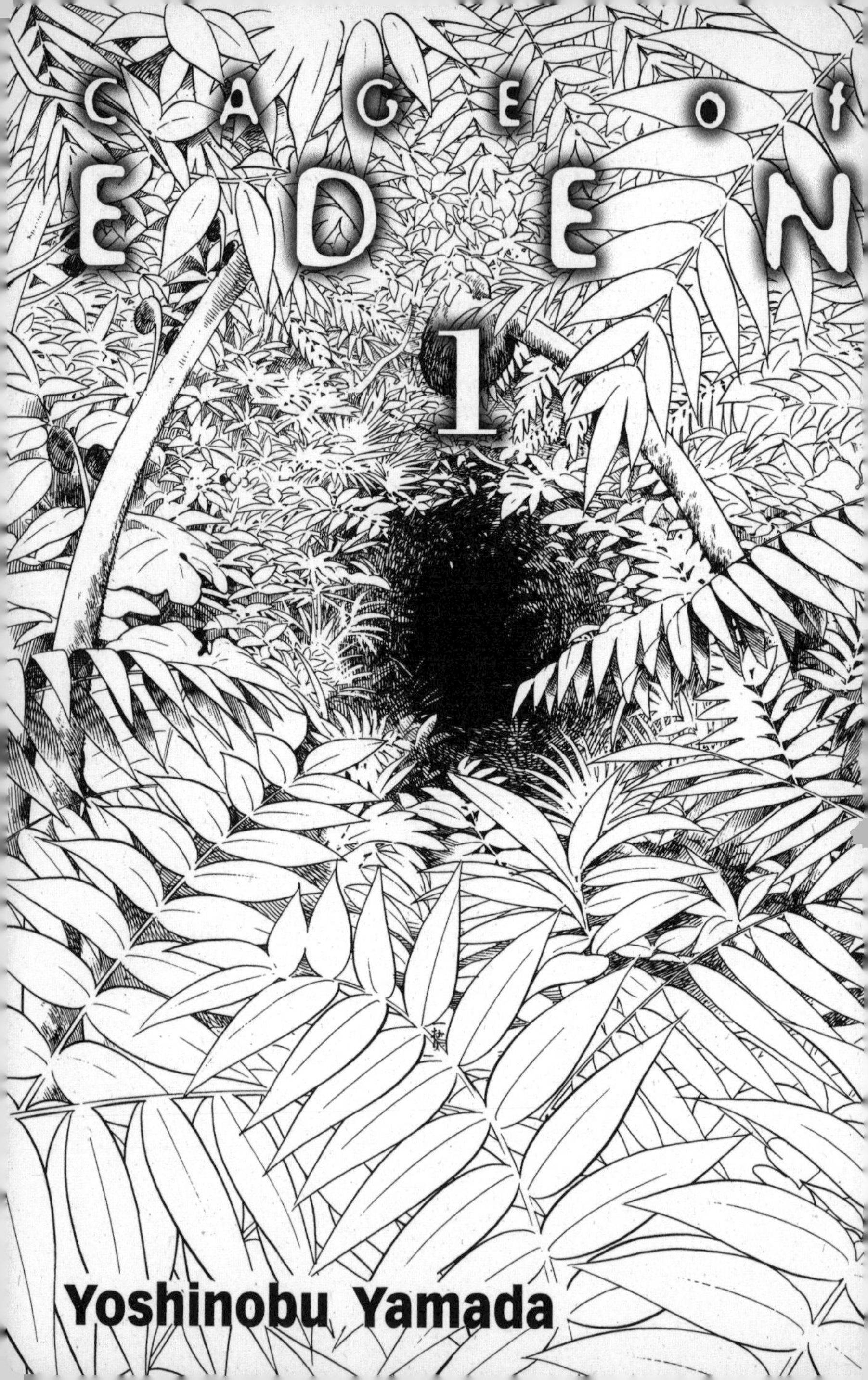
CAGE of
EDEN
1
Yoshinobu Yamada

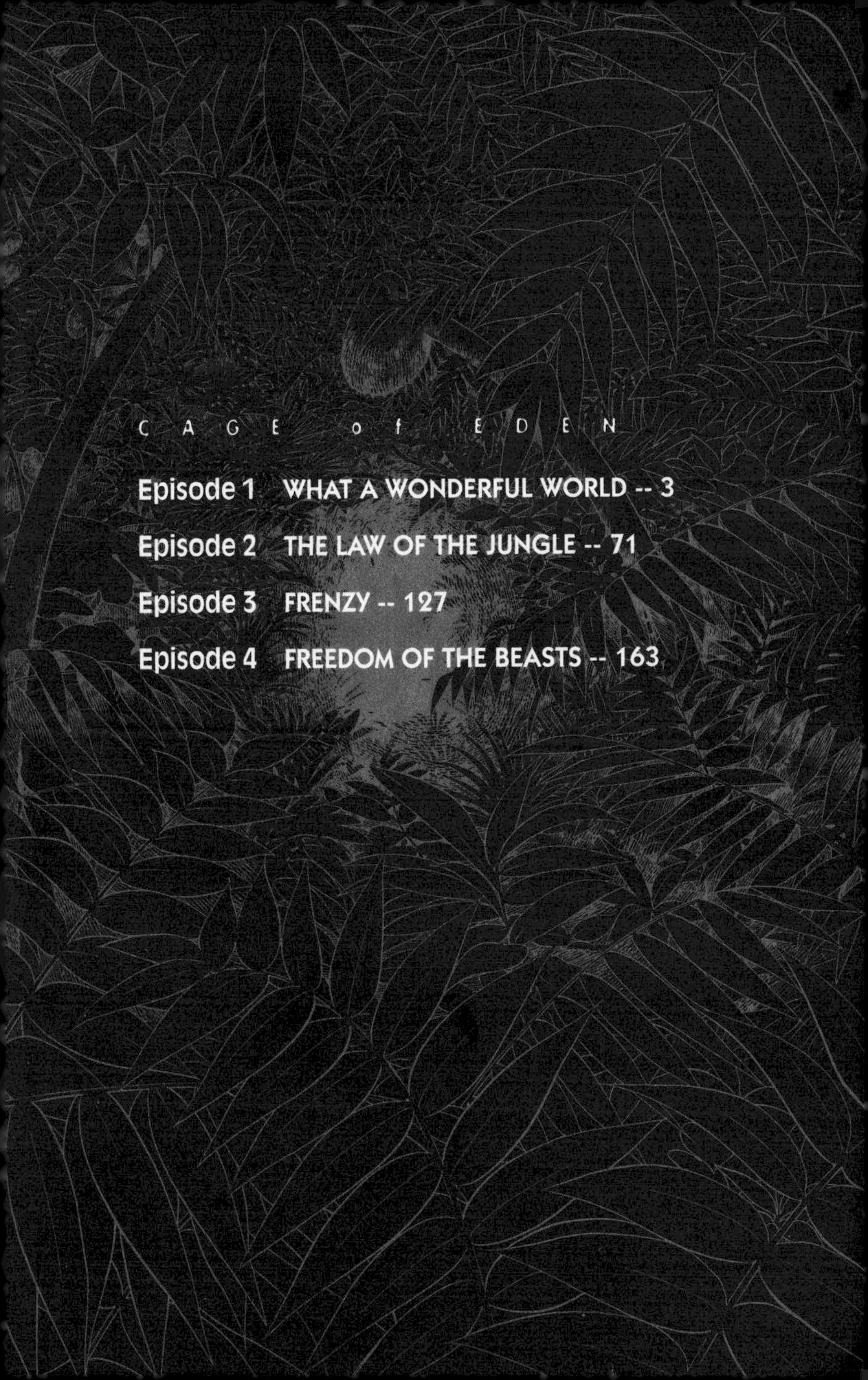

CAGE of EDEN

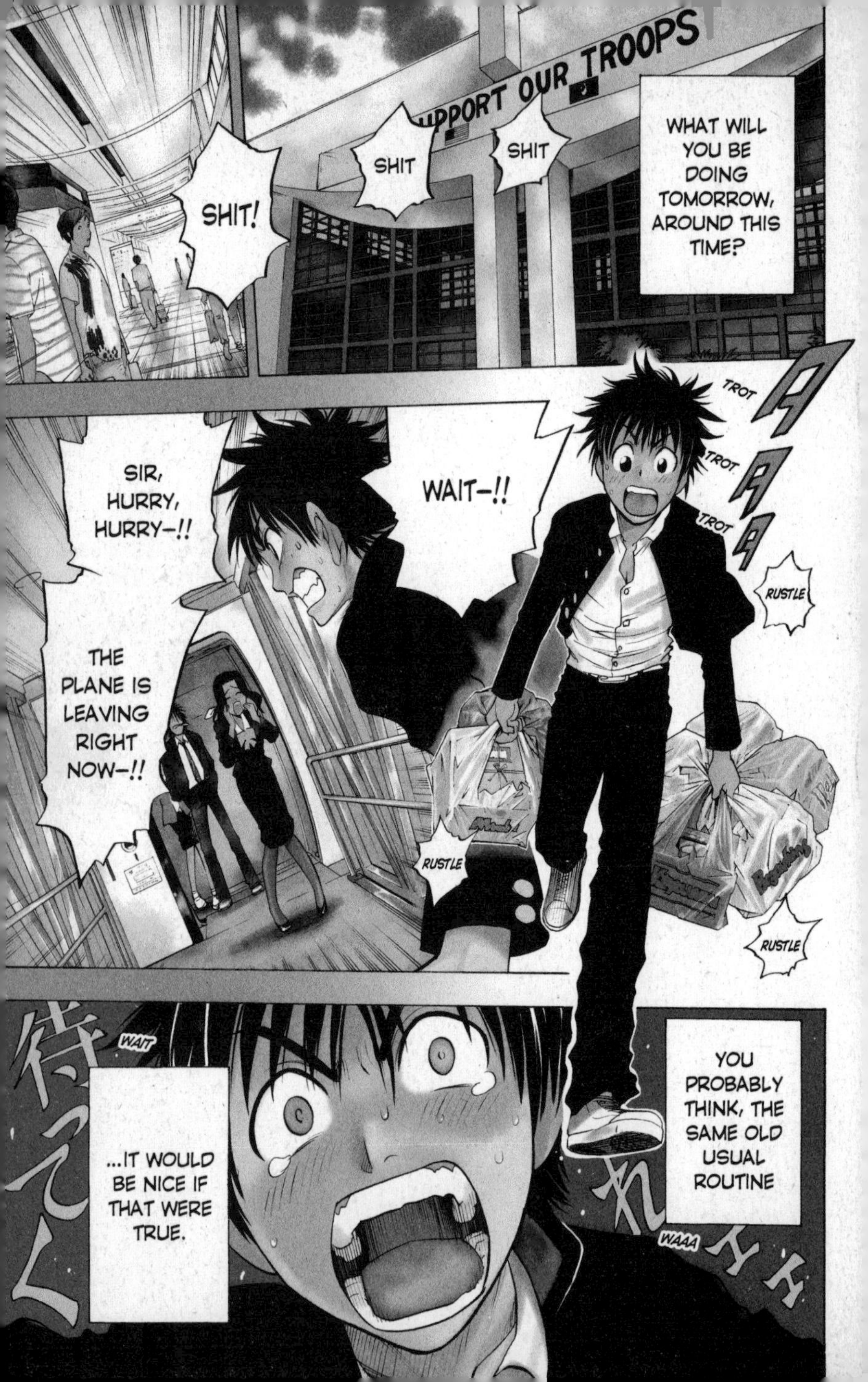
SUPPORT OUR TROOPS
WHAT WILL YOU BE DOING TOMORROW, AROUND THIS TIME?
SHIT
SHIT
SHIT!
TROT
TROT
TROT
RUSTLE
RUSTLE
RUSTLE
WAIT-!!
SIR, HURRY, HURRY-!!
THE PLANE IS LEAVING RIGHT NOW-!!
YOU PROBABLY THINK, THE SAME OLD USUAL ROUTINE
WAAA
WAIT
...IT WOULD BE NICE IF THAT WERE TRUE.

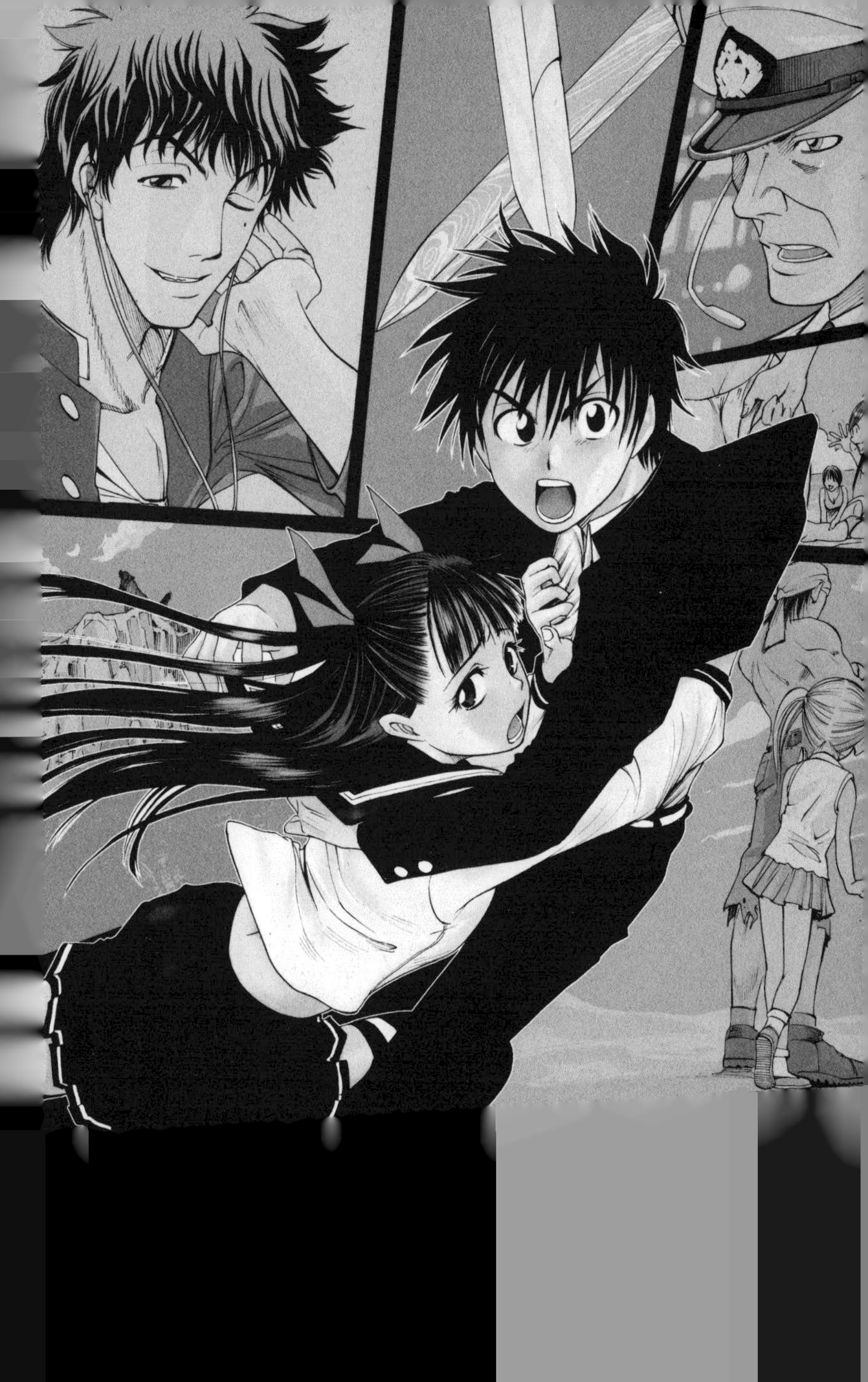

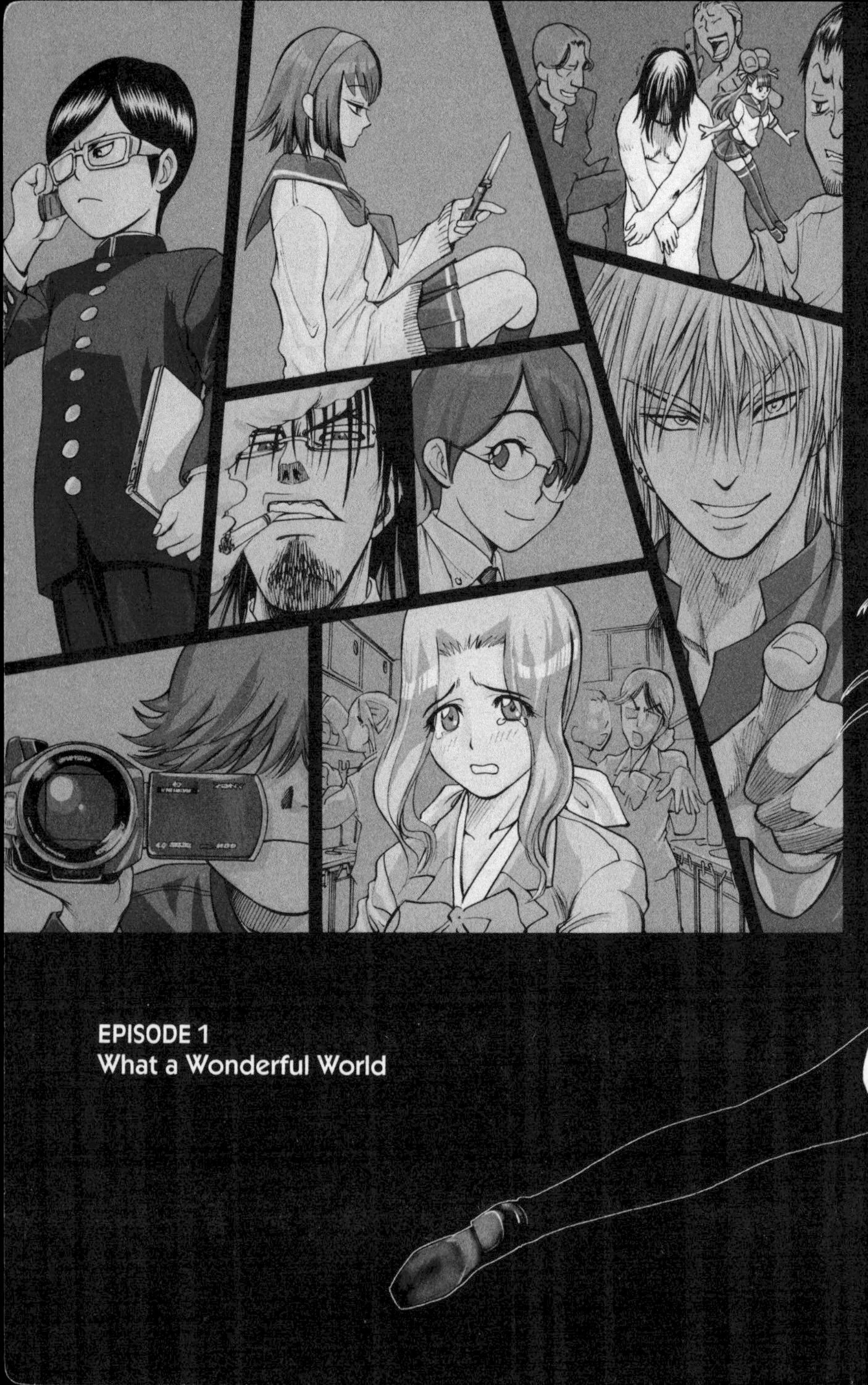

EPISODE 1
What a Wonderful World

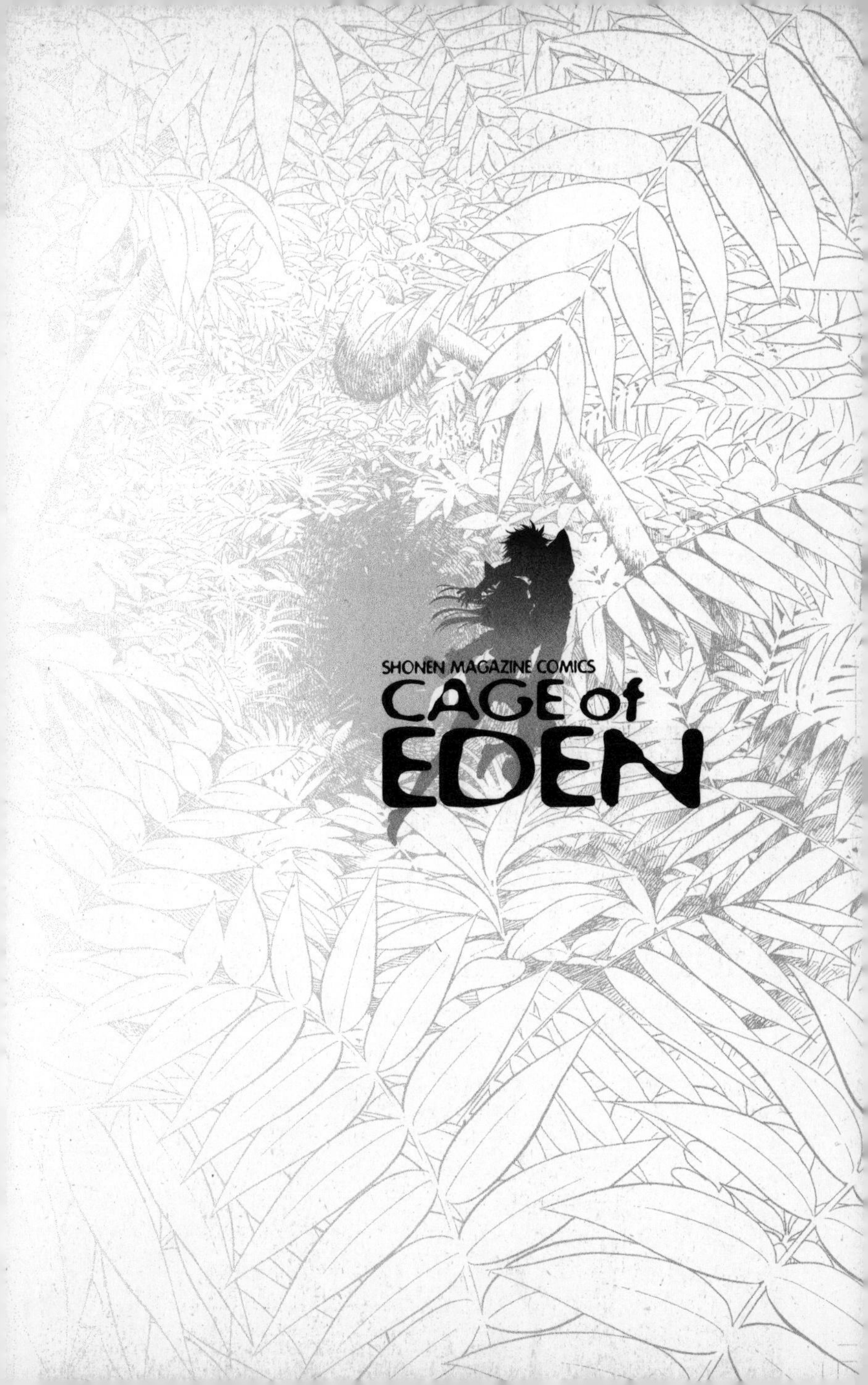
SHONEN MAGAZINE COMICS
CAGE of
EDEN

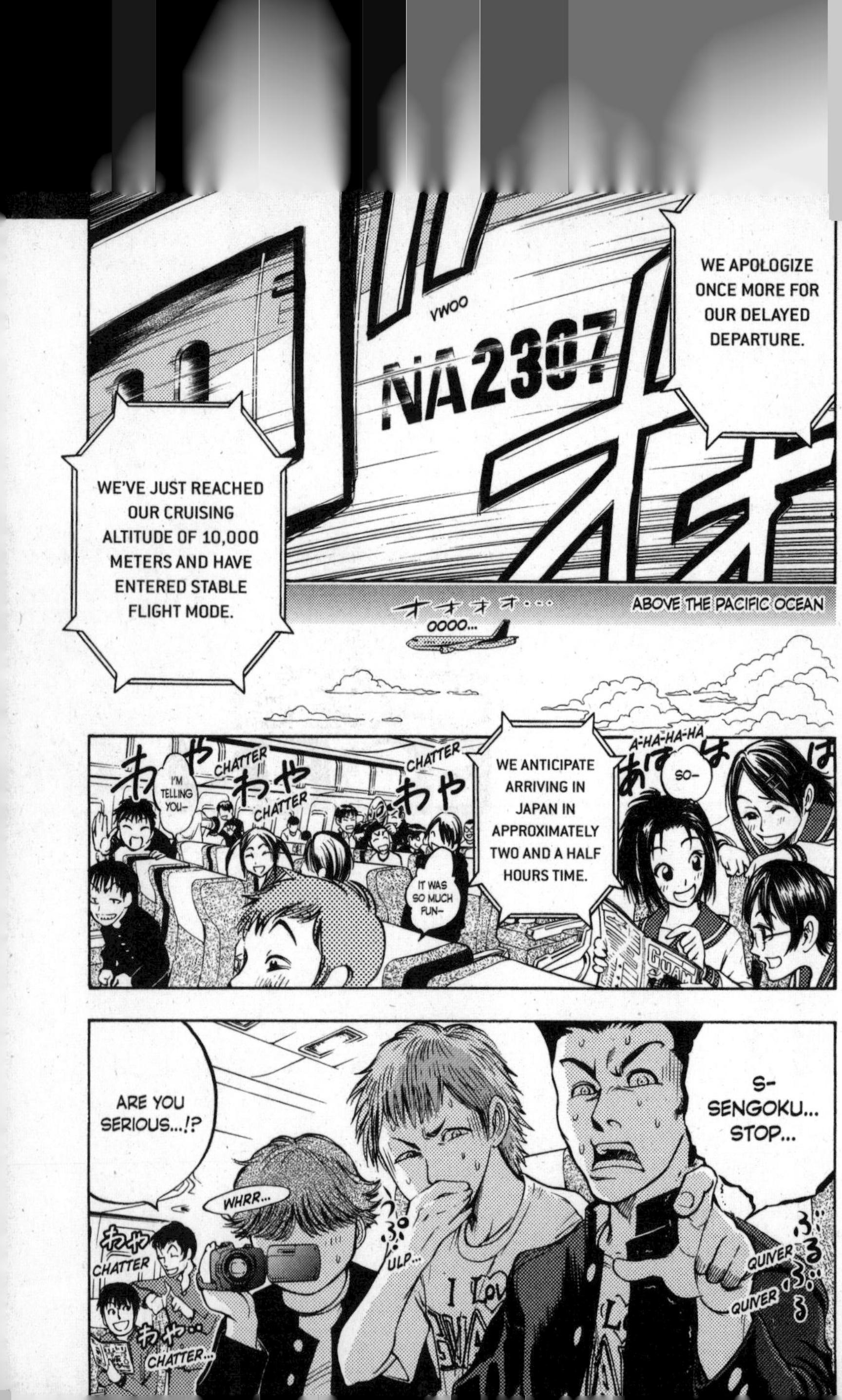

WE APOLOGIZE ONCE MORE FOR OUR DELAYED DEPARTURE.
VWOO
NA2307
オオ
WE'VE JUST REACHED OUR CRUISING ALTITUDE OF 10,000 METERS AND HAVE ENTERED STABLE FLIGHT MODE.
オオオオ…
OOOO...
ABOVE THE PACIFIC OCEAN
A-HA-HA-HA
SO-
WE ANTICIPATE ARRIVING IN JAPAN IN APPROXIMATELY TWO AND A HALF HOURS TIME.
IT WAS SO MUCH FUN-
CHATTER
CHATTER
I'M TELLING YOU-
CHATTER
S-SENGOKU... STOP...
QUIVER
QUIVER
ULP...
WHRR...
ARE YOU SERIOUS...!?
CHATTER
CHATTER...

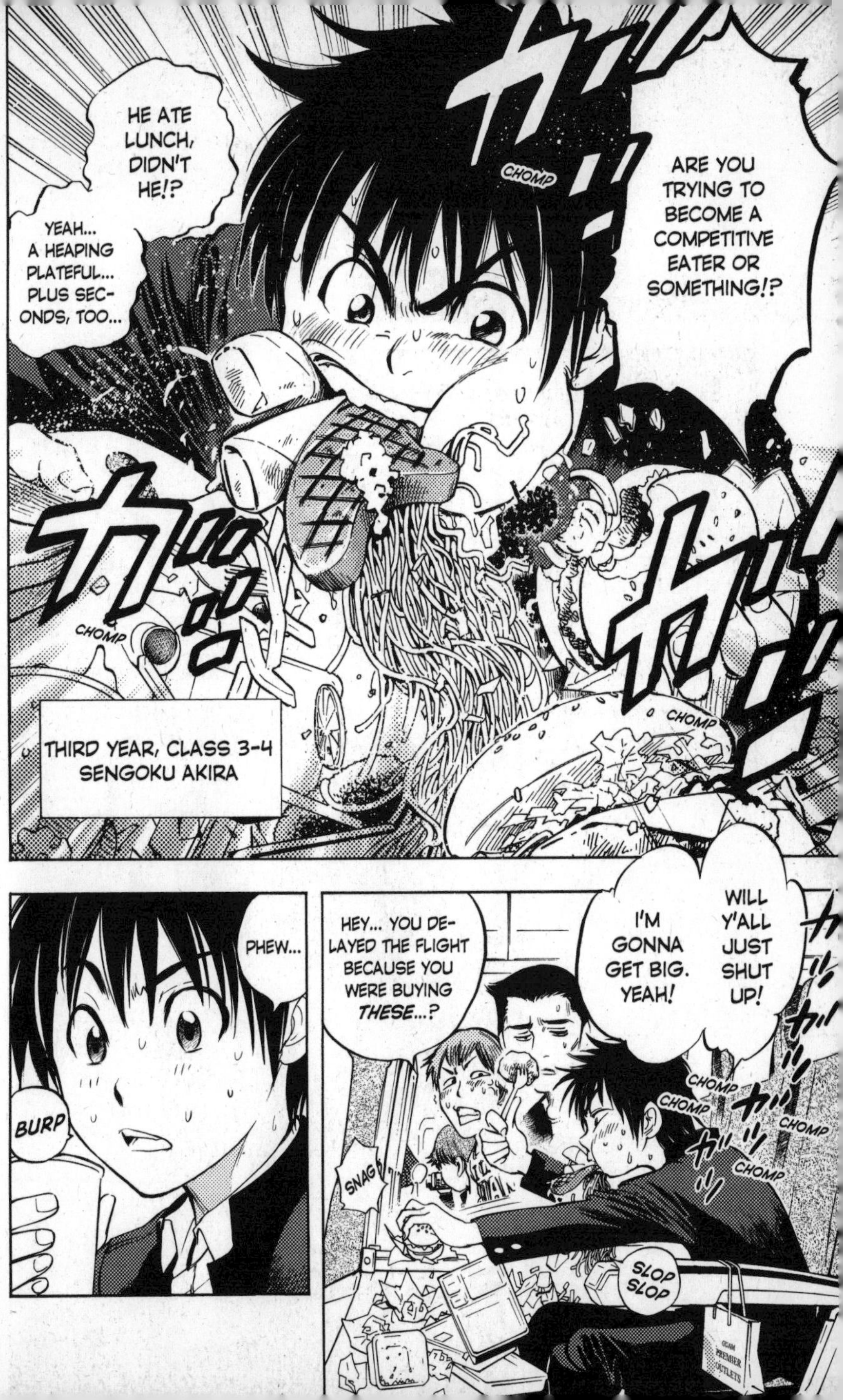
ARE YOU TRYING TO BECOME A COMPETITIVE EATER OR SOMETHING!?
HE ATE LUNCH, DIDN'T HE!?
CHOMP
YEAH... A HEAPING PLATEFUL... PLUS SEC-ONDS, TOO...
CHOMP
CHOMP
THIRD YEAR, CLASS 3-4 SENGOKU AKIRA
WILL Y'ALL JUST SHUT UP!
I'M GONNA GET BIG. YEAH!
HEY... YOU DE-LAYED THE FLIGHT BECAUSE YOU WERE BUYING *THESE*...?
CHOMP
CHOMP
CHOMP
CHOMP
SNAG
SLOP SLOP
PREMIER OUTLETS
PHEW...
BURP

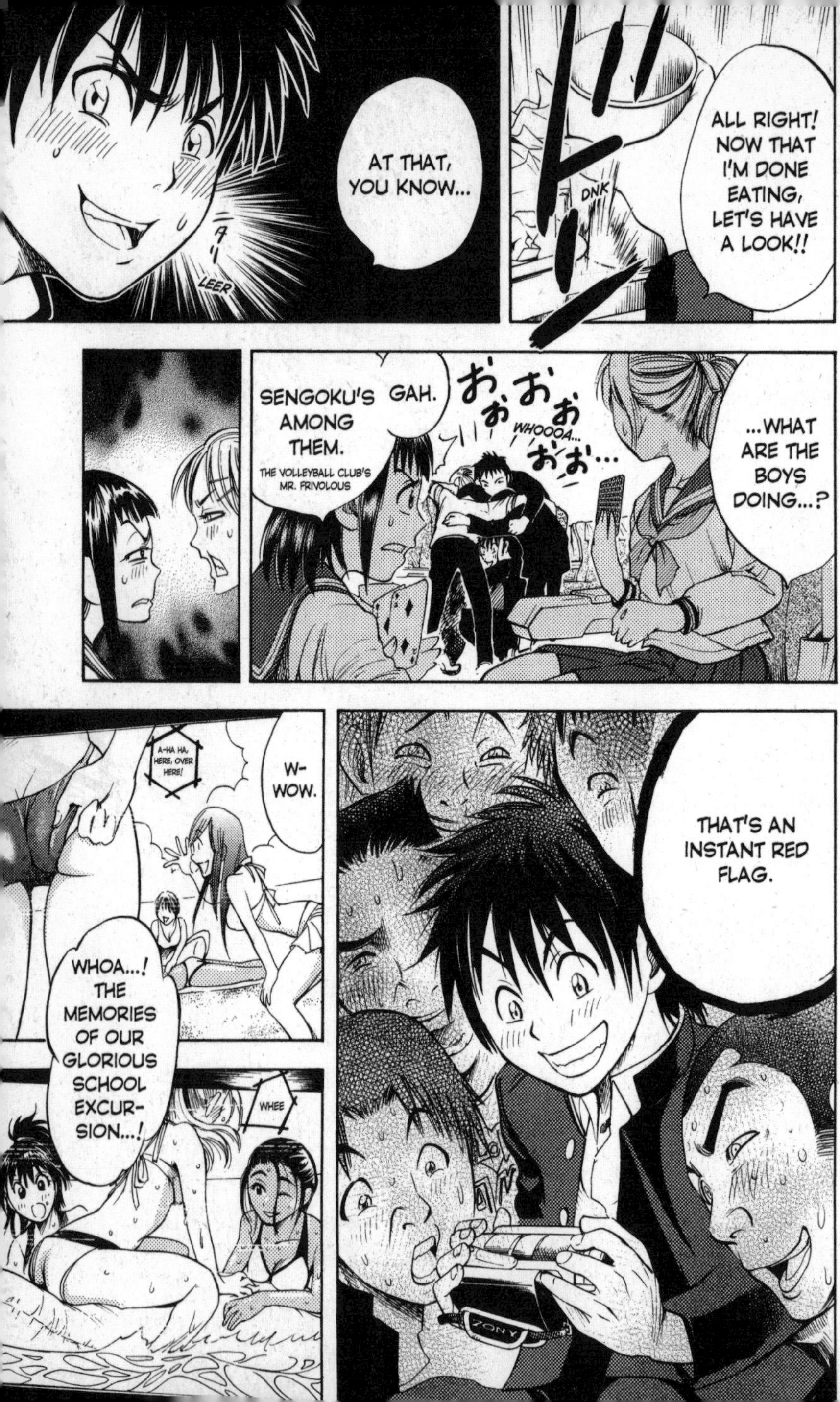
DNK
ALL RIGHT! NOW THAT I'M DONE EATING, LET'S HAVE A LOOK!!
AT THAT, YOU KNOW...
LEER
...WHAT ARE THE BOYS DOING...?
WHOOOA...
GAH.
SENGOKU'S AMONG THEM.
THE VOLLEYBALL CLUB'S MR. FRIVOLOUS
THAT'S AN INSTANT RED FLAG.
W-WOW.
A-HA HA, HERE, OVER HERE!
WHOA...! THE MEMORIES OF OUR GLORIOUS SCHOOL EXCURSION...!
WHEE

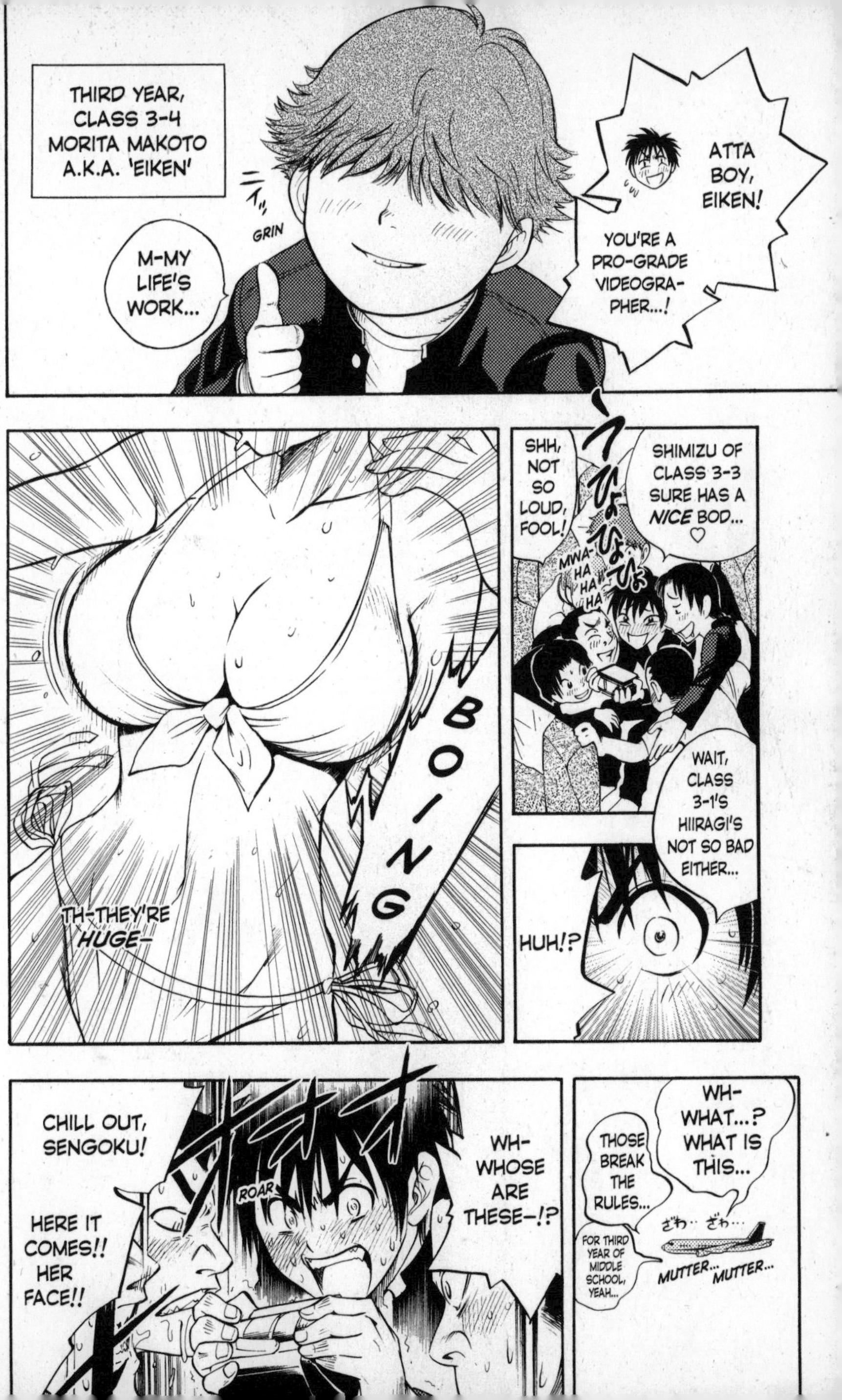
ATTA BOY, EIKEN!
YOU'RE A PRO-GRADE VIDEOGRA-PHER...!
THIRD YEAR, CLASS 3-4 MORITA MAKOTO A.K.A. 'EIKEN'
GRIN
M-MY LIFE'S WORK...
SHIMIZU OF CLASS 3-3 SURE HAS A NICE BOD... ♡
SHH, NOT SO LOUD, FOOL!
ひょひょひょ
MWA-HA HA HA HA
WAIT, CLASS 3-1'S HIIRAGI'S NOT SO BAD EITHER...
HUH!?
BOING
TH-THEY'RE HUGE-
WH- WHAT...? WHAT IS THIS...
THOSE BREAK THE RULES...
FOR THIRD YEAR OF MIDDLE SCHOOL, YEAH...
ざわ・・ざわ・・
MUTTER... MUTTER...
WH- WHOSE ARE THESE-!?
ROAR
CHILL OUT, SENGOKU!
HERE IT COMES!! HER FACE!!

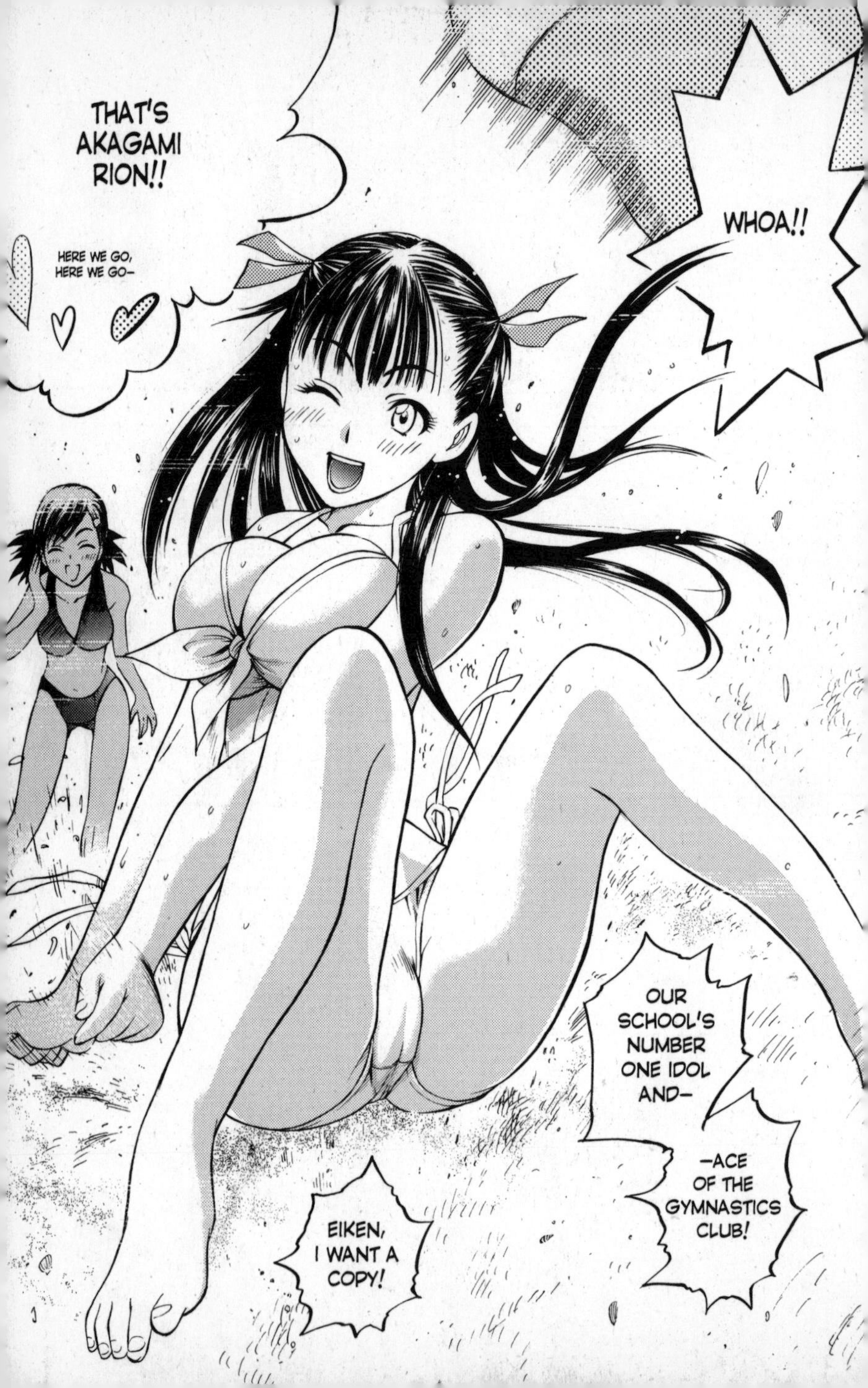
WHOA!!
THAT'S AKAGAMI RION!!
HERE WE GO, HERE WE GO–
OUR SCHOOL'S NUMBER ONE IDOL AND–
–ACE OF THE GYMNASTICS CLUB!
EIKEN, I WANT A COPY!

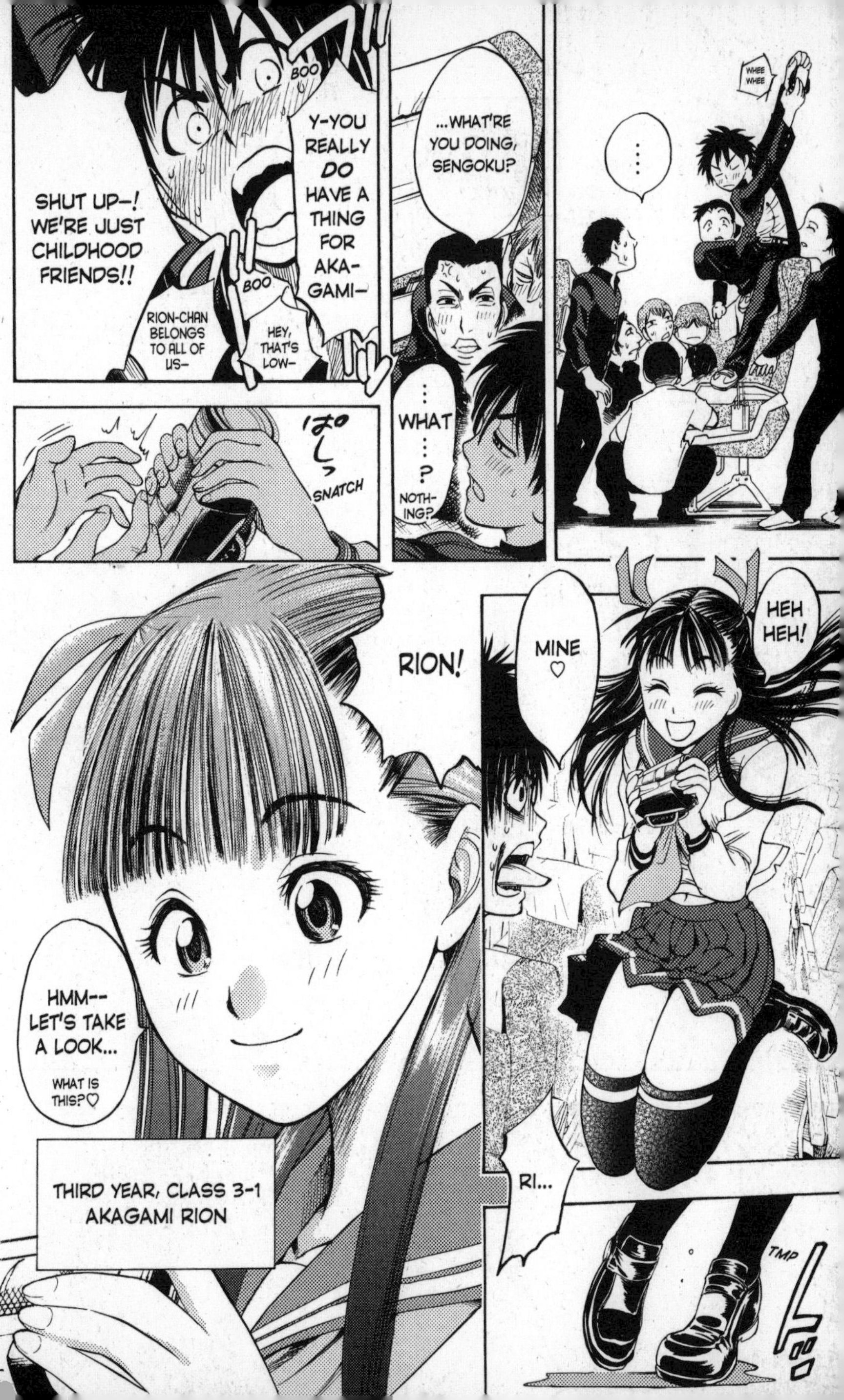
WHEE WHEE
...
...WHAT'RE YOU DOING, SENGOKU?
...WHAT...?
NOTH-ING?
Y-YOU REALLY DO HAVE A THING FOR AKA-GAMI–
BOO
SHUT UP–! WE'RE JUST CHILDHOOD FRIENDS!!
BOO
HEY, THAT'S LOW–
RION-CHAN BELONGS TO ALL OF US–
ぱしっ
SNATCH
HEH HEH!
MINE ♡
RI...
TMP
RION!
HMM-- LET'S TAKE A LOOK...
WHAT IS THIS?♡
THIRD YEAR, CLASS 3-1 AKAGAMI RION

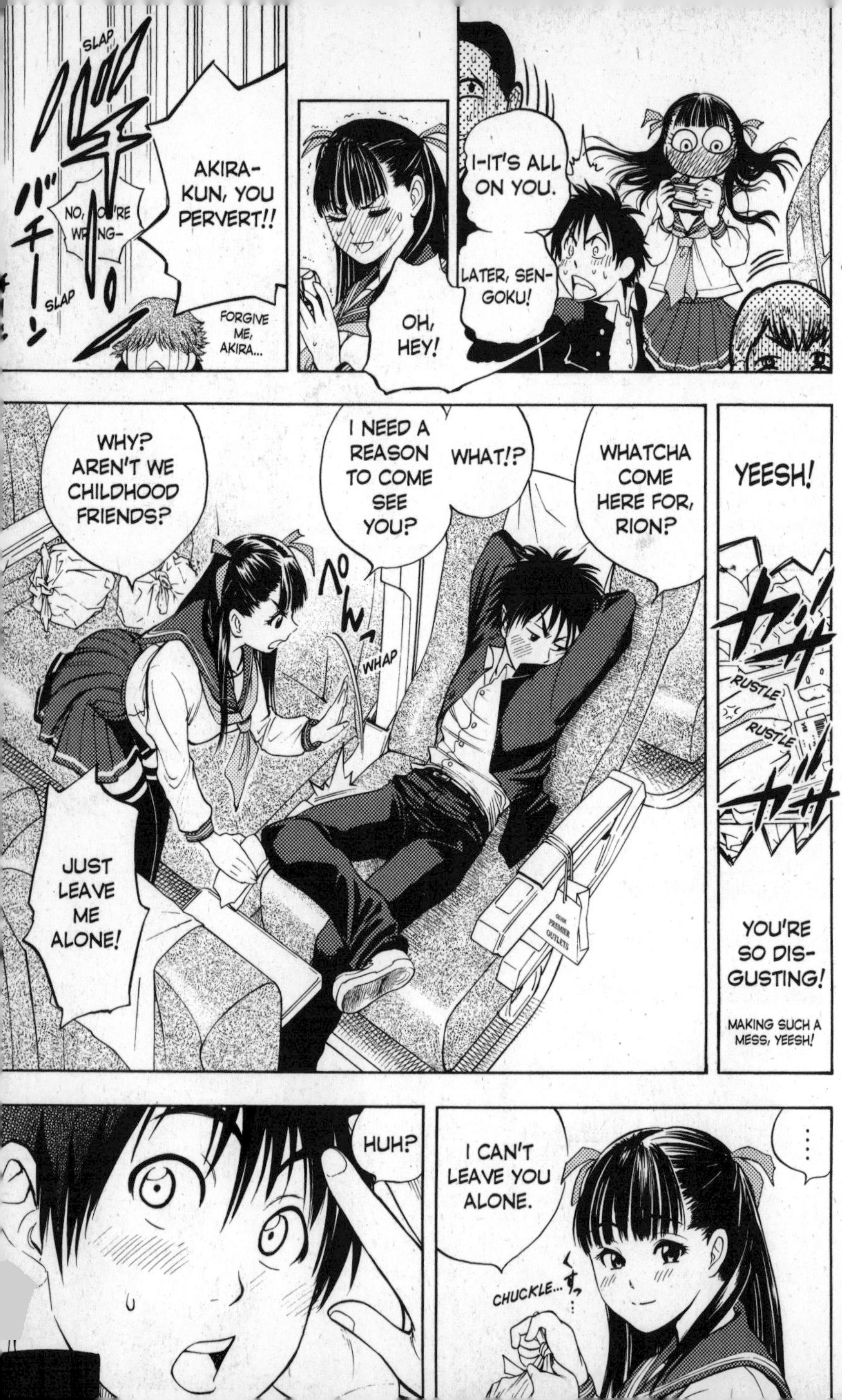
I-IT'S ALL ON YOU.
LATER, SEN-GOKU!
OH, HEY!
AKIRA-KUN, YOU PERVERT!!
SLAP
NO, O'RE WR NG-
SLAP
FORGIVE ME, AKIRA...
YEESH!
RUSTLE
RUSTLE
YOU'RE SO DIS-GUSTING!
MAKING SUCH A MESS, YEESH!
WHATCHA COME HERE FOR, RION?
WHAT!?
I NEED A REASON TO COME SEE YOU?
WHY? AREN'T WE CHILDHOOD FRIENDS?
WHAP
JUST LEAVE ME ALONE!
PREMIER OUTLETS
...
I CAN'T LEAVE YOU ALONE.
CHUCKLE...
HUH?

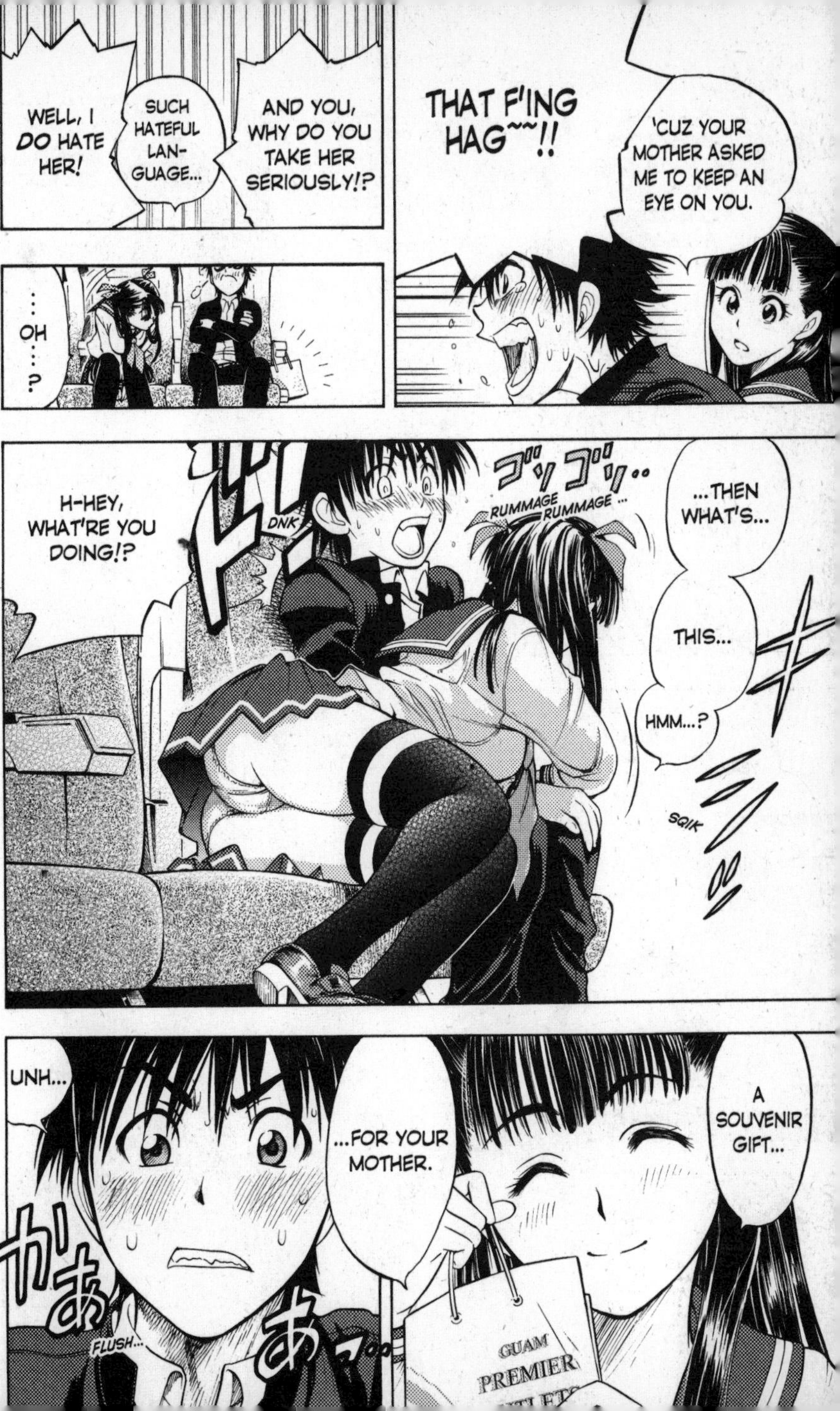

'CUZ YOUR MOTHER ASKED ME TO KEEP AN EYE ON YOU.
THAT F'ING HAG~~!!
AND YOU, WHY DO YOU TAKE HER SERIOUSLY!?
SUCH HATEFUL LAN-GUAGE...
WELL, I DO HATE HER!
... OH...?
...THEN WHAT'S...
THIS...
HMM...?
ゴソゴソ
RUMMAGE RUMMAGE...
SQIK
DNK
H-HEY, WHAT'RE YOU DOING!?
A SOUVENIR GIFT...
...FOR YOUR MOTHER.
UNH...
かあああっ
FLUSH...
GUAM
PREMIER

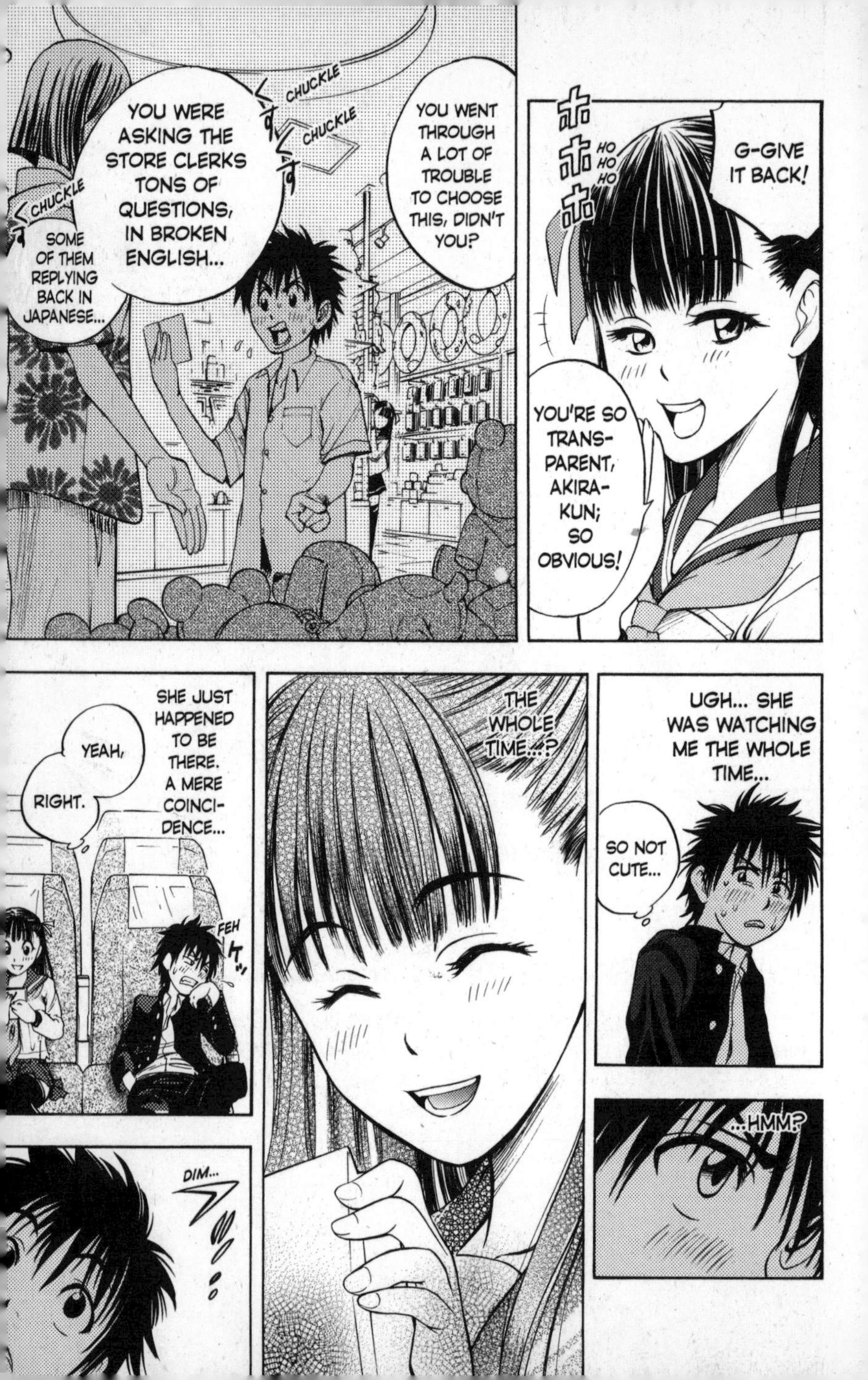
HO HO HO
G-GIVE IT BACK!
YOU'RE SO TRANS-PARENT, AKIRA-KUN; SO OBVIOUS!
YOU WENT THROUGH A LOT OF TROUBLE TO CHOOSE THIS, DIDN'T YOU?
CHUCKLE
CHUCKLE
YOU WERE ASKING THE STORE CLERKS TONS OF QUESTIONS, IN BROKEN ENGLISH...
CHUCKLE
SOME OF THEM REPLYING BACK IN JAPANESE...
UGH... SHE WAS WATCHING ME THE WHOLE TIME...
SO NOT CUTE...
...HMM?
THE WHOLE TIME...?
SHE JUST HAPPENED TO BE THERE. A MERE COINCI-DENCE...
YEAH, RIGHT.
FEH
DIM...

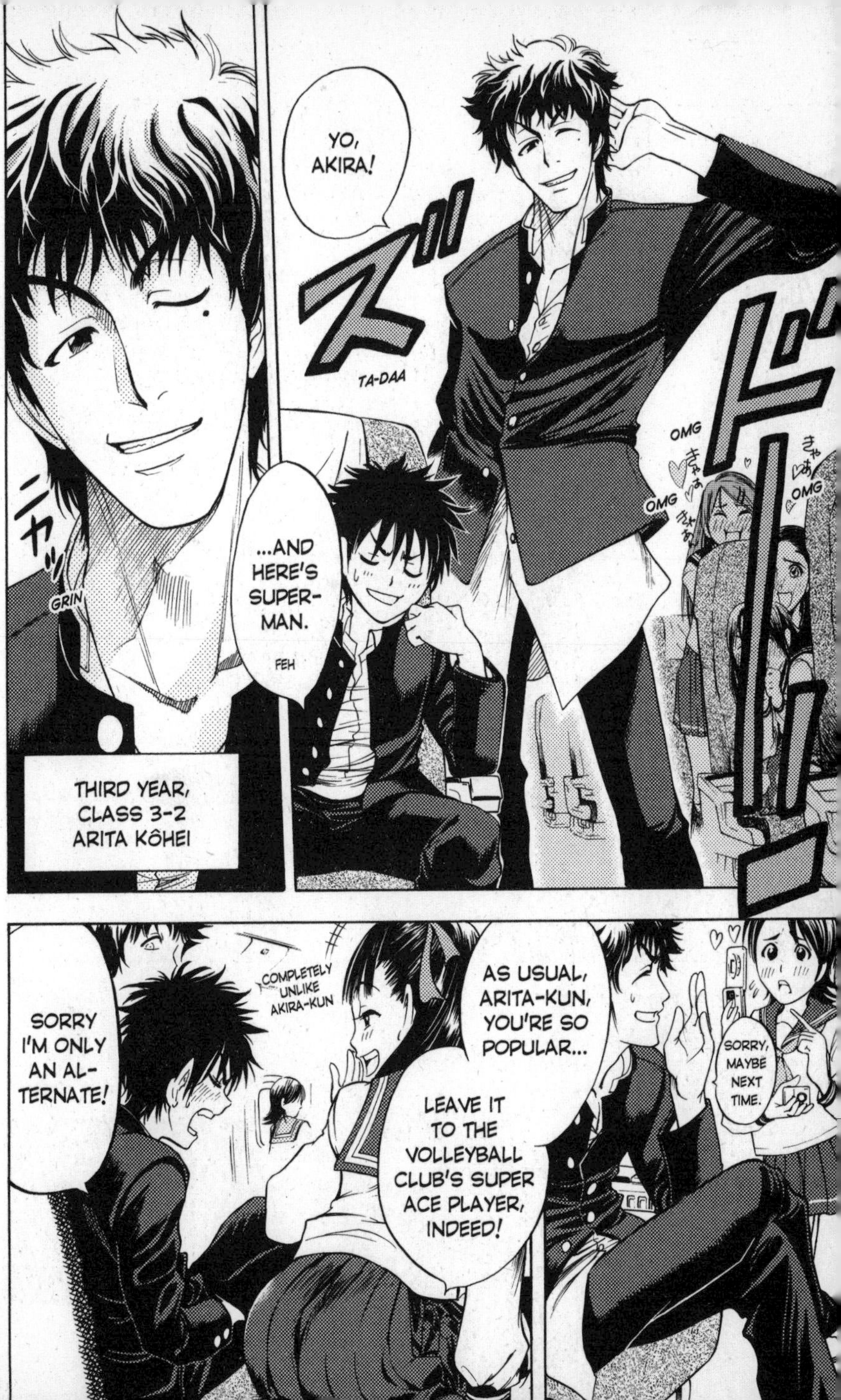
YO, AKIRA!
TA-DAA
OMG
OMG
OMG
...AND HERE'S SUPER-MAN.
FEH
GRIN
THIRD YEAR, CLASS 3-2 ARITA KÔHEI
SORRY, MAYBE NEXT TIME.
AS USUAL, ARITA-KUN, YOU'RE SO POPULAR...
LEAVE IT TO THE VOLLEYBALL CLUB'S SUPER ACE PLAYER, INDEED!
COMPLETELY UNLIKE AKIRA-KUN
SORRY I'M ONLY AN AL-TERNATE!

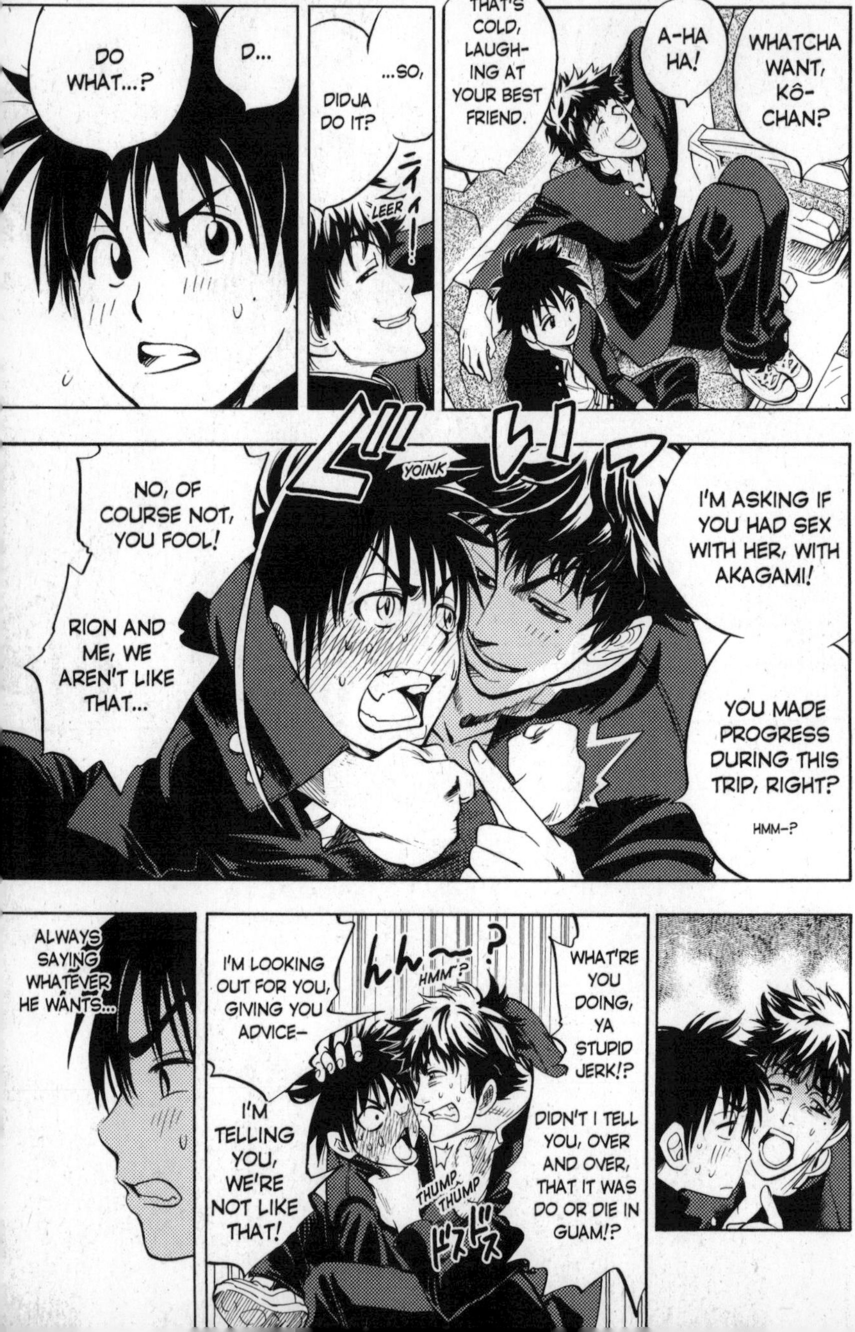
WHATCHA WANT, KÔ-CHAN?
A-HA HA!
THAT'S COLD, LAUGHING AT YOUR BEST FRIEND.
...SO, DIDJA DO IT?
LEER
D...
DO WHAT...?
YOINK
I'M ASKING IF YOU HAD SEX WITH HER, WITH AKAGAMI!
YOU MADE PROGRESS DURING THIS TRIP, RIGHT?
HMM-?
NO, OF COURSE NOT, YOU FOOL!
RION AND ME, WE AREN'T LIKE THAT...
WHAT'RE YOU DOING, YA STUPID JERK!?
んん～？
HMM?
I'M LOOKING OUT FOR YOU, GIVING YOU ADVICE–
DIDN'T I TELL YOU, OVER AND OVER, THAT IT WAS DO OR DIE IN GUAM!?
I'M TELLING YOU, WE'RE NOT LIKE THAT!
THUMP THUMP
ドスドス
ALWAYS SAYING WHATEVER HE WANTS...

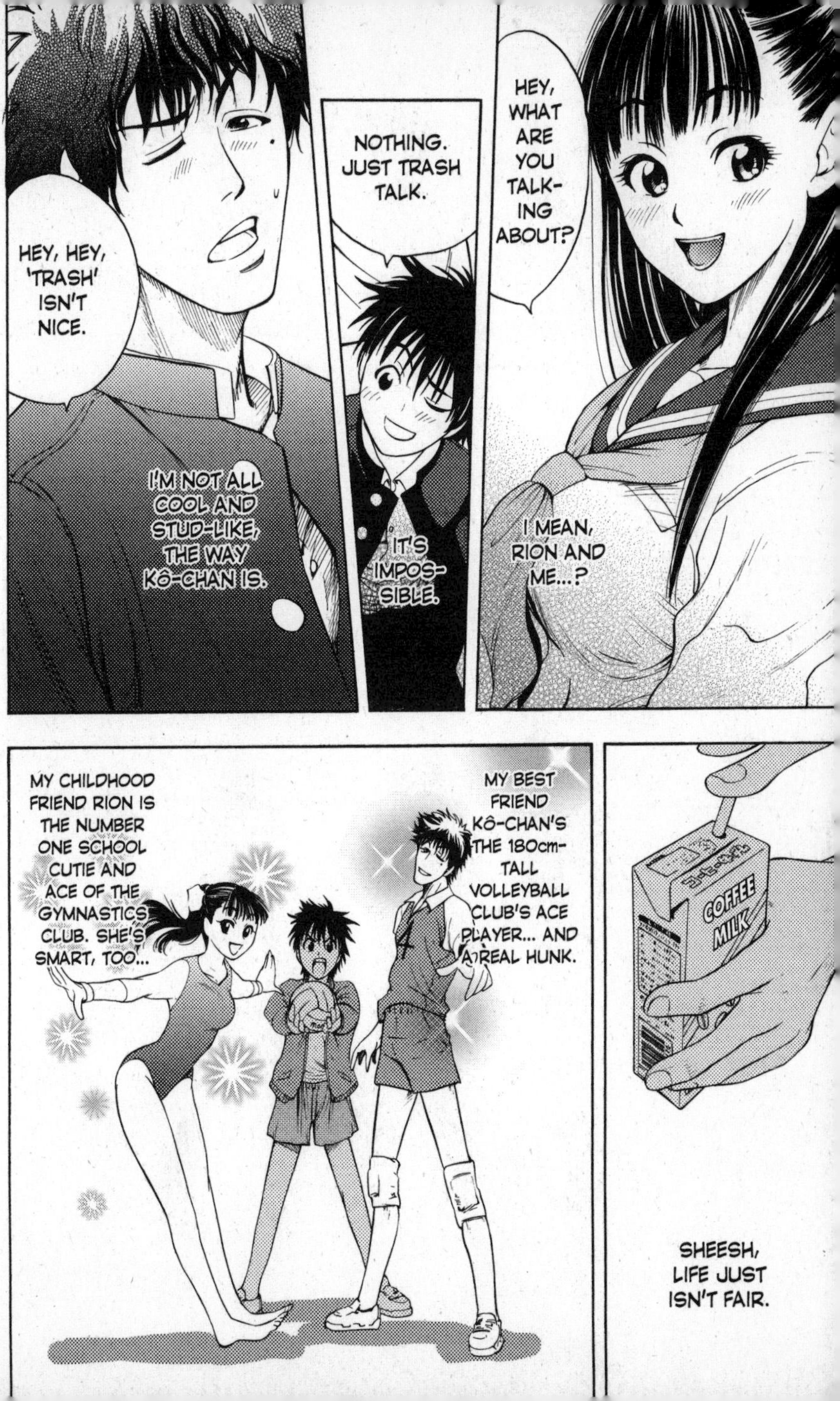
HEY, WHAT ARE YOU TALKING ABOUT?
I MEAN, RION AND ME...?
NOTHING. JUST TRASH TALK.
IT'S IMPOSSIBLE.
HEY, HEY, 'TRASH' ISN'T NICE.
I'M NOT ALL COOL AND STUD-LIKE, THE WAY KÔ-CHAN IS.
COFFEE MILK
SHEESH, LIFE JUST ISN'T FAIR.
MY BEST FRIEND KÔ-CHAN'S THE 180cm-TALL VOLLEYBALL CLUB'S ACE PLAYER... AND A REAL HUNK.
MY CHILDHOOD FRIEND RION IS THE NUMBER ONE SCHOOL CUTIE AND ACE OF THE GYMNASTICS CLUB. SHE'S SMART, TOO...

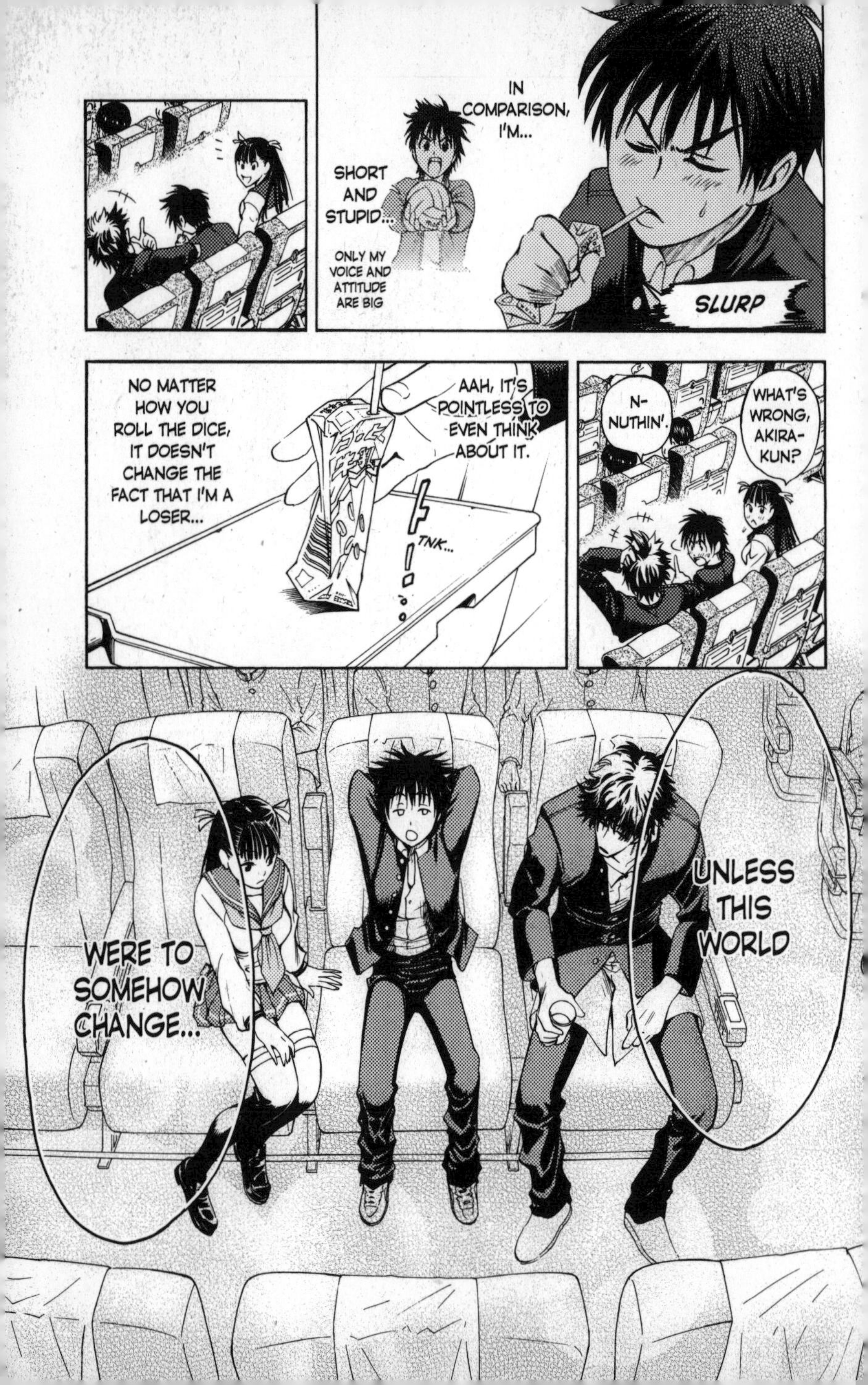
IN COMPARISON, I'M...
SHORT AND STUPID...
ONLY MY VOICE AND ATTITUDE ARE BIG
SLURP
WHAT'S WRONG, AKIRA-KUN?
N-NUTHIN'.
AAH, IT'S POINTLESS TO EVEN THINK ABOUT IT.
NO MATTER HOW YOU ROLL THE DICE, IT DOESN'T CHANGE THE FACT THAT I'M A LOSER...
TNK...
UNLESS THIS WORLD
WERE TO SOMEHOW CHANGE...

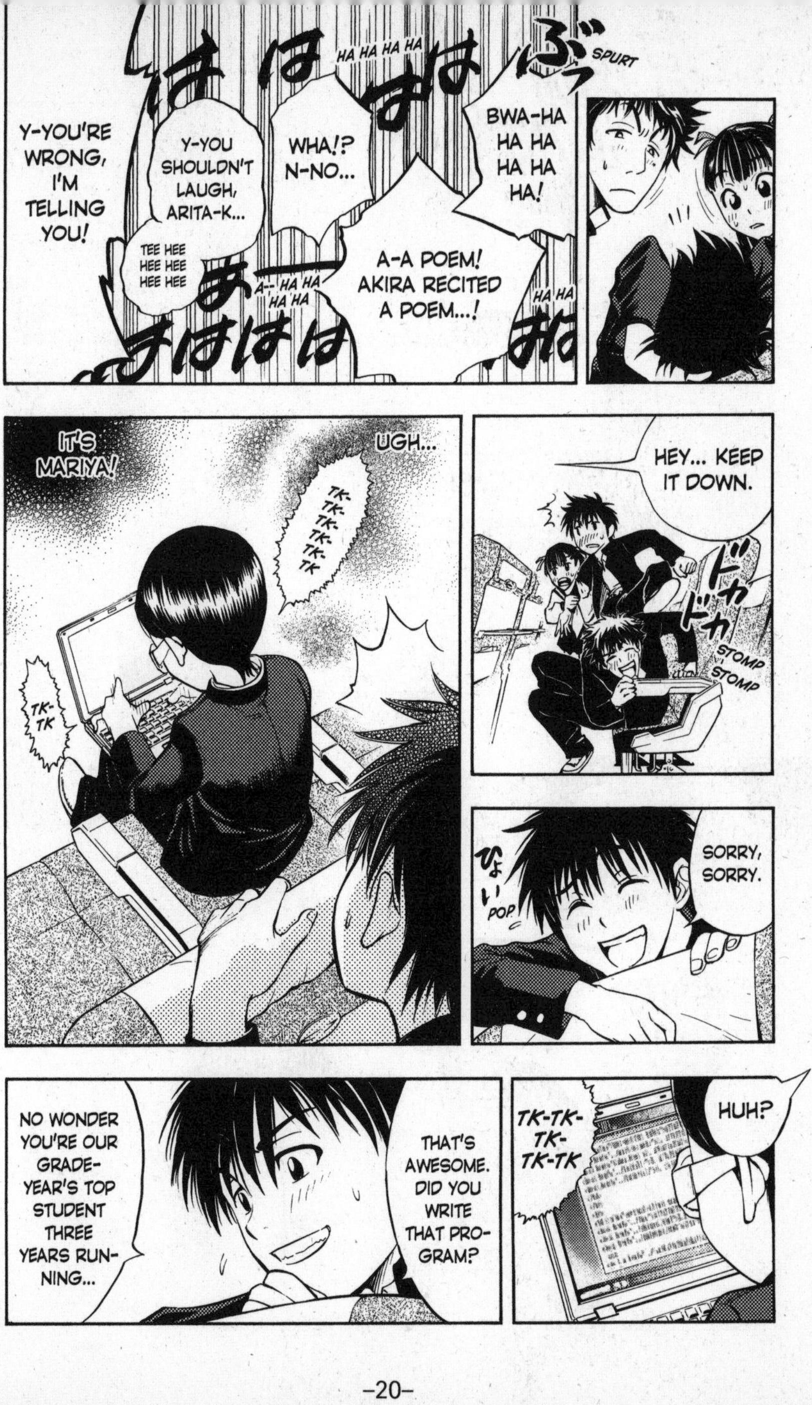
SPURT
BWA-HA HA HA HA HA HA!
HA HA HA HA
WHA!? N-NO...
Y-YOU SHOULDN'T LAUGH, ARITA-K...
Y-YOU'RE WRONG, I'M TELLING YOU!
A-A POEM! AKIRA RECITED A POEM...!
HA HA
A-- HA HA HA HA
TEE HEE HEE HEE HEE HEE
HEY... KEEP IT DOWN.
STOMP STOMP
SORRY, SORRY.
POP
UGH...
TK-TK-TK-TK-TK-TK
IT'S MARIYA!
TK-TK
HUH?
TK-TK-TK-TK-TK
THAT'S AWESOME. DID YOU WRITE THAT PRO-GRAM?
NO WONDER YOU'RE OUR GRADE-YEAR'S TOP STUDENT THREE YEARS RUN-NING...

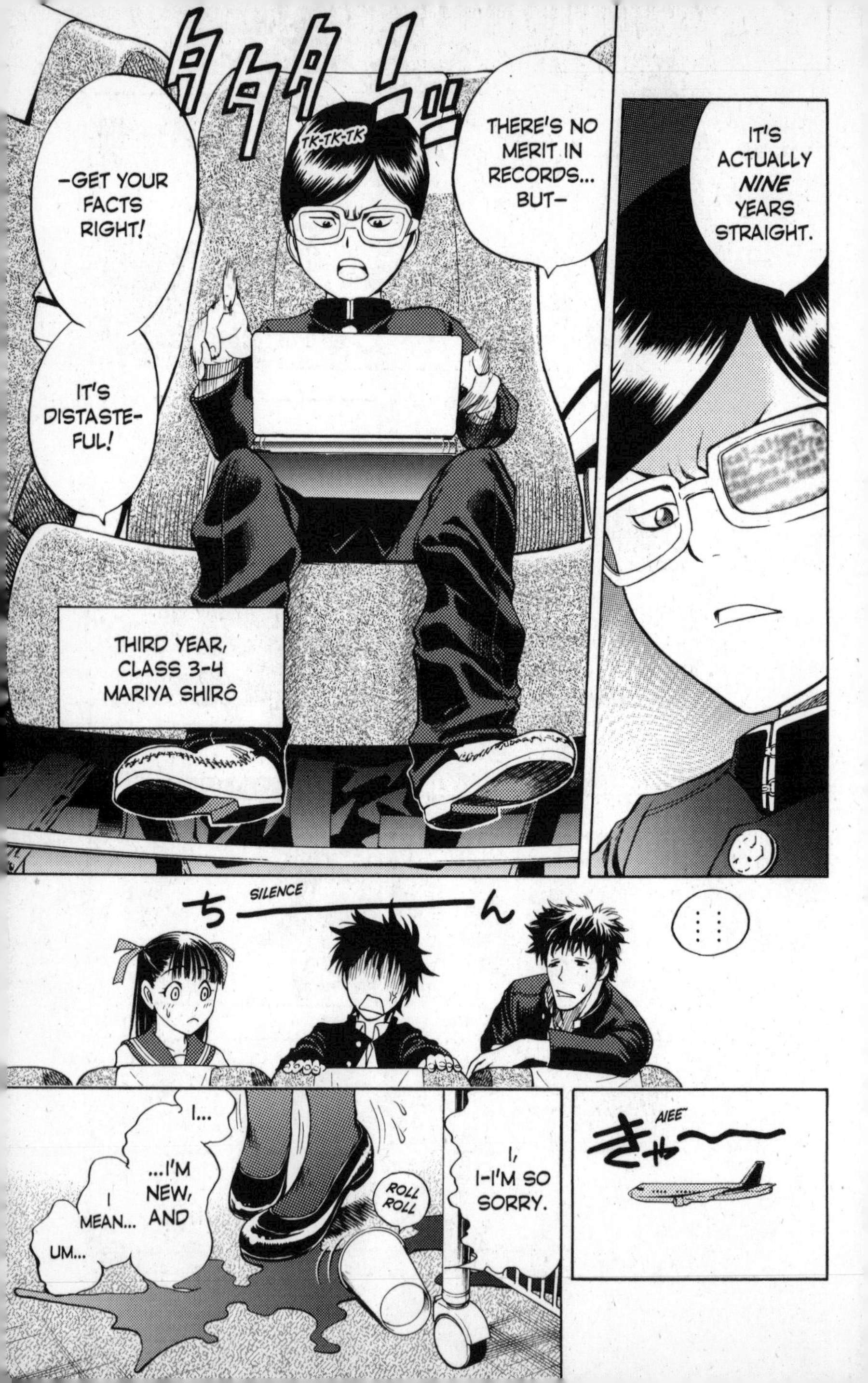
IT'S ACTUALLY NINE YEARS STRAIGHT.
THERE'S NO MERIT IN RECORDS... BUT–
TK-TK-TK
–GET YOUR FACTS RIGHT!
IT'S DISTASTEFUL!
THIRD YEAR, CLASS 3-4 MARIYA SHIRÔ
...
ち————ん
SILENCE
きゃ~~
AIEE
I, I-I'M SO SORRY.
ROLL ROLL
I...
...I'M NEW, AND
I MEAN...
UM...

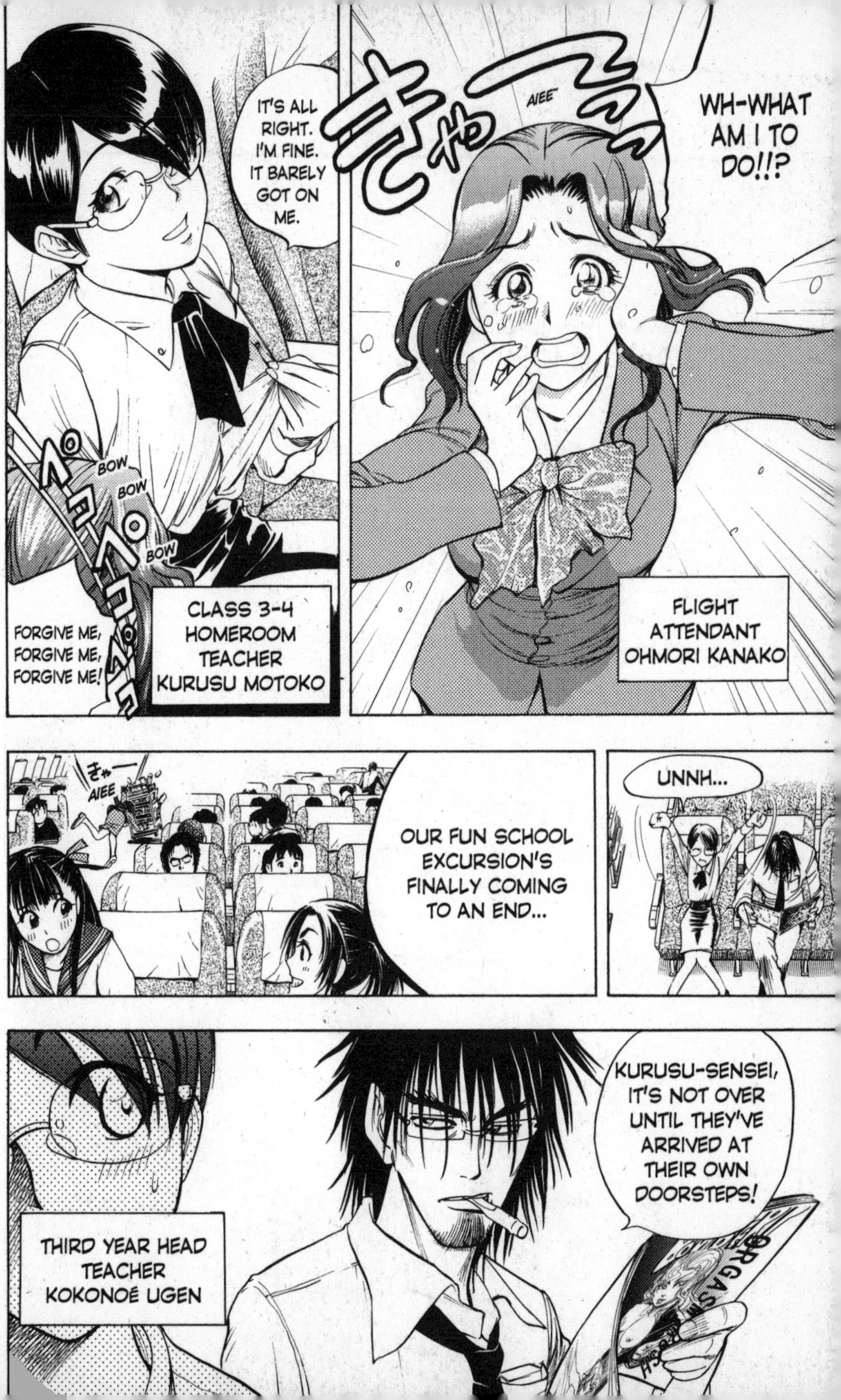
きゃ〜
AIEE
WH-WHAT AM I TO DO!!?
FLIGHT ATTENDANT OHMORI KANAKO
IT'S ALL RIGHT. I'M FINE. IT BARELY GOT ON ME.
BOW
BOW
BOW
FORGIVE ME, FORGIVE ME, FORGIVE ME!
CLASS 3-4 HOMEROOM TEACHER KURUSU MOTOKO
UNNH...
OUR FUN SCHOOL EXCURSION'S FINALLY COMING TO AN END...
きゃー
AIEE
KURUSU-SENSEI, IT'S NOT OVER UNTIL THEY'VE ARRIVED AT THEIR OWN DOORSTEPS!
THIRD YEAR HEAD TEACHER KOKONOÉ UGEN

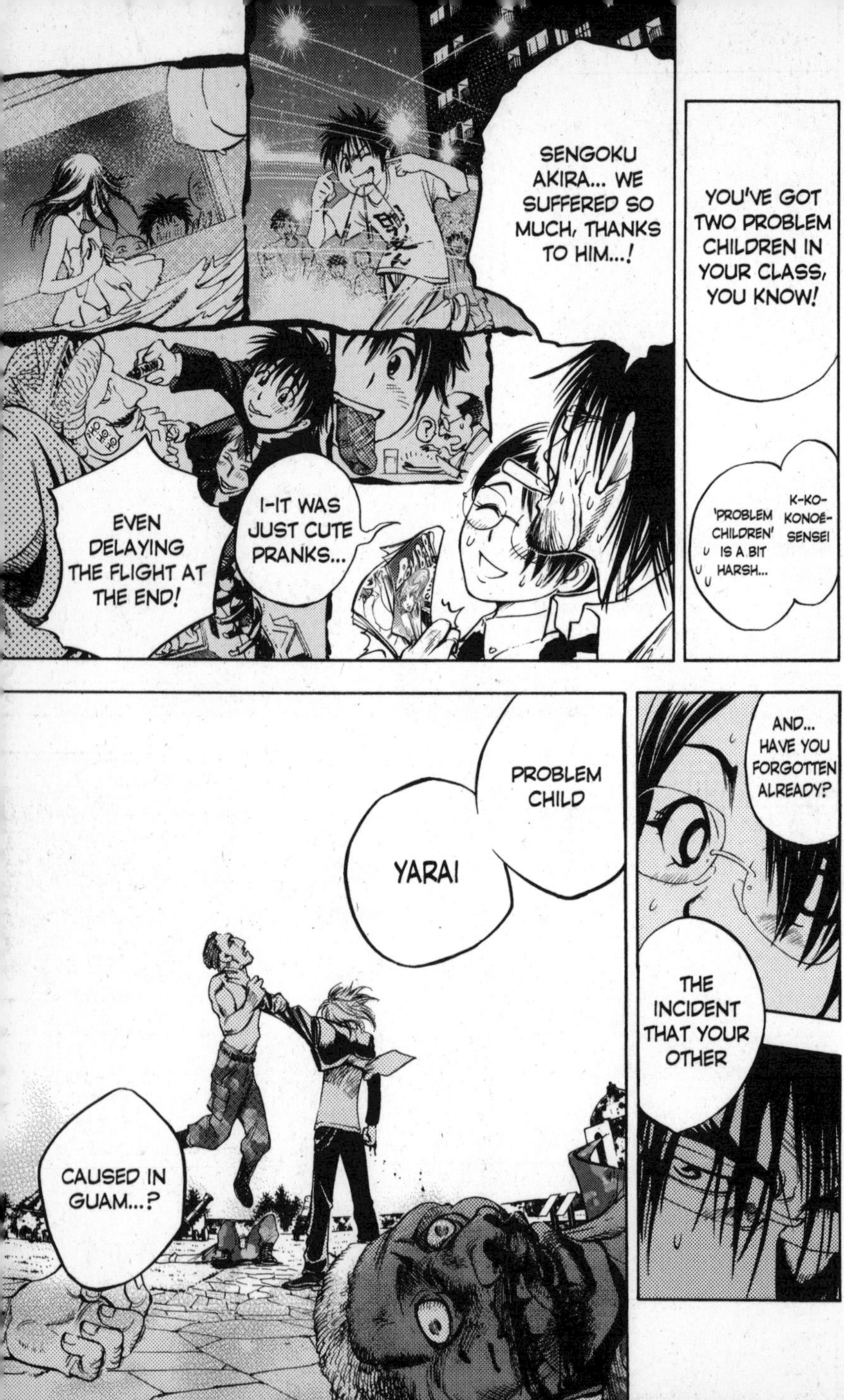
YOU'VE GOT TWO PROBLEM CHILDREN IN YOUR CLASS, YOU KNOW!
K-KO-KONOE-SENSEI
'PROBLEM CHILDREN' IS A BIT HARSH...
SENGOKU AKIRA... WE SUFFERED SO MUCH, THANKS TO HIM...!
I-IT WAS JUST CUTE PRANKS...
EVEN DELAYING THE FLIGHT AT THE END!
AND... HAVE YOU FORGOTTEN ALREADY?
THE INCIDENT THAT YOUR OTHER
PROBLEM CHILD
YARAI
CAUSED IN GUAM...?

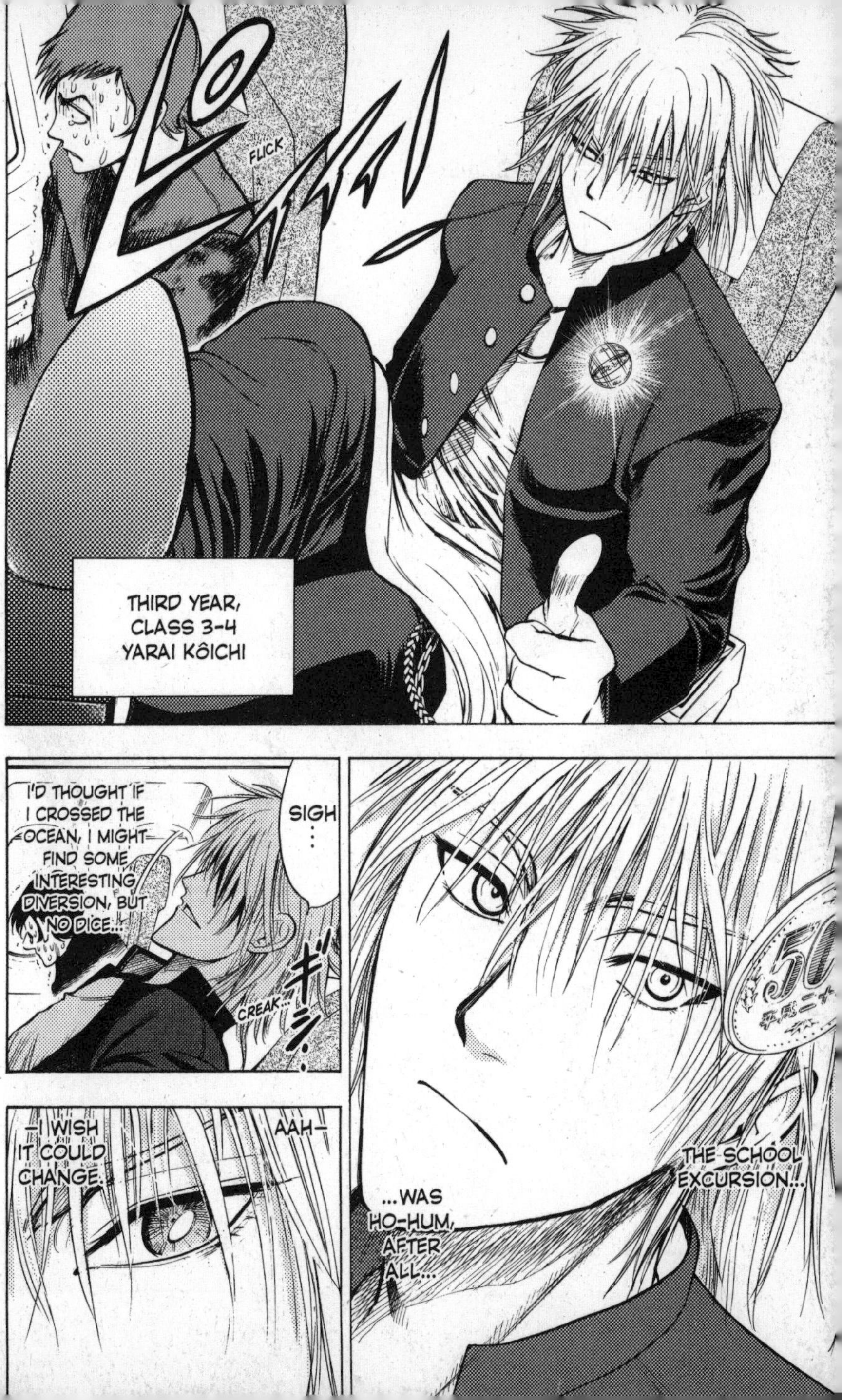
FLICK
THIRD YEAR, CLASS 3-4 YARAI KÔICHI
THE SCHOOL EXCURSION...
...WAS HO-HUM, AFTER ALL...
SIGH...
I'D THOUGHT IF I CROSSED THE OCEAN, I MIGHT FIND SOME INTERESTING DIVERSION, BUT NO DICE...
CREAK...
AAH—
—I WISH IT COULD CHANGE...

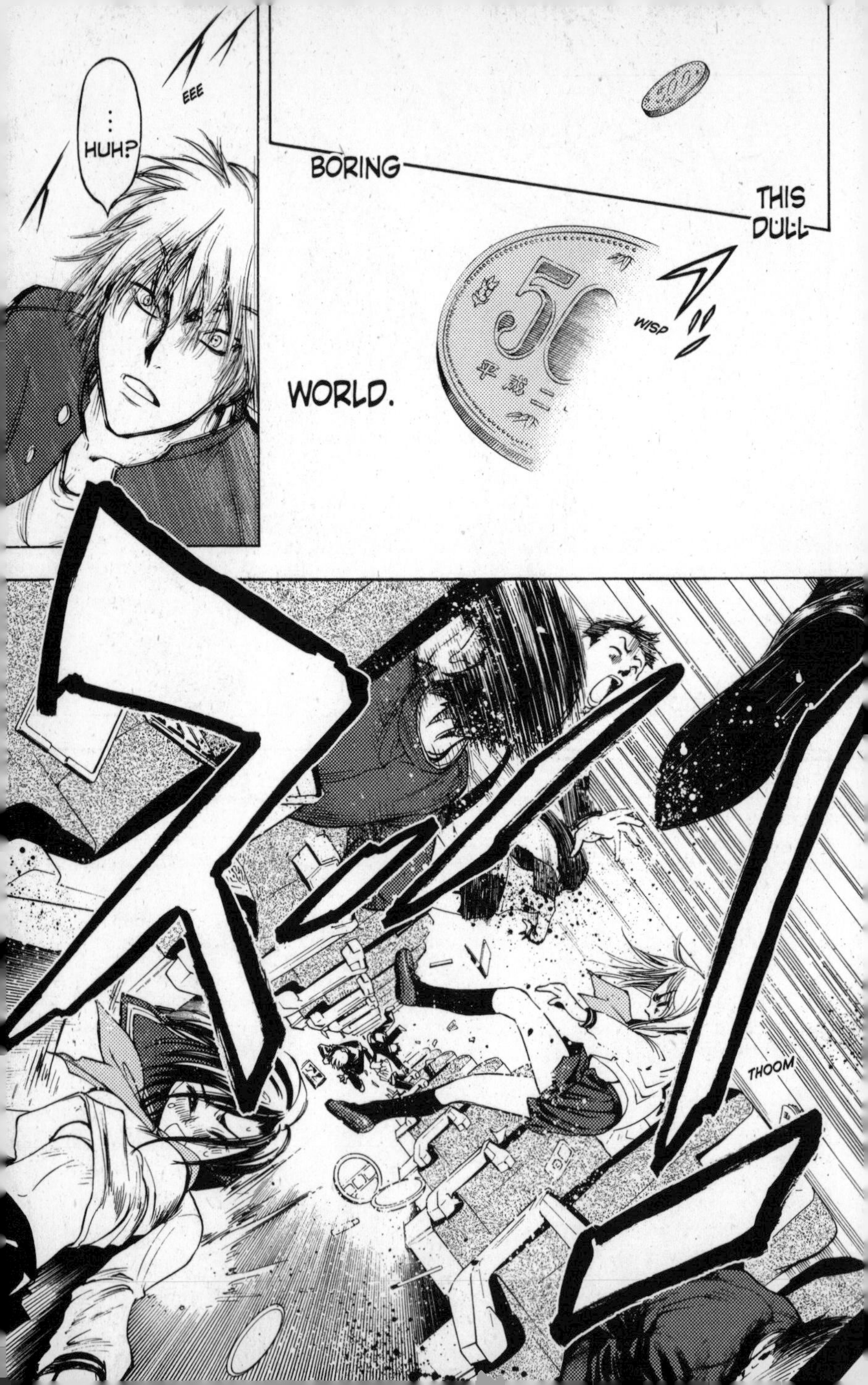
THIS DULL
BORING
WISP
WORLD.
EEE
...HUH?
THOOM

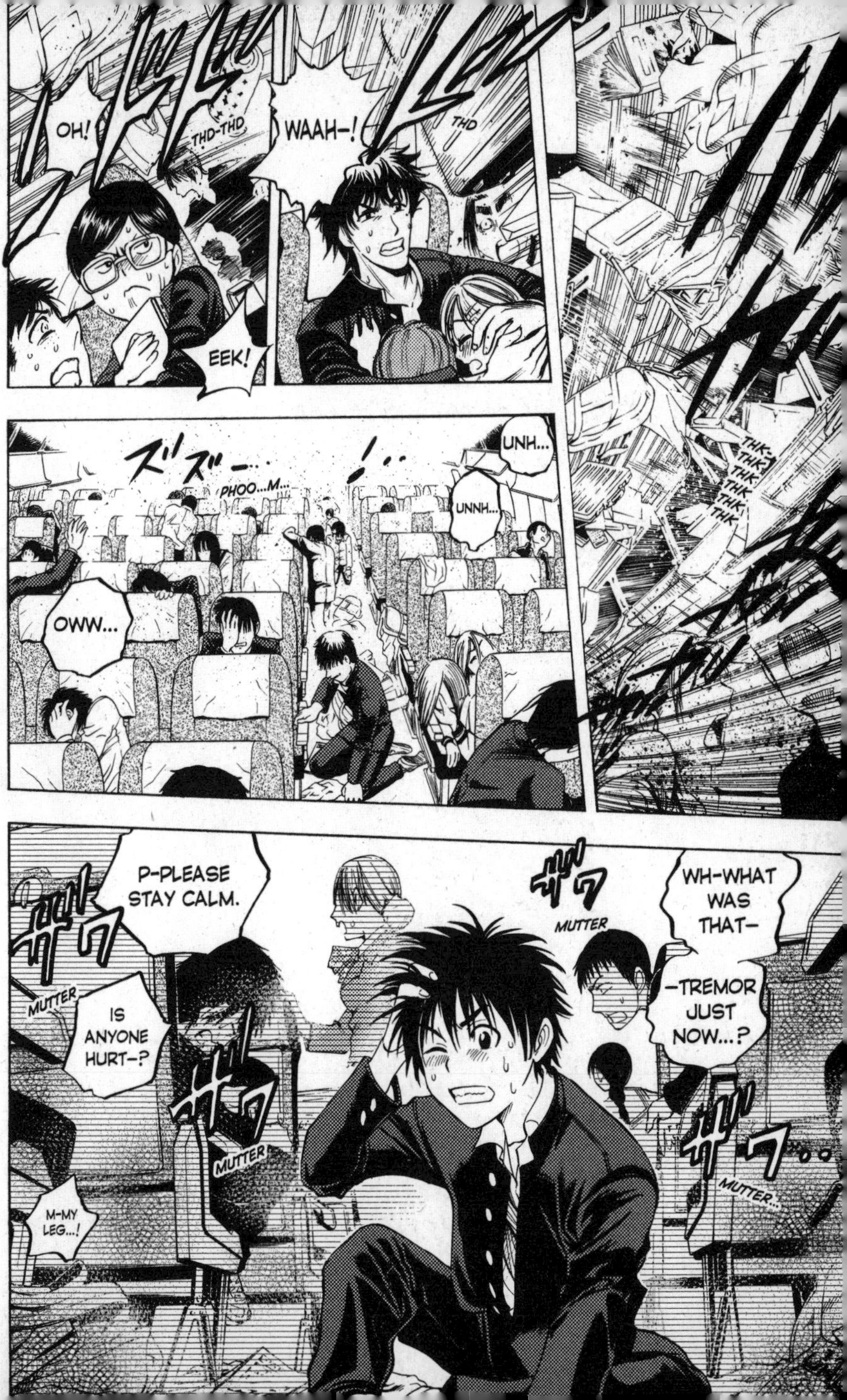
THK-THK-THK-THK-THK-THK
THD
WAAH-!
THD-THD
OH!
EEK!
UNH...
UNNH...
PHOO...M...
ズズー…
OWW...
WH-WHAT WAS THAT-
-TREMOR JUST NOW...?
MUTTER...
MUTTER
P-PLEASE STAY CALM.
MUTTER
IS ANYONE HURT-?
MUTTER
M-MY LEG...!

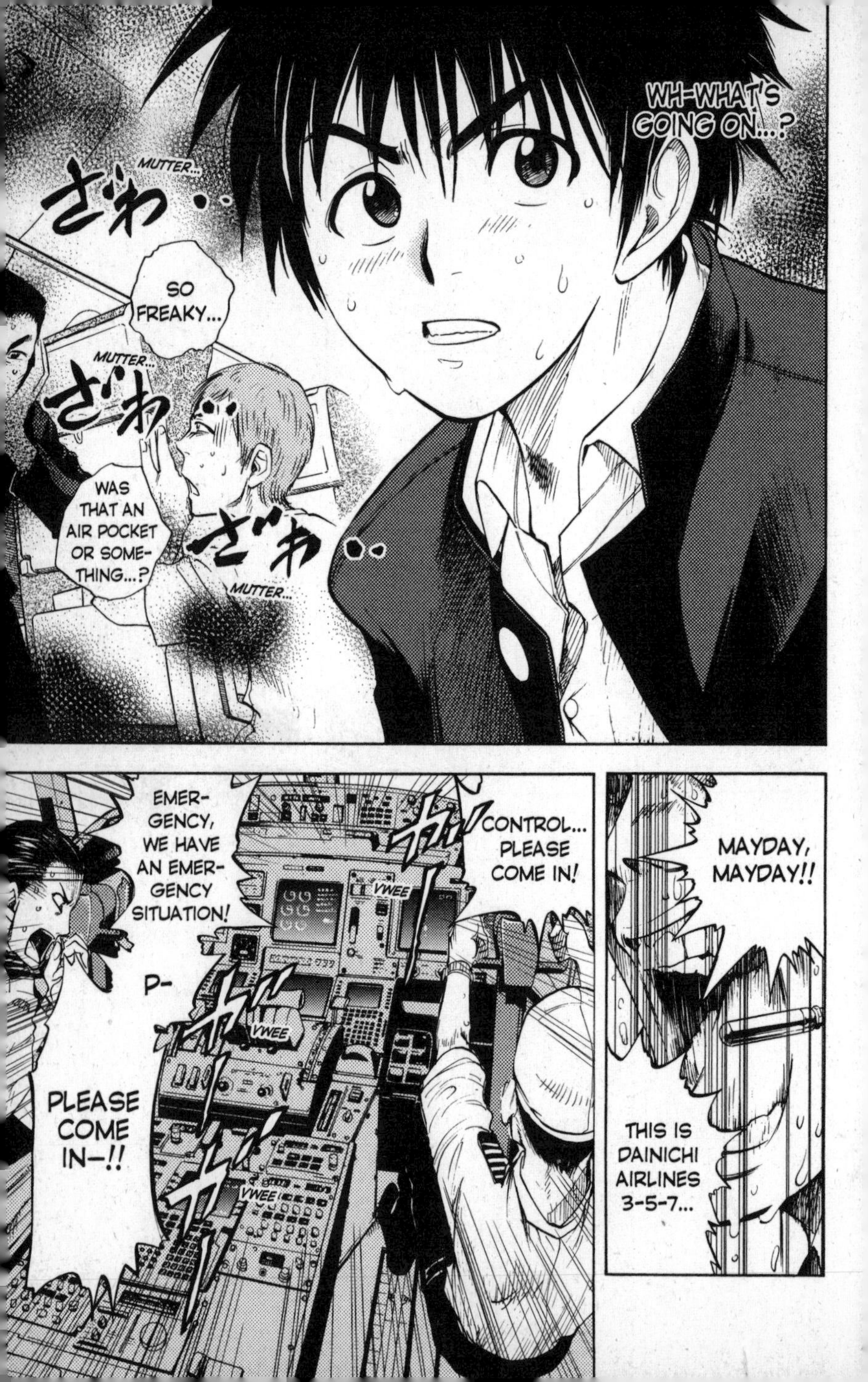
WH-WHAT'S GOING ON...?
MUTTER...
SO FREAKY...
MUTTER...
WAS THAT AN AIR POCKET OR SOME-THING...?
MUTTER...
MAYDAY, MAYDAY!!
THIS IS DAINICHI AIRLINES 3-5-7...
CONTROL... PLEASE COME IN!
EMER-GENCY, WE HAVE AN EMER-GENCY SITUATION!
VWEE
P-
VWEE
PLEASE COME IN--!!
VWEE

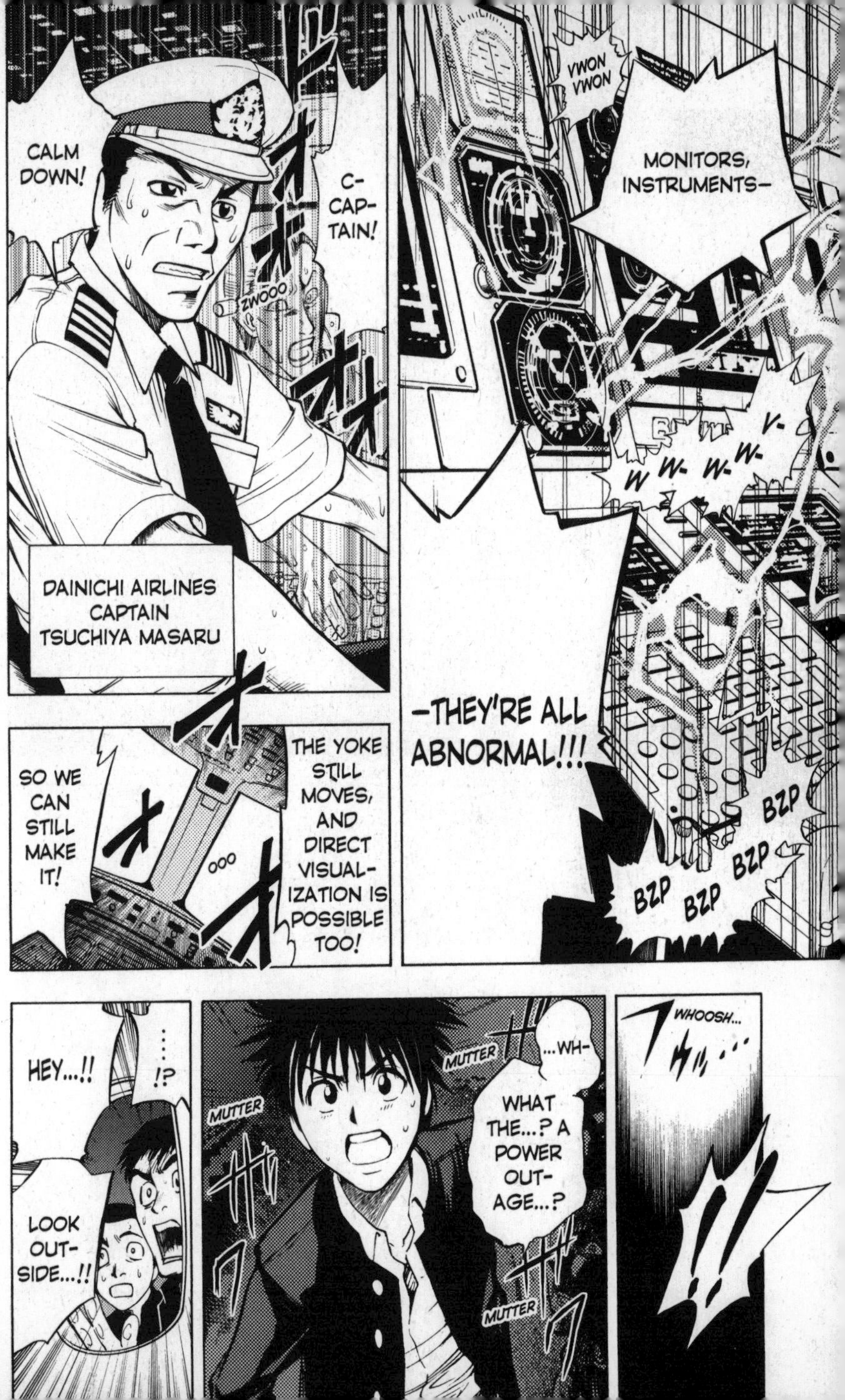
VWON VWON
MONITORS, INSTRUMENTS—
V- W- W- W- W
—THEY'RE ALL ABNORMAL!!!
BZP BZP BZP BZP BZP
C-CAPTAIN!
CALM DOWN!
ZWOOO
DAINICHI AIRLINES CAPTAIN TSUCHIYA MASARU
THE YOKE STILL MOVES, AND DIRECT VISUALIZATION IS POSSIBLE TOO!
SO WE CAN STILL MAKE IT!
OOO
WHOOSH...
!!
MUTTER
...WH-
WHAT THE...? A POWER OUTAGE...?
MUTTER
MUTTER
.....!?
HEY...!!
LOOK OUTSIDE...!!

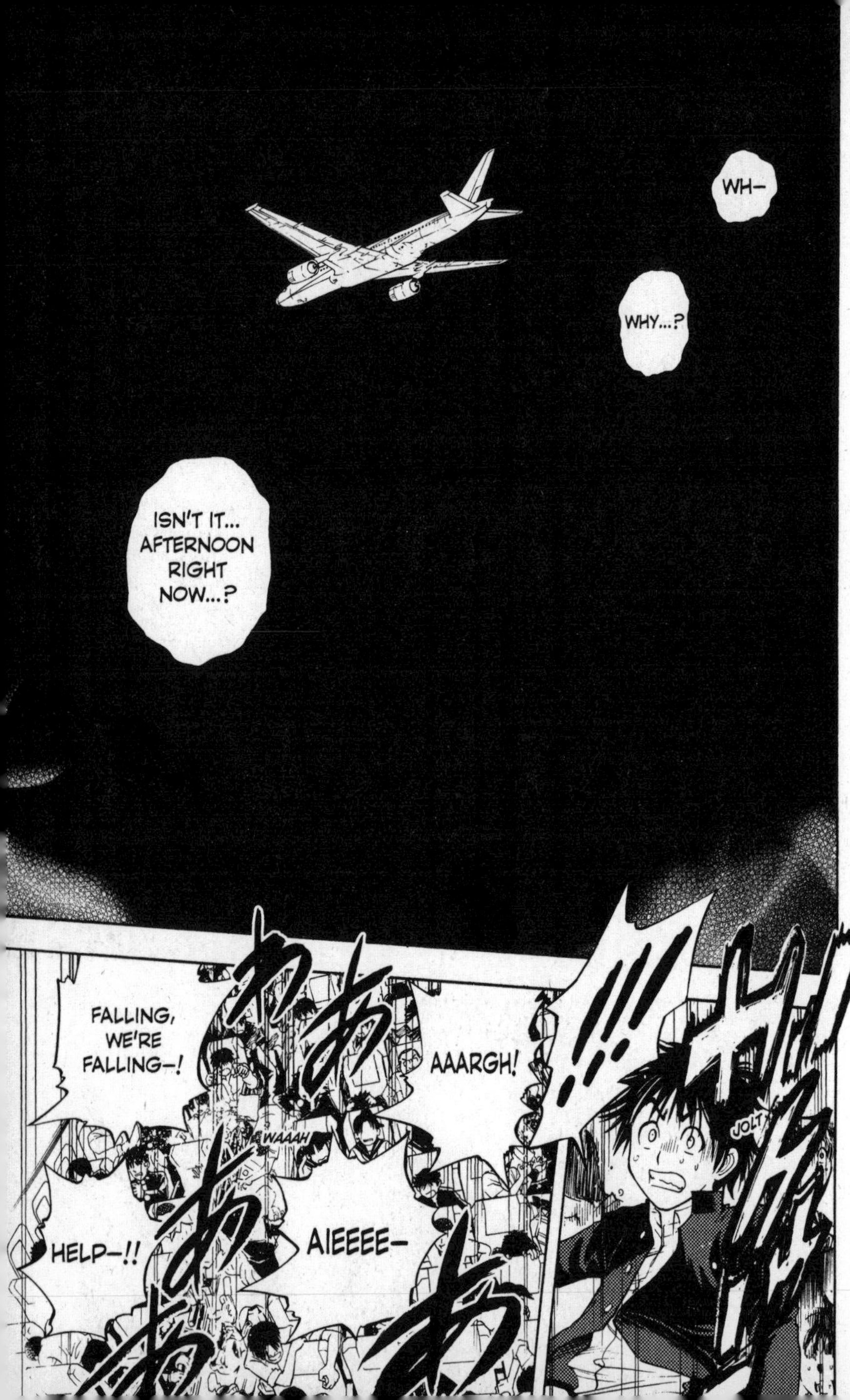
WH-
WHY...?
ISN'T IT... AFTERNOON RIGHT NOW...?
JOLT
!!!
AAARGH!
FALLING, WE'RE FALLING-!
WAAAH
AIEEEE-
HELP-!!

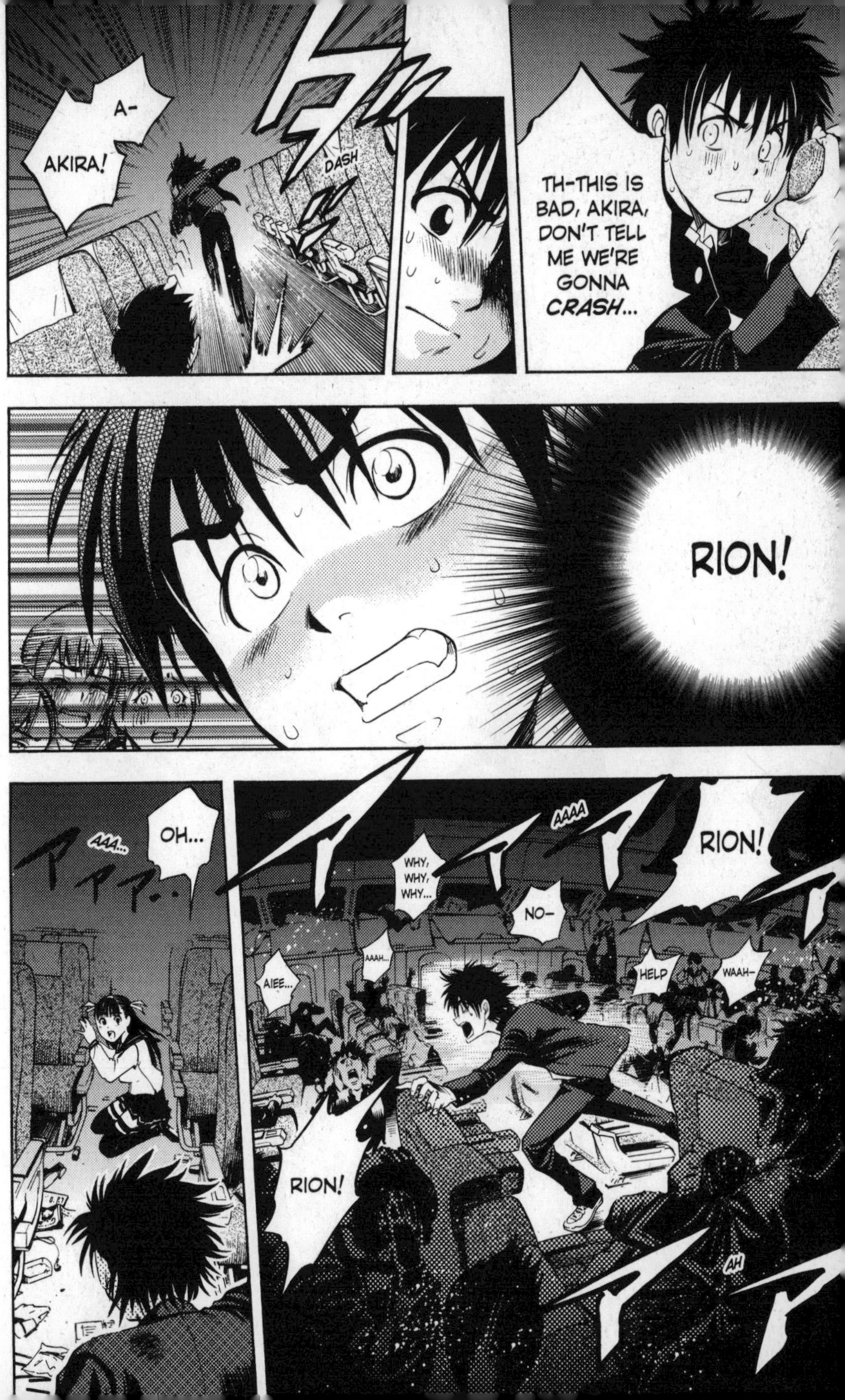
TH-THIS IS BAD, AKIRA, DON'T TELL ME WE'RE GONNA *CRASH*...
DASH
A-
AKIRA!
RION!
RION!
AAAA
WHY, WHY, WHY...
NO-
WAAH-
HELP
AAAH...
AIEE...
RION!
AH
OH...
AAA...

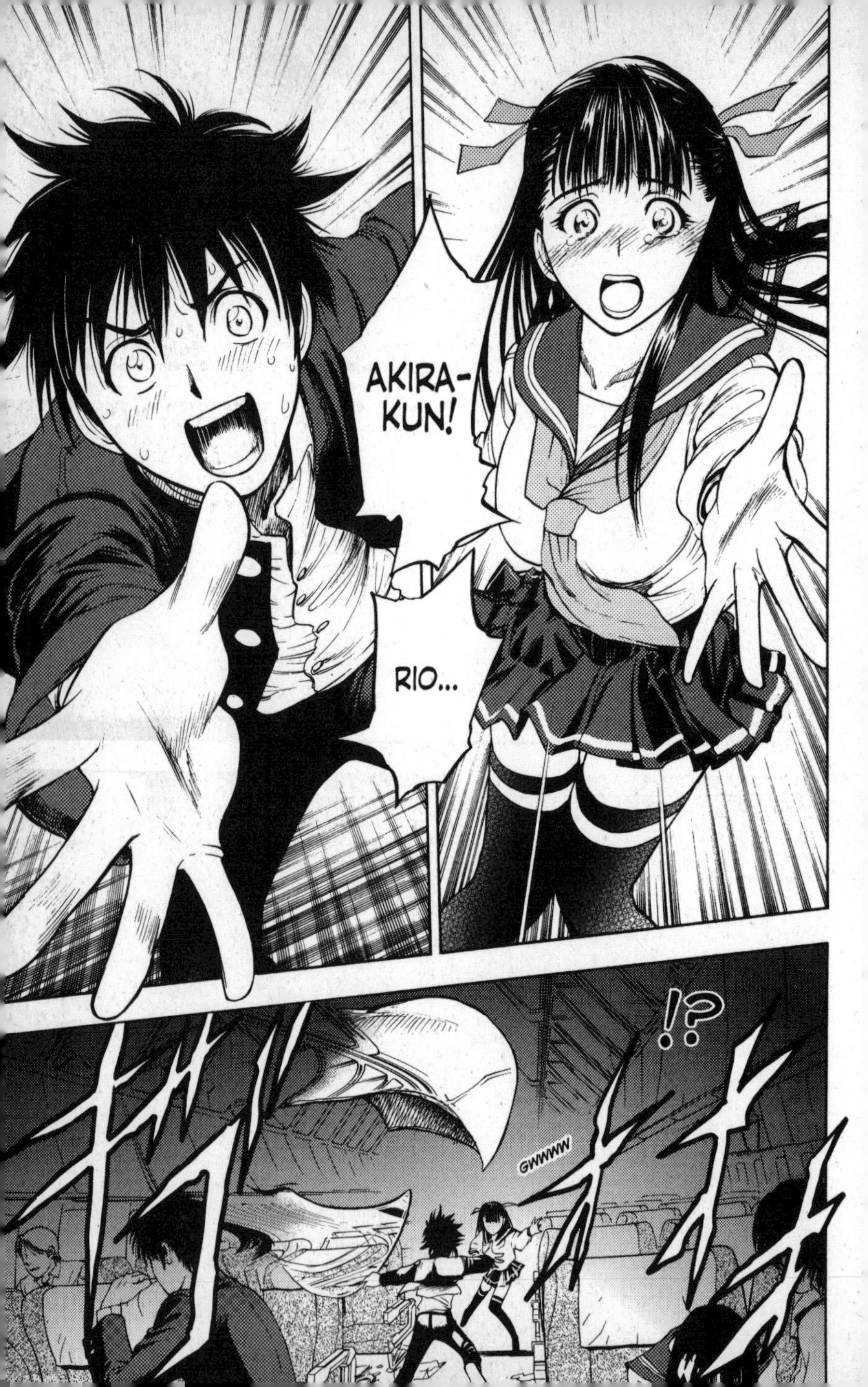
AKIRA-KUN!
RIO...
!?
GWWWW

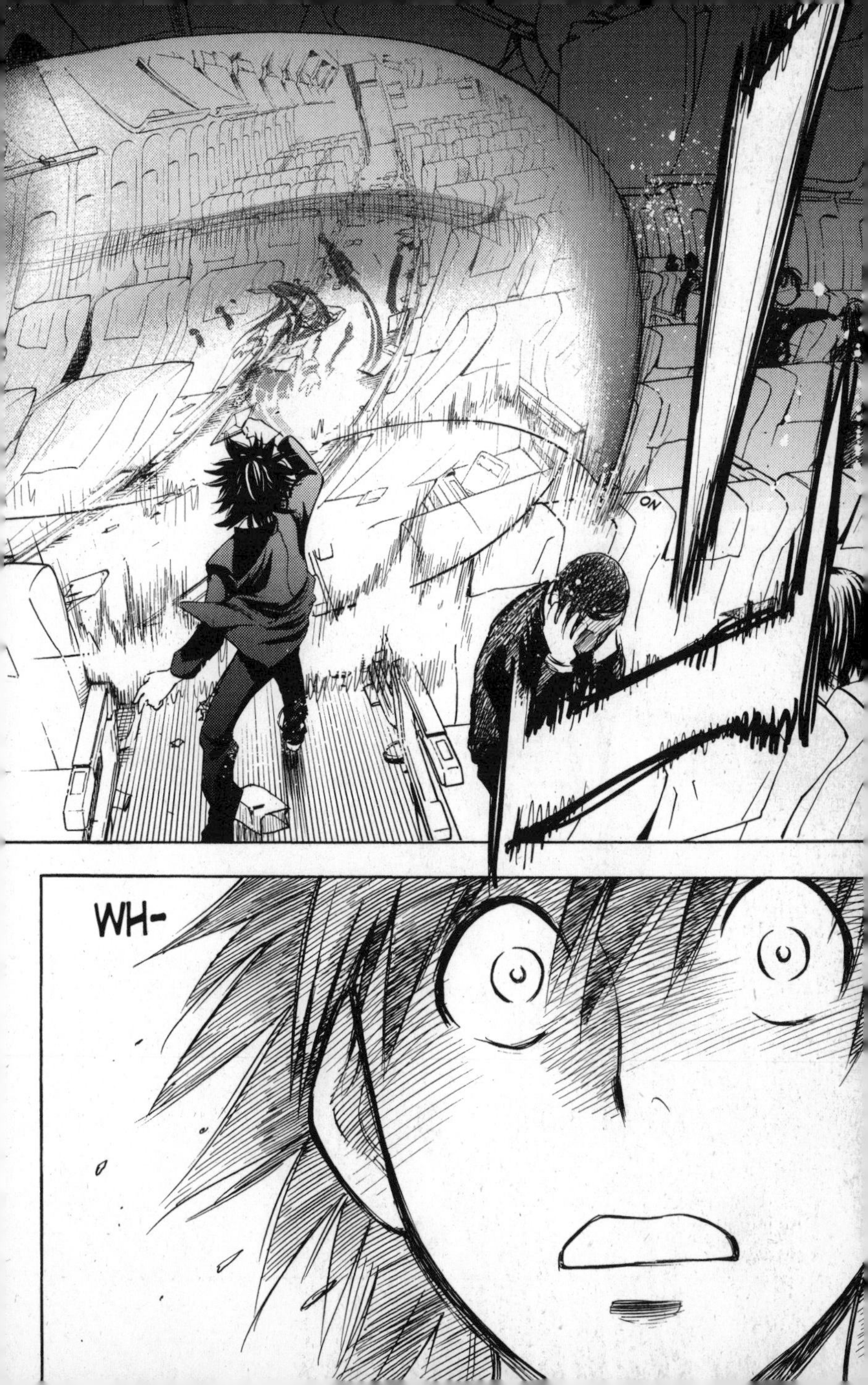
ON
WH-

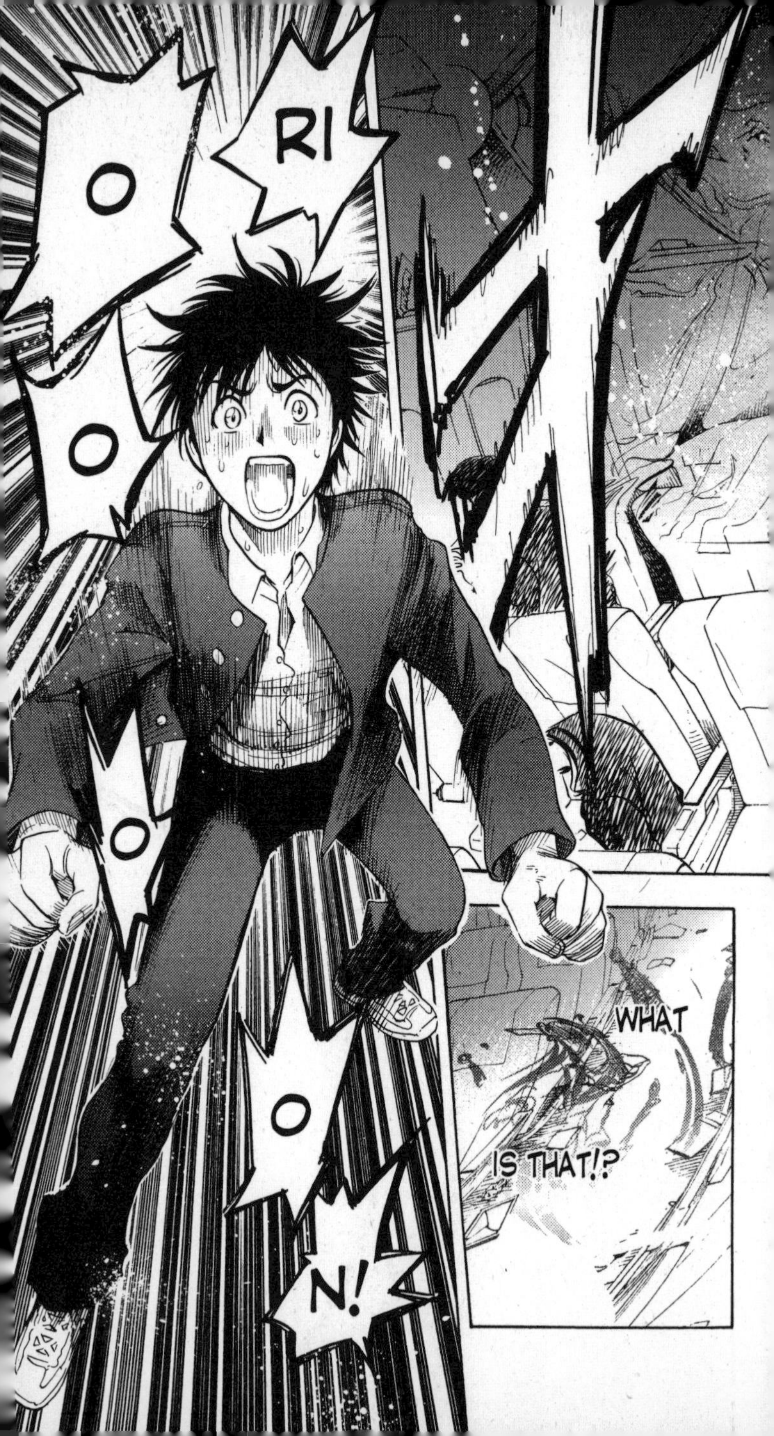
O RI
O
O
O
N!
WHAT IS THAT!?

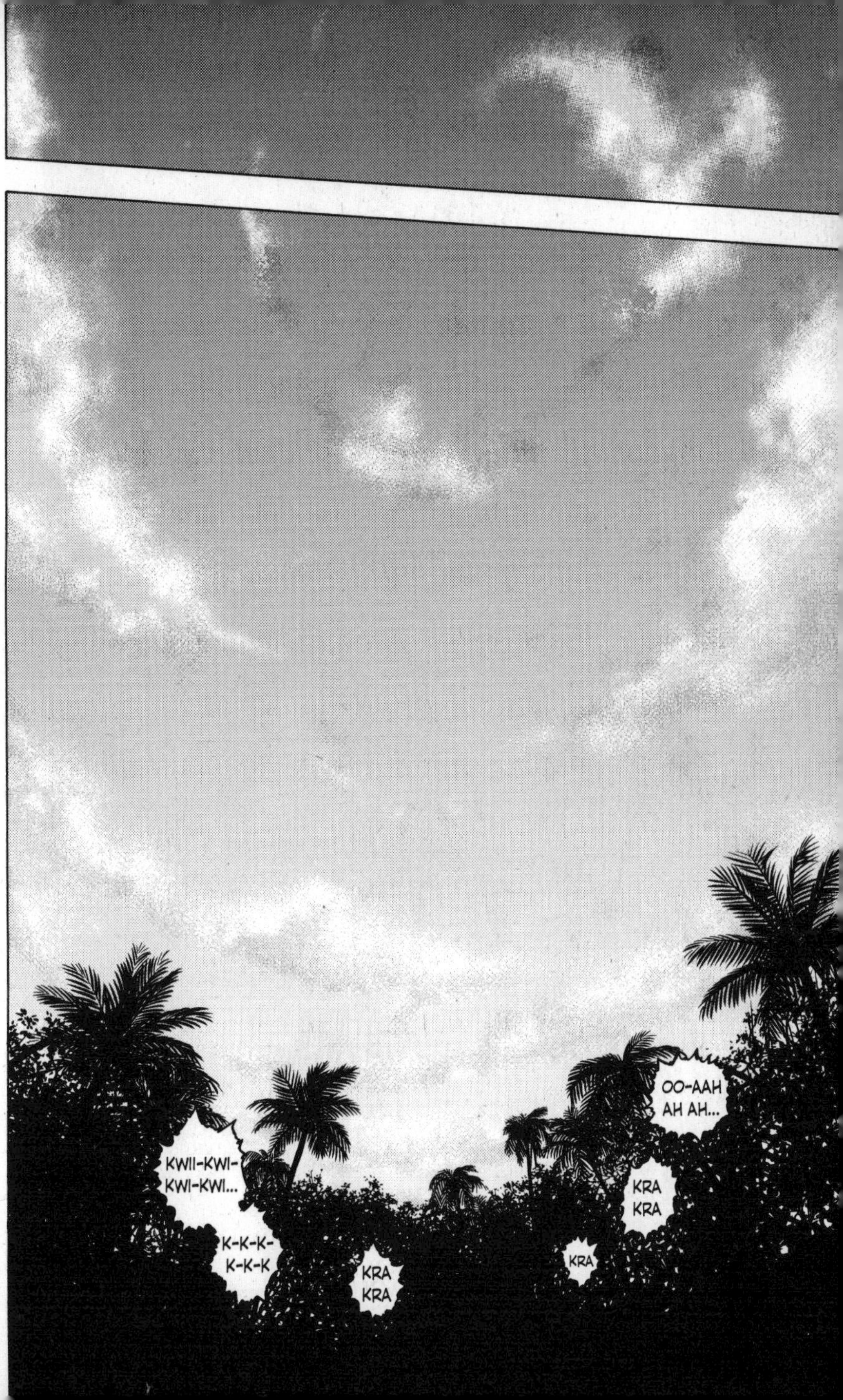
OO-AAH AH AH...
KRA KRA
KRA
KRA KRA
KWII-KWI-KWI-KWI...
K-K-K-K-K-K

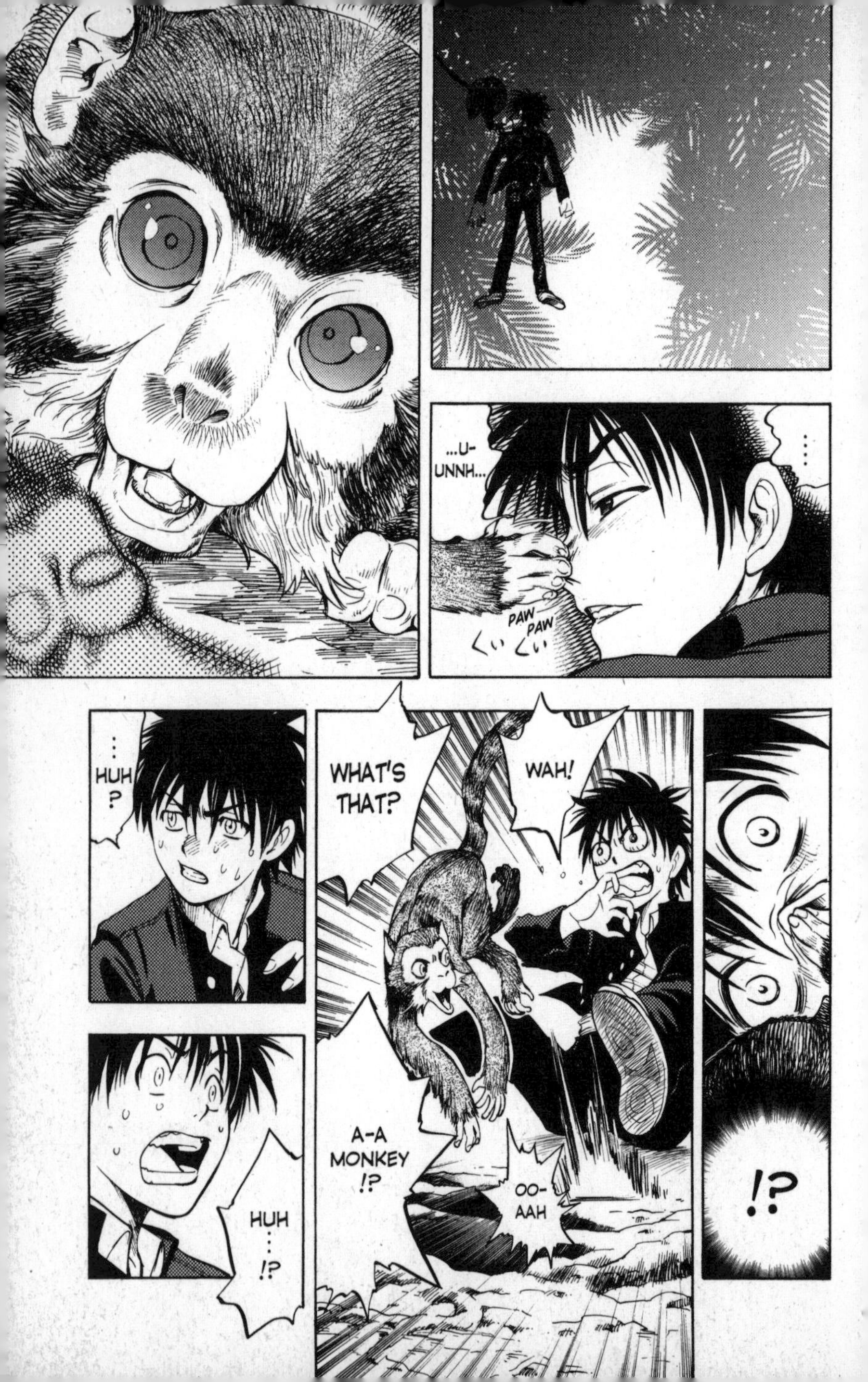
....
...U-UNNH...
PAW PAW
くいくい
!?
WAH!
WHAT'S THAT?
A-A MONKEY !?
OO-AAH
...HUH?
HUH... !?

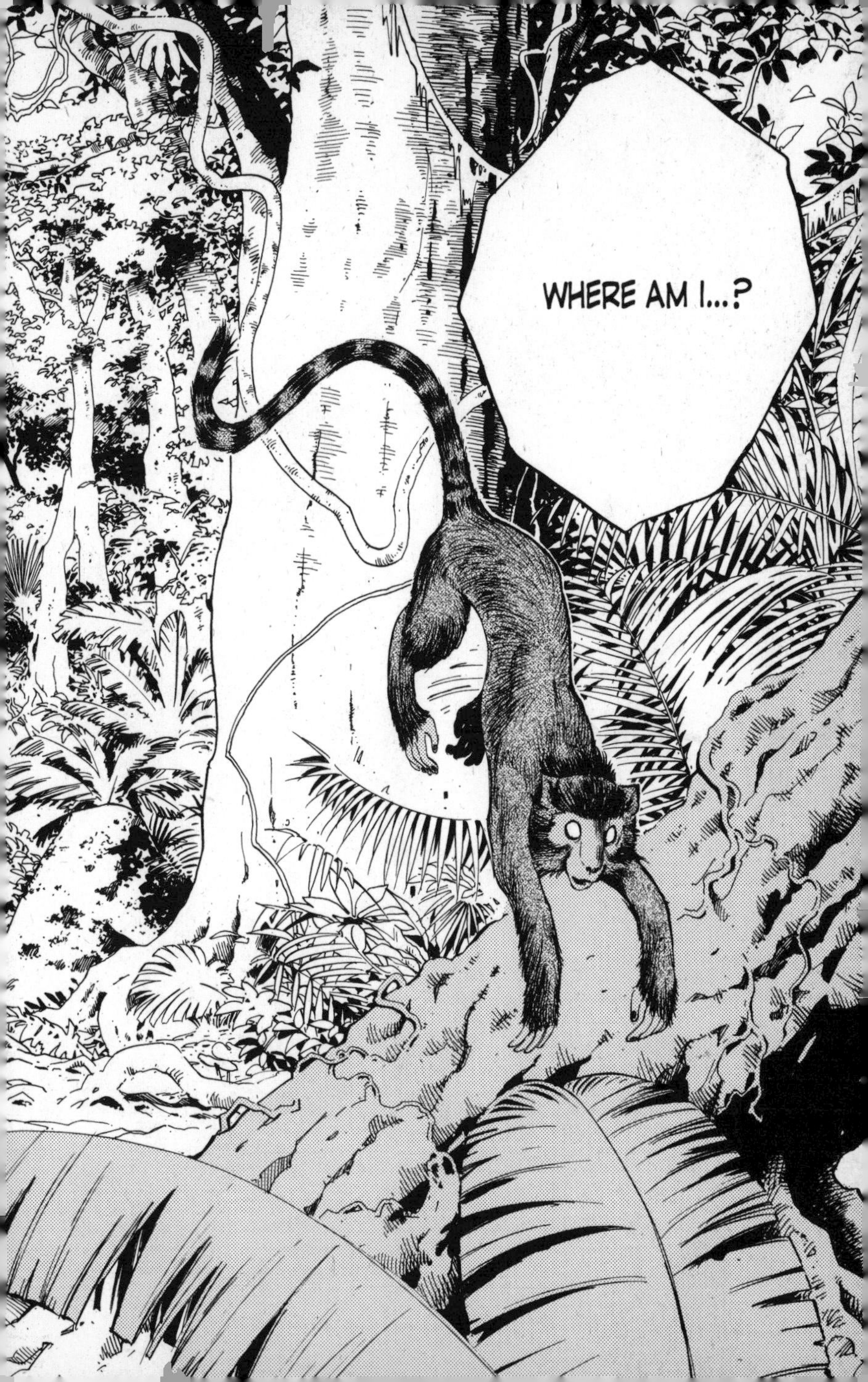
WHERE AM I...?

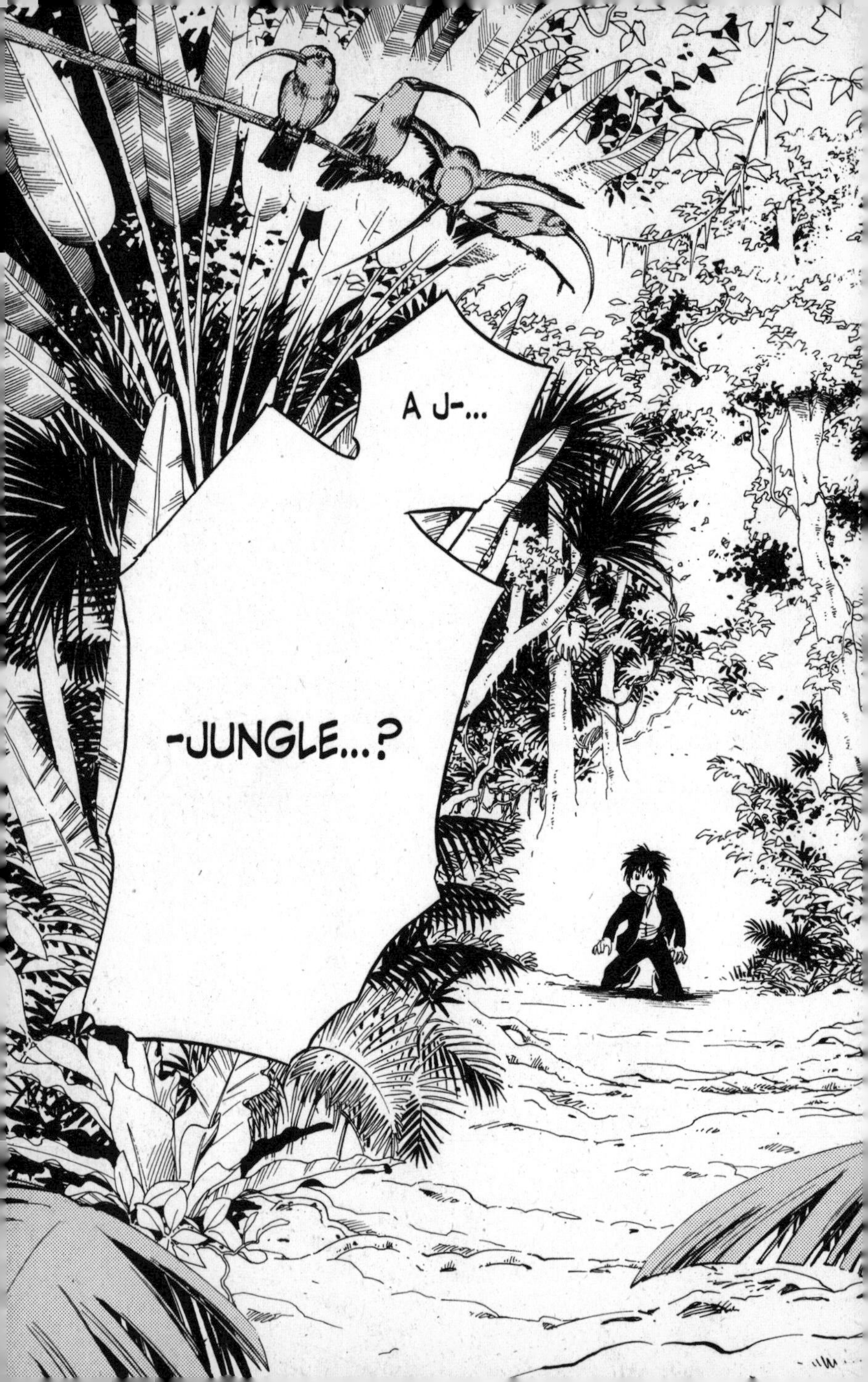
A J-...
-JUNGLE...?

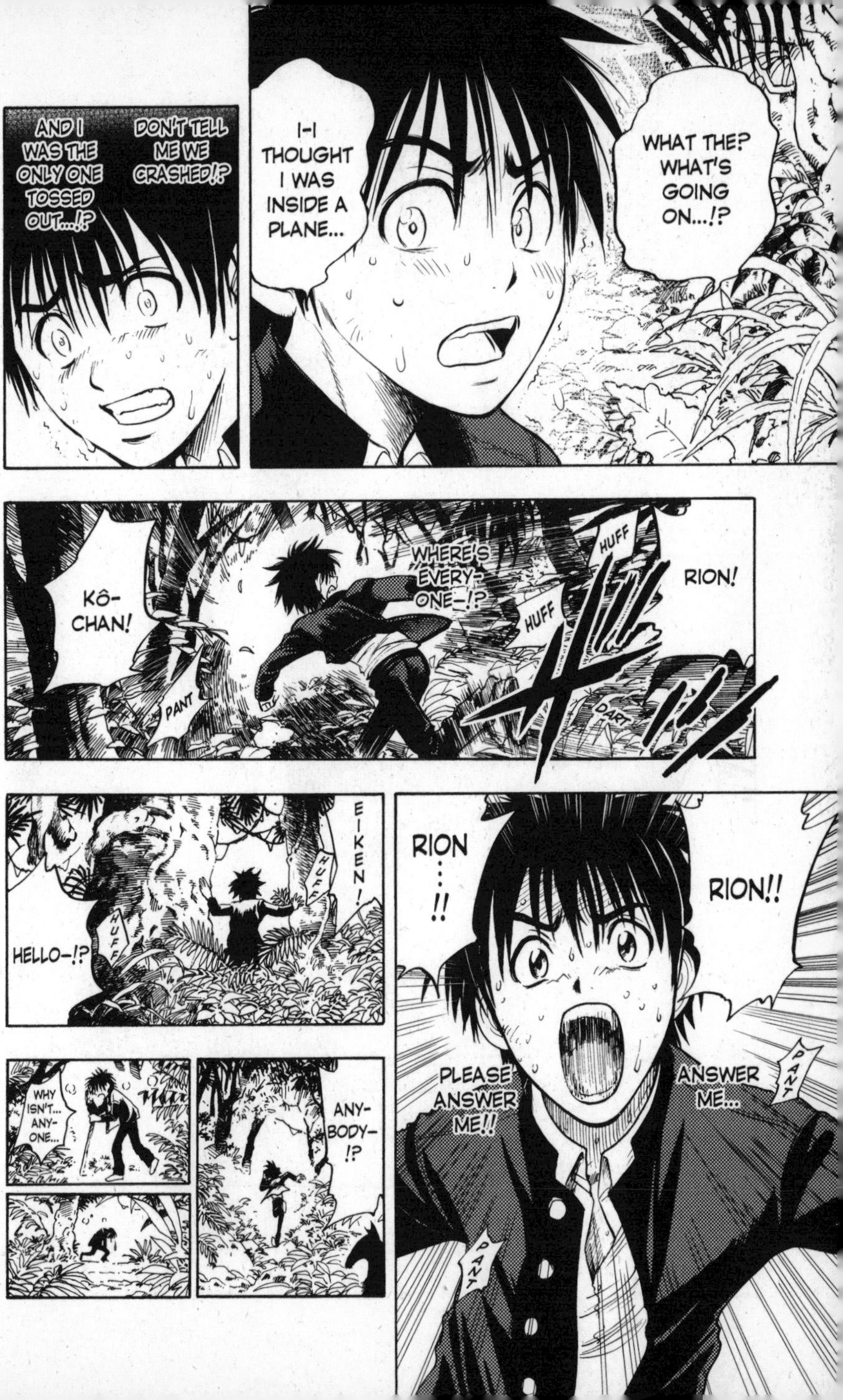
WHAT THE? WHAT'S GOING ON...!?
I-I THOUGHT I WAS INSIDE A PLANE...
DON'T TELL ME WE CRASHED!?
AND I WAS THE ONLY ONE TOSSED OUT...!?
RION!
HUFF
HUFF
WHERE'S EVERY-ONE–!?
DART
KÔ-CHAN!
PANT
RION!!
RION...!!
ANSWER ME...
PANT
PLEASE ANSWER ME!!
PANT
EIKEN!
HUFF
HUFF
HELLO–!?
ANY-BODY–!?
WHY ISN'T... ANY-ONE...

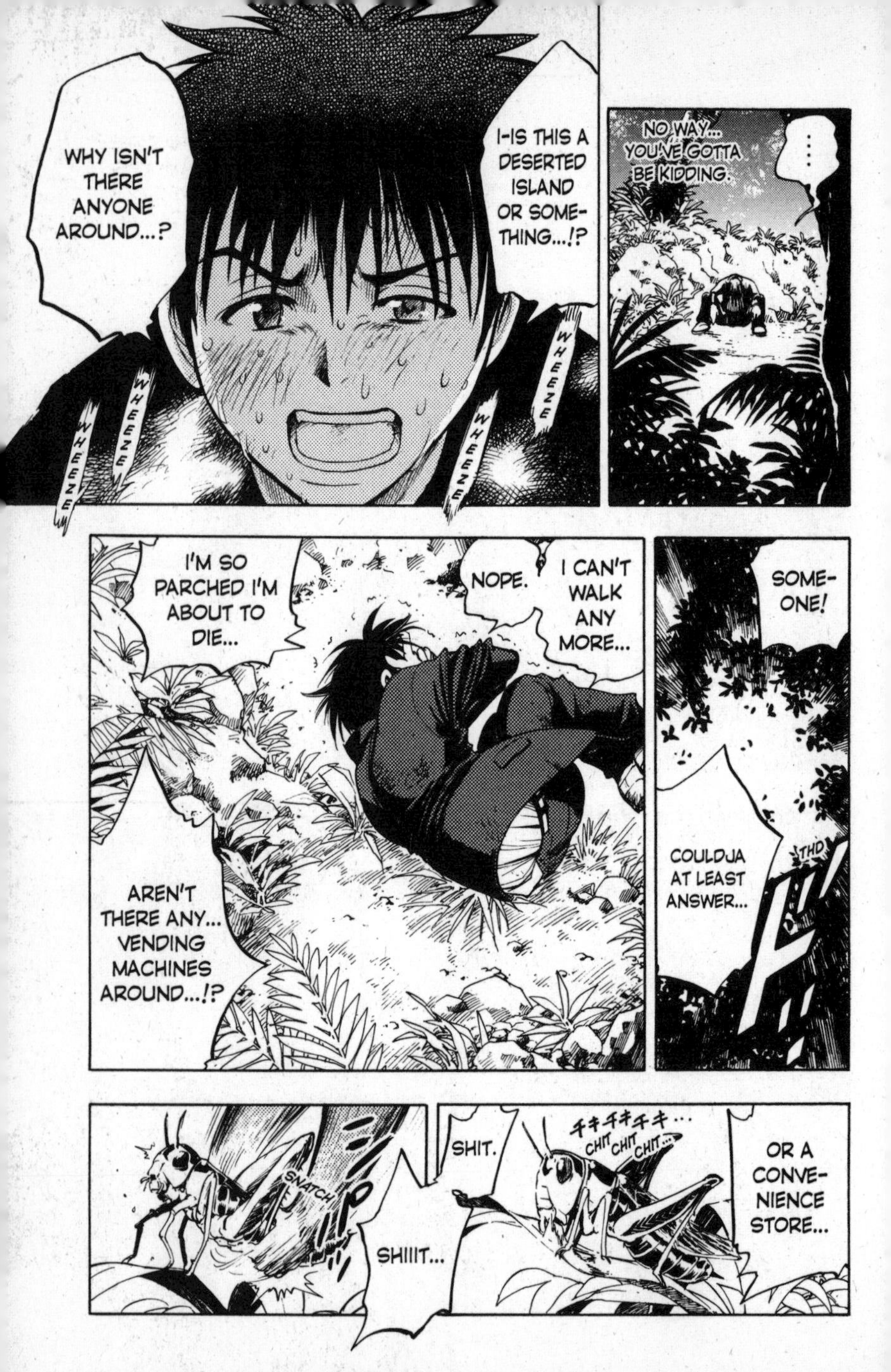
....
NO WAY... YOU'VE GOTTA BE KIDDING.
I-IS THIS A DESERTED ISLAND OR SOME-THING...!?
WHY ISN'T THERE ANYONE AROUND...?
WHEEZE
WHEEZE
WHEEZE
WHEEZE
SOME-ONE!
COULDJA AT LEAST ANSWER...
THD
I CAN'T WALK ANY MORE...
NOPE.
I'M SO PARCHED I'M ABOUT TO DIE...
AREN'T THERE ANY... VENDING MACHINES AROUND...!?
OR A CONVE-NIENCE STORE...
チキチキチキ…
CHIT CHIT CHIT...
SHIT.
SHIIIT...
SNATCH

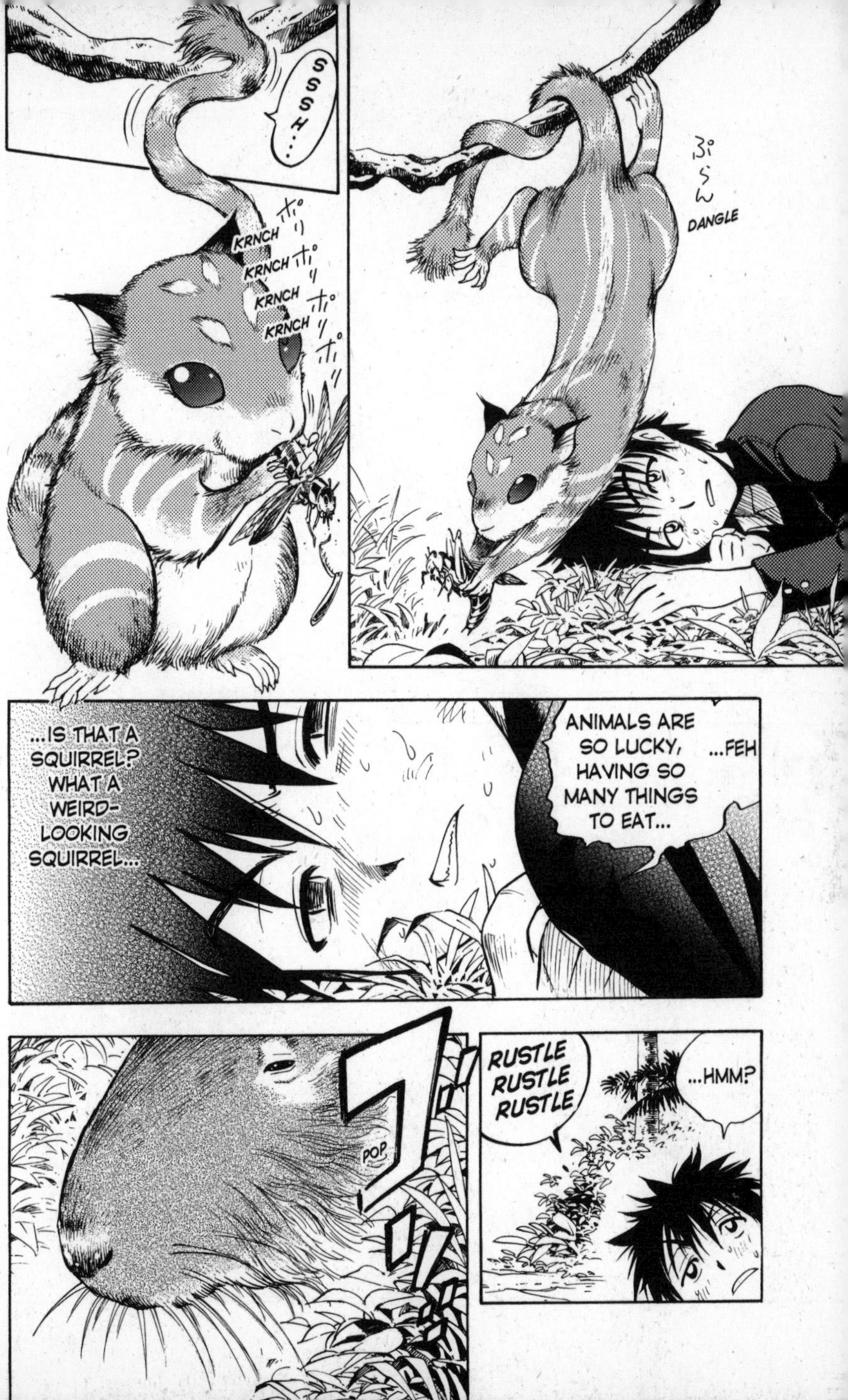

ぷらん
DANGLE
SSSH...
KRNCH
ポリ
KRNCH
ポリ
KRNCH
ポリ
KRNCH
ポリ
...FEH
ANIMALS ARE SO LUCKY, HAVING SO MANY THINGS TO EAT...
...IS THAT A SQUIRREL? WHAT A WEIRD-LOOKING SQUIRREL...
...HMM?
RUSTLE RUSTLE RUSTLE
POP

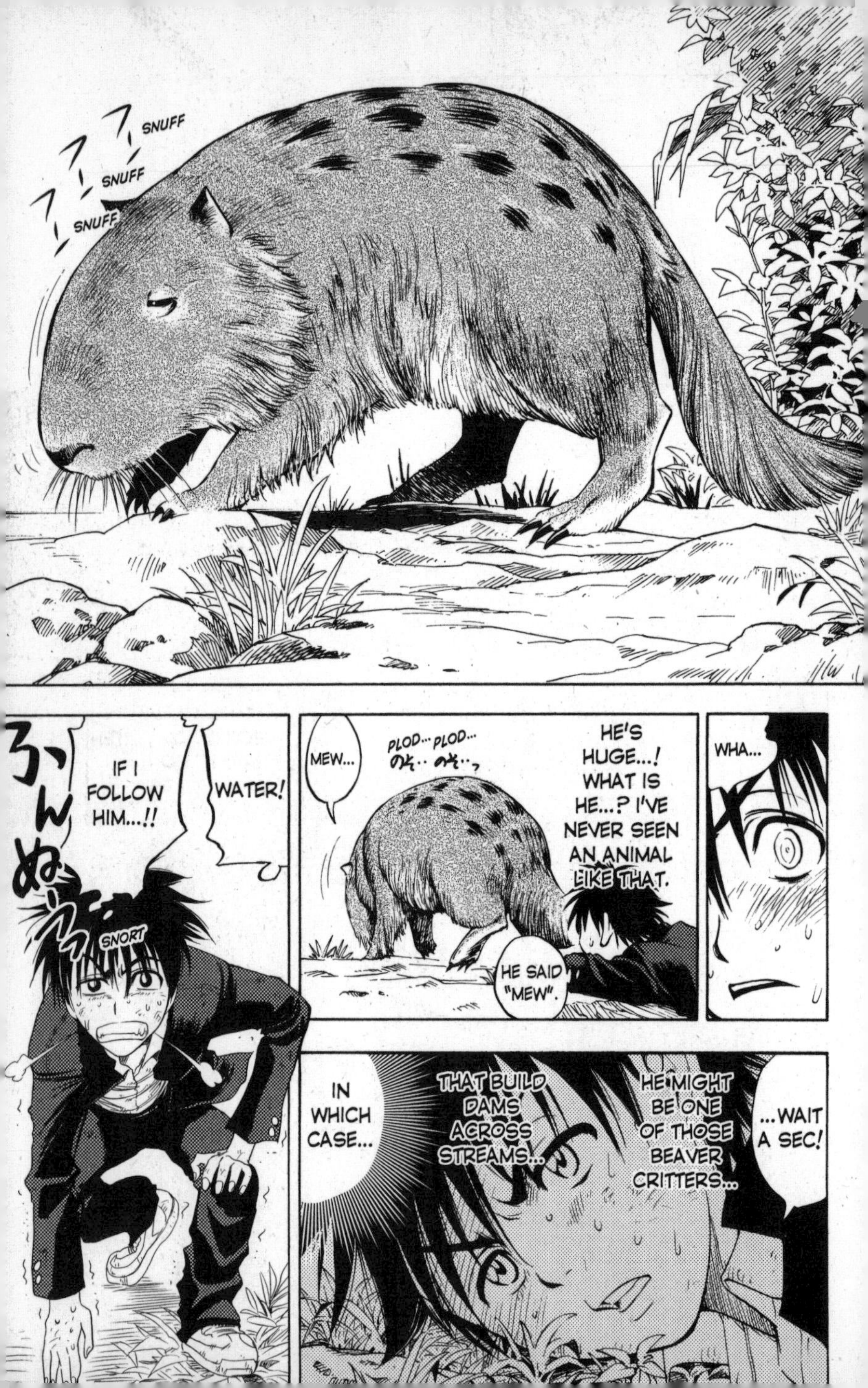

フ
SNUFF
フ
SNUFF
フ
SNUFF
WHA...
HE'S HUGE...! WHAT IS HE...? I'VE NEVER SEEN AN ANIMAL LIKE THAT.
PLOD... PLOD...
のそ… のそ…っ
MEW...
HE SAID "MEW".
...WAIT A SEC!
HE MIGHT BE ONE OF THOSE BEAVER CRITTERS...
THAT BUILD DAMS ACROSS STREAMS...
IN WHICH CASE...
WATER!
IF I FOLLOW HIM...!!
ふんぬぇぇ
SNORT

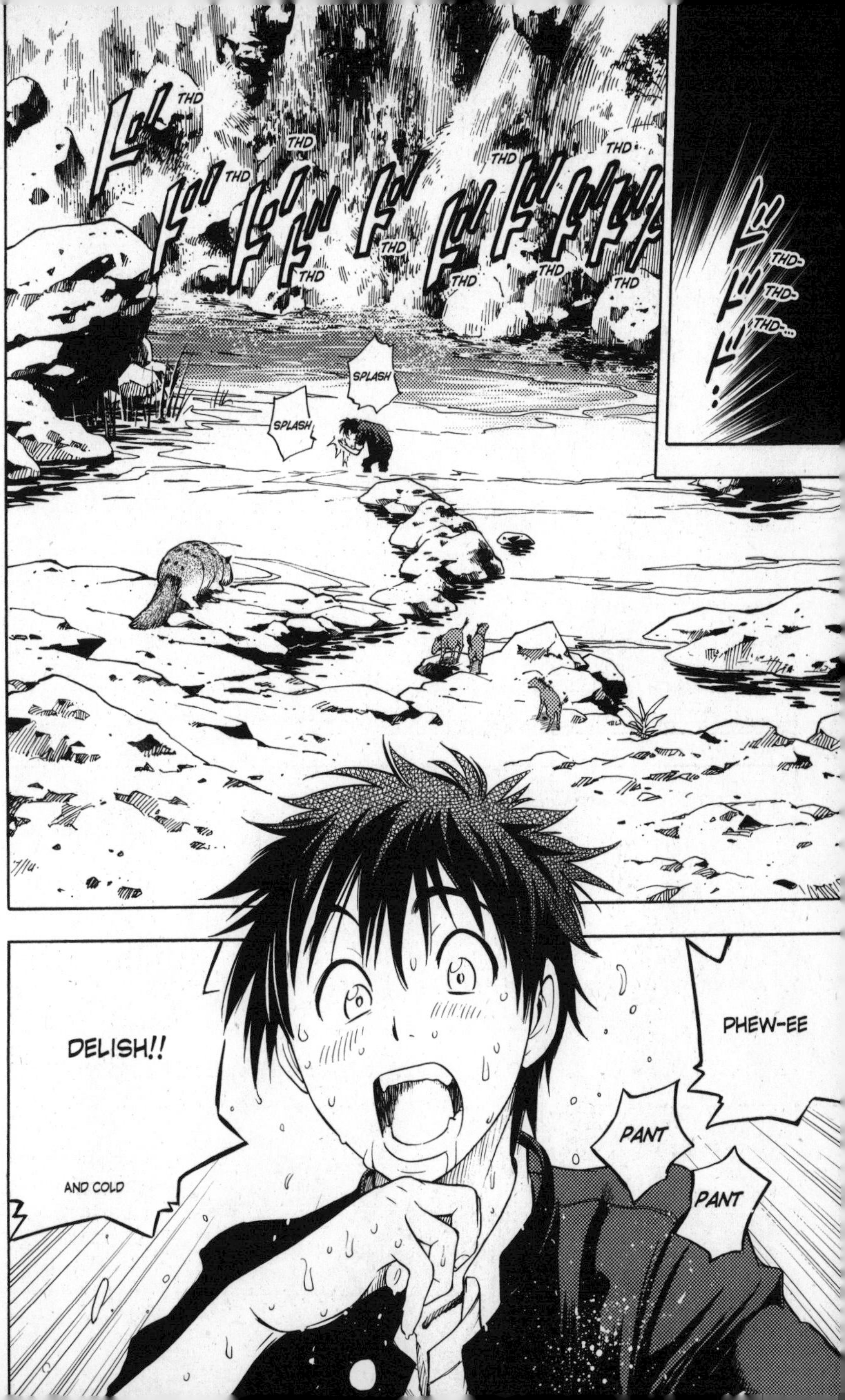
THD-
THD-
THD-...
THD
THD
THD
THD
THD
THD
THD
THD
THD
THD
SPLASH
SPLASH
PHEW-EE
PANT
PANT
DELISH!!
AND COLD

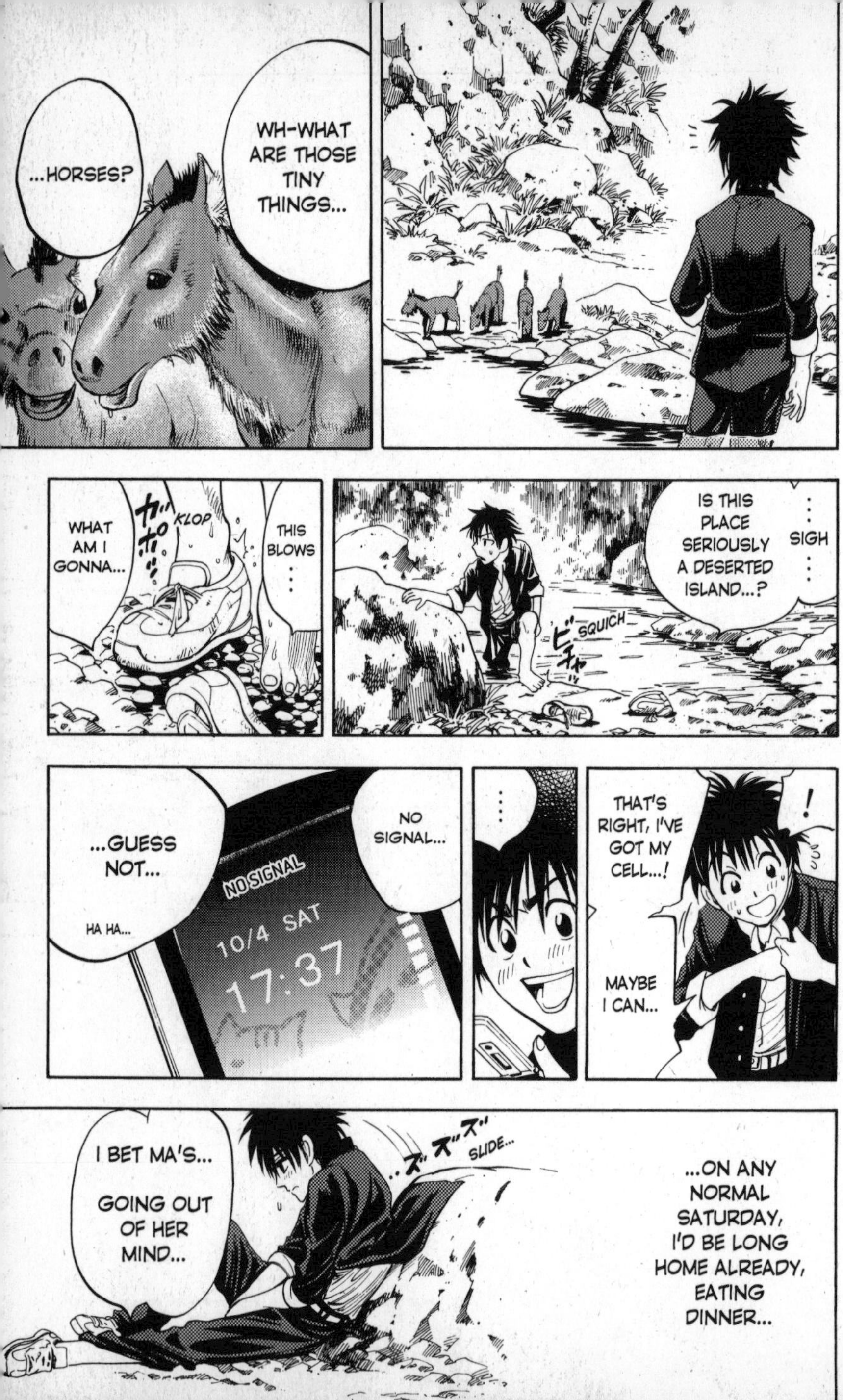

WH-WHAT ARE THOSE TINY THINGS...
...HORSES?
IS THIS PLACE SERIOUSLY A DESERTED ISLAND...?
...SIGH...
SQUICH
THIS BLOWS...
KLOP
WHAT AM I GONNA...
!
THAT'S RIGHT, I'VE GOT MY CELL...!
MAYBE I CAN...
...
NO SIGNAL...
NO SIGNAL
10/4 SAT
17:37
...GUESS NOT...
HA HA...
...ON ANY NORMAL SATURDAY, I'D BE LONG HOME ALREADY, EATING DINNER...
SLIDE...
I BET MA'S...
GOING OUT OF HER MIND...

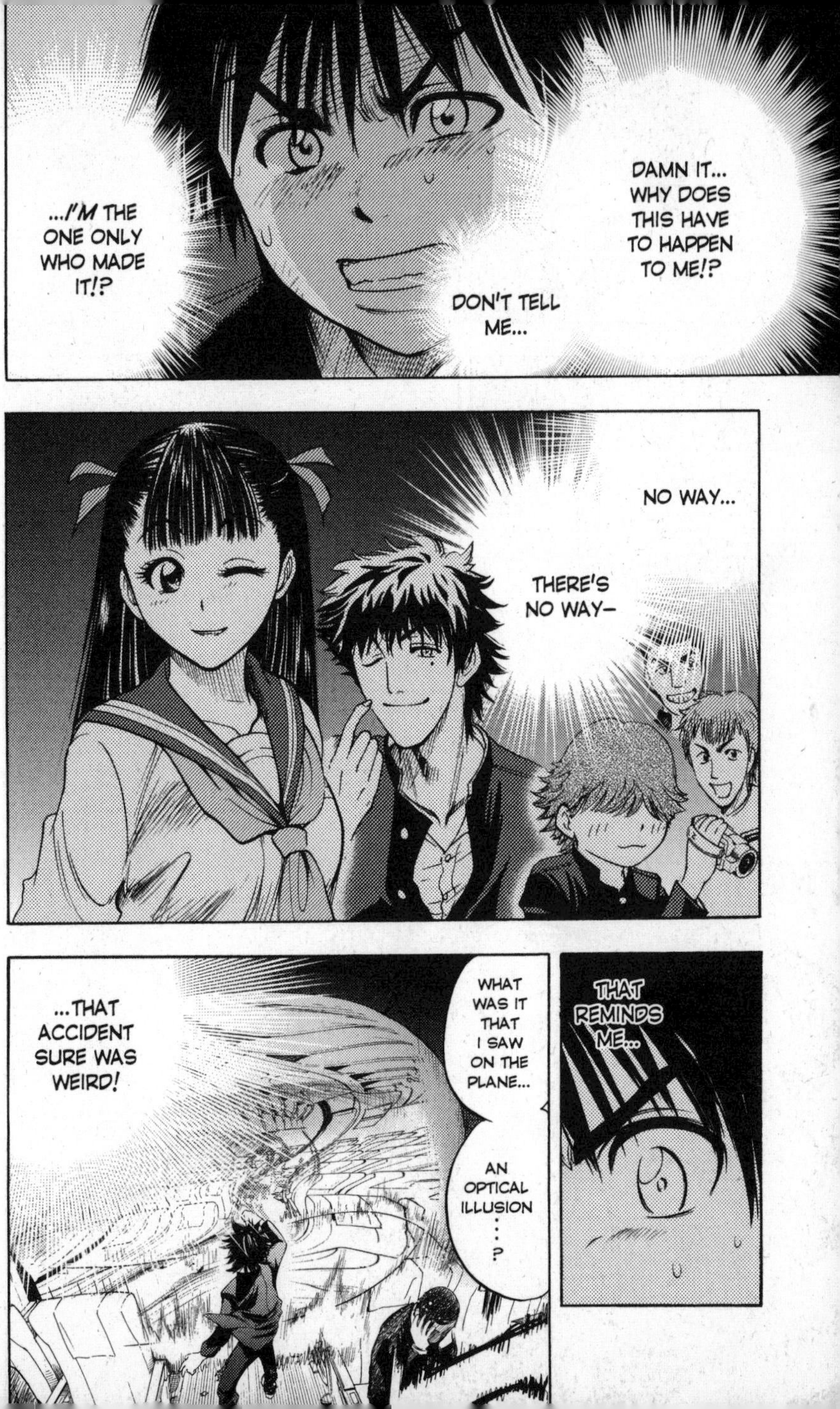
DAMN IT... WHY DOES THIS HAVE TO HAPPEN TO ME!?
DON'T TELL ME...
...I'M THE ONE ONLY WHO MADE IT!?
NO WAY...
THERE'S NO WAY–
THAT REMINDS ME...
WHAT WAS IT THAT I SAW ON THE PLANE...
AN OPTICAL ILLUSION...?
...THAT ACCIDENT SURE WAS WEIRD!

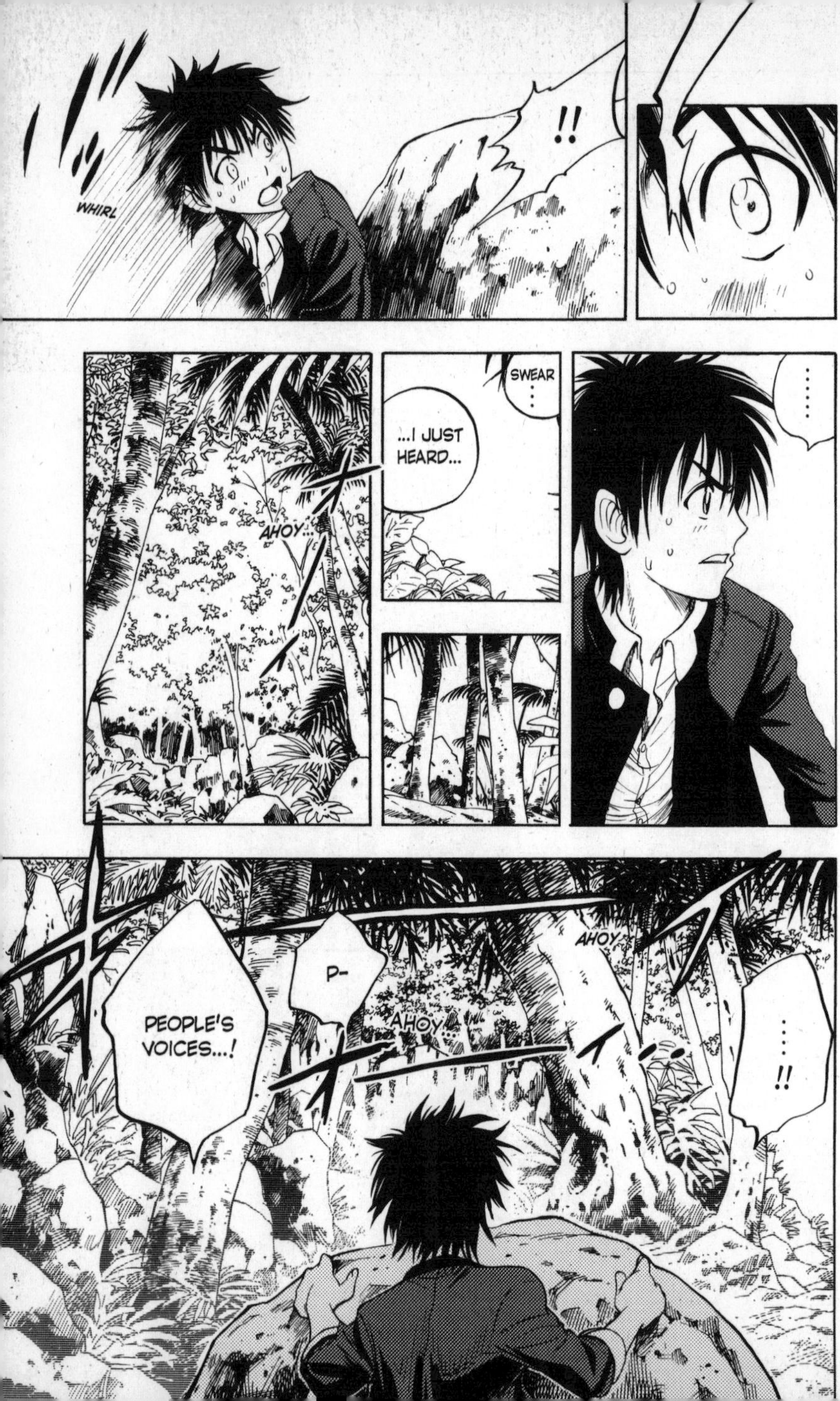
!!
WHIRL
......
SWEAR...
...I JUST HEARD...
AHOY...
AHOY
....!!
P-
AHOY...
PEOPLE'S VOICES...!

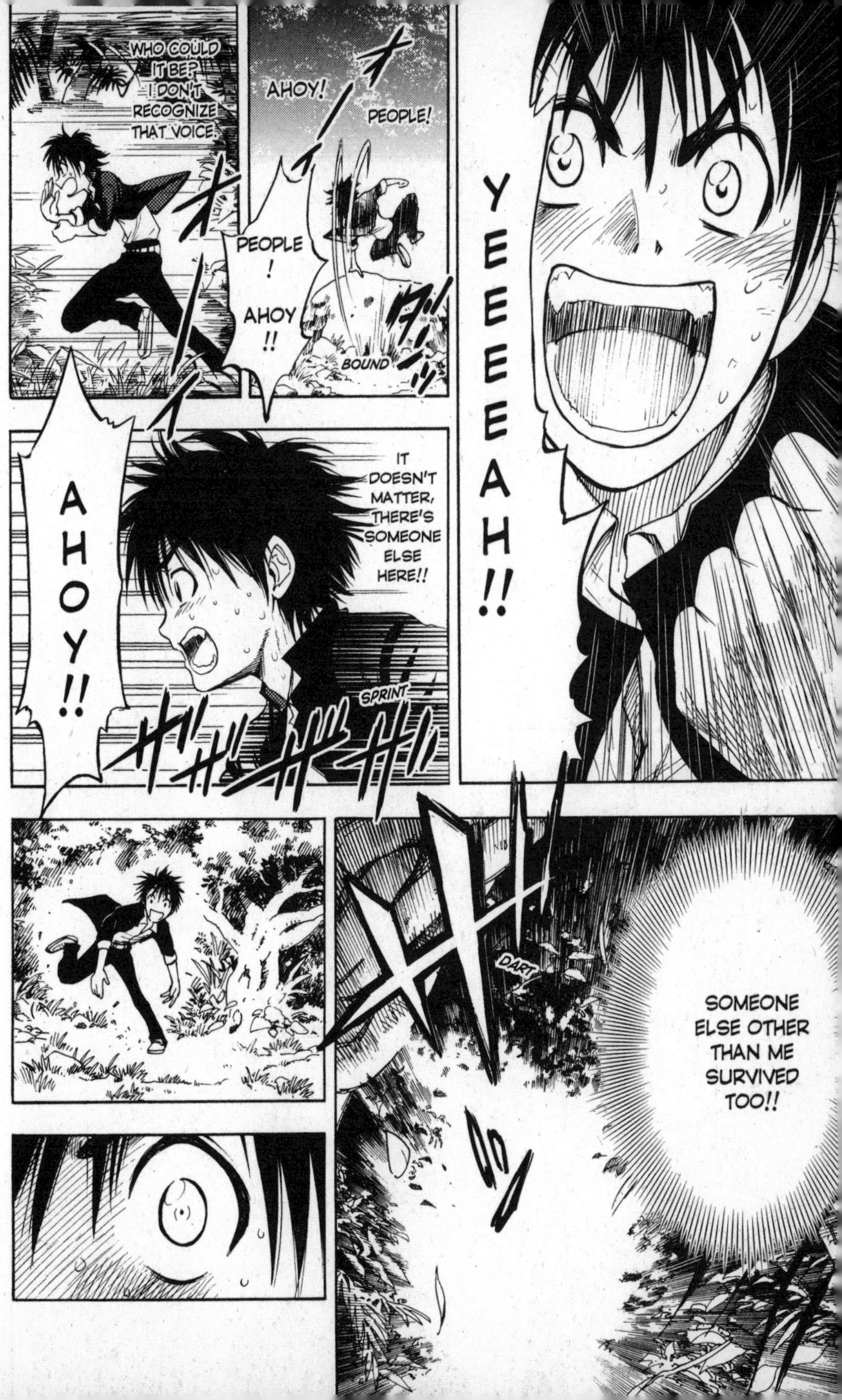
YEEEEAH!!
AHOY!
PEOPLE!
PEOPLE!
AHOY!!
BOUND
WHO COULD IT BE? I DON'T RECOGNIZE THAT VOICE.
IT DOESN'T MATTER, THERE'S SOMEONE ELSE HERE!!
SPRINT
AHOY!!
SOMEONE ELSE OTHER THAN ME SURVIVED TOO!!
DART

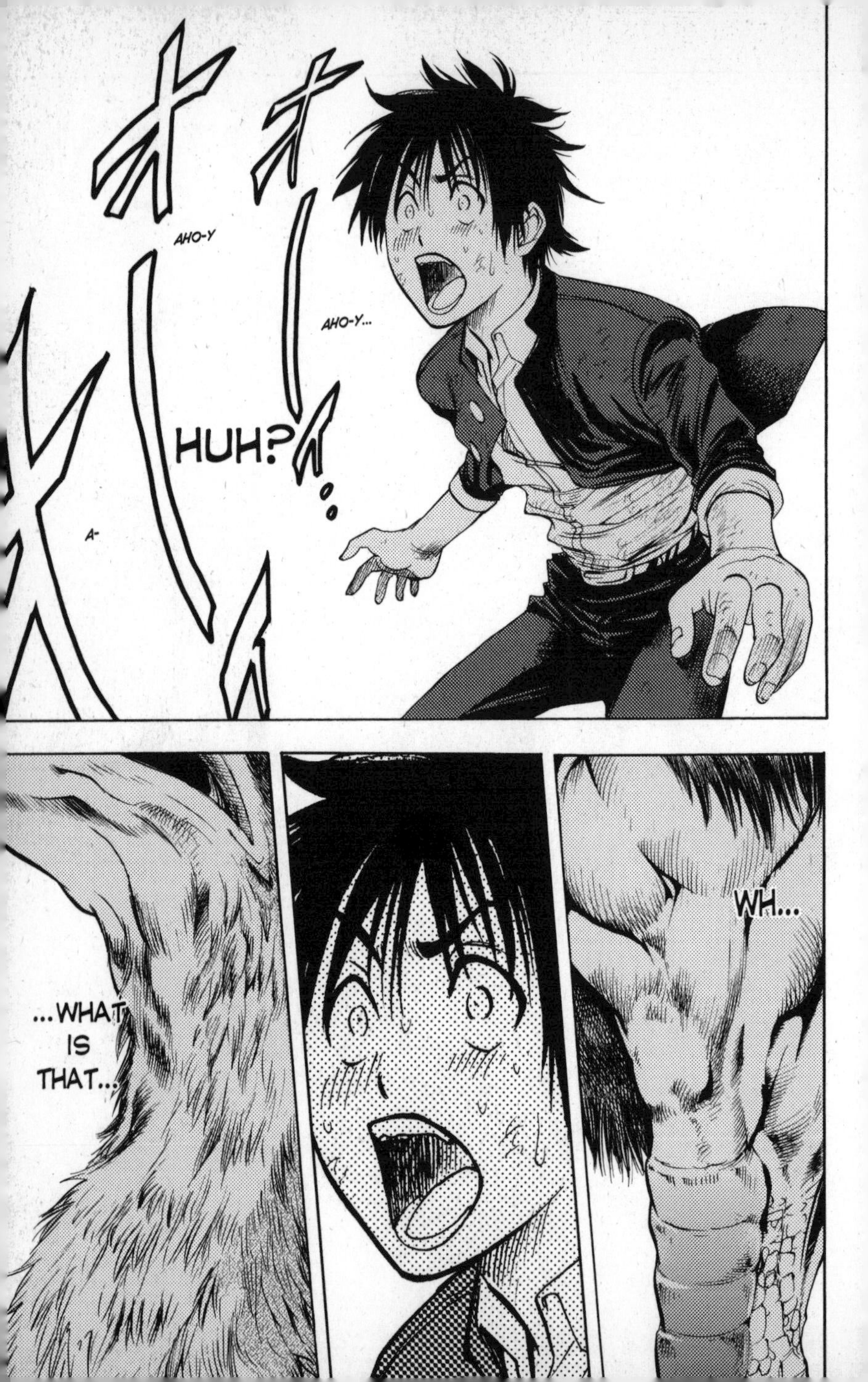
AHO-Y
AHO-Y...
HUH?
A-
WH...
...WHAT IS THAT...

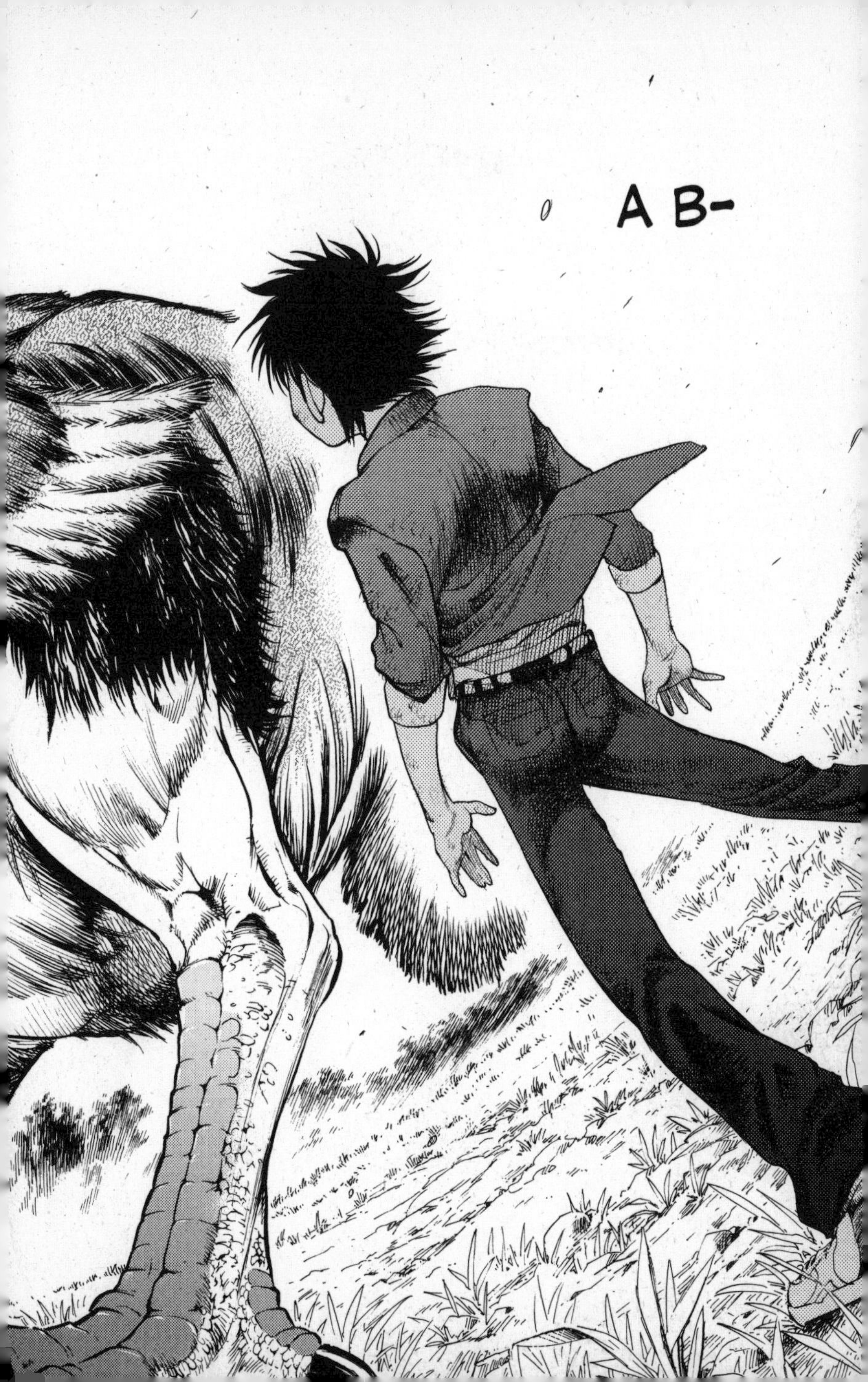
A B-

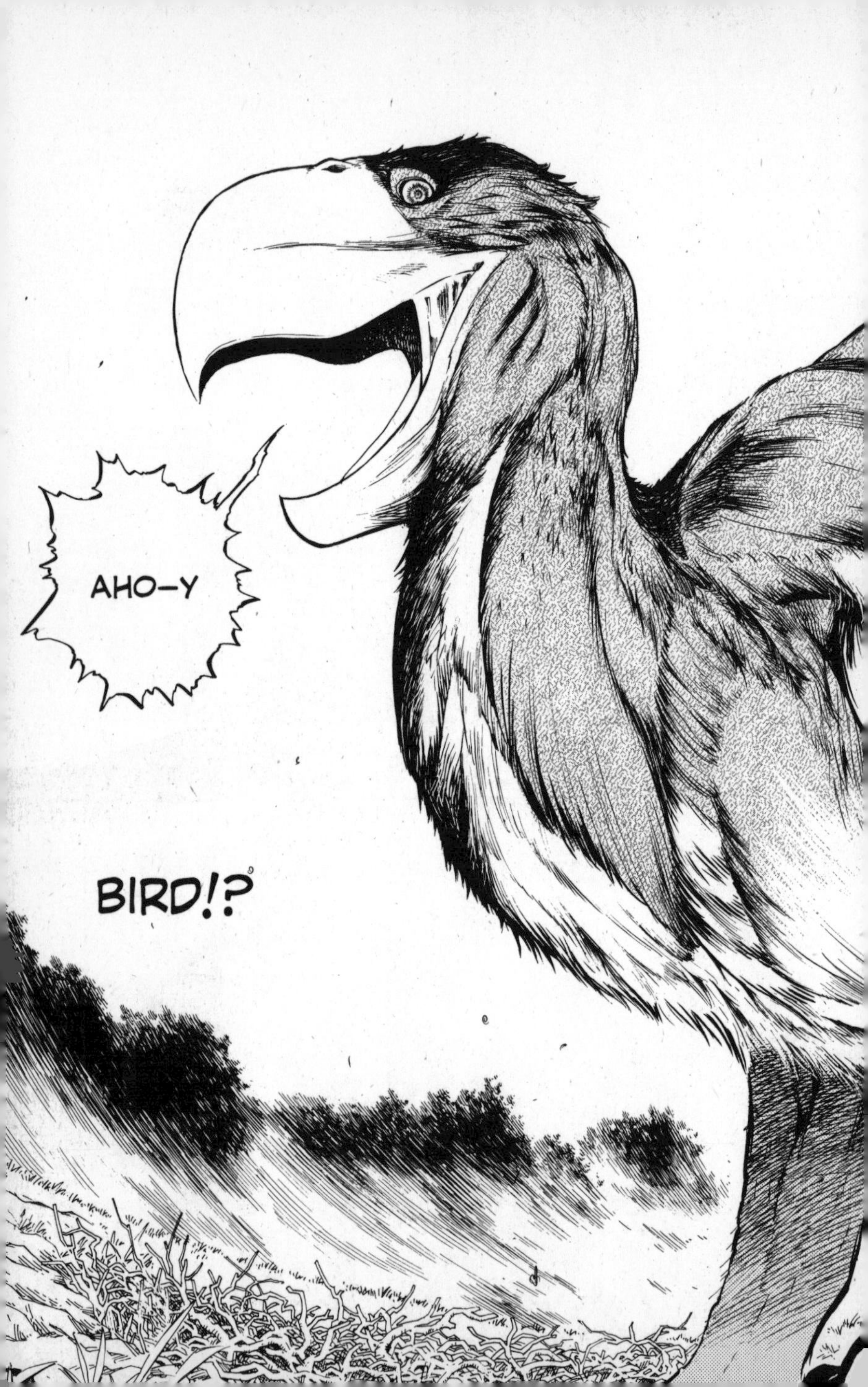
AHO-Y
BIRD!?

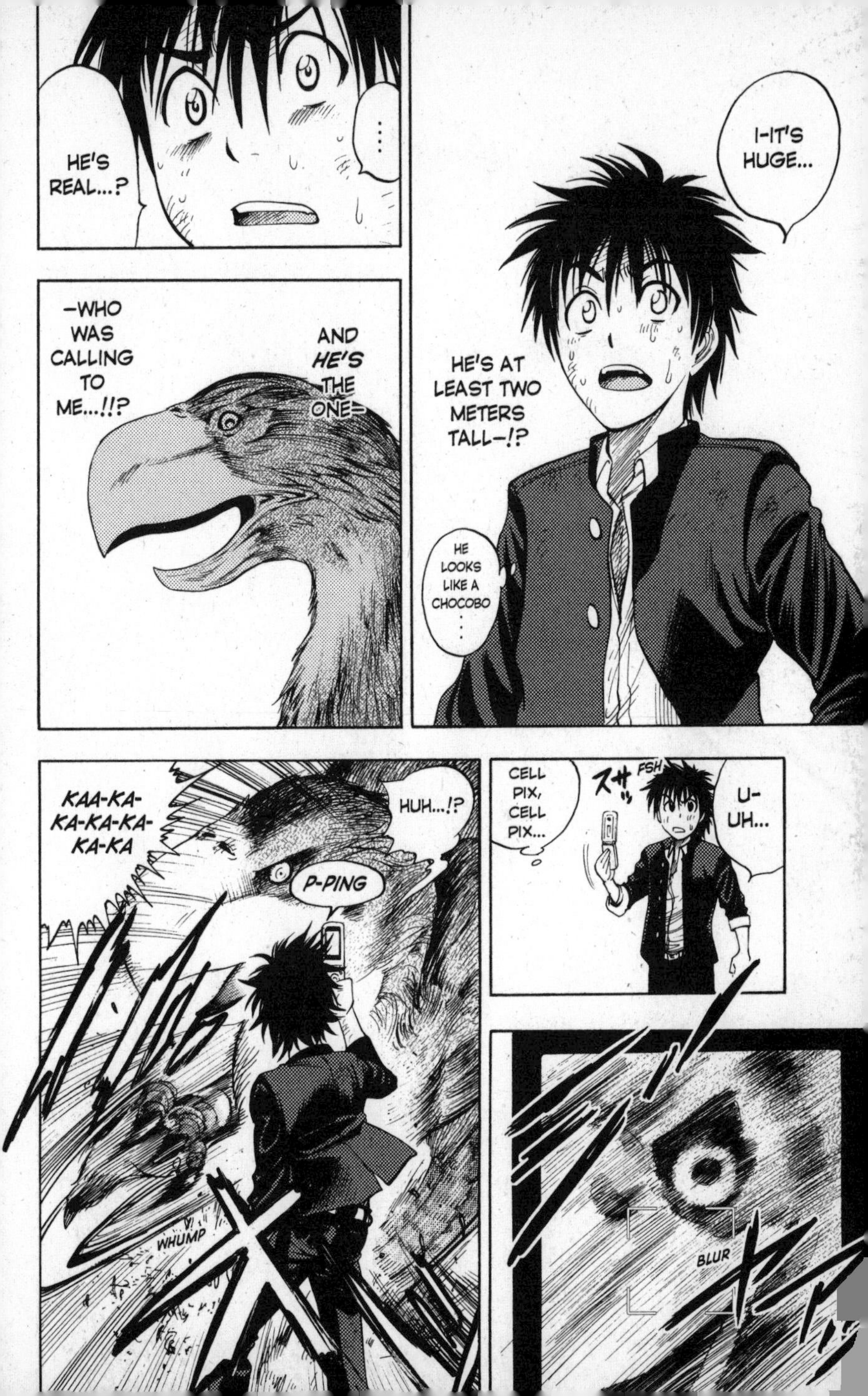

I-IT'S HUGE...
HE'S AT LEAST TWO METERS TALL–!?
HE LOOKS LIKE A CHOCOBO...
HE'S REAL...?
AND *HE'S* THE ONE–
–WHO WAS CALLING TO ME...!!?
U-UH...
スサ FSH
CELL PIX, CELL PIX...
BLUR
HUH...!?
P-PING
KAA-KA-KA-KA-KA-KA-KA-KA
WHUMP

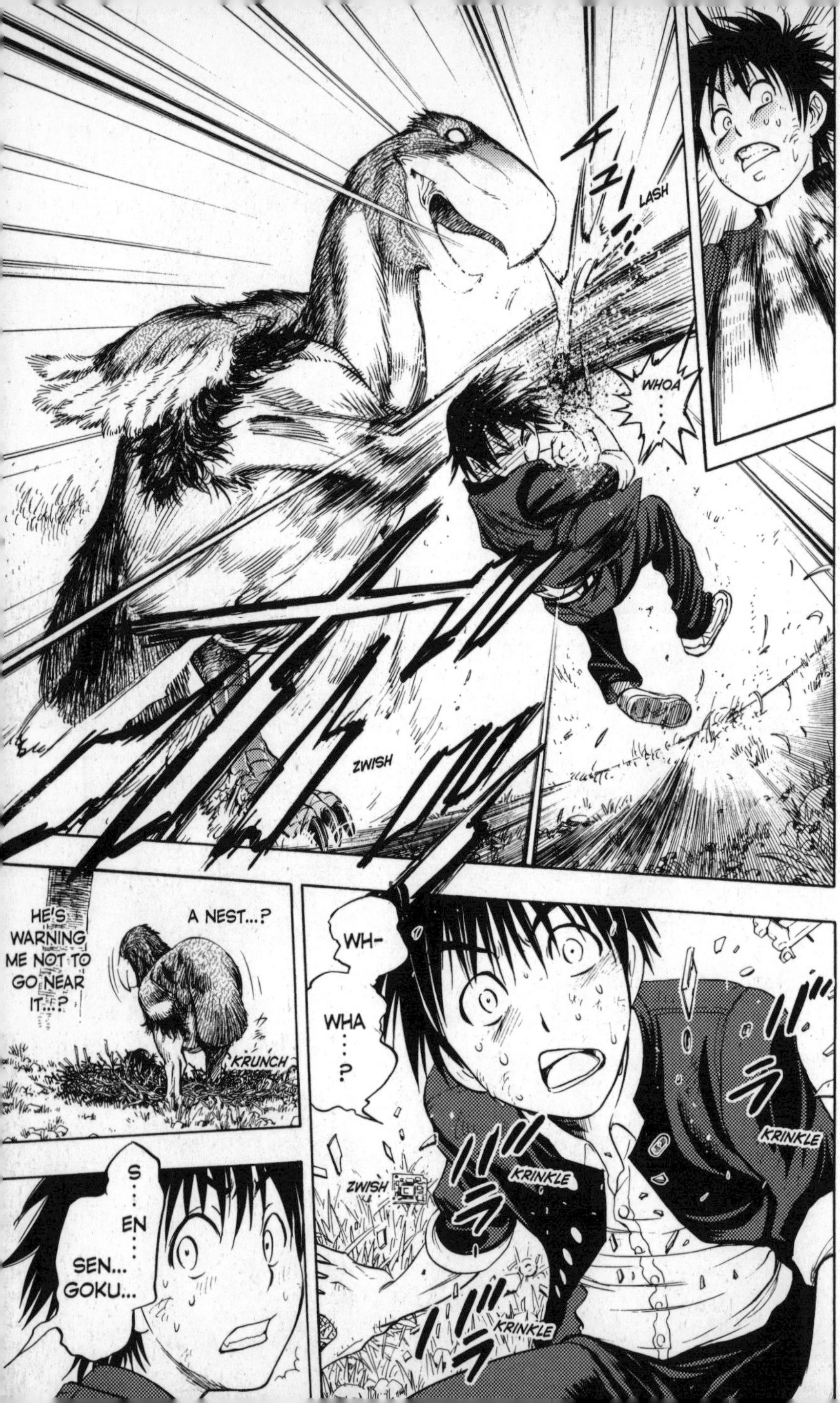

LASH
WHOA...!
ZWISH
WH-
WHA...?
KRINKLE
KRINKLE
KRINKLE
ZWISH
A NEST...?
HE'S WARNING ME NOT TO GO NEAR IT...?
KRUNCH
S... EN...
SEN... GOKU...

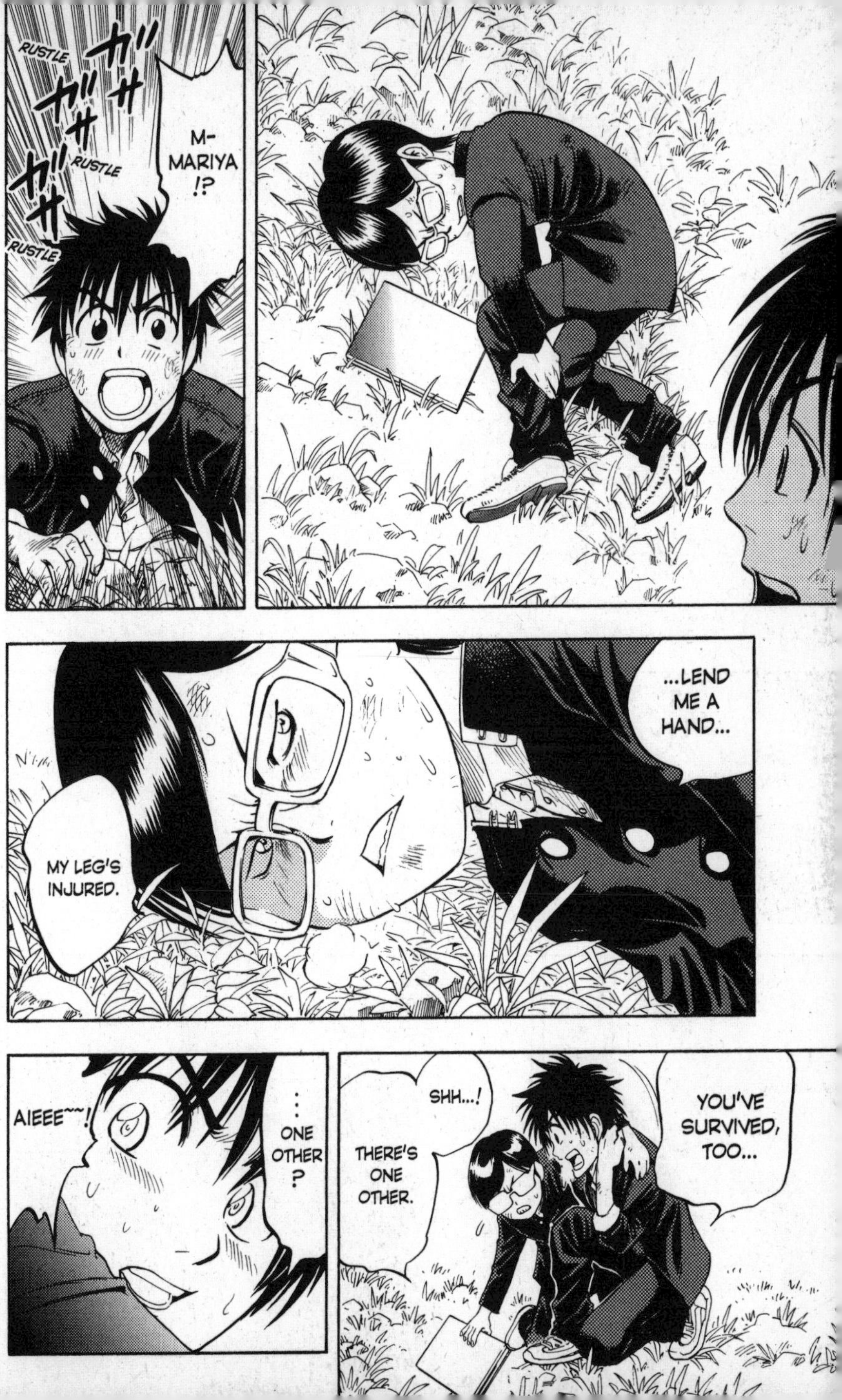
RUSTLE
RUSTLE
RUSTLE
M-MARIYA!?
...LEND ME A HAND...
MY LEG'S INJURED.
YOU'VE SURVIVED, TOO...
SHH...!
THERE'S ONE OTHER.
...ONE OTHER?
AIEEE~~!

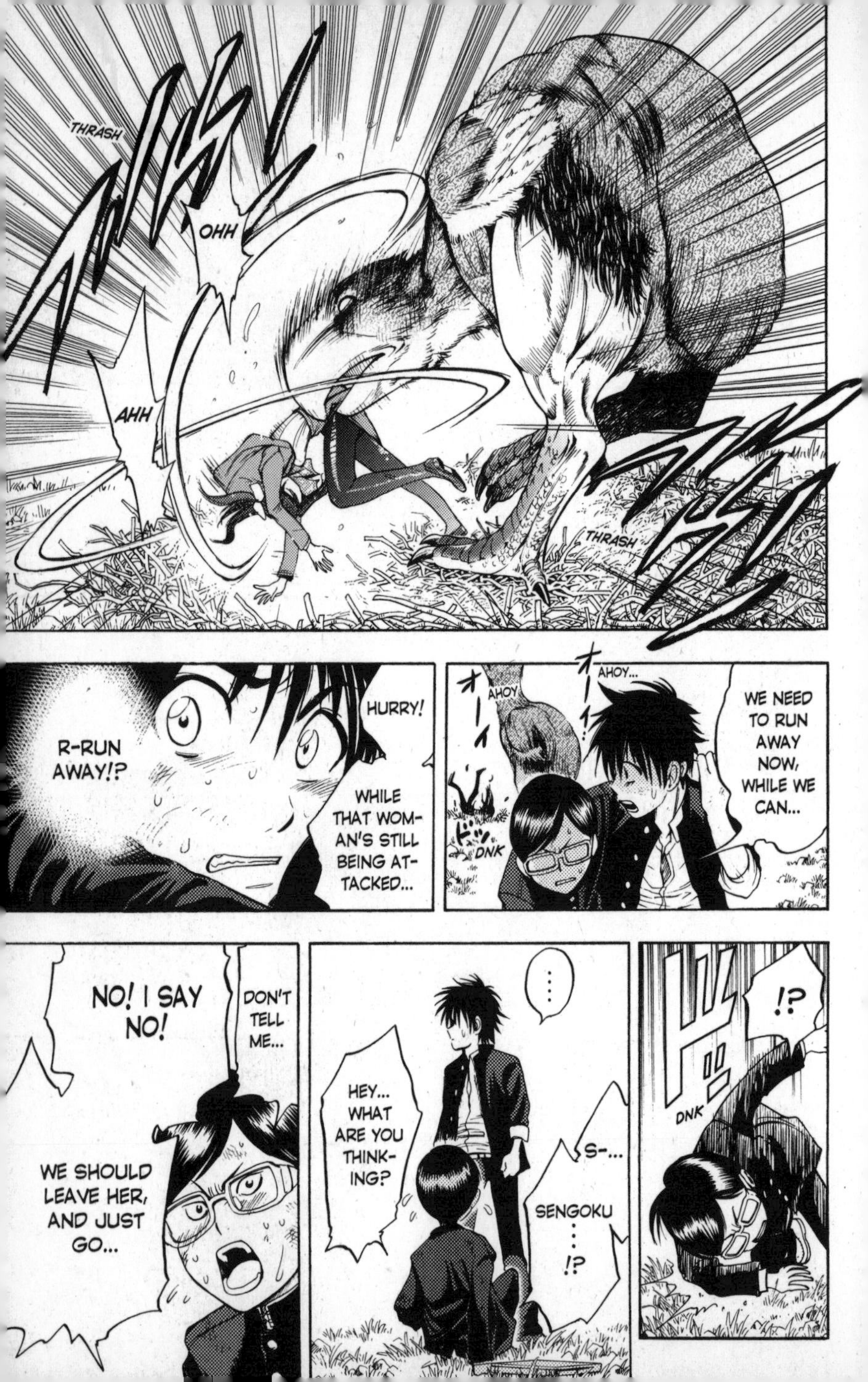
THRASH
OHH
AHH
THRASH
AHOY...
AHOY
オーイ
WE NEED TO RUN AWAY NOW, WHILE WE CAN...
ドッ
DNK
HURRY!
WHILE THAT WOM-AN'S STILL BEING AT-TACKED...
R-RUN AWAY!?
!?
DNK
....
HEY... WHAT ARE YOU THINK-ING?
S-...
SENGOKU ...!?
DON'T TELL ME...
NO! I SAY NO!
WE SHOULD LEAVE HER, AND JUST GO...

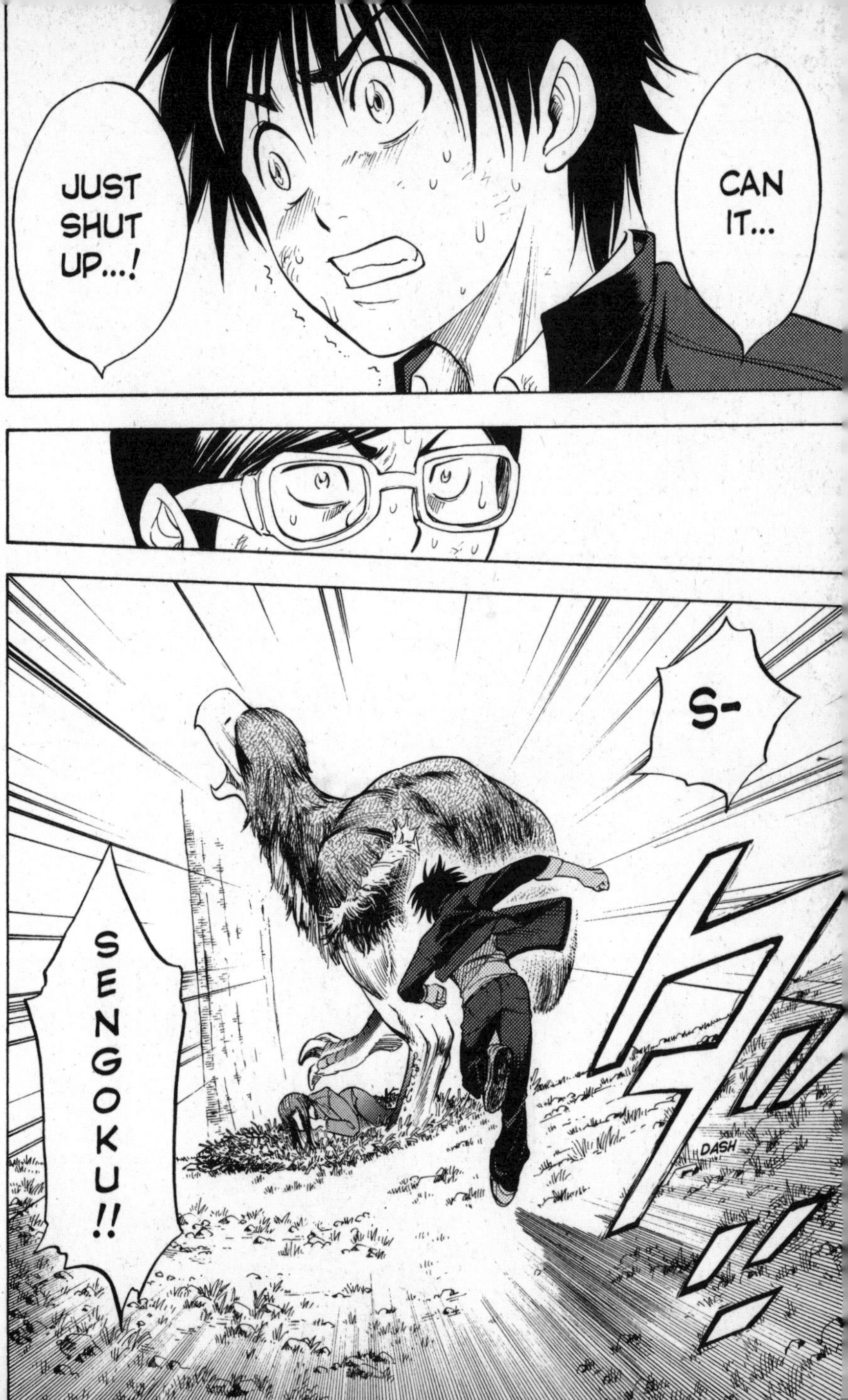
CAN IT...
JUST SHUT UP...!
S-
SENGOKU!!
DASH

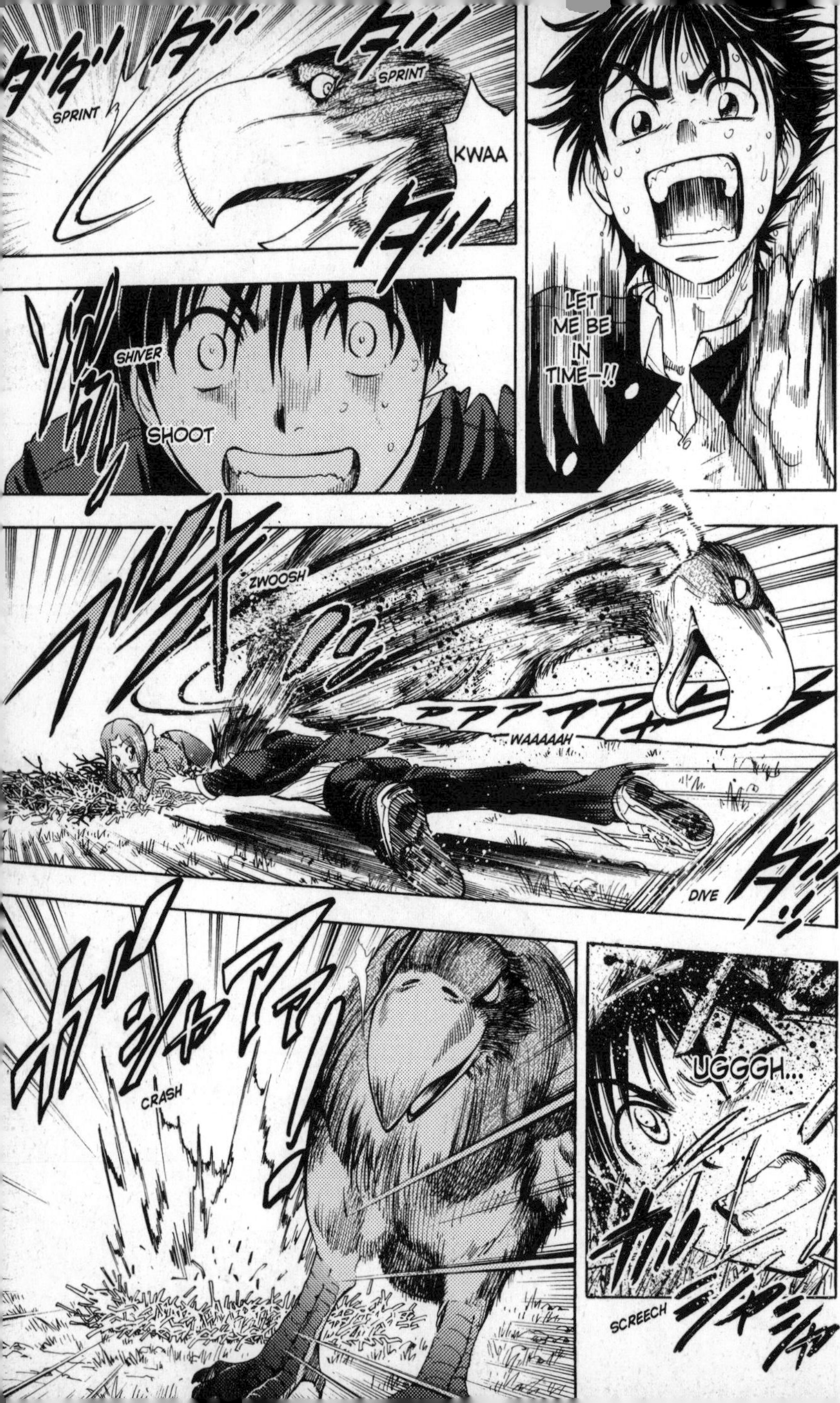
LET ME BE IN TIME—!!
SPRINT
SPRINT
KWAA
SHIVER
SHOOT
ZWOOSH
WAAAAAH
DIVE
UGGGH...
SCREECH
CRASH

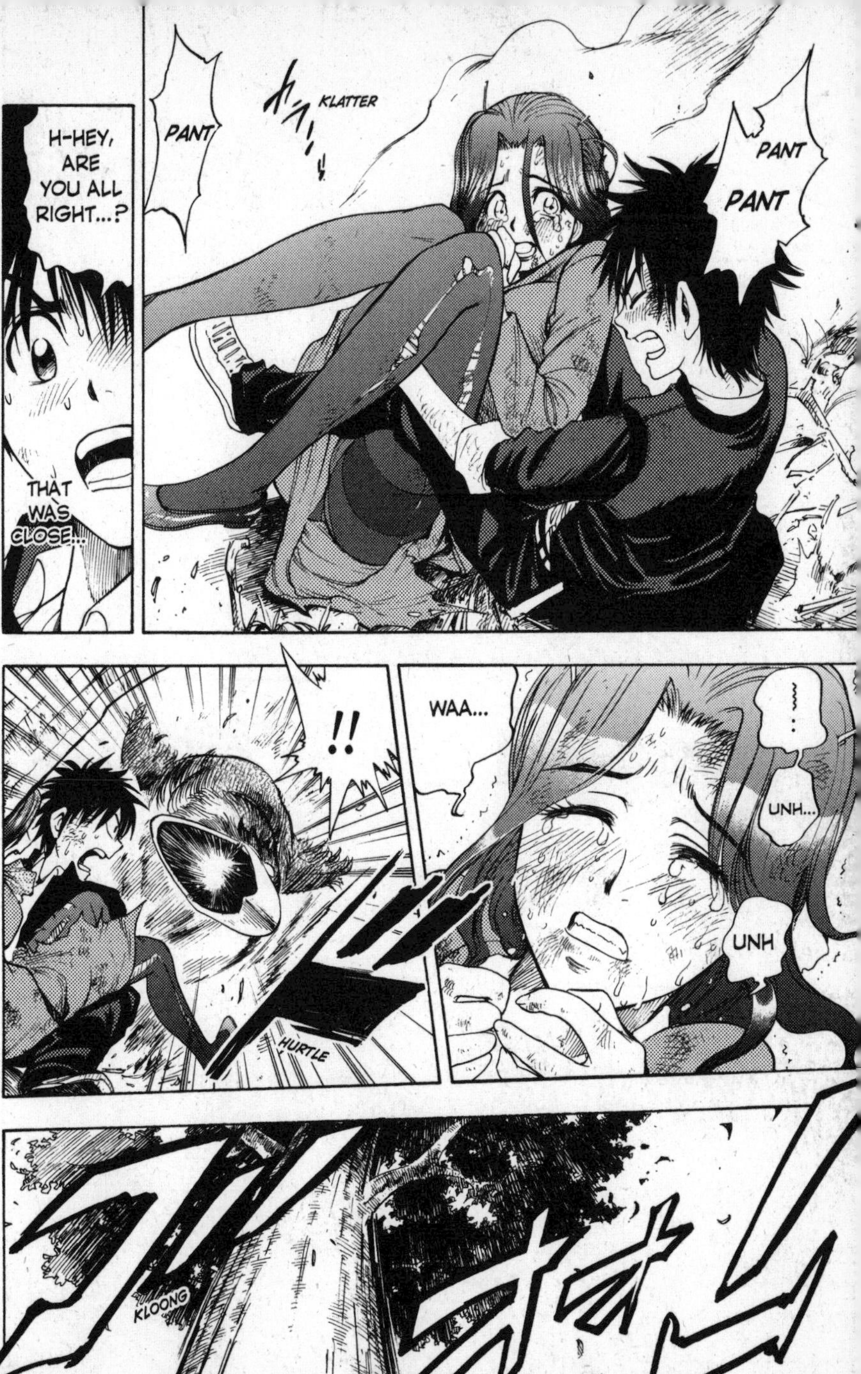
PANT
PANT
KLATTER
PANT
H-HEY, ARE YOU ALL RIGHT...?
THAT WAS CLOSE...
...
UNH...
UNH
WAA...
!!
HURTLE
KLOONG

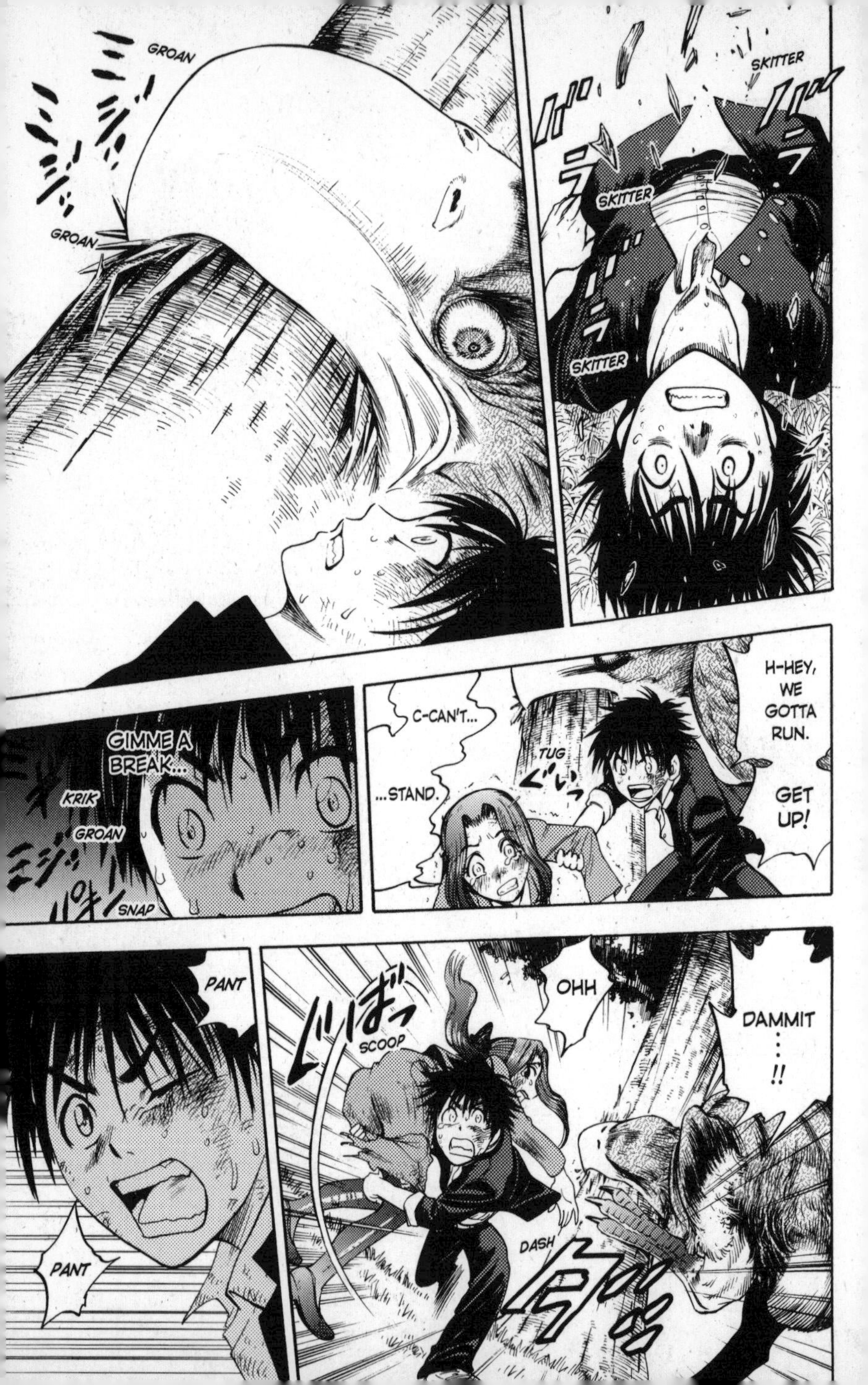
SKITTER
SKITTER
SKITTER
GROAN
GROAN
H-HEY, WE GOTTA RUN.
GET UP!
TUG
C-CAN'T...
...STAND.
GIMME A BREAK...
KRIK
GROAN
SNAP
DAMMIT ...!!
OHH
SCOOP
DASH
PANT
PANT

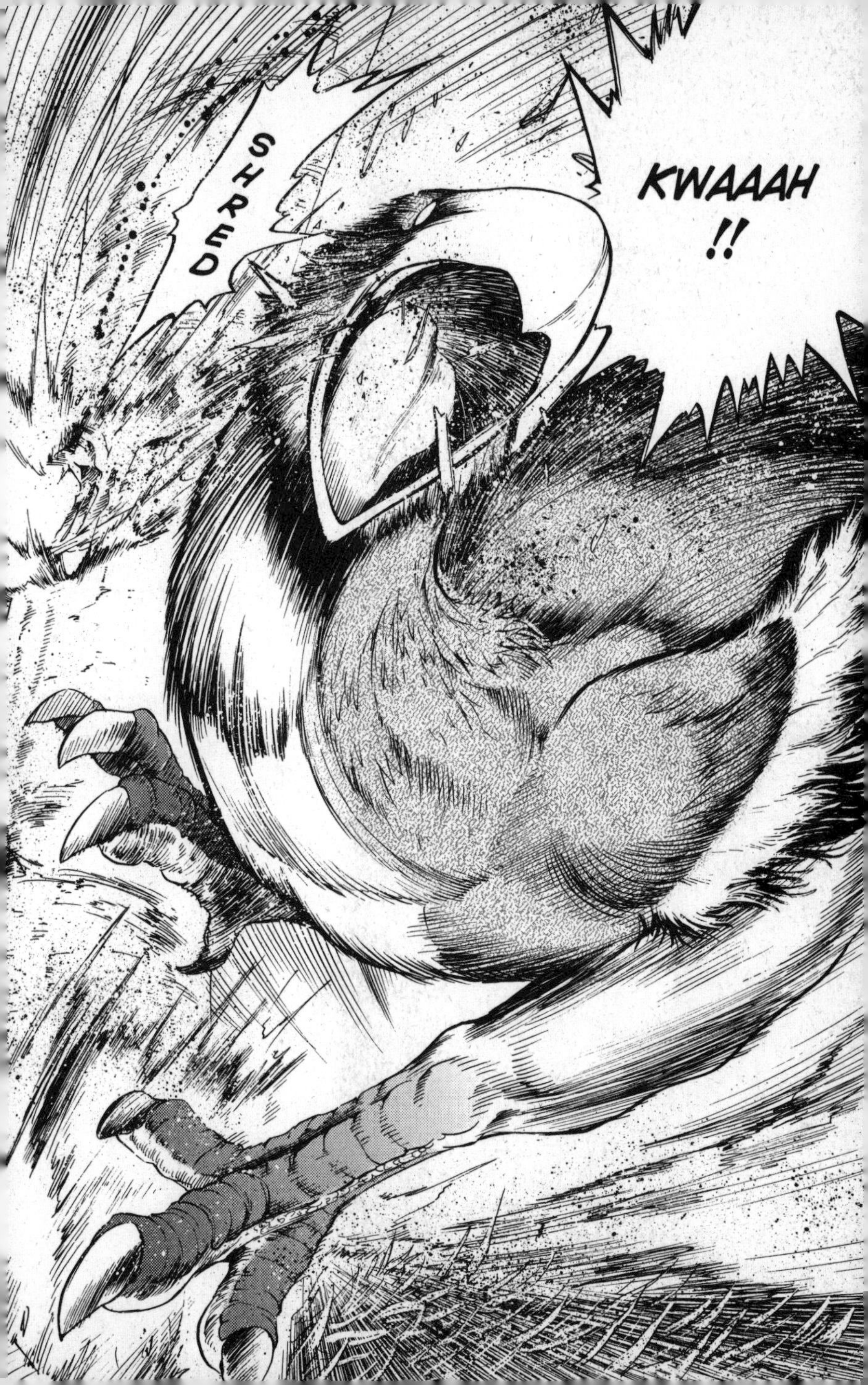
SHRED
KWAAAH !!

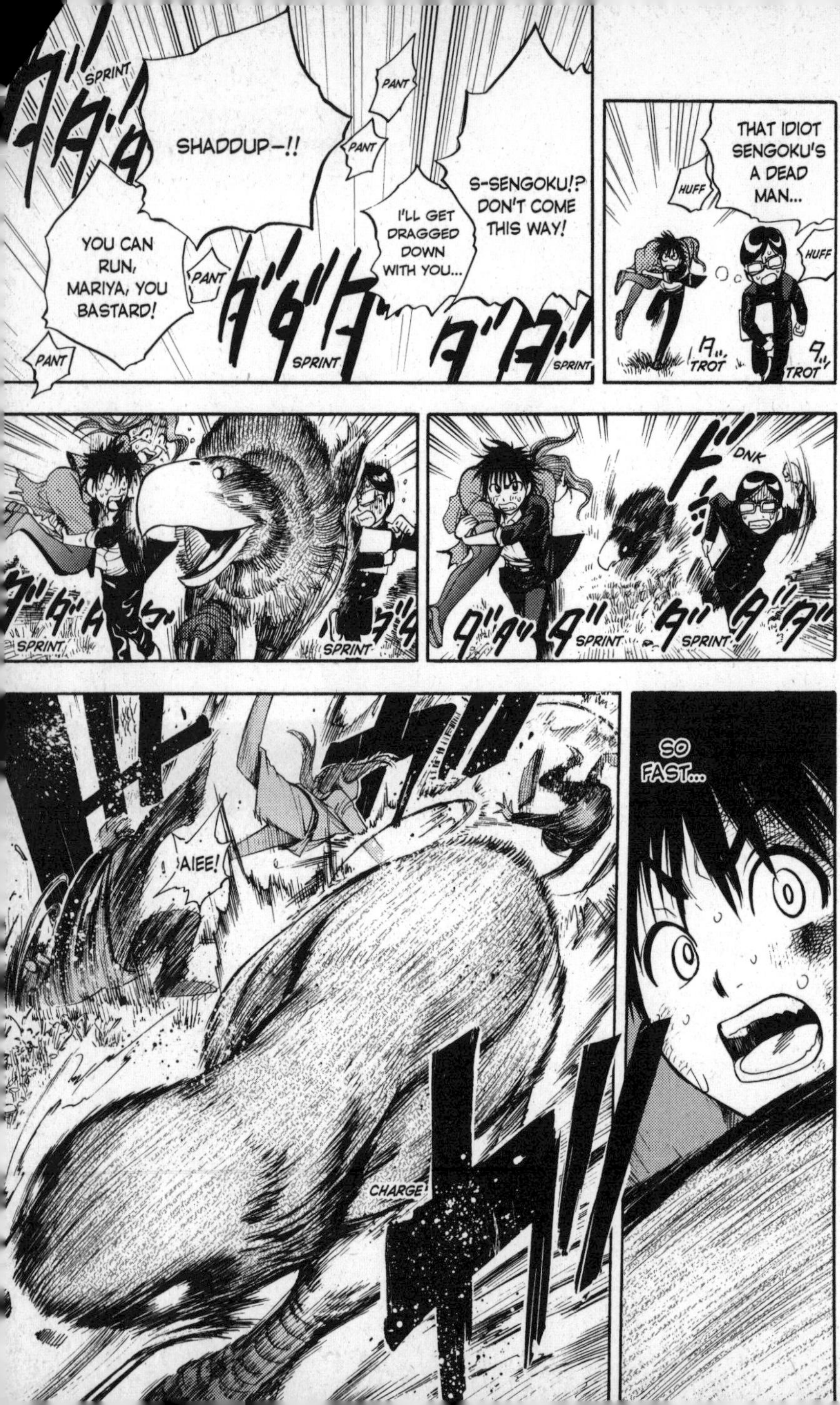
THAT IDIOT SENGOKU'S A DEAD MAN...
HUFF
HUFF
TROT
TROT
S-SENGOKU!? DON'T COME THIS WAY!
I'LL GET DRAGGED DOWN WITH YOU...
PANT
PANT
SHADDUP—!!
SPRINT
PANT
YOU CAN RUN, MARIYA, YOU BASTARD!
PANT
SPRINT
SPRINT
DNK
SPRINT
SPRINT
SPRINT
SPRINT
SO FAST...
AIEE!
CHARGE

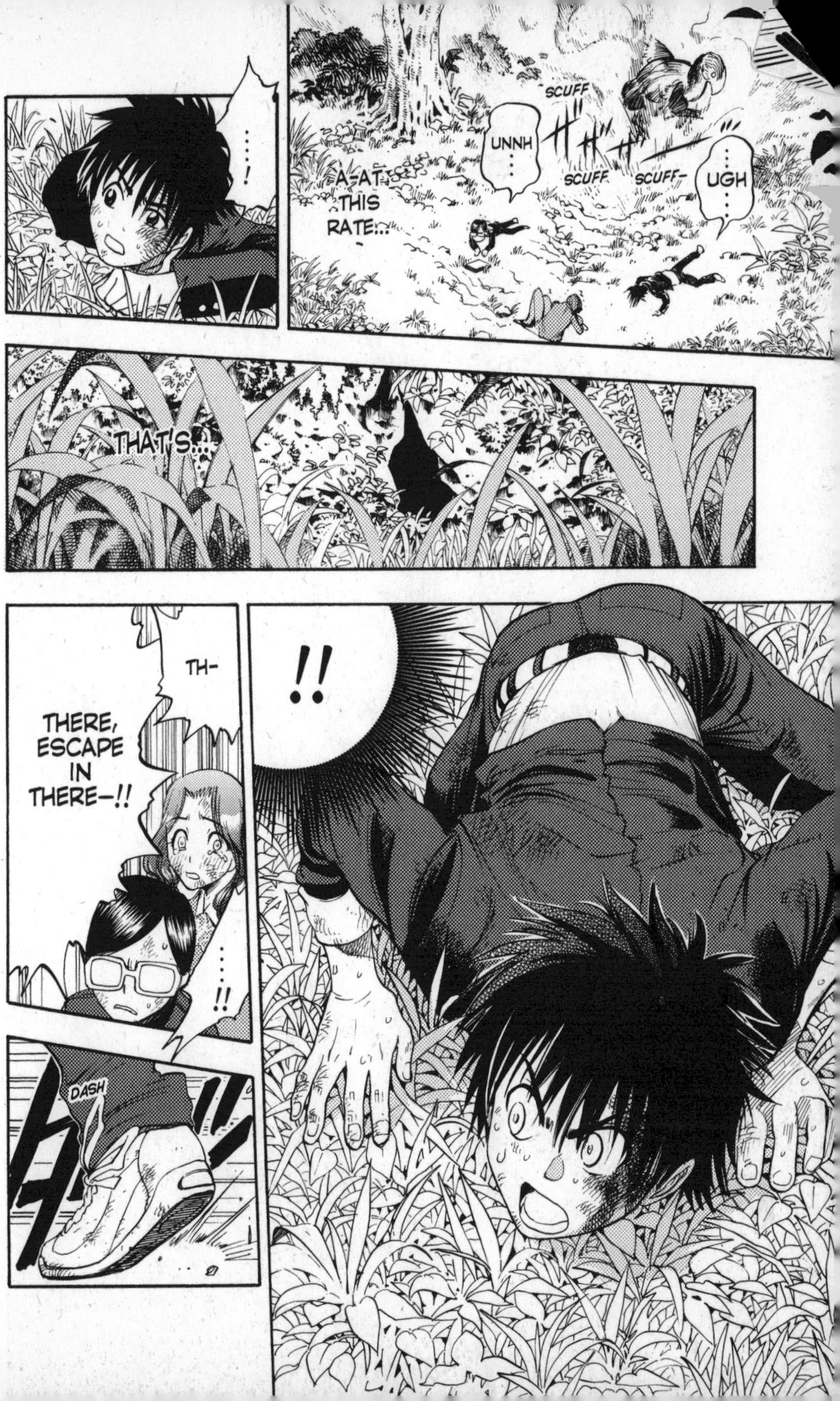
SCUFF
...UGH...
UNNH...
SCUFF
SCUFF-
A-AT THIS RATE...
...!
THAT'S...
!!
TH-
THERE, ESCAPE IN THERE–!!
...!!
DASH

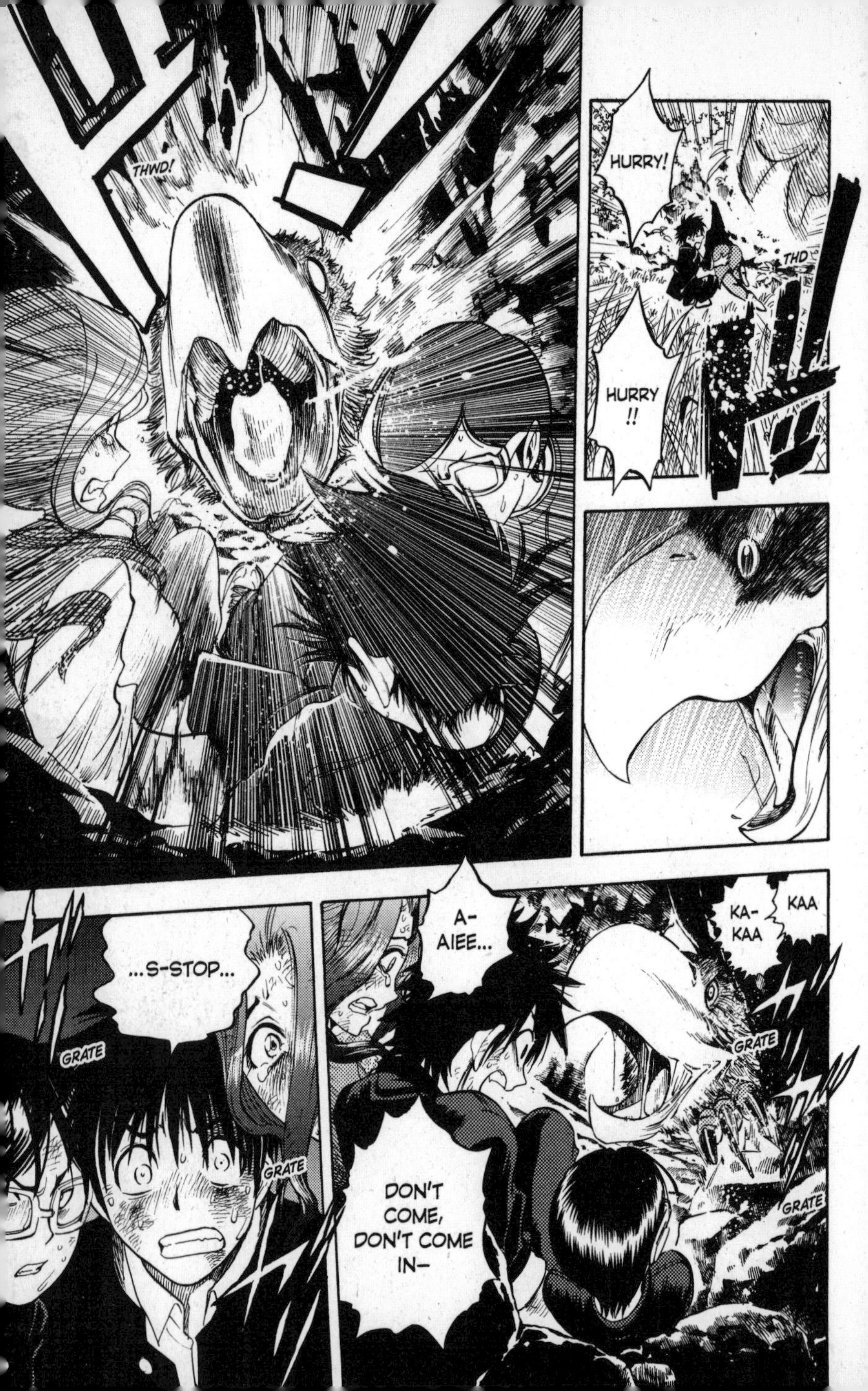
HURRY!
THD
HURRY !!
THWD!
A- AIEE...
KAA
KA- KAA
GRATE
GRATE
DON'T COME, DON'T COME IN–
...S-STOP...
GRATE
GRATE

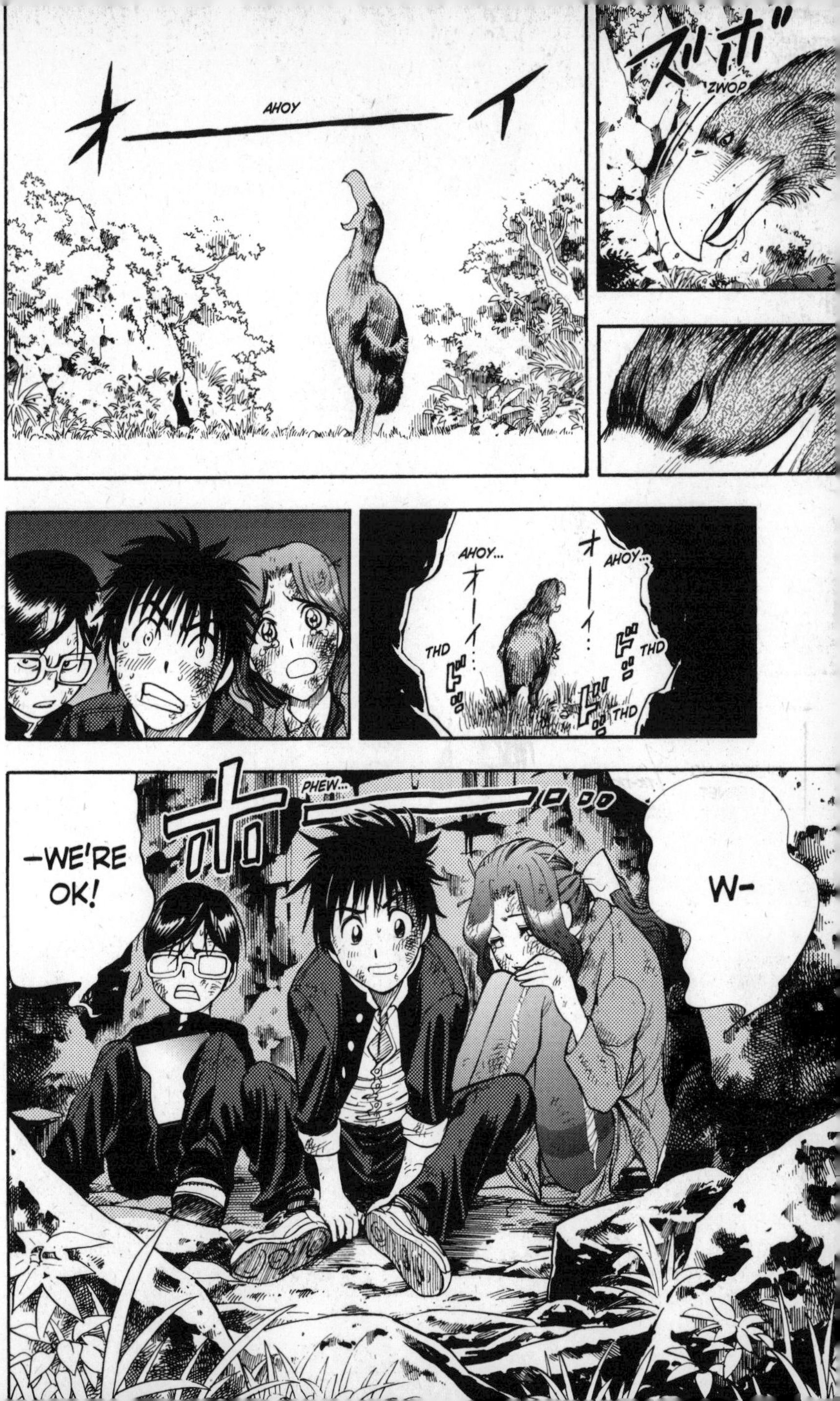
ズボ
ZWOP
オーーーイ
AHOY
オーイ…
AHOY...
オーイ…
AHOY...
ドッ
THD
ドッ
THD
ドッ
THD
ホーーっっっ
PHEW...
W-
-WE'RE OK!

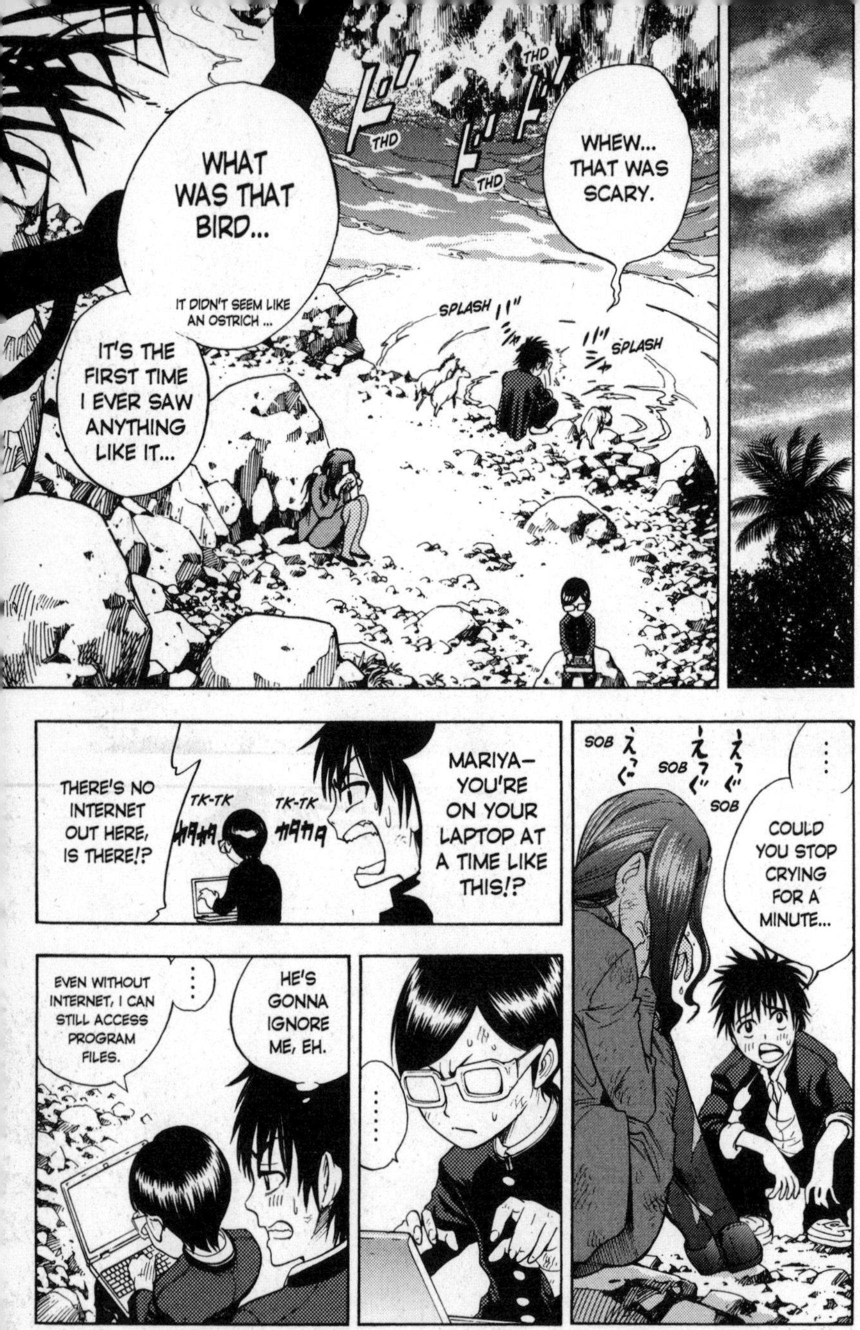
THD
THD
THD
WHEW... THAT WAS SCARY.
WHAT WAS THAT BIRD...
SPLASH
SPLASH
IT DIDN'T SEEM LIKE AN OSTRICH ...
IT'S THE FIRST TIME I EVER SAW ANYTHING LIKE IT...
...
SOB
SOB
SOB
COULD YOU STOP CRYING FOR A MINUTE...
MARIYA— YOU'RE ON YOUR LAPTOP AT A TIME LIKE THIS!?
TK-TK
TK-TK
THERE'S NO INTERNET OUT HERE, IS THERE!?
......
HE'S GONNA IGNORE ME, EH.
...
EVEN WITHOUT INTERNET, I CAN STILL ACCESS PROGRAM FILES.

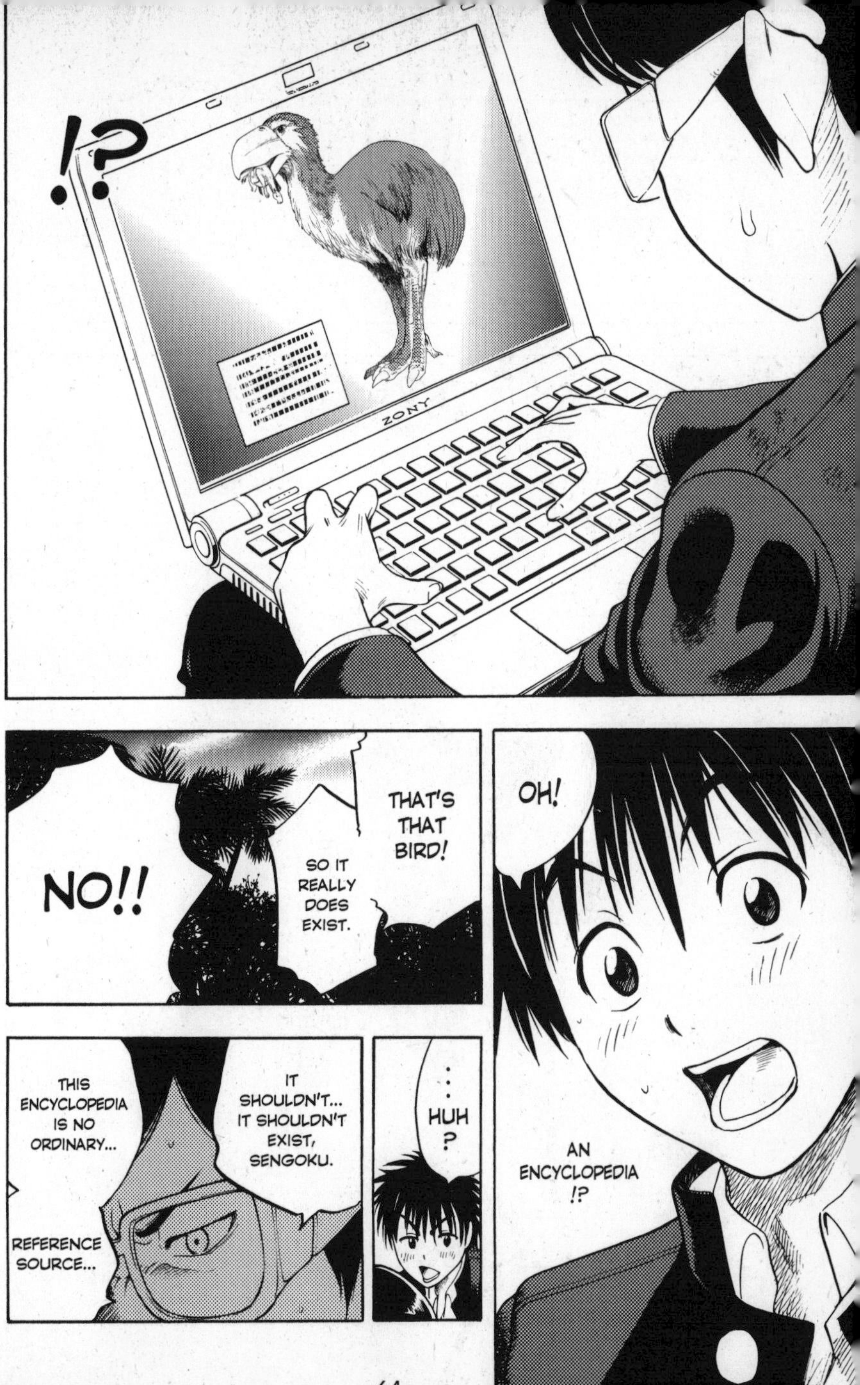
!?
OH!
AN ENCYCLOPEDIA !?
THAT'S THAT BIRD!
SO IT REALLY DOES EXIST.
NO!!
... HUH?
IT SHOULDN'T... IT SHOULDN'T EXIST, SENGOKU.
THIS ENCYCLOPEDIA IS NO ORDINARY...
REFERENCE SOURCE...

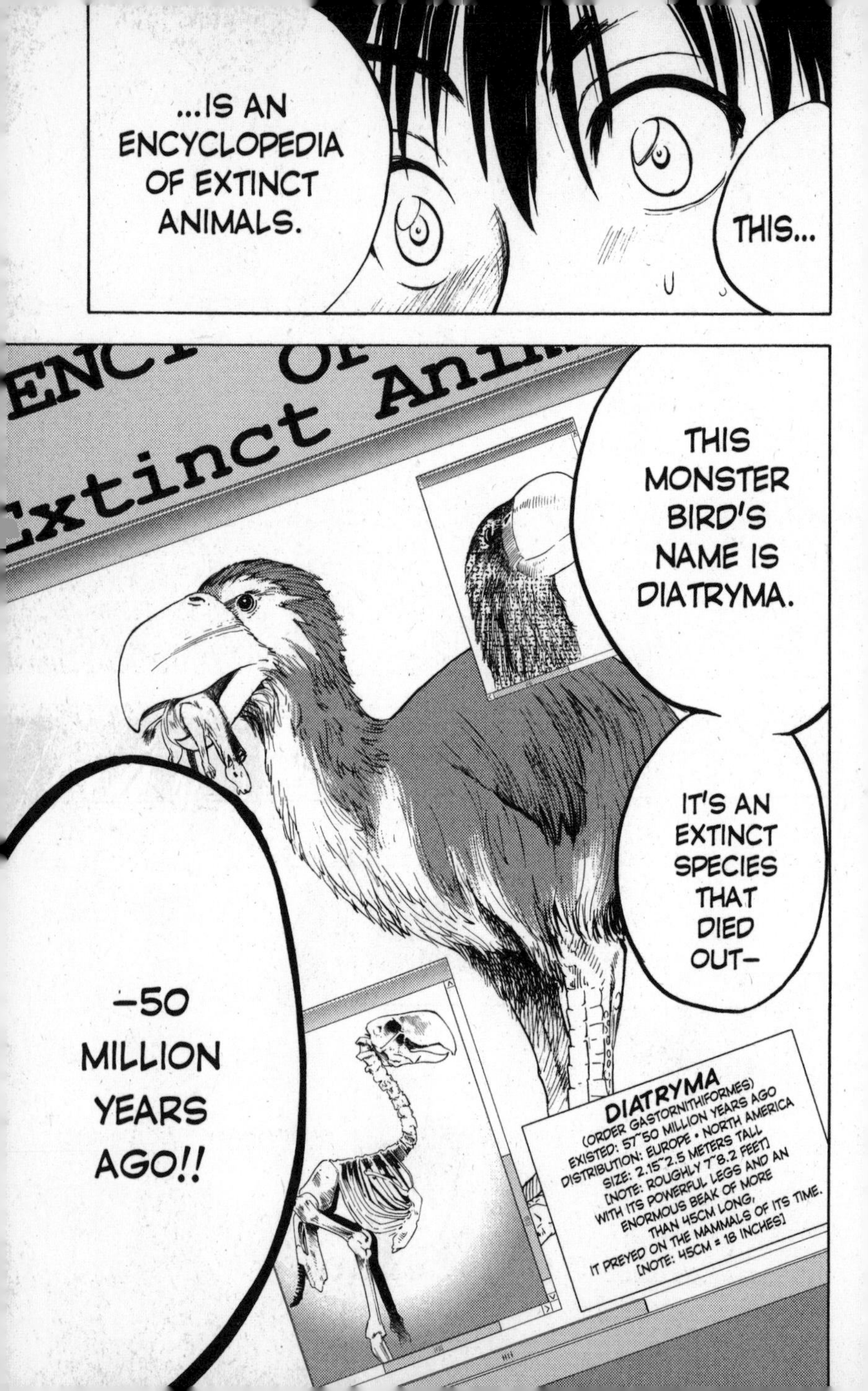
THIS...
...IS AN ENCYCLOPEDIA OF EXTINCT ANIMALS.
ENCY OF Extinct Ani
THIS MONSTER BIRD'S NAME IS DIATRYMA.
IT'S AN EXTINCT SPECIES THAT DIED OUT–
–50 MILLION YEARS AGO!!
DIATRYMA
(ORDER GASTORNITHIFORMES)
EXISTED: 57~50 MILLION YEARS AGO
DISTRIBUTION: EUROPE • NORTH AMERICA
SIZE: 2.15~2.5 METERS TALL
[NOTE: ROUGHLY 7~8.2 FEET]
WITH ITS POWERFUL LEGS AND AN ENORMOUS BEAK OF MORE THAN 45CM LONG, IT PREYED ON THE MAMMALS OF ITS TIME.
[NOTE: 45CM = 18 INCHES]

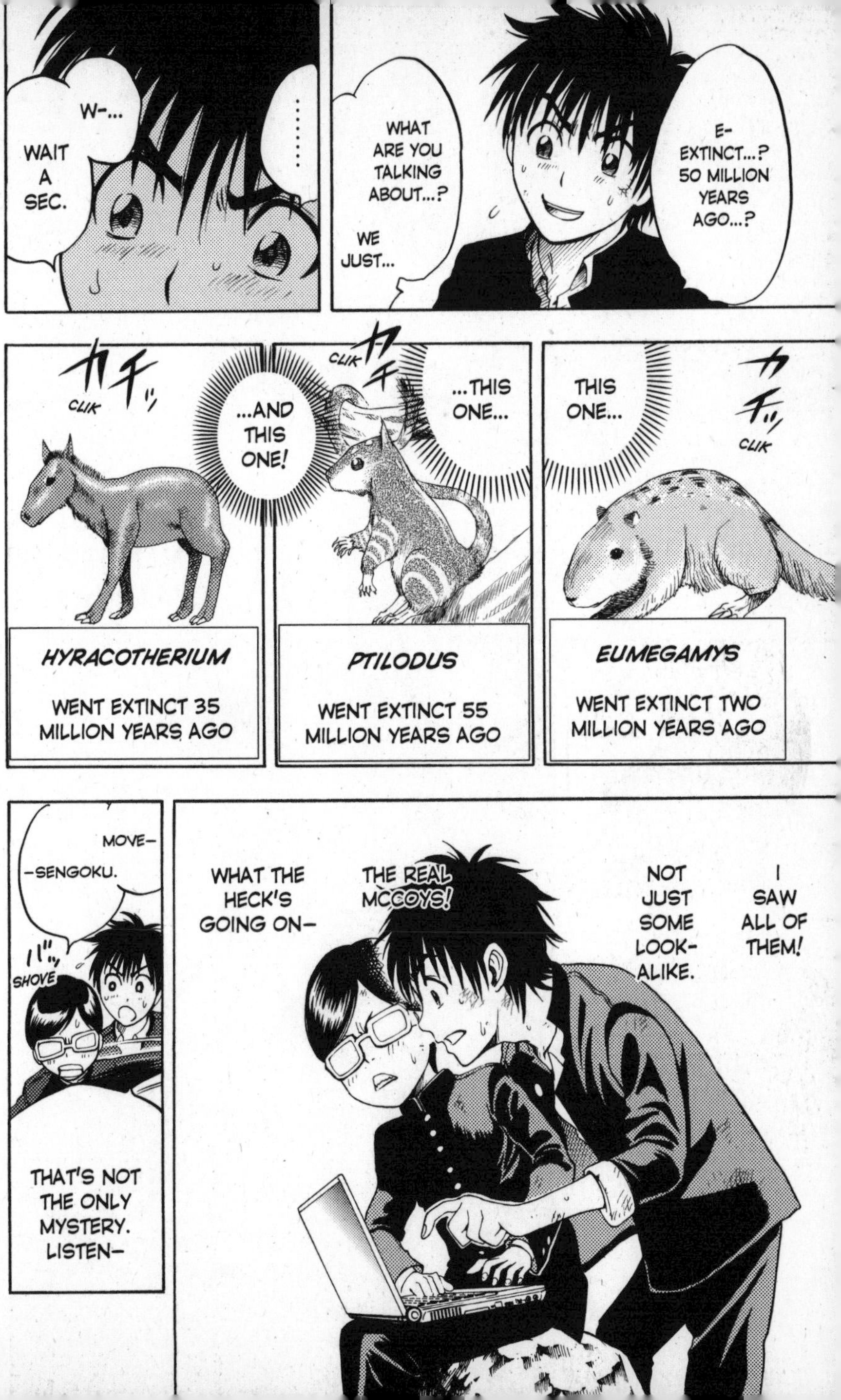
E- EXTINCT...? 50 MILLION YEARS AGO...?
WHAT ARE YOU TALKING ABOUT...?
WE JUST...
......
W-... WAIT A SEC.
カチッ
CLIK
THIS ONE...
EUMEGAMYS
WENT EXTINCT TWO MILLION YEARS AGO
...THIS ONE...
カチ
CLIK
PTILODUS
WENT EXTINCT 55 MILLION YEARS AGO
カチッ
CLIK
...AND THIS ONE!
HYRACOTHERIUM
WENT EXTINCT 35 MILLION YEARS AGO
I SAW ALL OF THEM!
NOT JUST SOME LOOK-ALIKE.
THE REAL MCCOYS!
WHAT THE HECK'S GOING ON—
MOVE—
—SENGOKU.
バッ
SHOVE
THAT'S NOT THE ONLY MYSTERY. LISTEN—

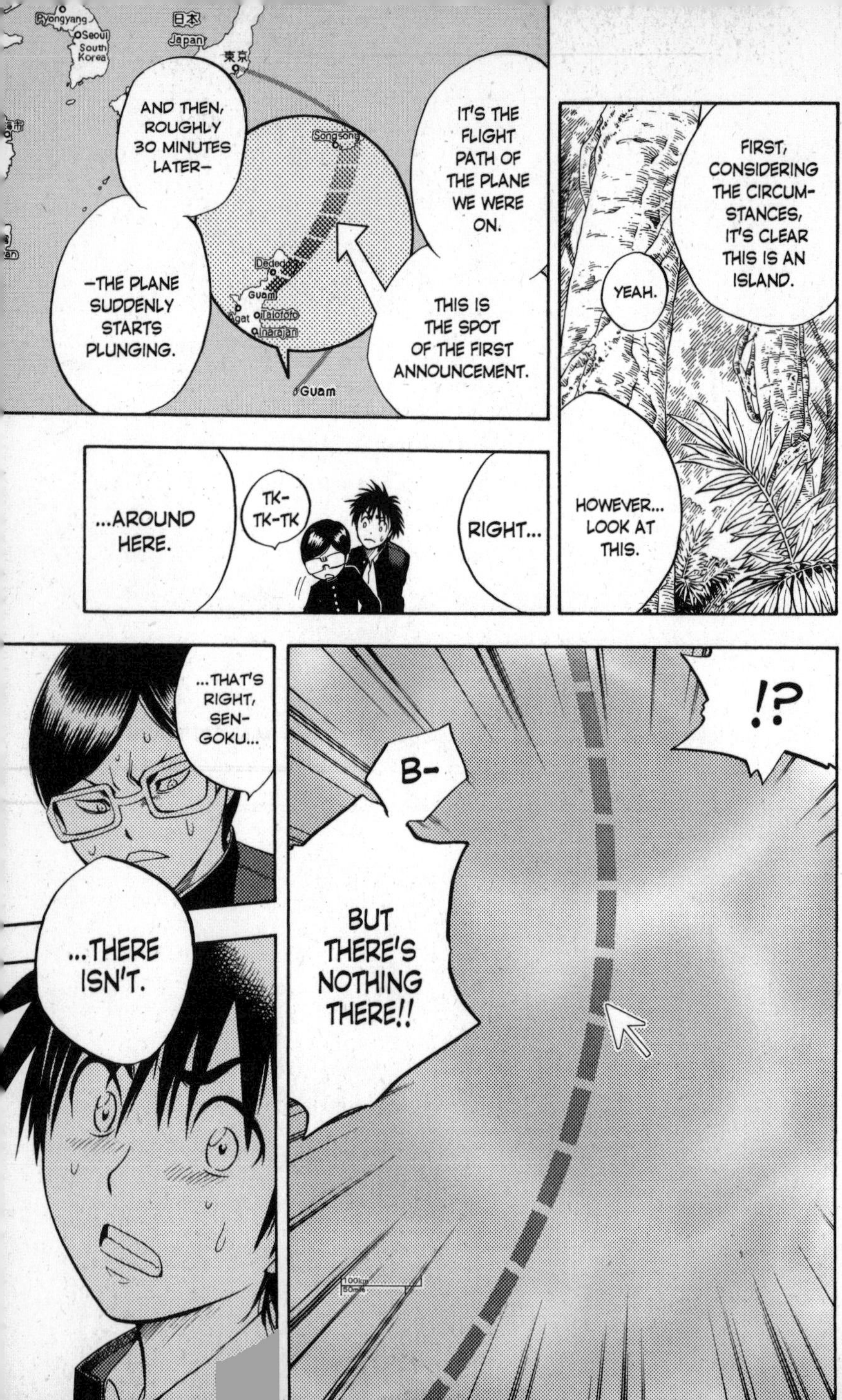
FIRST, CONSIDERING THE CIRCUM-STANCES, IT'S CLEAR THIS IS AN ISLAND.
YEAH.
HOWEVER... LOOK AT THIS.
Pyongyang
Seoul
South Korea
日本
Japan
東京
IT'S THE FLIGHT PATH OF THE PLANE WE WERE ON.
Songsong
Dededo
Guam
Agat
Talofofo
Inarajan
Guam
THIS IS THE SPOT OF THE FIRST ANNOUNCEMENT.
AND THEN, ROUGHLY 30 MINUTES LATER—
—THE PLANE SUDDENLY STARTS PLUNGING.
RIGHT...
TK-TK-TK
...AROUND HERE.
!?
B-
BUT THERE'S NOTHING THERE!!
...THAT'S RIGHT, SEN-GOKU...
...THERE ISN'T.

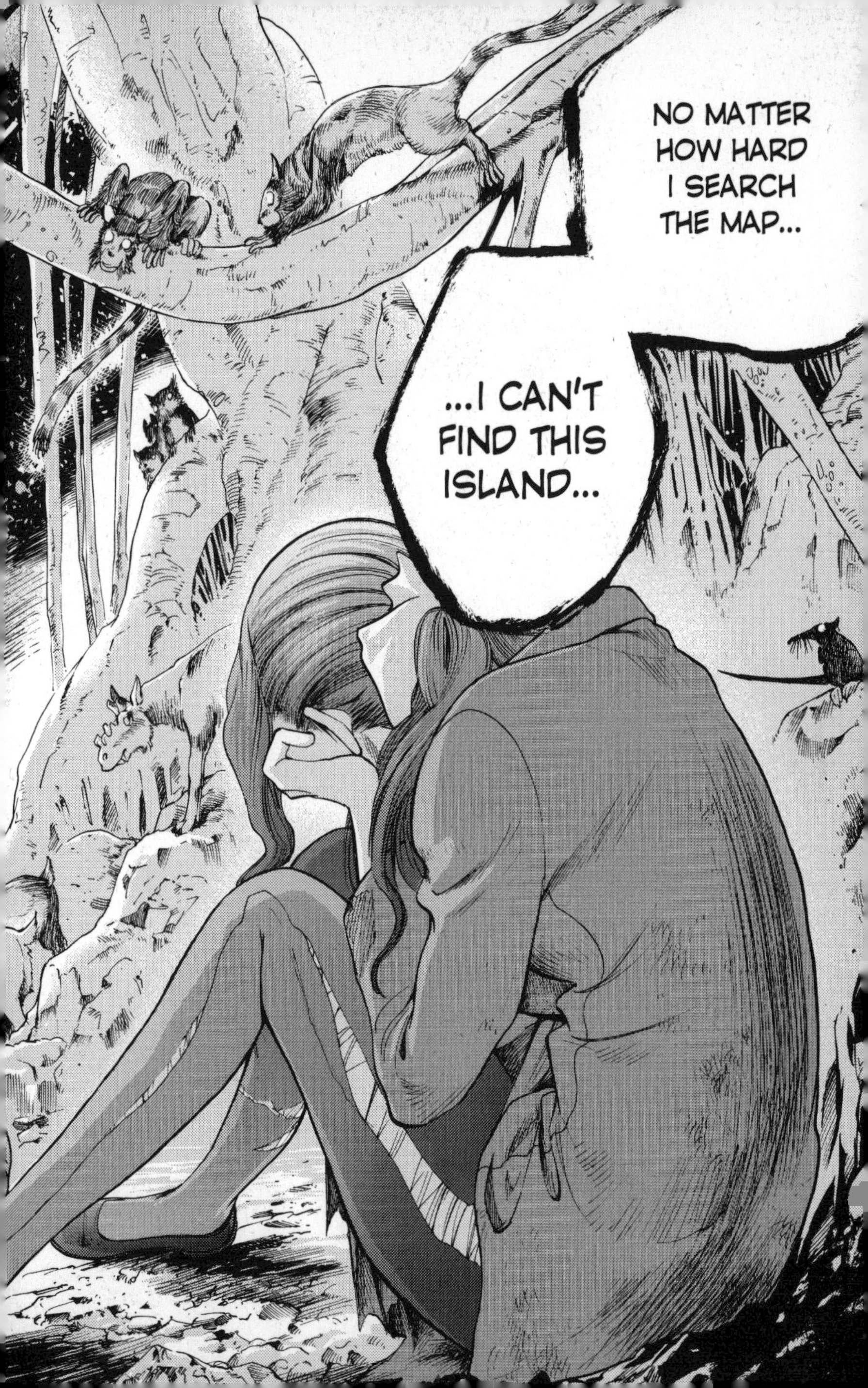
NO MATTER HOW HARD I SEARCH THE MAP...
...I CAN'T FIND THIS ISLAND...

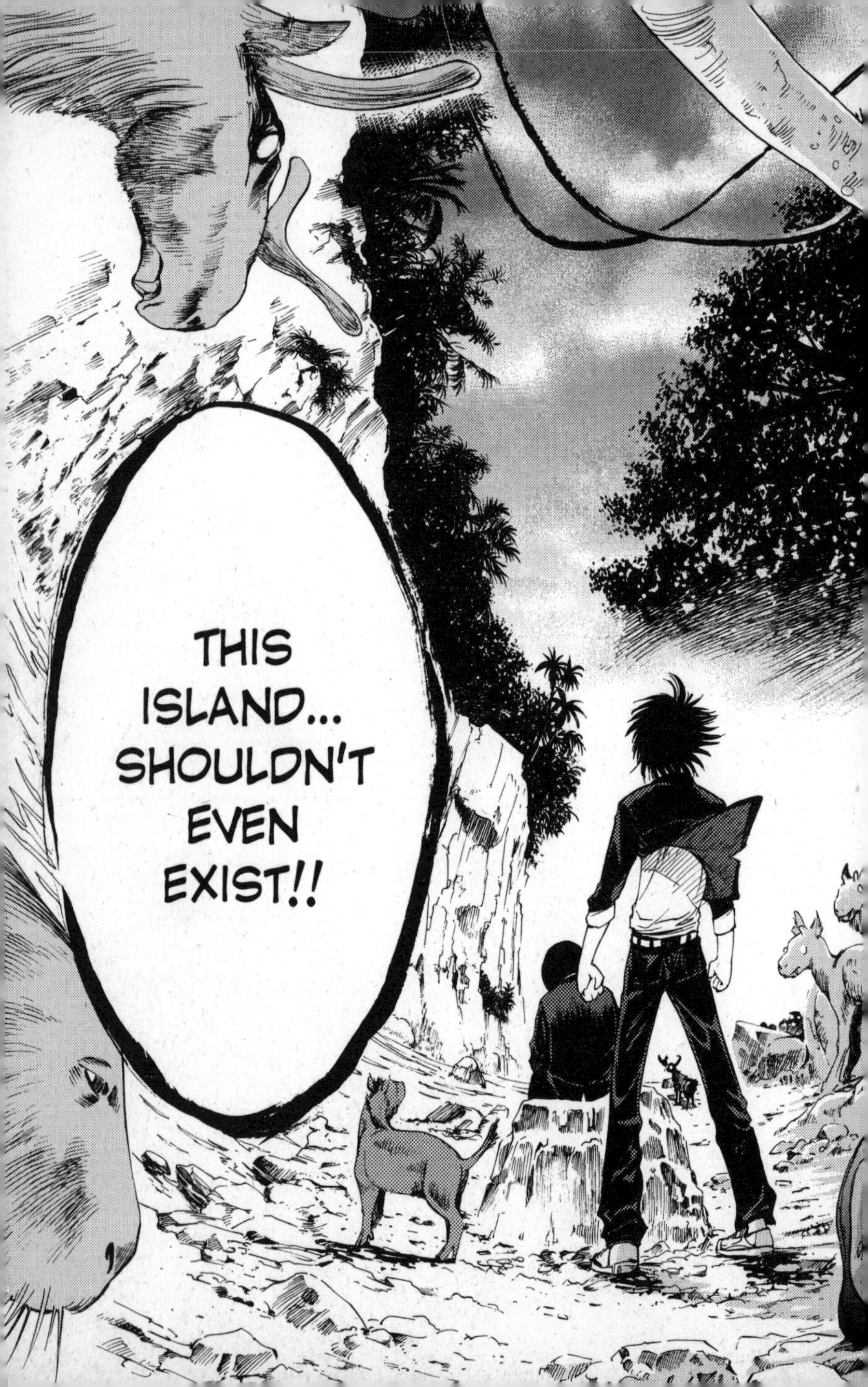
THIS ISLAND... SHOULDN'T EVEN EXIST!!

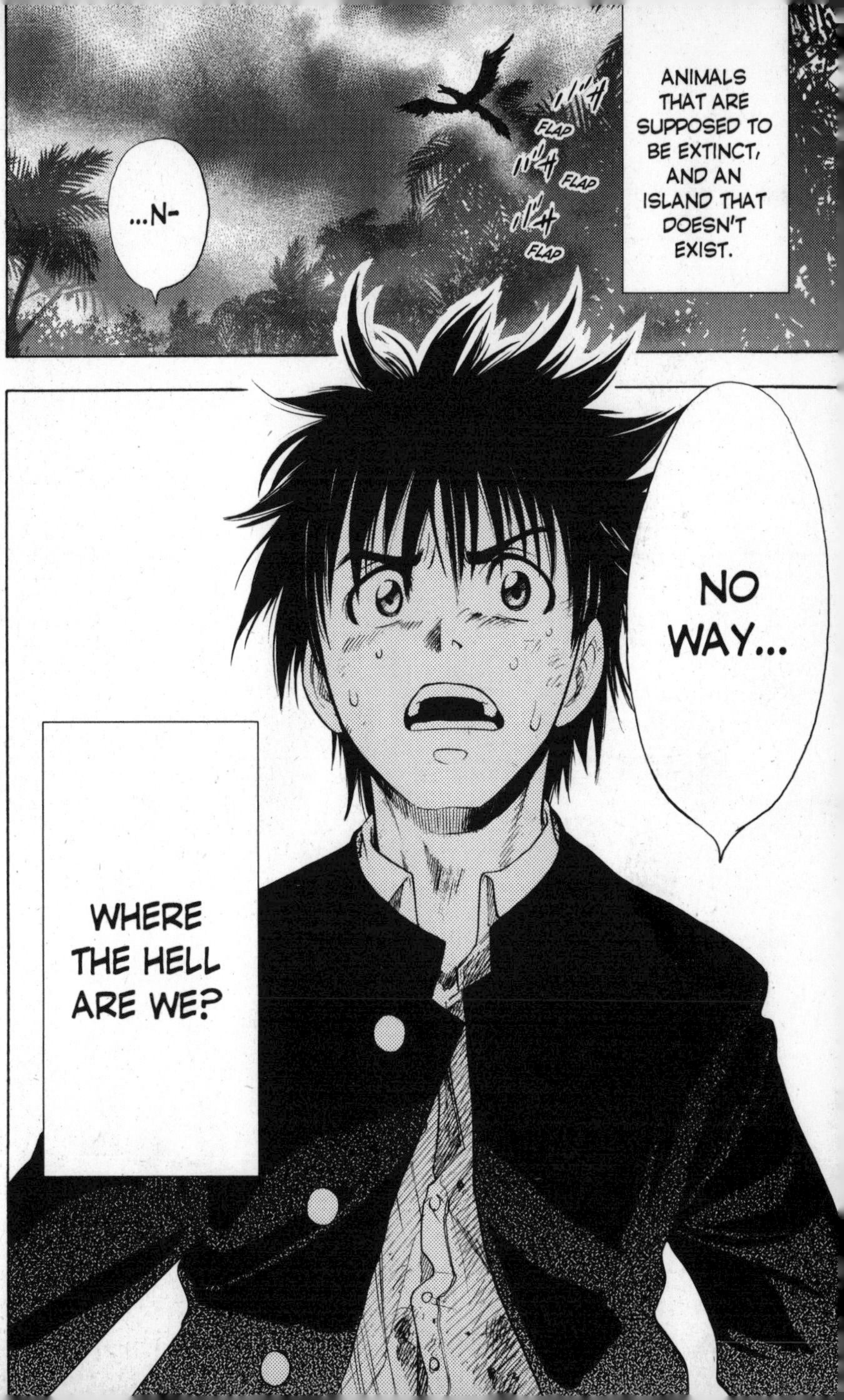
ANIMALS THAT ARE SUPPOSED TO BE EXTINCT, AND AN ISLAND THAT DOESN'T EXIST.
FLAP
FLAP
FLAP
...N-
NO WAY...
WHERE THE HELL ARE WE?

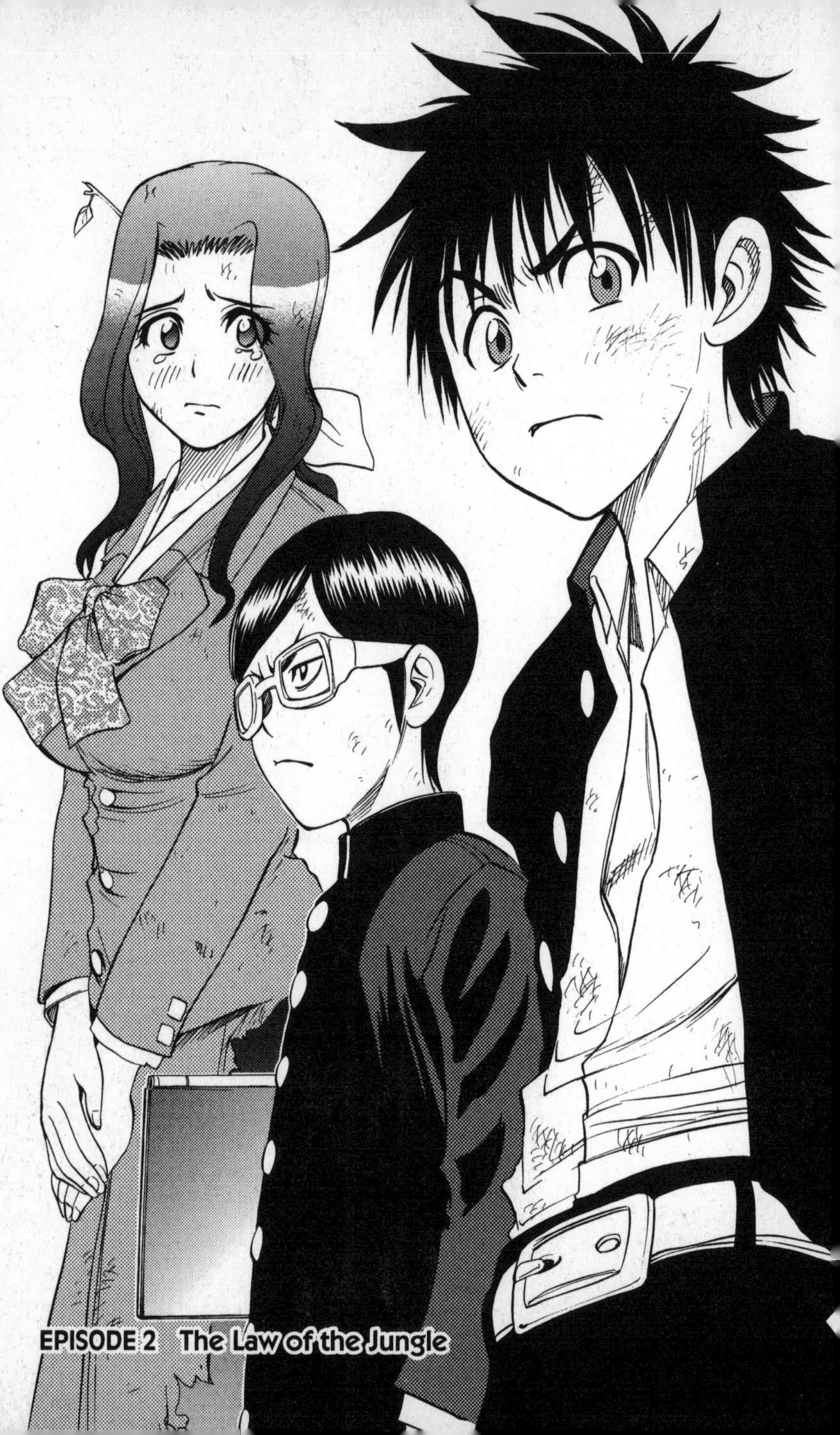

EPISODE 2 The Law of the Jungle

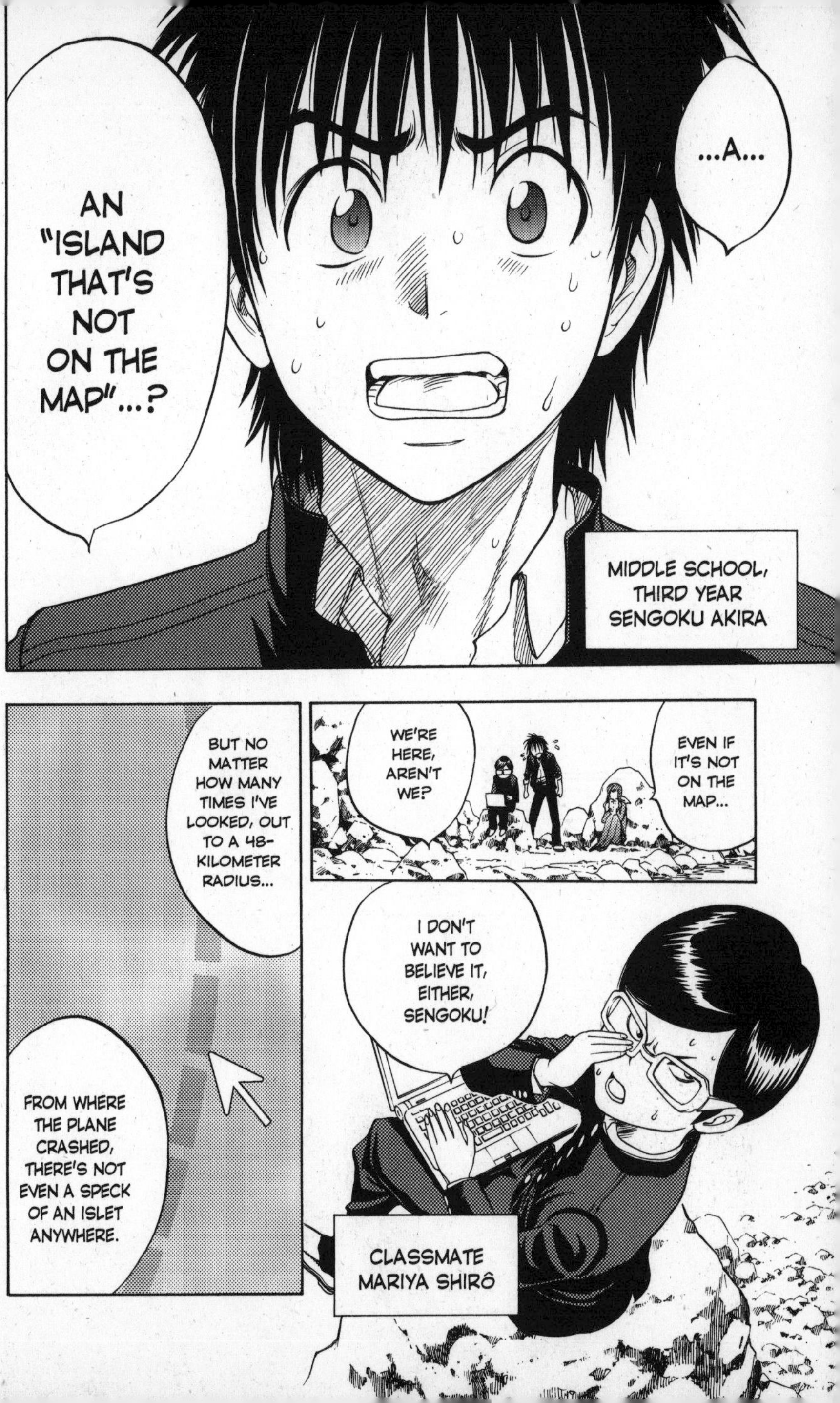
...A...
AN "ISLAND THAT'S NOT ON THE MAP"...?
MIDDLE SCHOOL, THIRD YEAR SENGOKU AKIRA
EVEN IF IT'S NOT ON THE MAP...
WE'RE HERE, AREN'T WE?
I DON'T WANT TO BELIEVE IT, EITHER, SENGOKU!
CLASSMATE MARIYA SHIRÔ
BUT NO MATTER HOW MANY TIMES I'VE LOOKED, OUT TO A 48-KILOMETER RADIUS...
FROM WHERE THE PLANE CRASHED, THERE'S NOT EVEN A SPECK OF AN ISLET ANYWHERE.

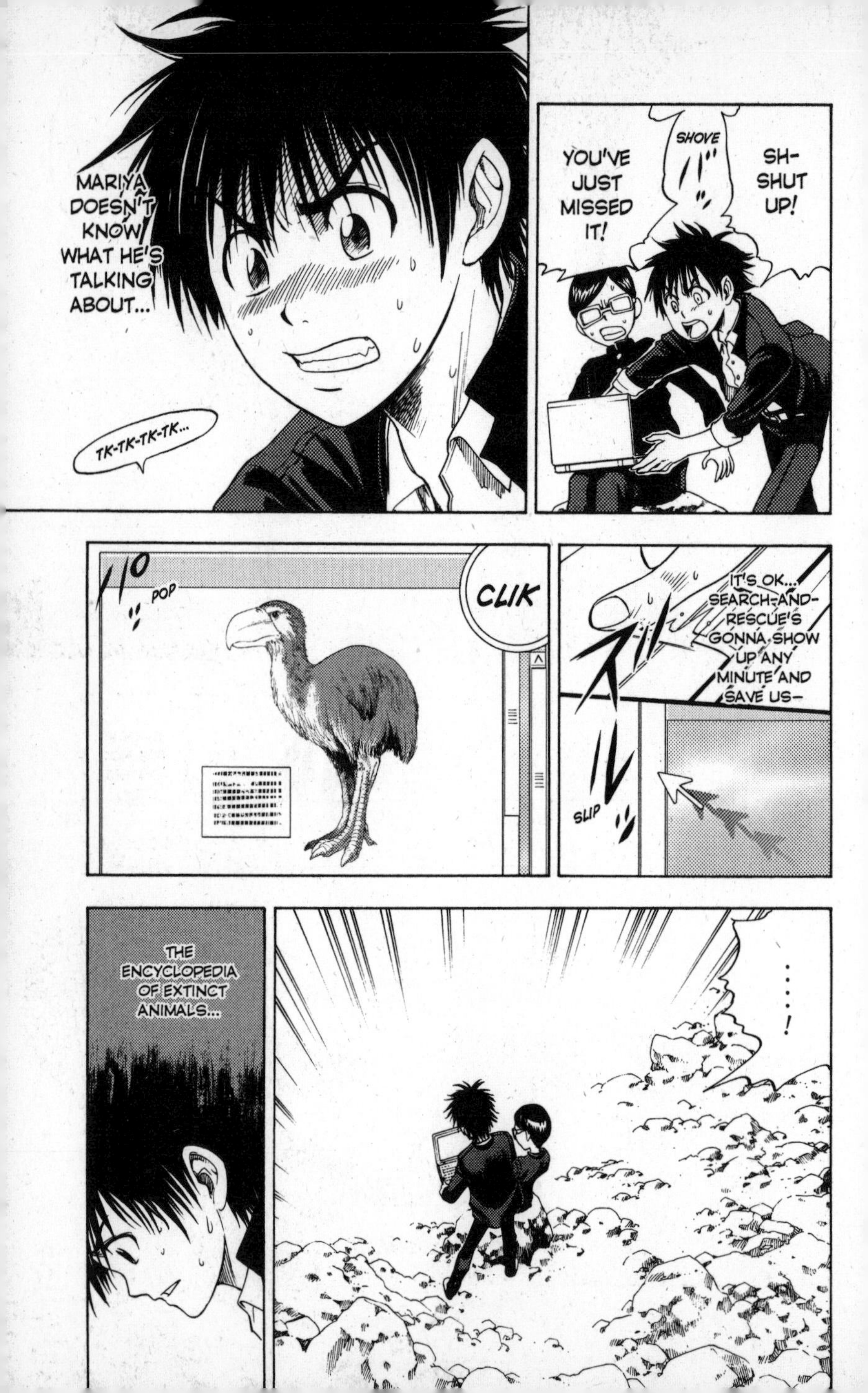
SH-SHUT UP!
SHOVE
YOU'VE JUST MISSED IT!
MARIYA DOESN'T KNOW WHAT HE'S TALKING ABOUT...
TK-TK-TK-TK...
IT'S OK... SEARCH-AND-RESCUE'S GONNA SHOW UP ANY MINUTE AND SAVE US—
SLIP
CLIK
POP
....!
THE ENCYCLOPEDIA OF EXTINCT ANIMALS...

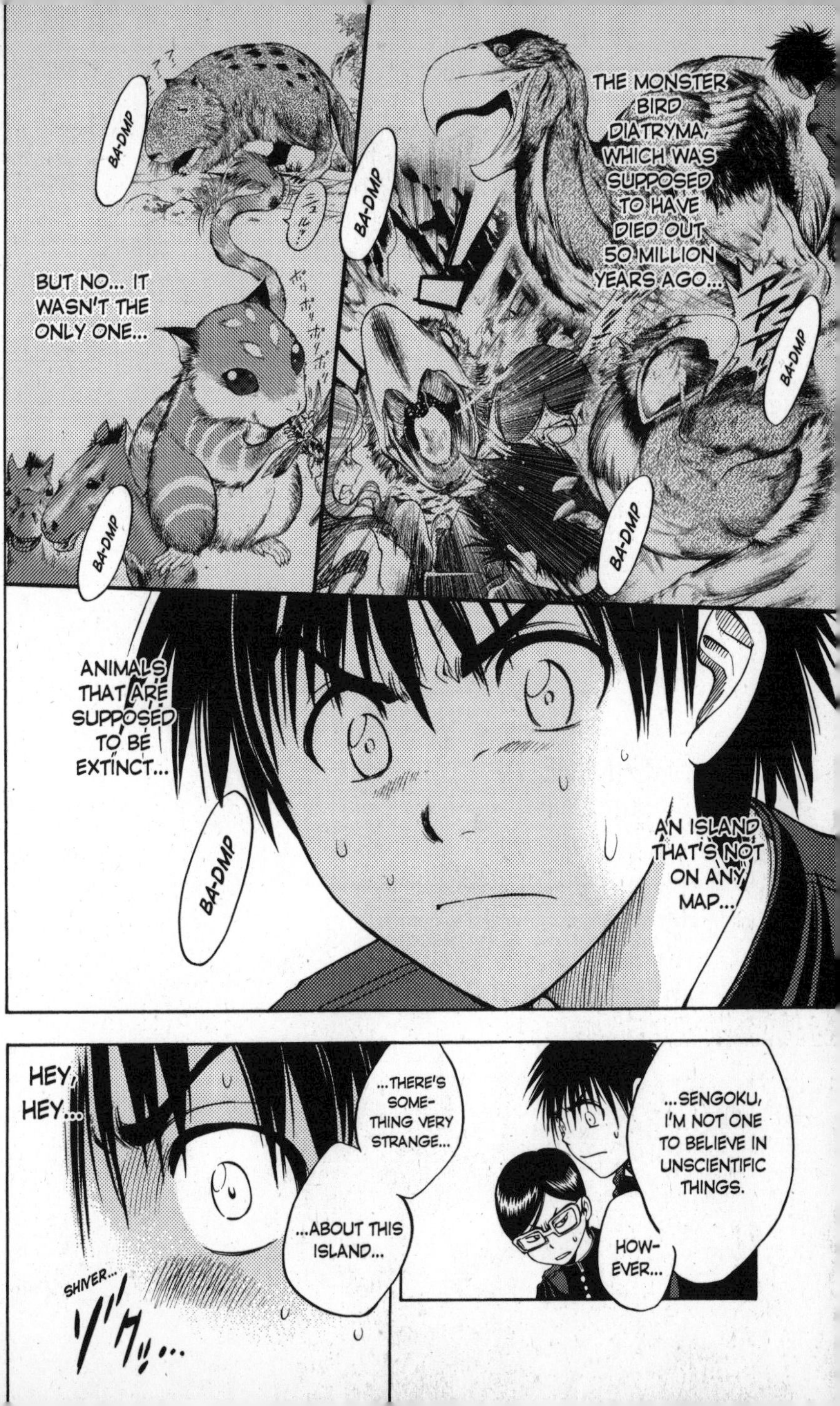
THE MONSTER BIRD DIATRYMA, WHICH WAS SUPPOSED TO HAVE DIED OUT 50 MILLION YEARS AGO...
BA-DMP
BA-DMP
BA-DMP
BA-DMP
BUT NO... IT WASN'T THE ONLY ONE...
BA-DMP
ANIMALS THAT ARE SUPPOSED TO BE EXTINCT...
BA-DMP
AN ISLAND THAT'S NOT ON ANY MAP...
...SENGOKU, I'M NOT ONE TO BELIEVE IN UNSCIENTIFIC THINGS.
HOW-EVER...
HEY, HEY...
...THERE'S SOME-THING VERY STRANGE...
...ABOUT THIS ISLAND...
SHIVER...
ゾクッ…

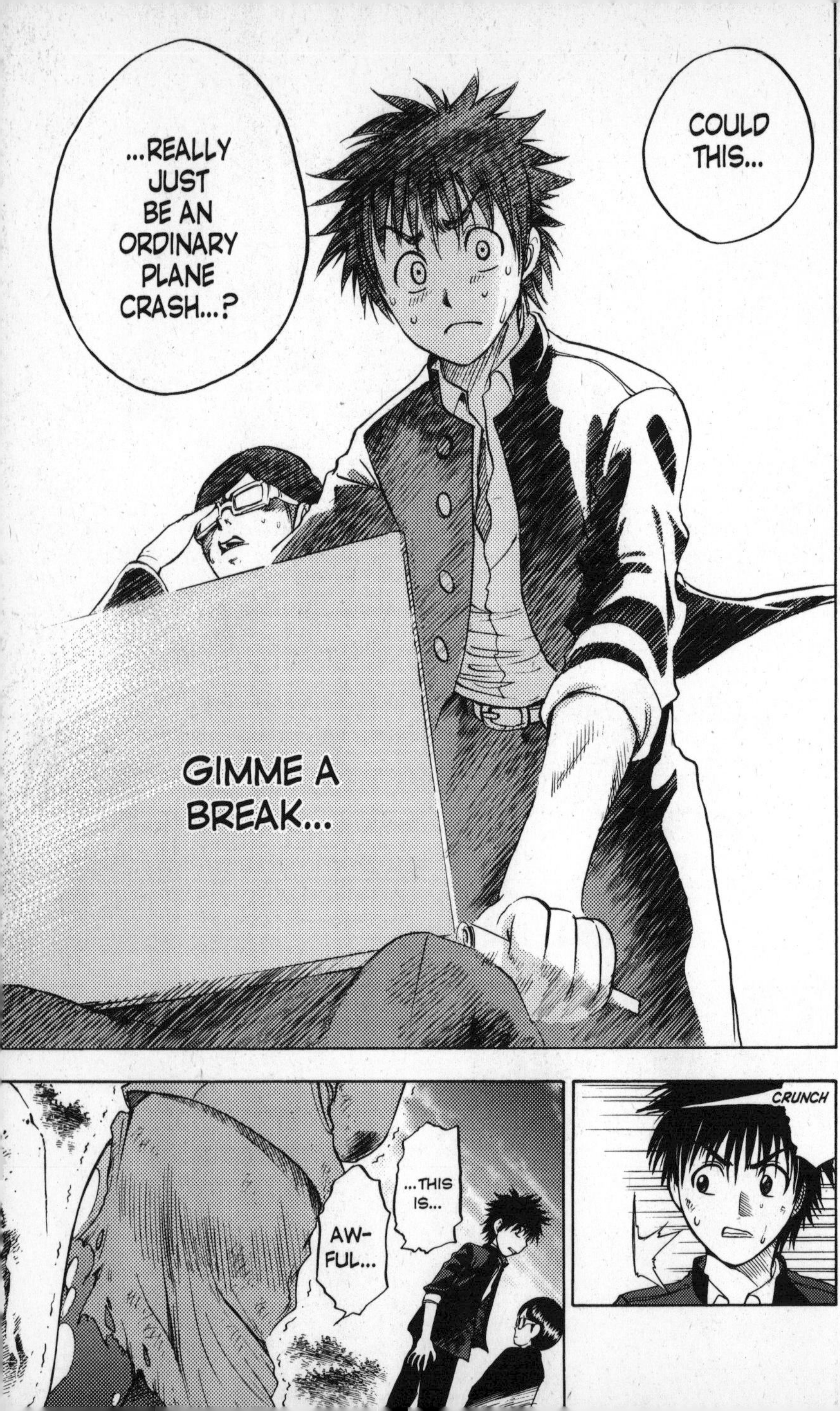
COULD THIS...
...REALLY JUST BE AN ORDINARY PLANE CRASH...?
GIMME A BREAK...
CRUNCH
...THIS IS...
AW-FUL...

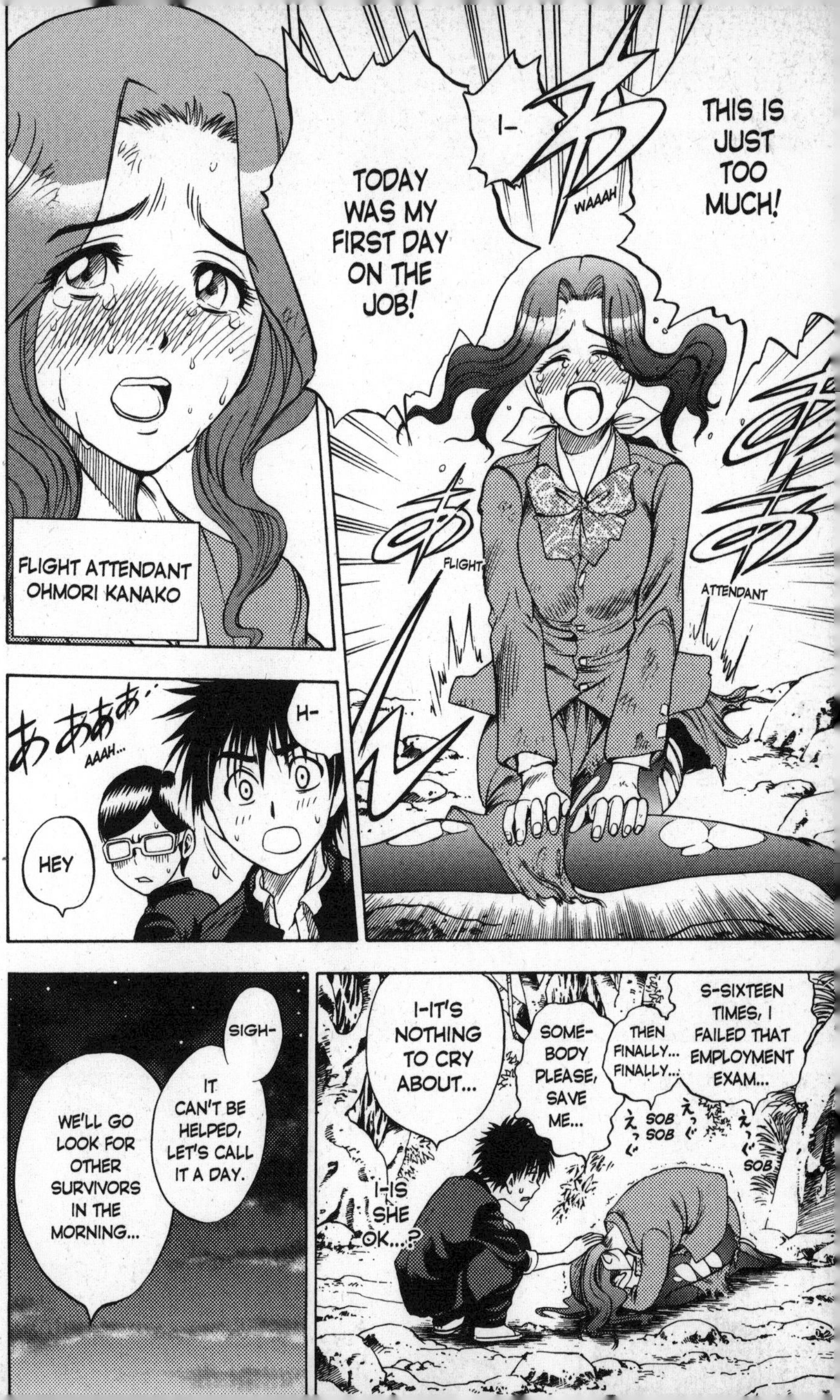

I-
WAAAH
THIS IS JUST TOO MUCH!
TODAY WAS MY FIRST DAY ON THE JOB!
FLIGHT
ATTENDANT
FLIGHT ATTENDANT OHMORI KANAKO
H-
AAAH...
HEY
S-SIXTEEN TIMES, I FAILED THAT EMPLOYMENT EXAM...
THEN FINALLY... FINALLY...
SOME-BODY PLEASE, SAVE ME...
I-IT'S NOTHING TO CRY ABOUT...
SOB SOB
SOB
I-IS SHE OK...?
SIGH-
IT CAN'T BE HELPED, LET'S CALL IT A DAY.
WE'LL GO LOOK FOR OTHER SURVIVORS IN THE MORNING...

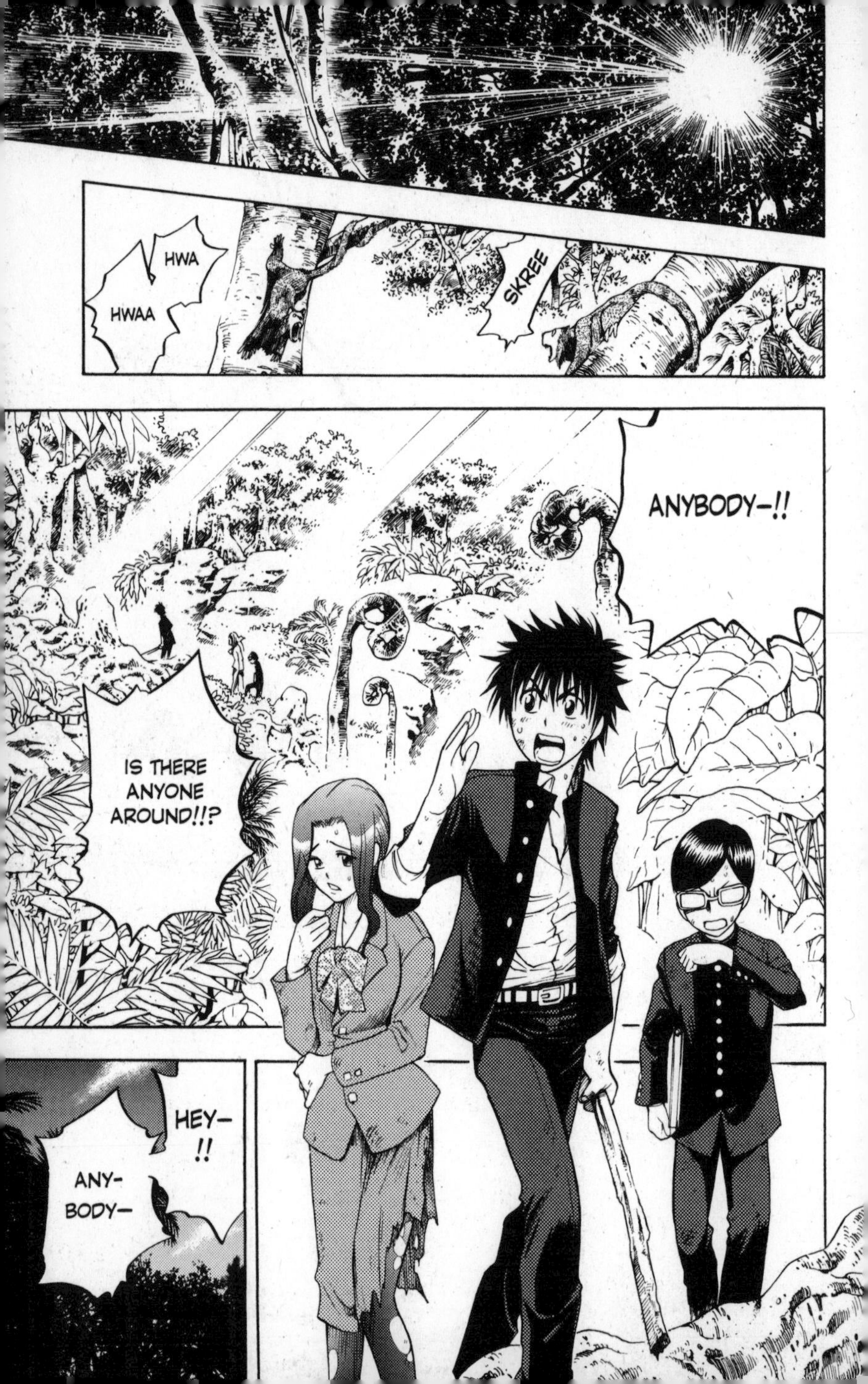
SKREE
HWA
HWAA
ANYBODY-!!
IS THERE ANYONE AROUND!!?
HEY-!!
ANY-BODY-

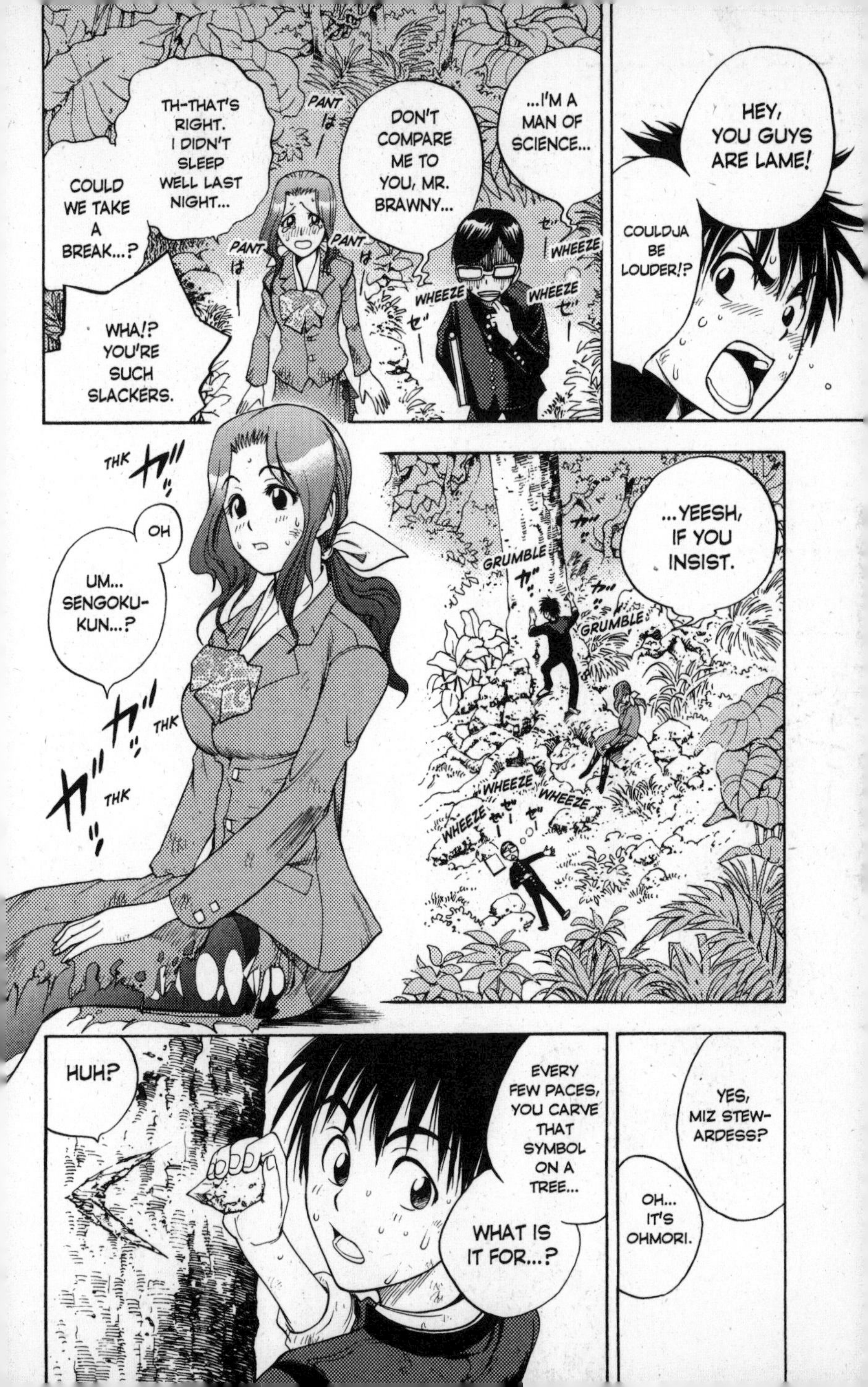
HEY, YOU GUYS ARE LAME!
COULDJA BE LOUDER!?
...I'M A MAN OF SCIENCE...
WHEEZE ゼ
WHEEZE ゼー
WHEEZE ゼー
DON'T COMPARE ME TO YOU, MR. BRAWNY...
PANT はー
PANT はー
TH-THAT'S RIGHT. I DIDN'T SLEEP WELL LAST NIGHT...
PANT はー
COULD WE TAKE A BREAK...?
WHA!? YOU'RE SUCH SLACKERS.
...YEESH, IF YOU INSIST.
GRUMBLE ガ
GRUMBLE ガ
WHEEZE
WHEEZE ゼー ゼー
WHEEZE
THK ガッ
OH
UM... SENGOKU-KUN...?
THK ガッ
THK ガッ
YES, MIZ STEW-ARDESS?
OH... IT'S OHMORI.
EVERY FEW PACES, YOU CARVE THAT SYMBOL ON A TREE...
WHAT IS IT FOR...?
HUH?

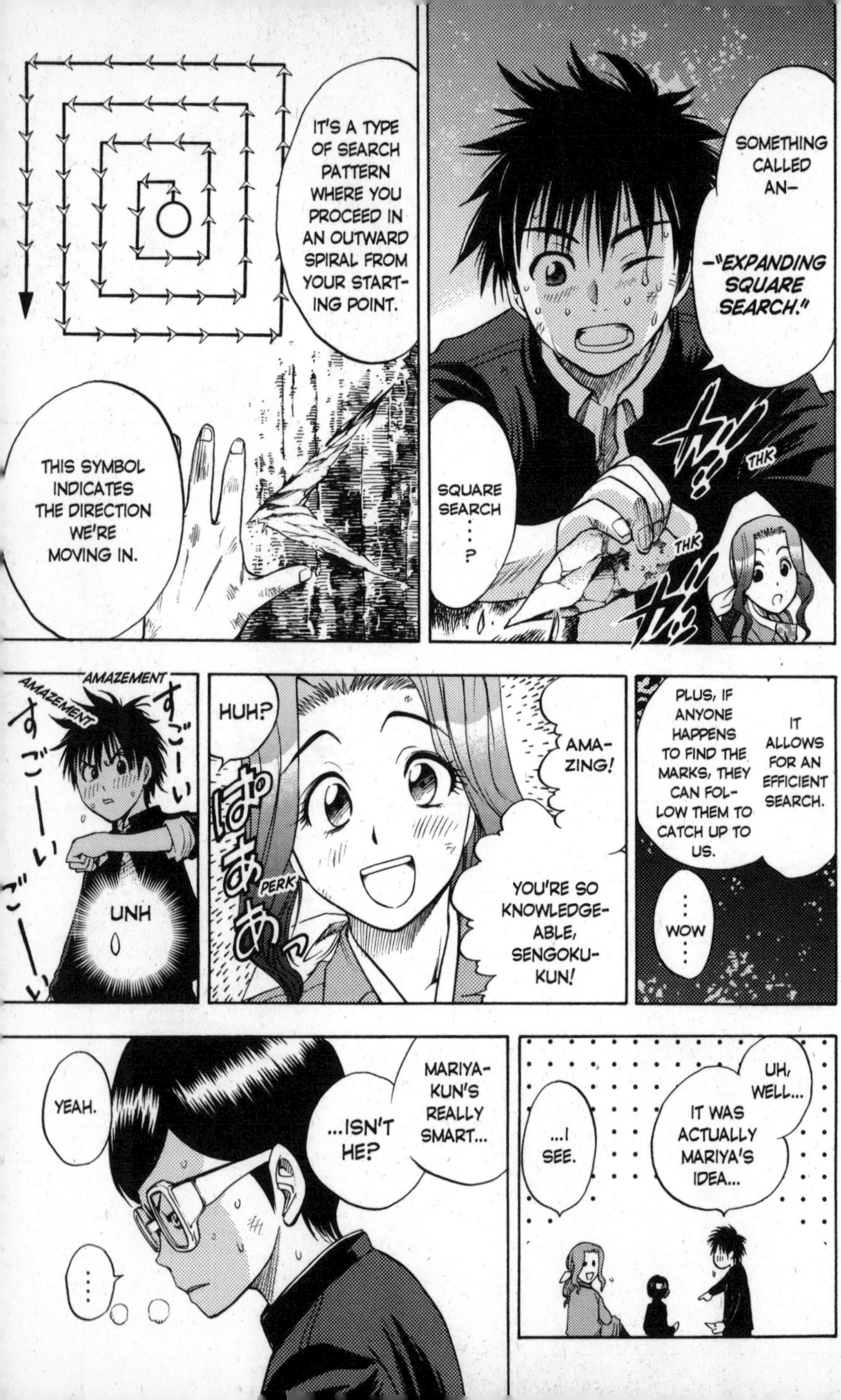
SOMETHING CALLED AN—
—"EXPANDING SQUARE SEARCH."
THK
THK
SQUARE SEARCH ...?
IT'S A TYPE OF SEARCH PATTERN WHERE YOU PROCEED IN AN OUTWARD SPIRAL FROM YOUR START-ING POINT.
THIS SYMBOL INDICATES THE DIRECTION WE'RE MOVING IN.
IT ALLOWS FOR AN EFFICIENT SEARCH.
PLUS, IF ANYONE HAPPENS TO FIND THE MARKS, THEY CAN FOL-LOW THEM TO CATCH UP TO US.
...WOW...
HUH?
PERK
ぱあぁ
AMA-ZING!
YOU'RE SO KNOWLEDGE-ABLE, SENGOKU-KUN!
AMAZEMENT
AMAZEMENT
すごーい
UNH
UH, WELL...
IT WAS ACTUALLY MARIYA'S IDEA...
...I SEE.
MARIYA-KUN'S REALLY SMART...
...ISN'T HE?
YEAH.
......

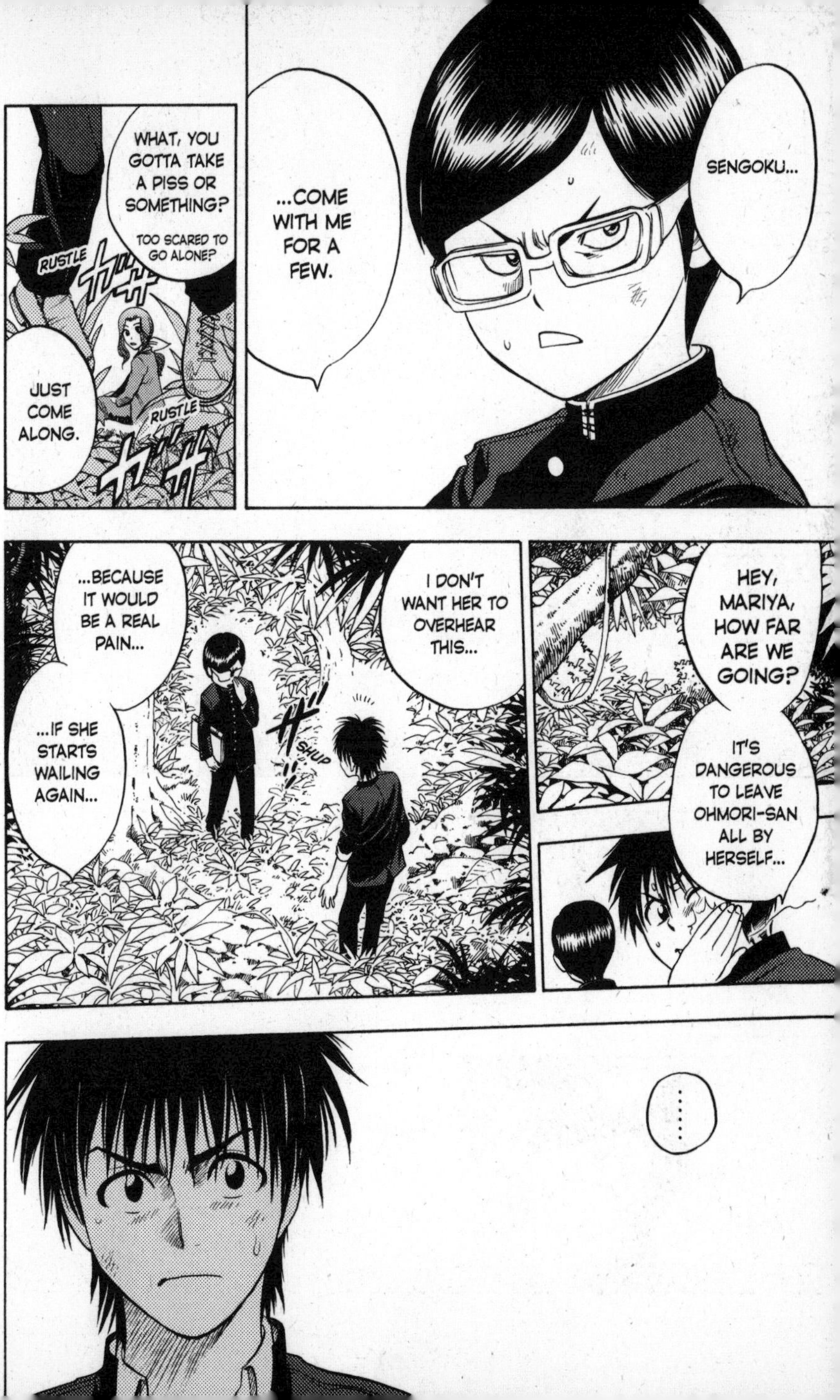
SENGOKU...
...COME WITH ME FOR A FEW.
WHAT, YOU GOTTA TAKE A PISS OR SOMETHING?
TOO SCARED TO GO ALONE?
RUSTLE
JUST COME ALONG.
RUSTLE
HEY, MARIYA, HOW FAR ARE WE GOING?
IT'S DANGEROUS TO LEAVE OHMORI-SAN ALL BY HERSELF...
I DON'T WANT HER TO OVERHEAR THIS...
SHUP
...BECAUSE IT WOULD BE A REAL PAIN...
...IF SHE STARTS WAILING AGAIN...
......

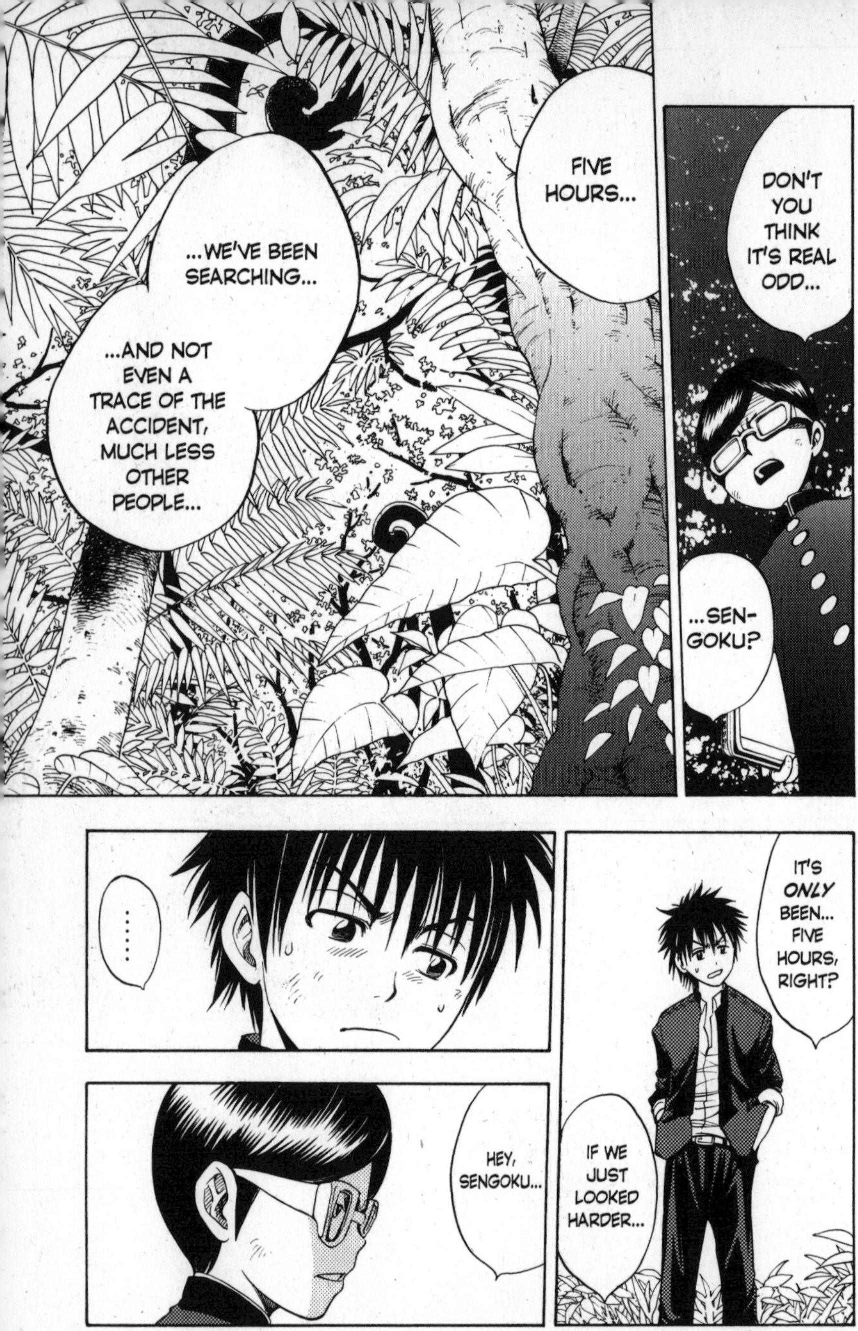
DON'T YOU THINK IT'S REAL ODD...
...SEN-GOKU?
FIVE HOURS...
...WE'VE BEEN SEARCHING...
...AND NOT EVEN A TRACE OF THE ACCIDENT, MUCH LESS OTHER PEOPLE...
IT'S *ONLY* BEEN... FIVE HOURS, RIGHT?
IF WE JUST LOOKED HARDER...
......
HEY, SENGOKU...

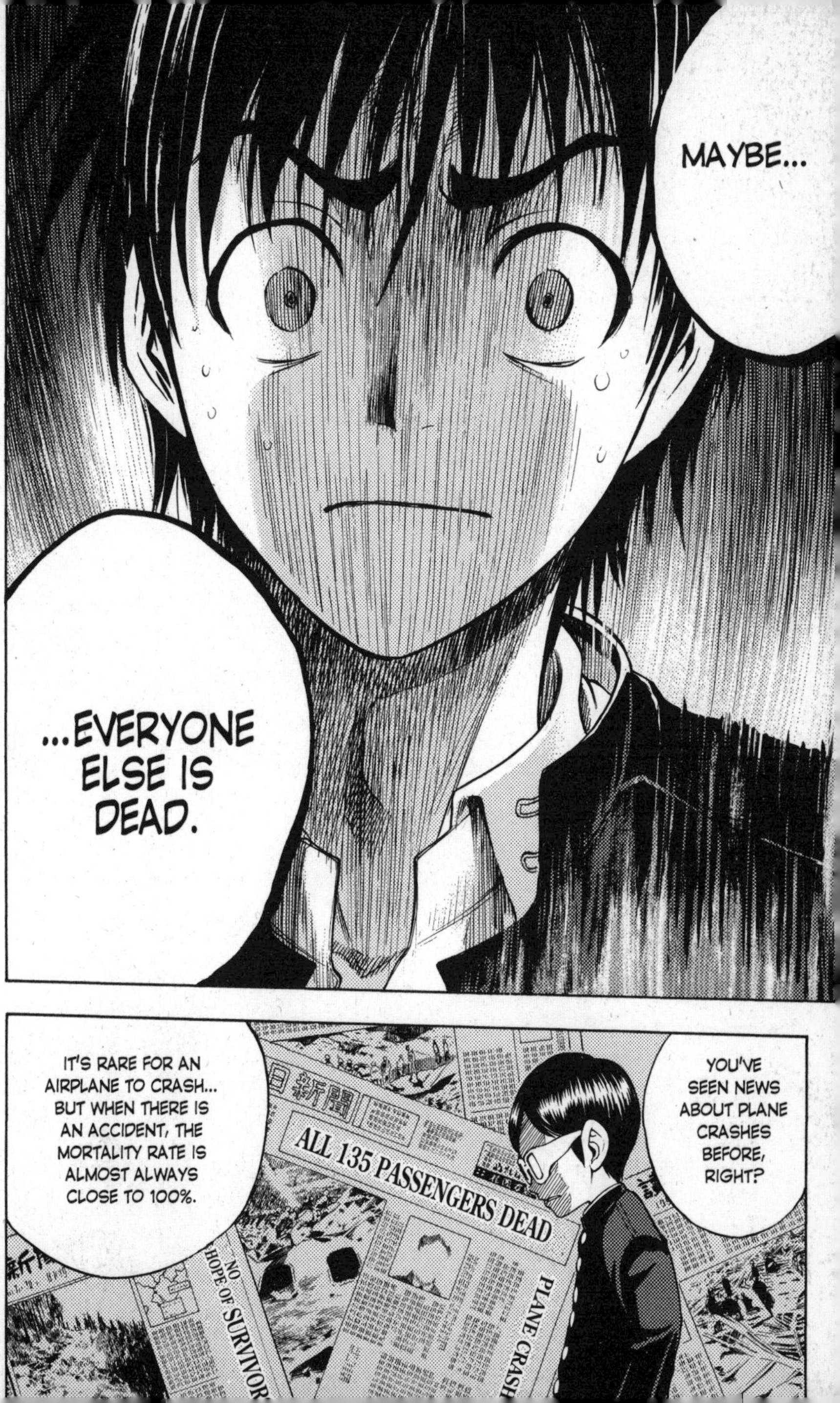

MAYBE...
...EVERYONE ELSE IS DEAD.
YOU'VE SEEN NEWS ABOUT PLANE CRASHES BEFORE, RIGHT?
IT'S RARE FOR AN AIRPLANE TO CRASH... BUT WHEN THERE IS AN ACCIDENT, THE MORTALITY RATE IS ALMOST ALWAYS CLOSE TO 100%.
ALL 135 PASSENGERS DEAD
NO HOPE OF SURVIVOR
PLANE CRASH

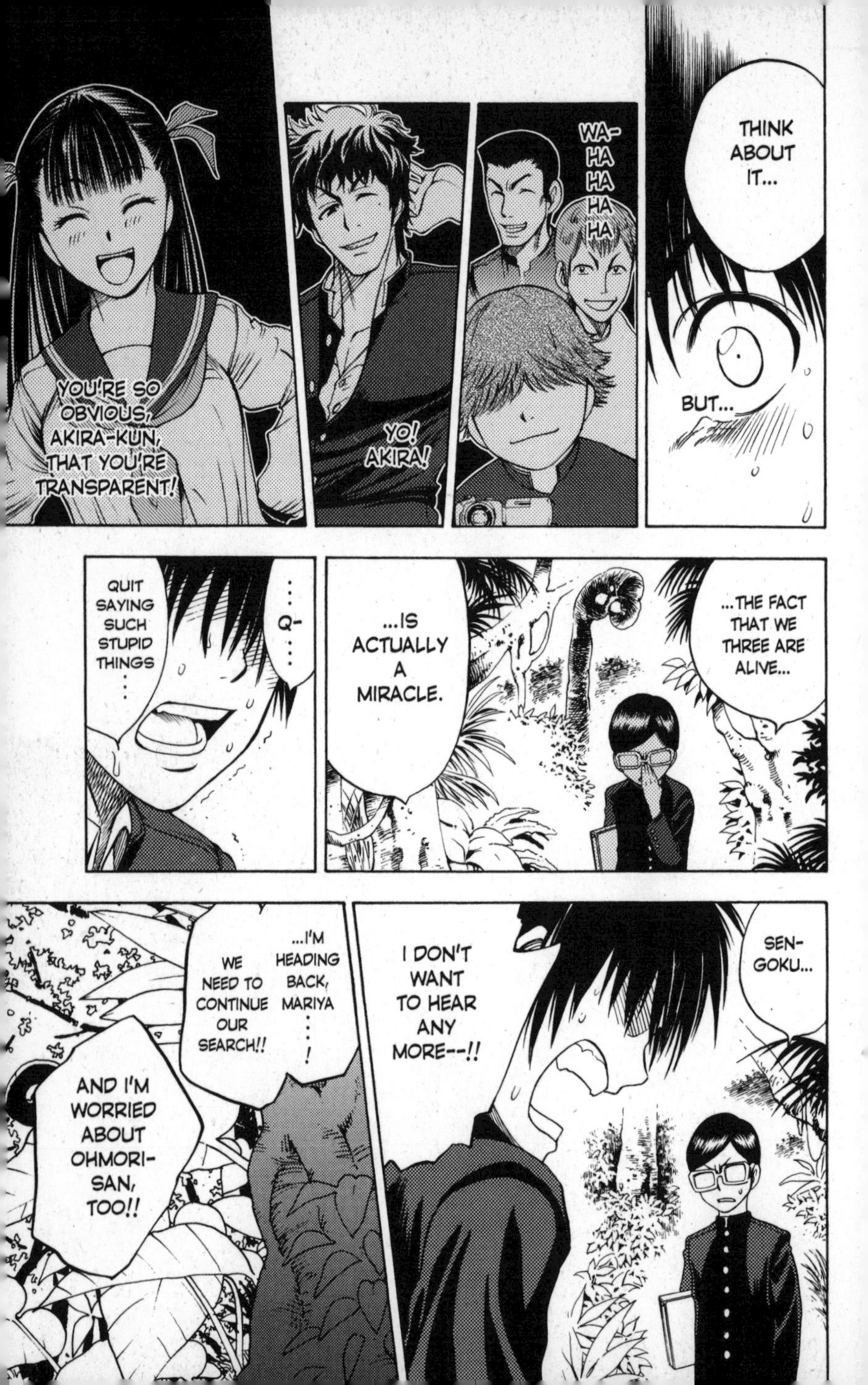
THINK ABOUT IT...
BUT...
WA-HA HA HA HA
YO! AKIRA!
YOU'RE SO OBVIOUS, AKIRA-KUN, THAT YOU'RE TRANSPARENT!
...THE FACT THAT WE THREE ARE ALIVE...
...IS ACTUALLY A MIRACLE.
...Q-...
QUIT SAYING SUCH STUPID THINGS...
SEN-GOKU...
I DON'T WANT TO HEAR ANY MORE--!!
...I'M HEADING BACK, MARIYA...!
WE NEED TO CONTINUE OUR SEARCH!!
AND I'M WORRIED ABOUT OHMORI-SAN, TOO!!

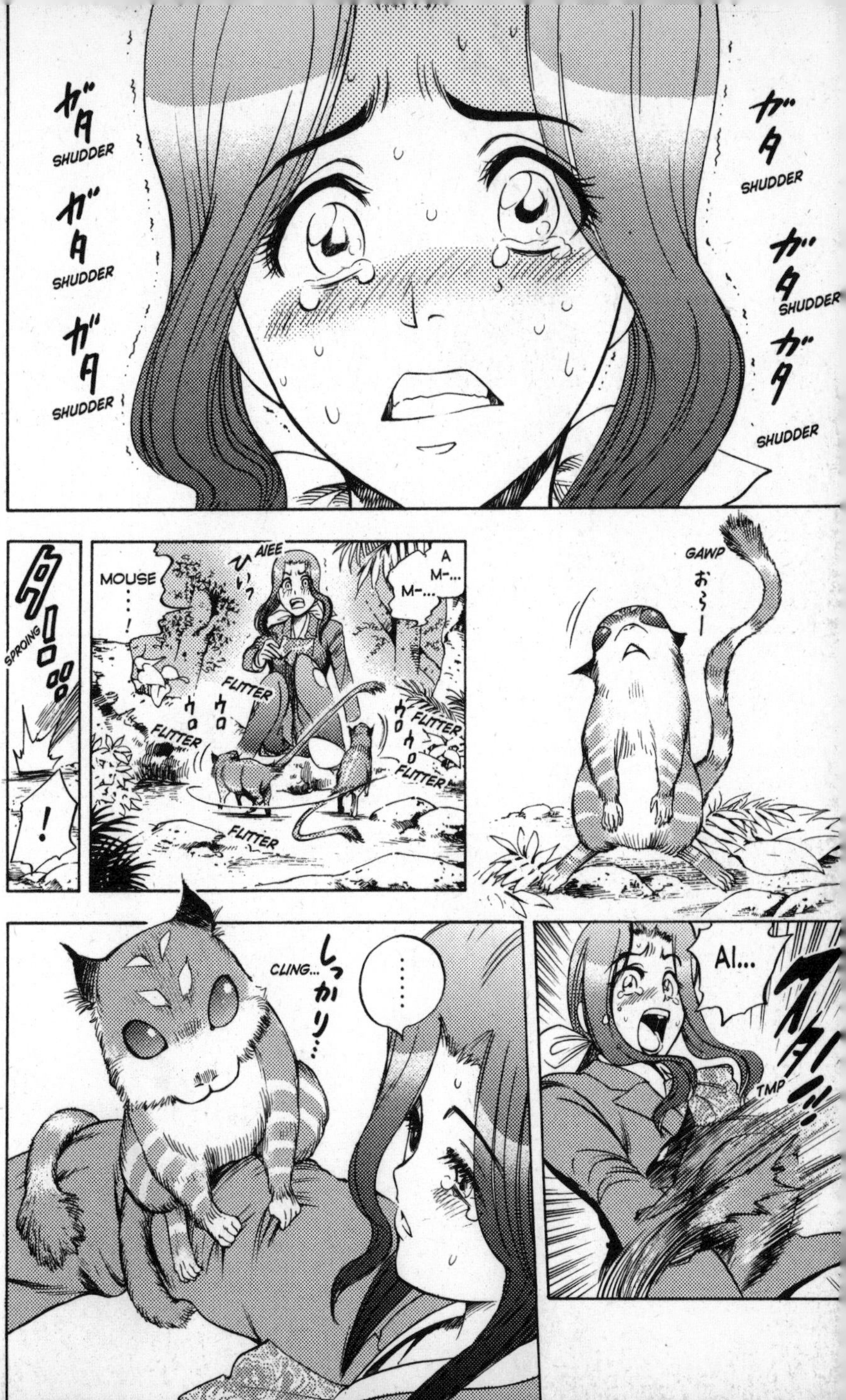

ガタ
SHUDDER
ガタ
SHUDDER
ガタ
SHUDDER
ガタ
SHUDDER
ガタ
SHUDDER
ガタ
SHUDDER
GAWP
おら~
A M-... M-...
AIEE
ひぃっ
MOUSE
...!
FLUTTER
ウロ
ウロ
FLUTTER
ウロ
FLUTTER
ウロ ウロ
FLUTTER
FLUTTER
SPROING
!
AI...
スタ!!
TMP
CLING...
しっかり...
......

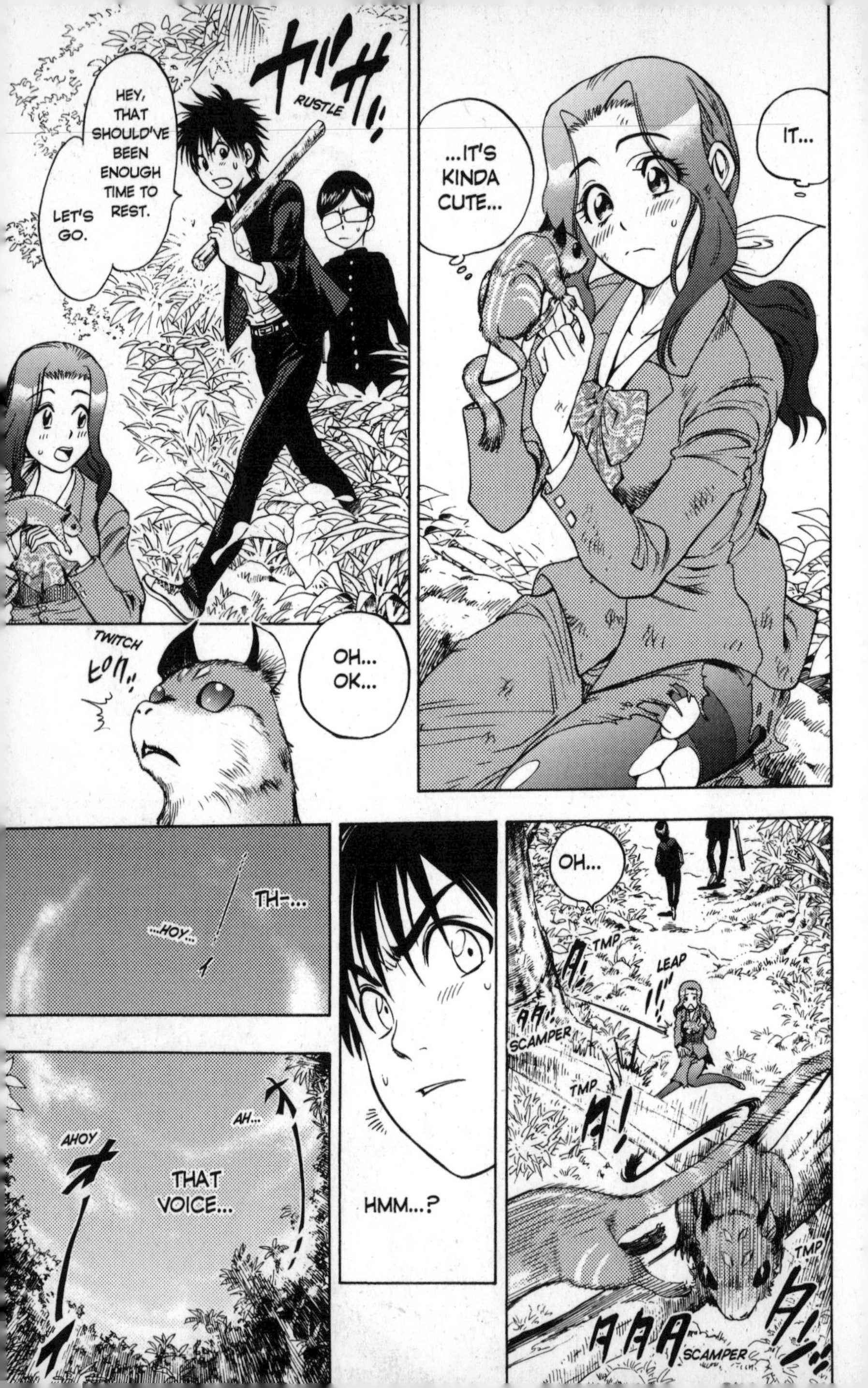
IT...
...IT'S KINDA CUTE...
RUSTLE
HEY, THAT SHOULD'VE BEEN ENOUGH TIME TO REST.
LET'S GO.
TWITCH
OH... OK...
OH...
TMP
LEAP
SCAMPER
TMP
TMP
SCAMPER
HMM...?
TH-...
...HOY...
AH...
AHOY
THAT VOICE...

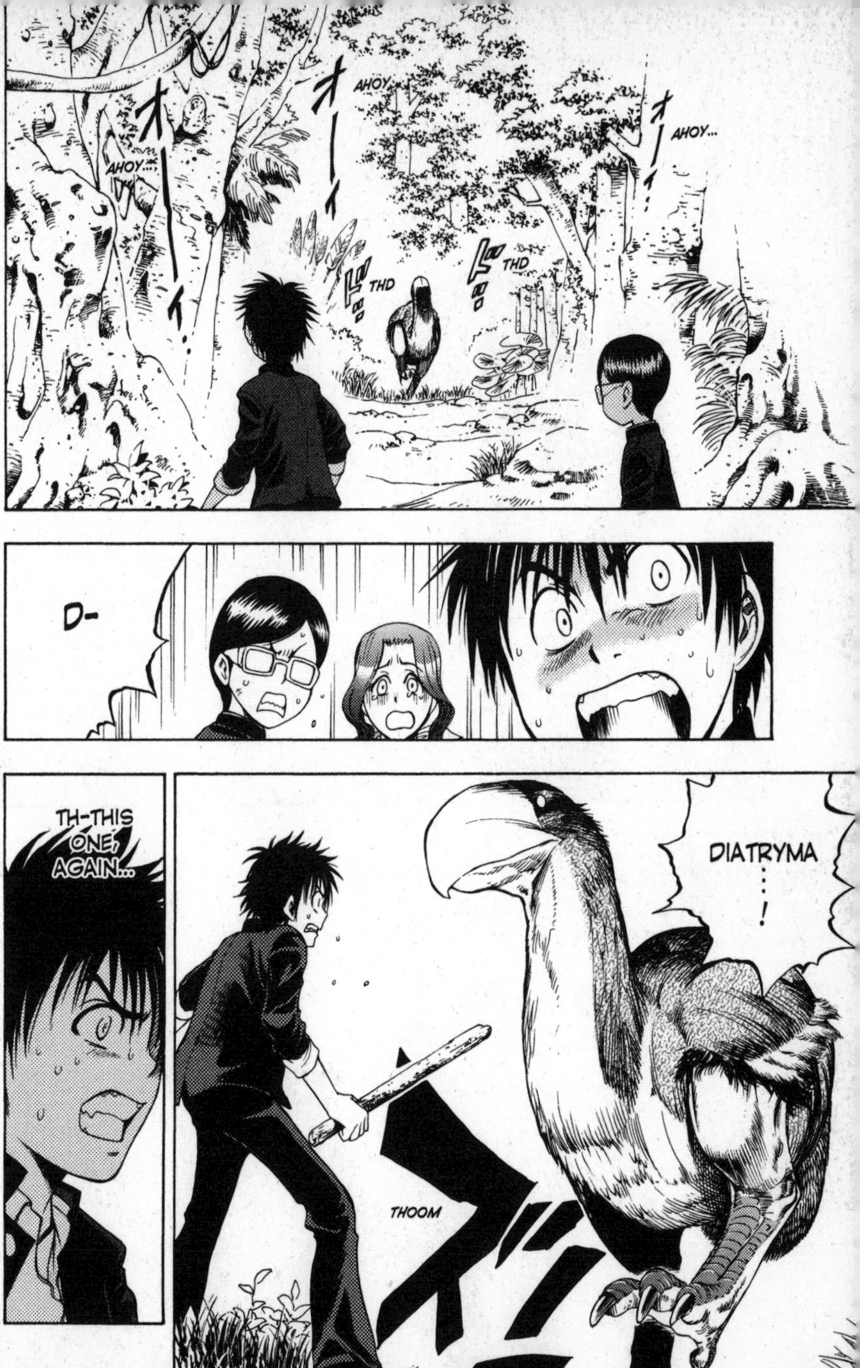
AHOY...
AHOY
AHOY...
THD
THD
D-
DIATRYMA
...!
TH-THIS ONE, AGAIN...
THOOM

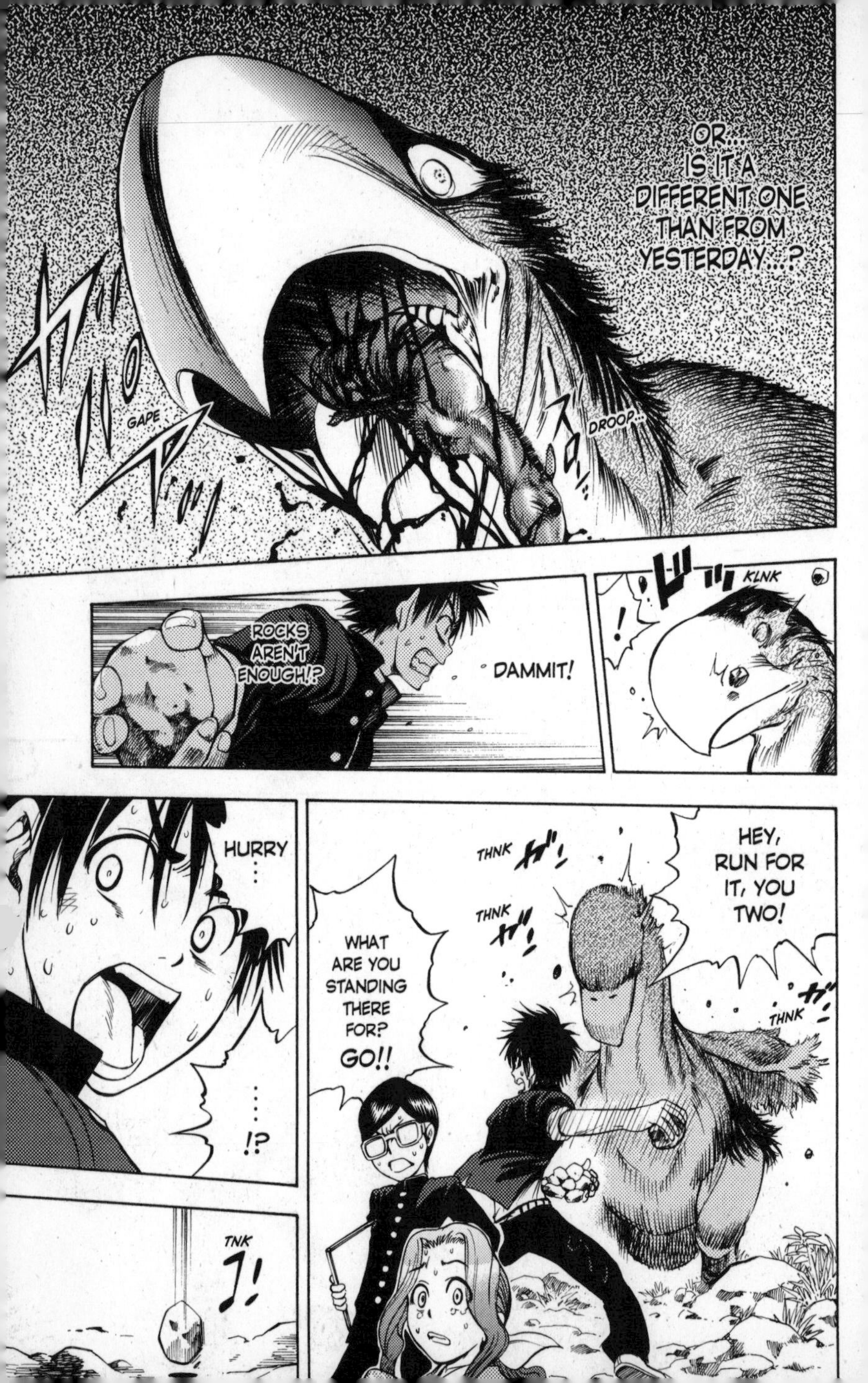
OR... IS IT A DIFFERENT ONE THAN FROM YESTERDAY...?
DROOP...
GAPE
KLNK
DAMMIT!
ROCKS AREN'T ENOUGH!?
THNK
HEY, RUN FOR IT, YOU TWO!
THNK
THNK
WHAT ARE YOU STANDING THERE FOR? GO!!
HURRY...
......!?
TNK

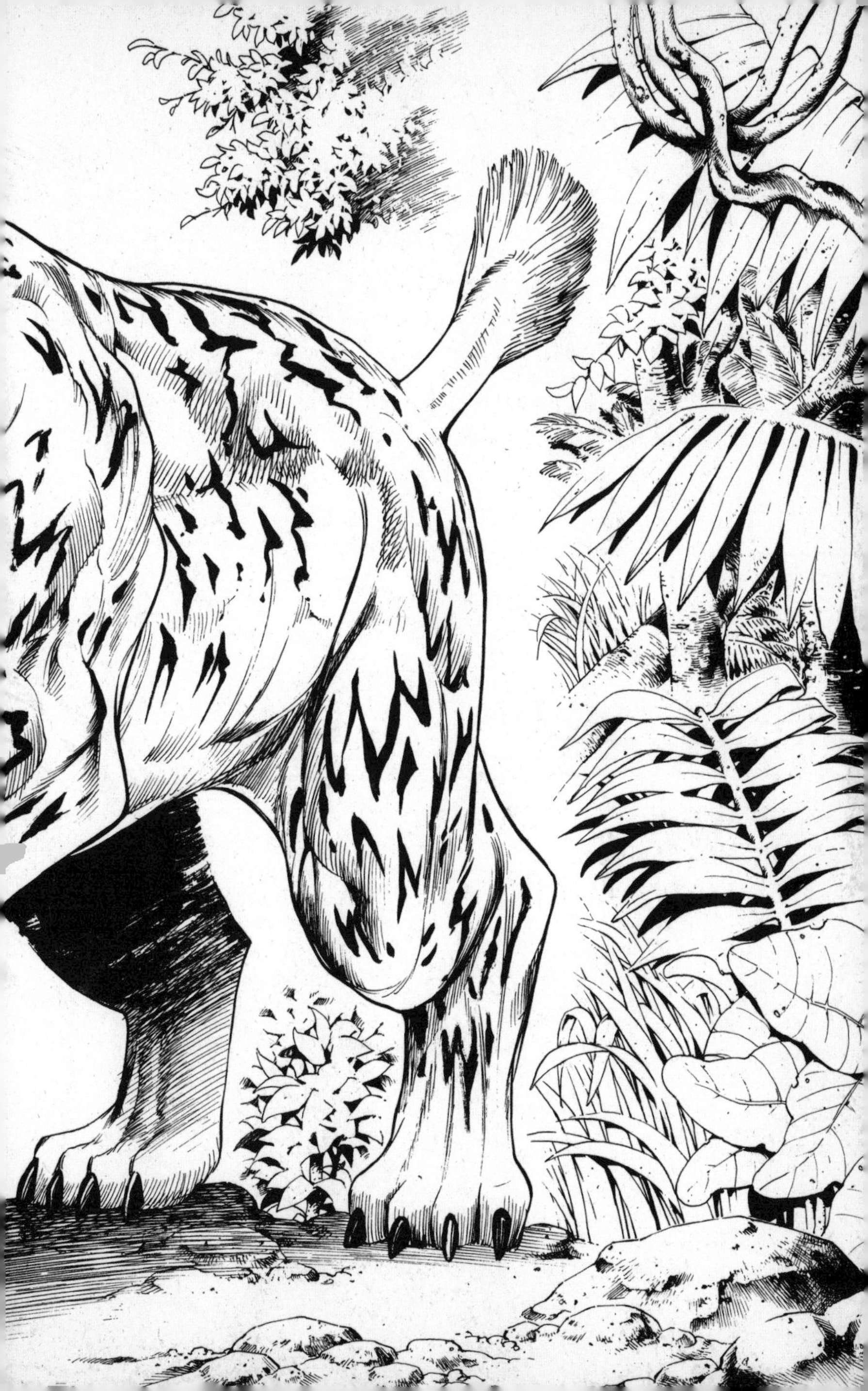

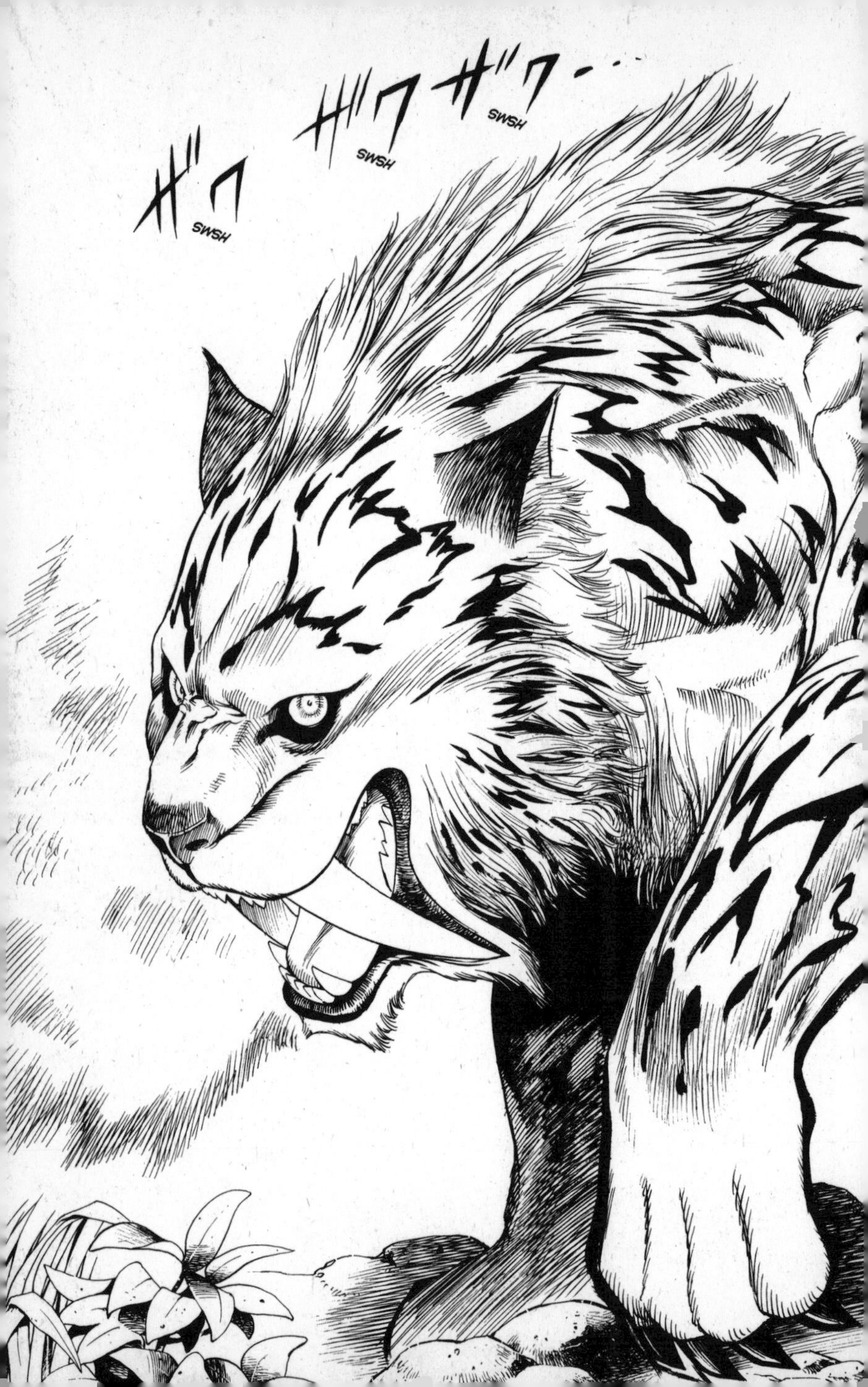
ザク
SWSH
ザク
SWSH
ザク‥
SWSH

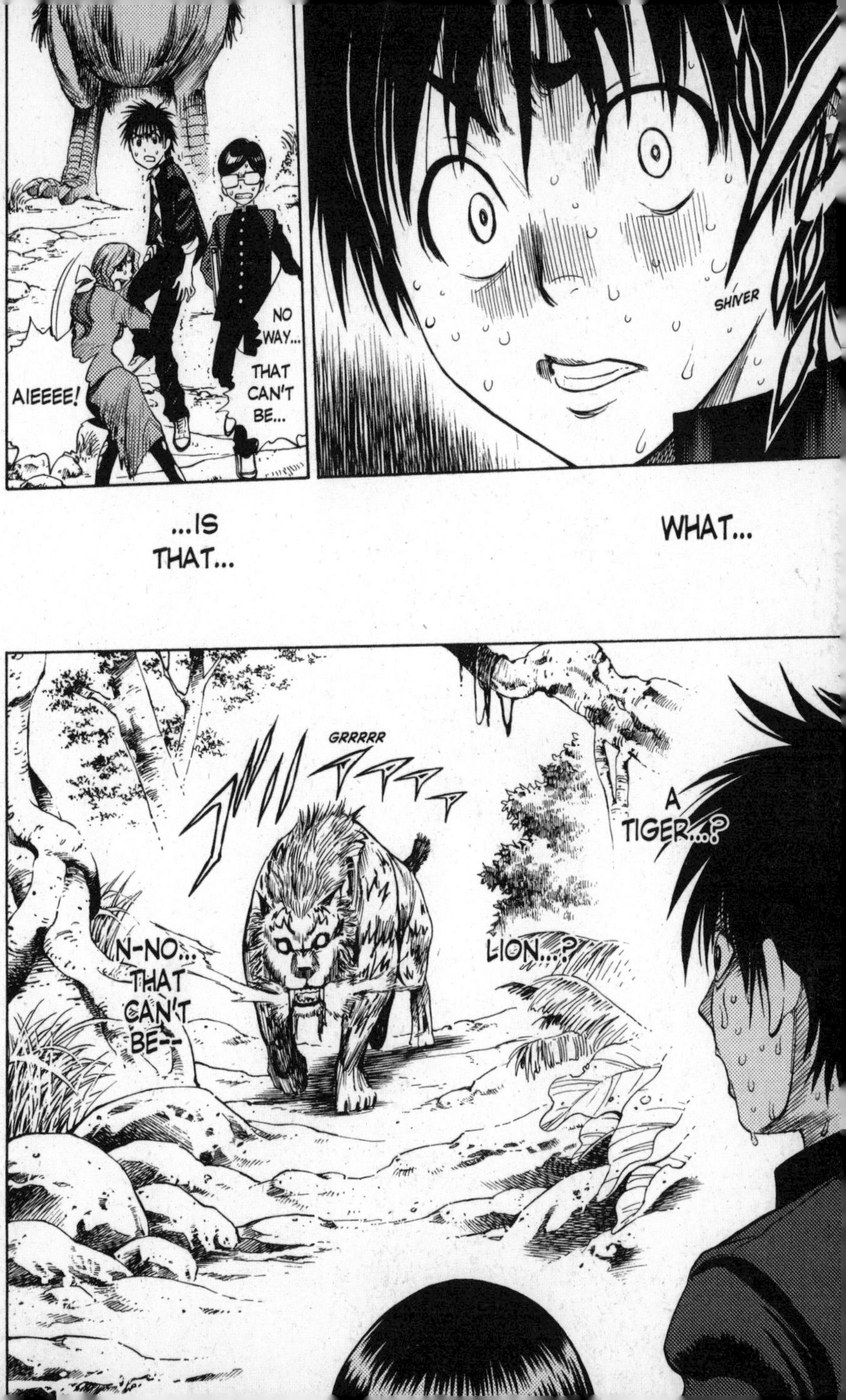
SHIVER
NO WAY...
THAT CAN'T BE...
AIEEEE!
WHAT...
...IS THAT...
A TIGER...?
LION...?
GRRRRR
N-NO... THAT CAN'T BE--

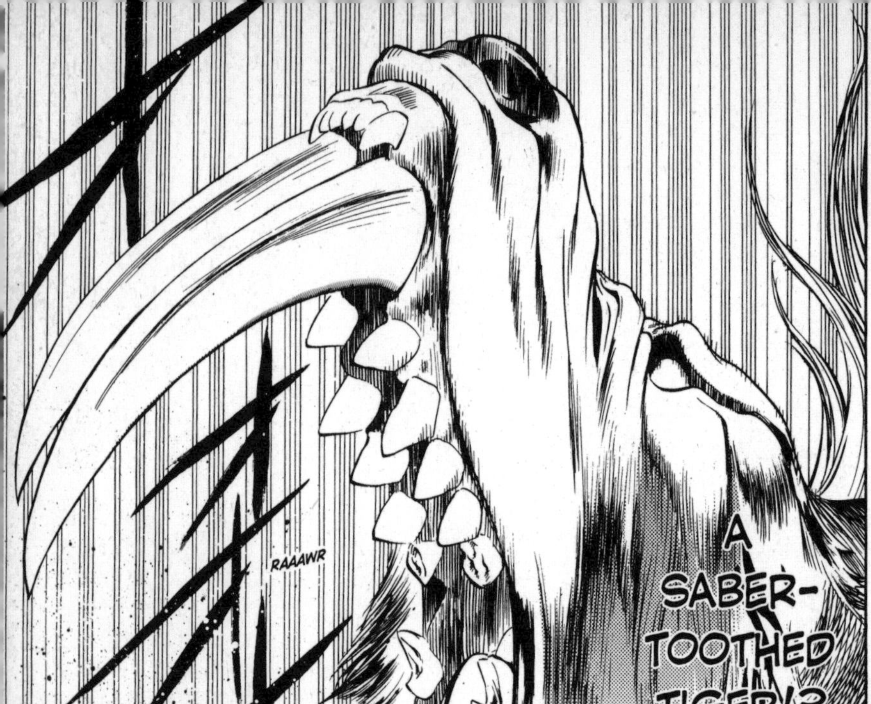
A SABER-TOOTHED TIGER!?
RAAAWR
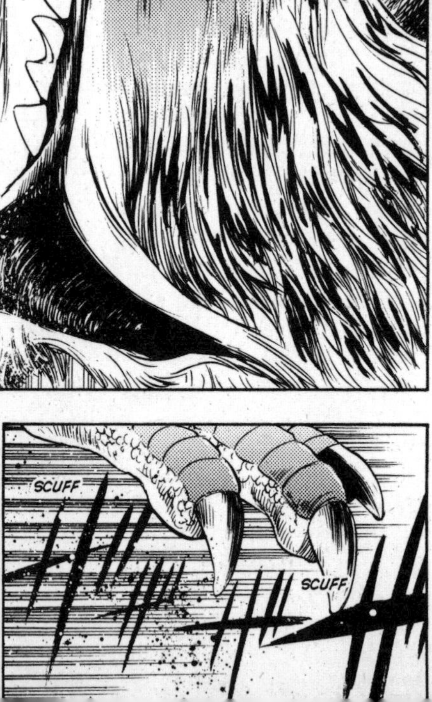
SCUFF
SCUFF
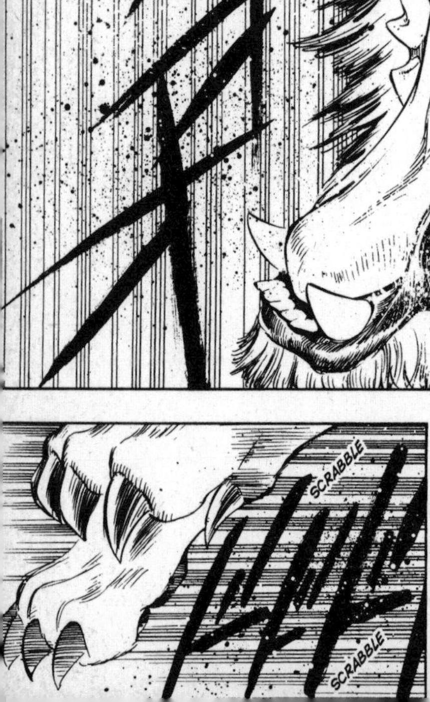
SCRABBLE
SCRABBLE

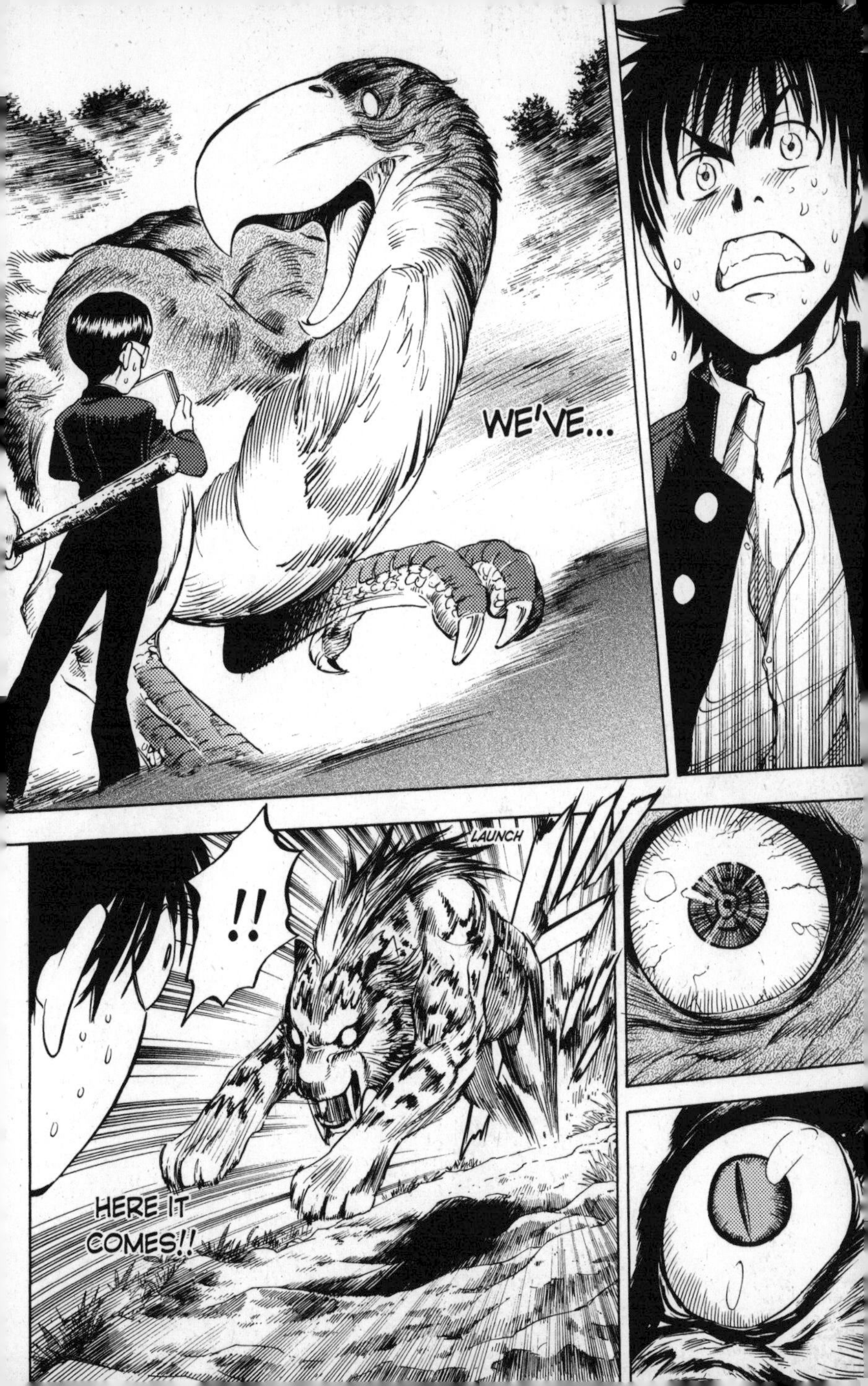
WE'VE...
LAUNCH
!!
HERE IT COMES!!

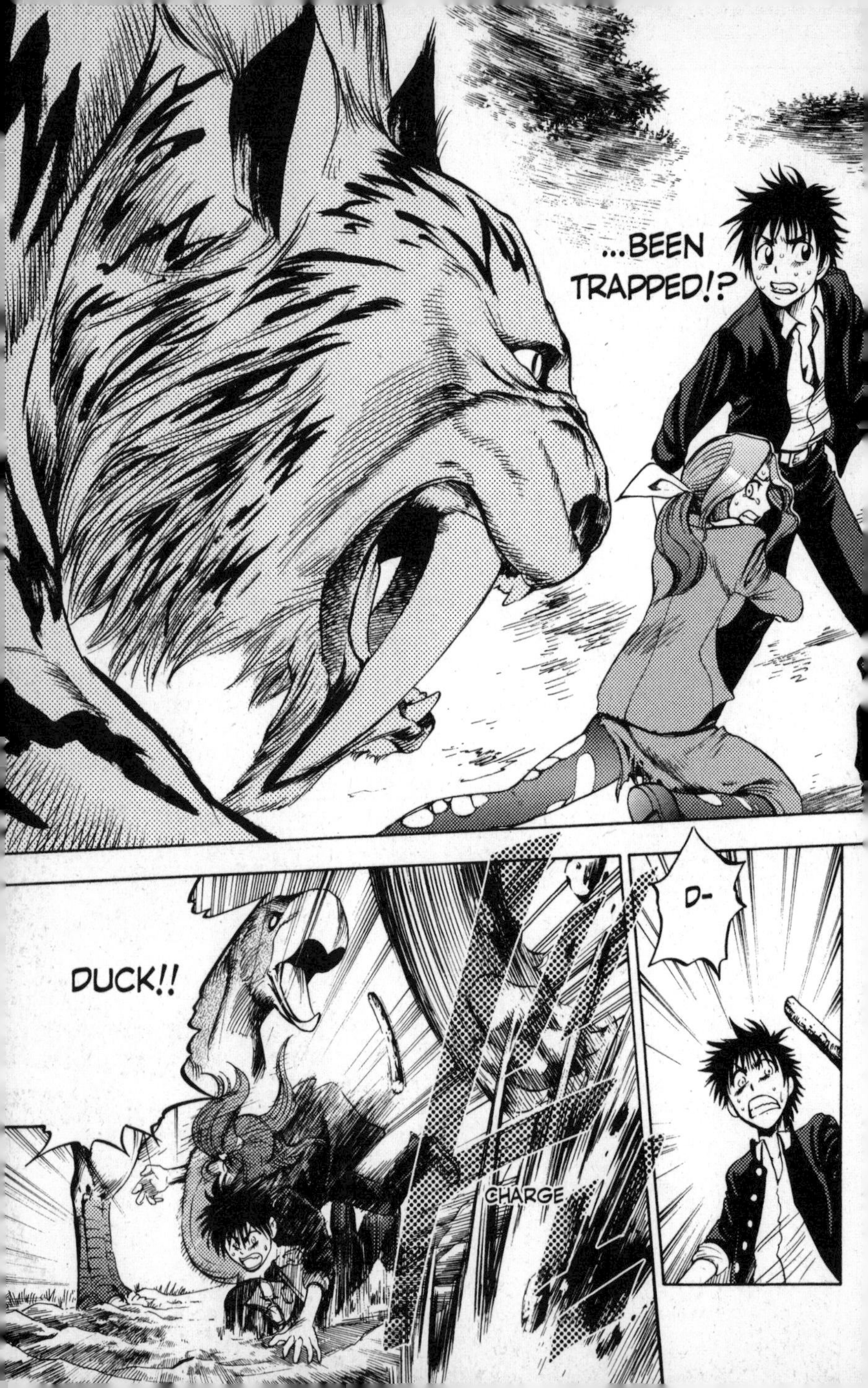
...BEEN TRAPPED!?
D-
DUCK!!
CHARGE

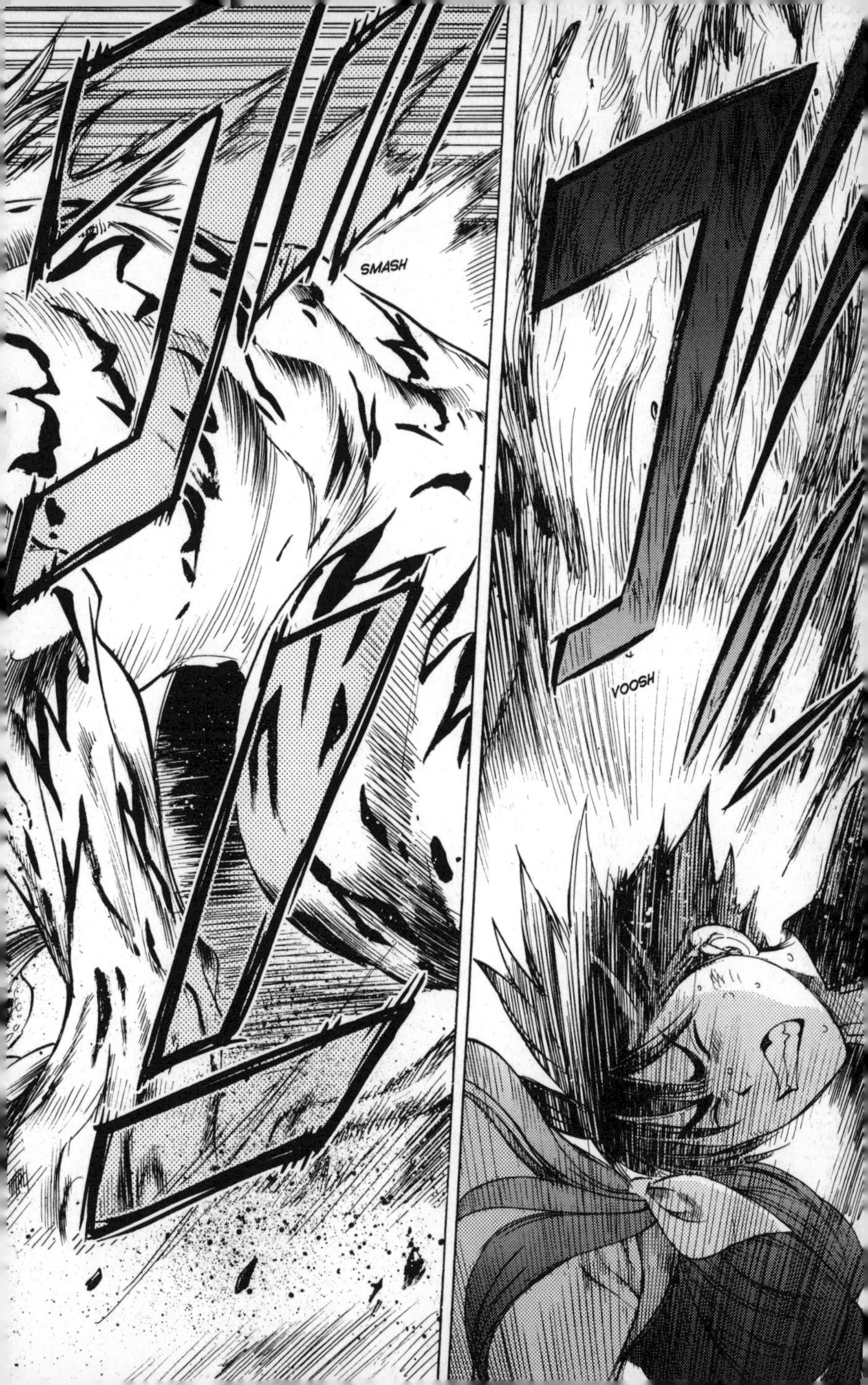
VOOSH
SMASH

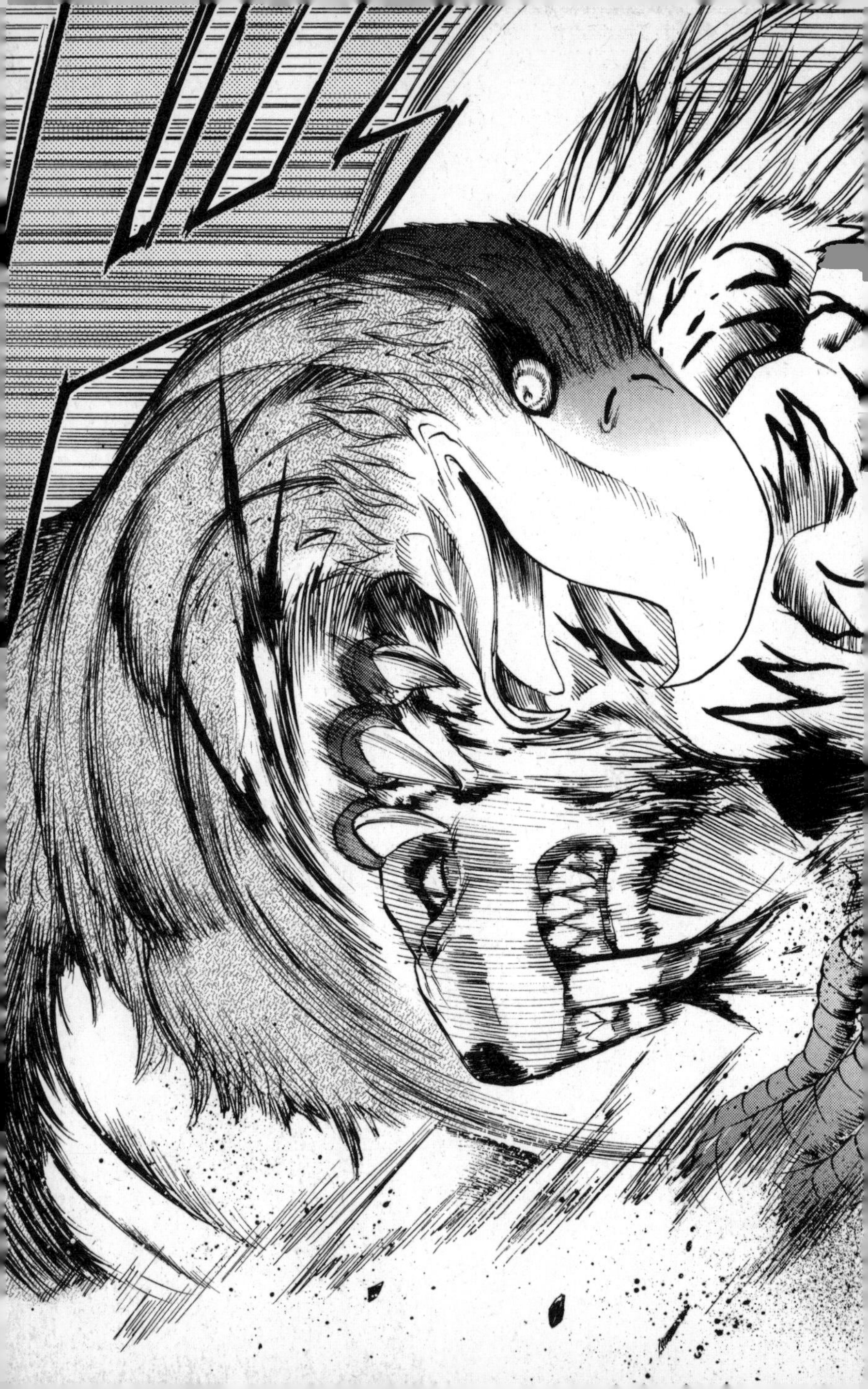

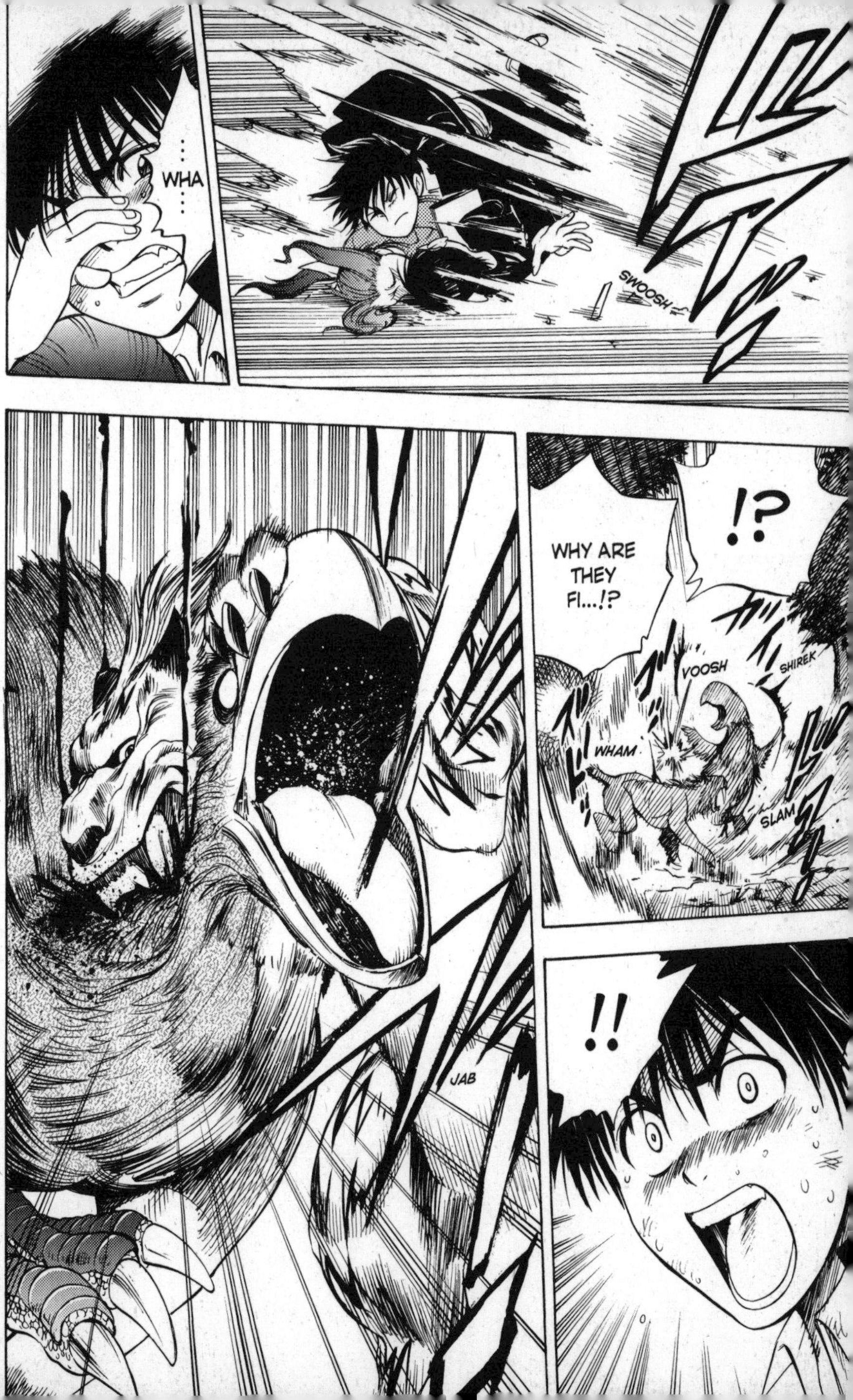
SWOOSH
WHA......
!?
WHY ARE THEY FI...!?
SHIREK
VOOSH
WHAM
SLAM
!!
JAB

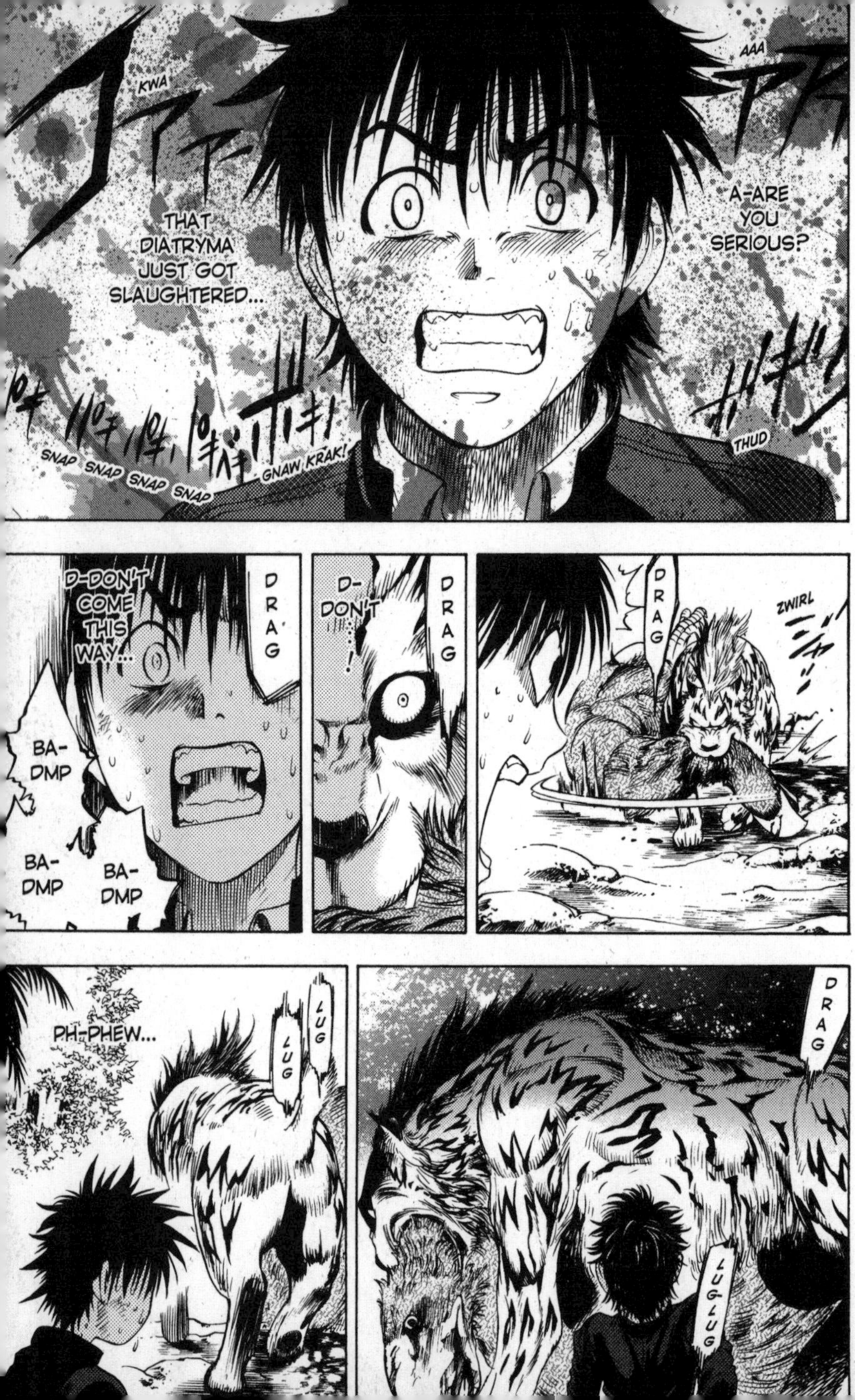
AAA
A-ARE YOU SERIOUS?
KWA
THAT DIATRYMA JUST GOT SLAUGHTERED...
THUD
GNAW KRAK!
SNAP SNAP SNAP SNAP
DRAG
ZWIRL
DRAG
D-DON'T...!
DRAG
D-DON'T COME THIS WAY...
BA-DMP
BA-DMP
BA-DMP
DRAG
LUGLUG
LUG
LUG
PH-PHEW...

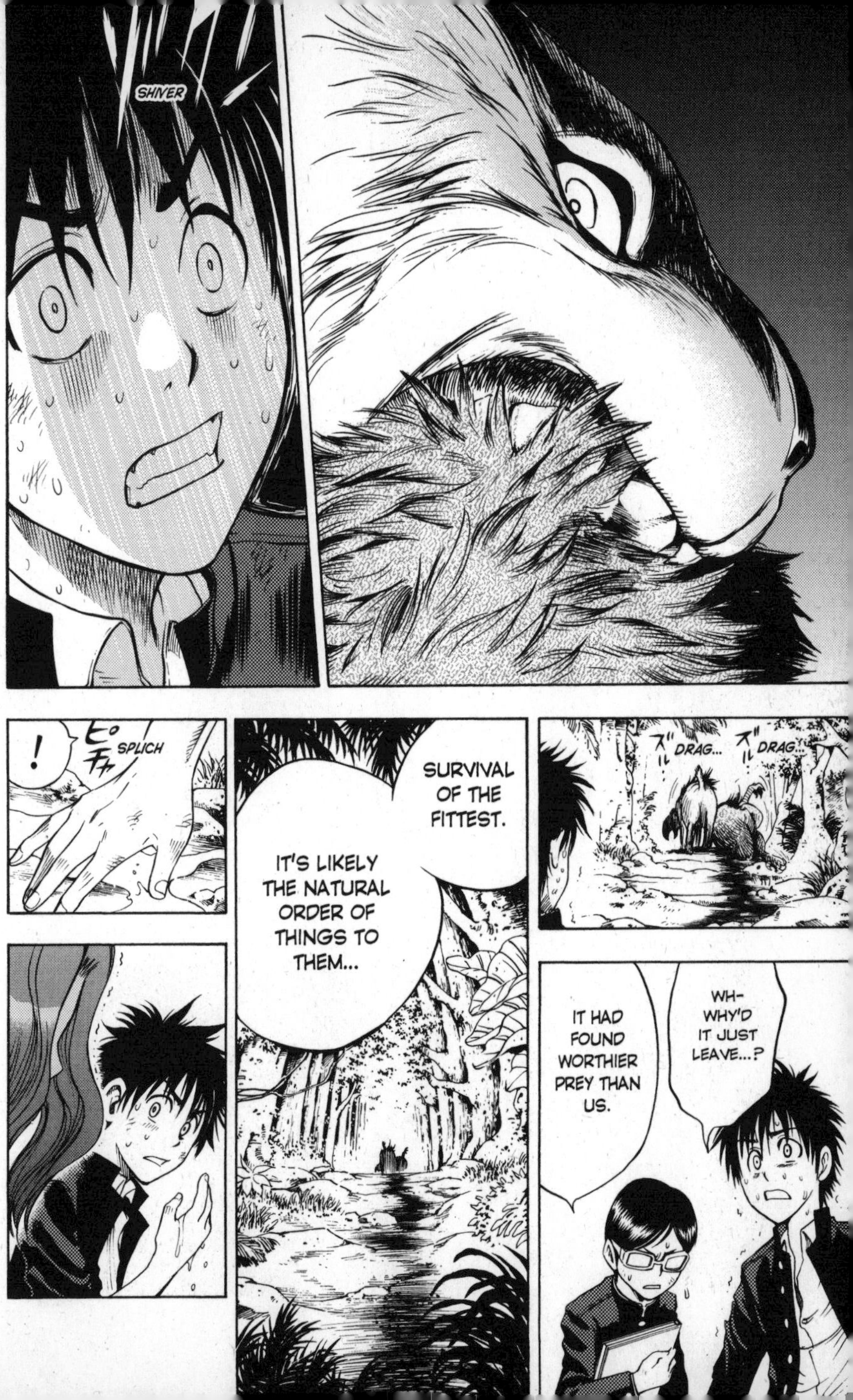
SHIVER
ズル DRAG...
ズル DRAG...
WH- WHY'D IT JUST LEAVE...?
IT HAD FOUND WORTHIER PREY THAN US.
SURVIVAL OF THE FITTEST.
IT'S LIKELY THE NATURAL ORDER OF THINGS TO THEM...
!
ピチャ SPLICH

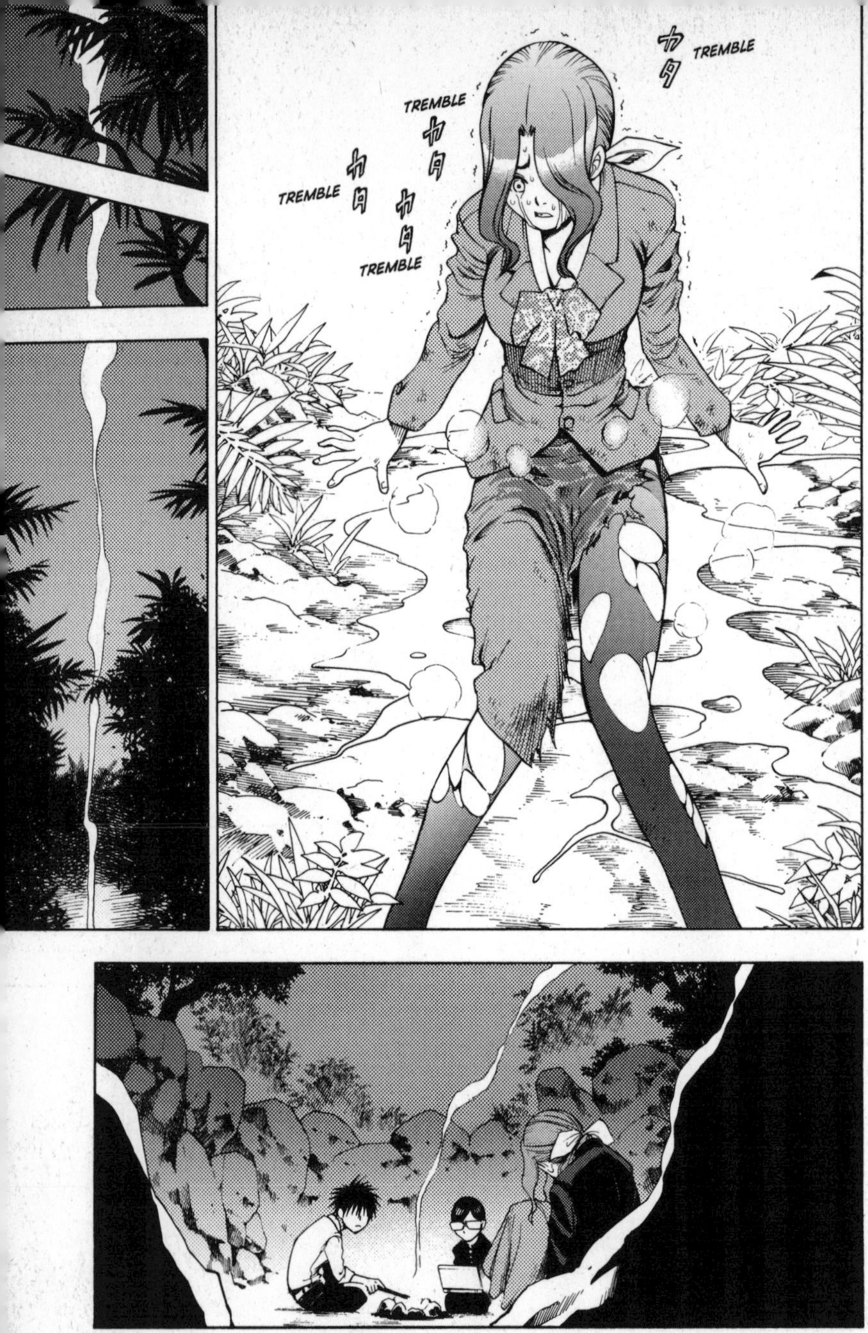
カタ
TREMBLE
TREMBLE
カタ
カタ
カタ
TREMBLE
TREMBLE

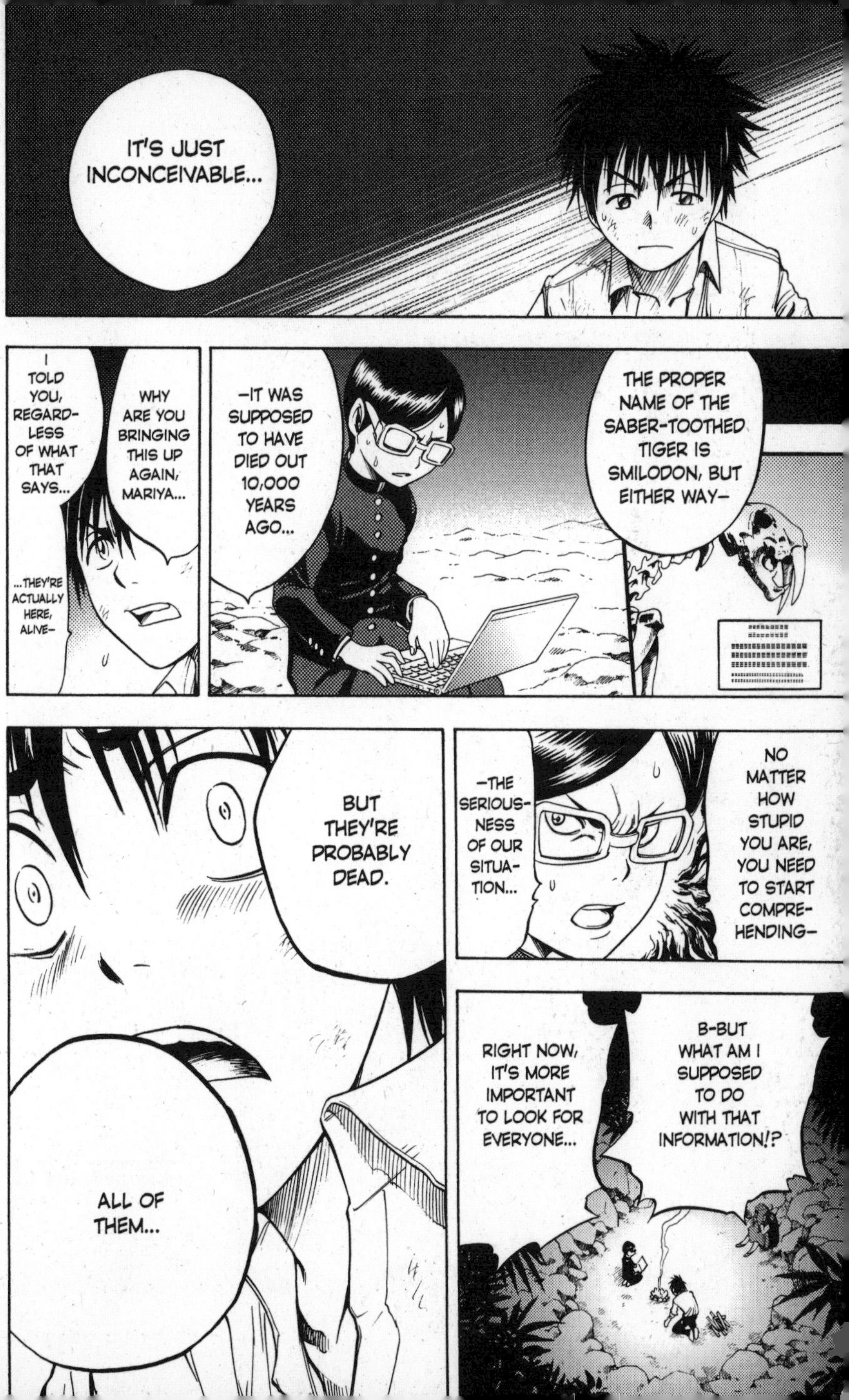
IT'S JUST INCONCEIVABLE...
THE PROPER NAME OF THE SABER-TOOTHED TIGER IS SMILODON, BUT EITHER WAY—
—IT WAS SUPPOSED TO HAVE DIED OUT 10,000 YEARS AGO...
WHY ARE YOU BRINGING THIS UP AGAIN, MARIYA...
I TOLD YOU, REGARDLESS OF WHAT THAT SAYS...
...THEY'RE ACTUALLY HERE, ALIVE—
NO MATTER HOW STUPID YOU ARE, YOU NEED TO START COMPREHENDING—
—THE SERIOUSNESS OF OUR SITUATION...
B-BUT WHAT AM I SUPPOSED TO DO WITH THAT INFORMATION!?
RIGHT NOW, IT'S MORE IMPORTANT TO LOOK FOR EVERYONE...
BUT THEY'RE PROBABLY DEAD.
ALL OF THEM...

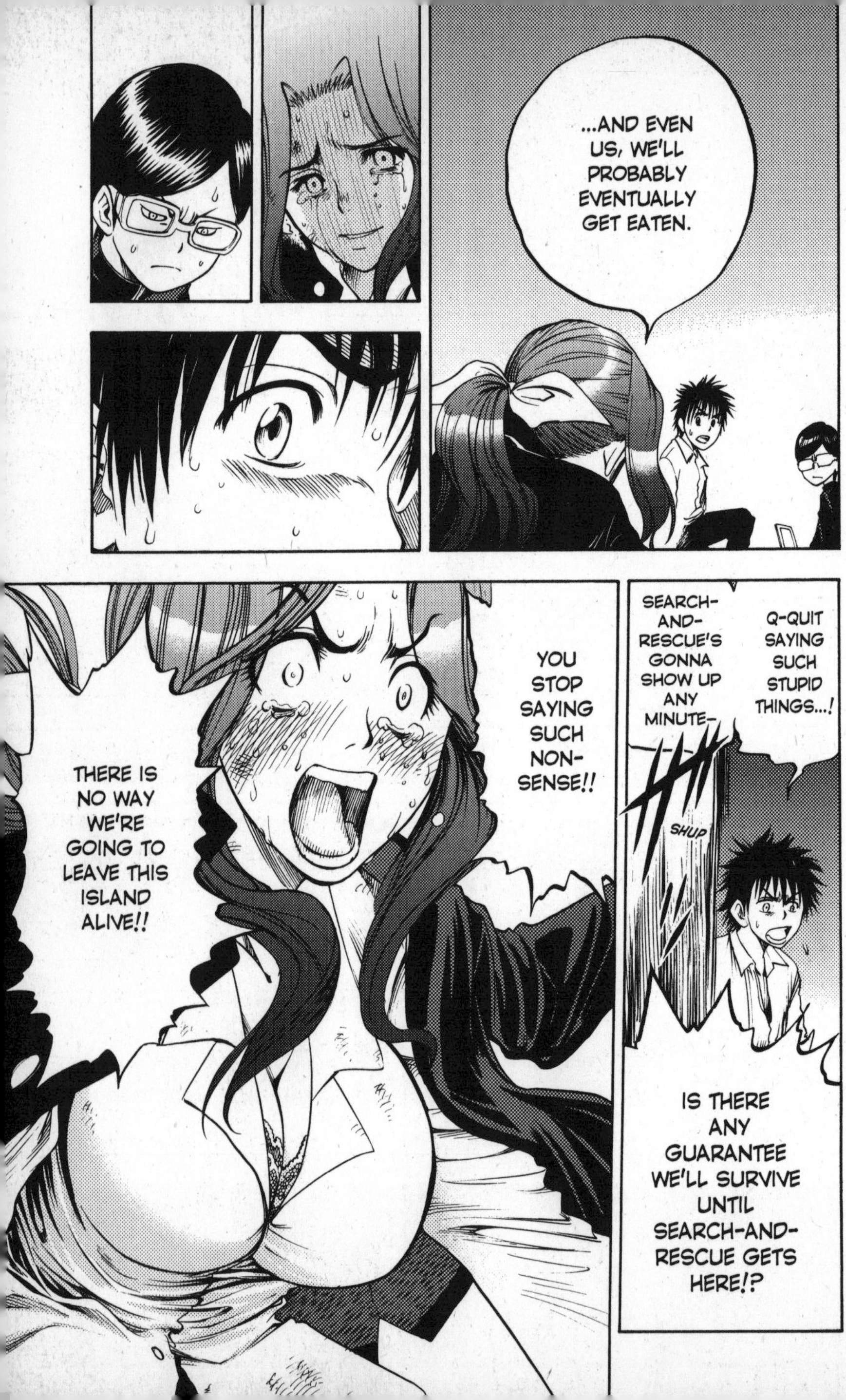
...AND EVEN US, WE'LL PROBABLY EVENTUALLY GET EATEN.
Q-QUIT SAYING SUCH STUPID THINGS...!
SEARCH-AND-RESCUE'S GONNA SHOW UP ANY MINUTE—
SHUP
IS THERE ANY GUARANTEE WE'LL SURVIVE UNTIL SEARCH-AND-RESCUE GETS HERE!?
YOU STOP SAYING SUCH NON-SENSE!!
THERE IS NO WAY WE'RE GOING TO LEAVE THIS ISLAND ALIVE!!

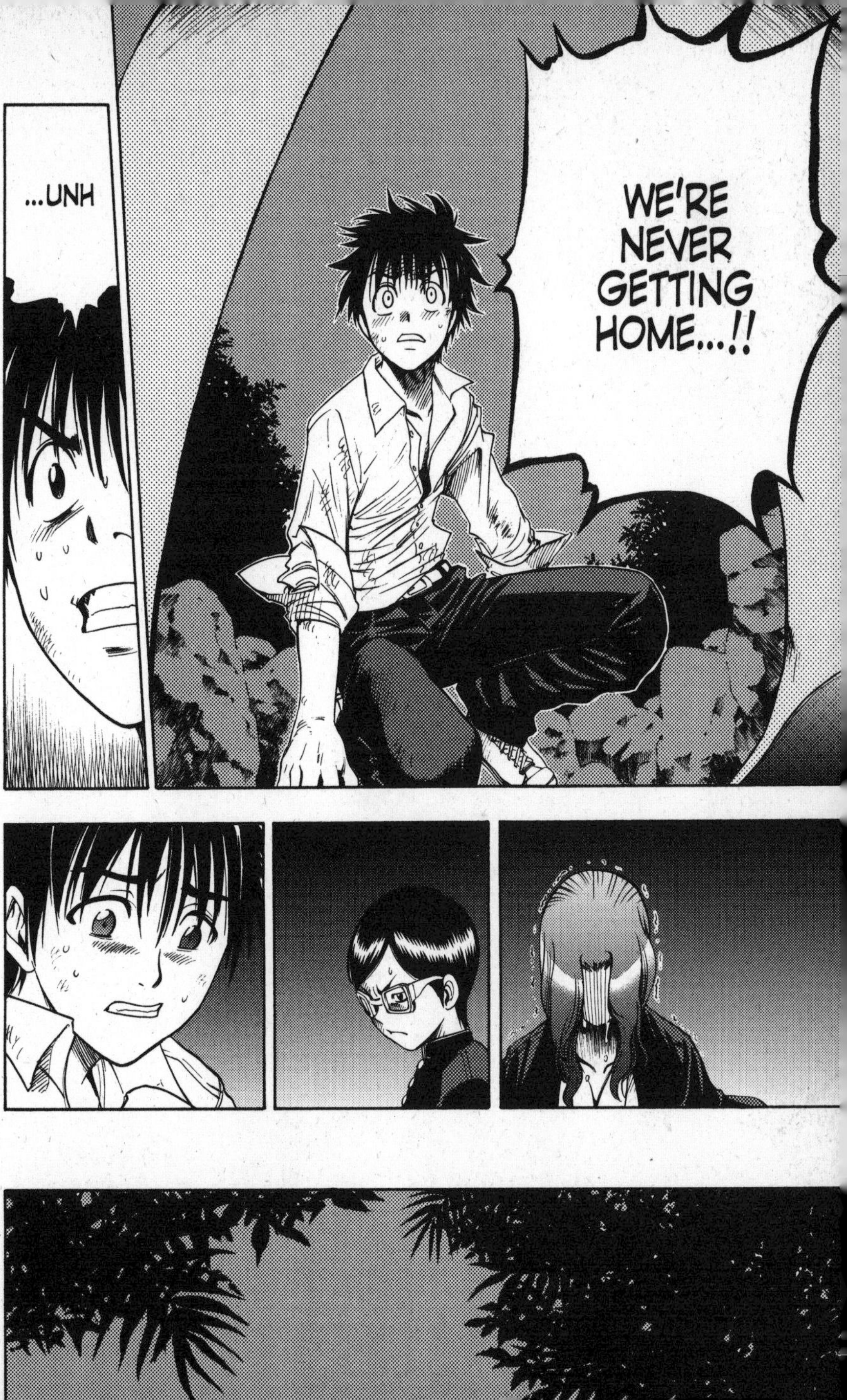
WE'RE NEVER GETTING HOME...!!
...UNH

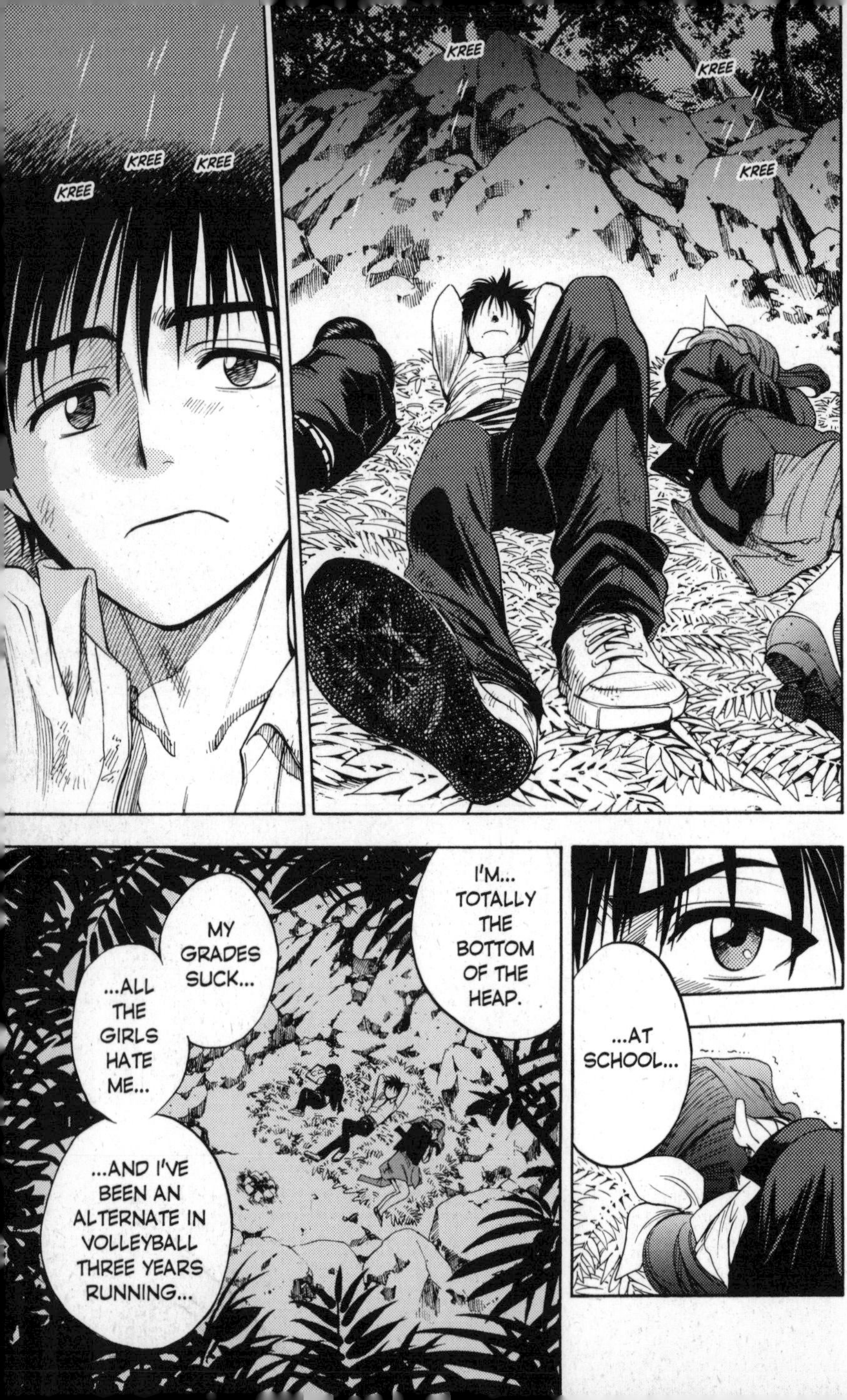
KREE
KREE
KREE
KREE
KREE
KREE
KREE
...AT SCHOOL...
I'M... TOTALLY THE BOTTOM OF THE HEAP.
MY GRADES SUCK...
...ALL THE GIRLS HATE ME...
...AND I'VE BEEN AN ALTERNATE IN VOLLEYBALL THREE YEARS RUNNING...

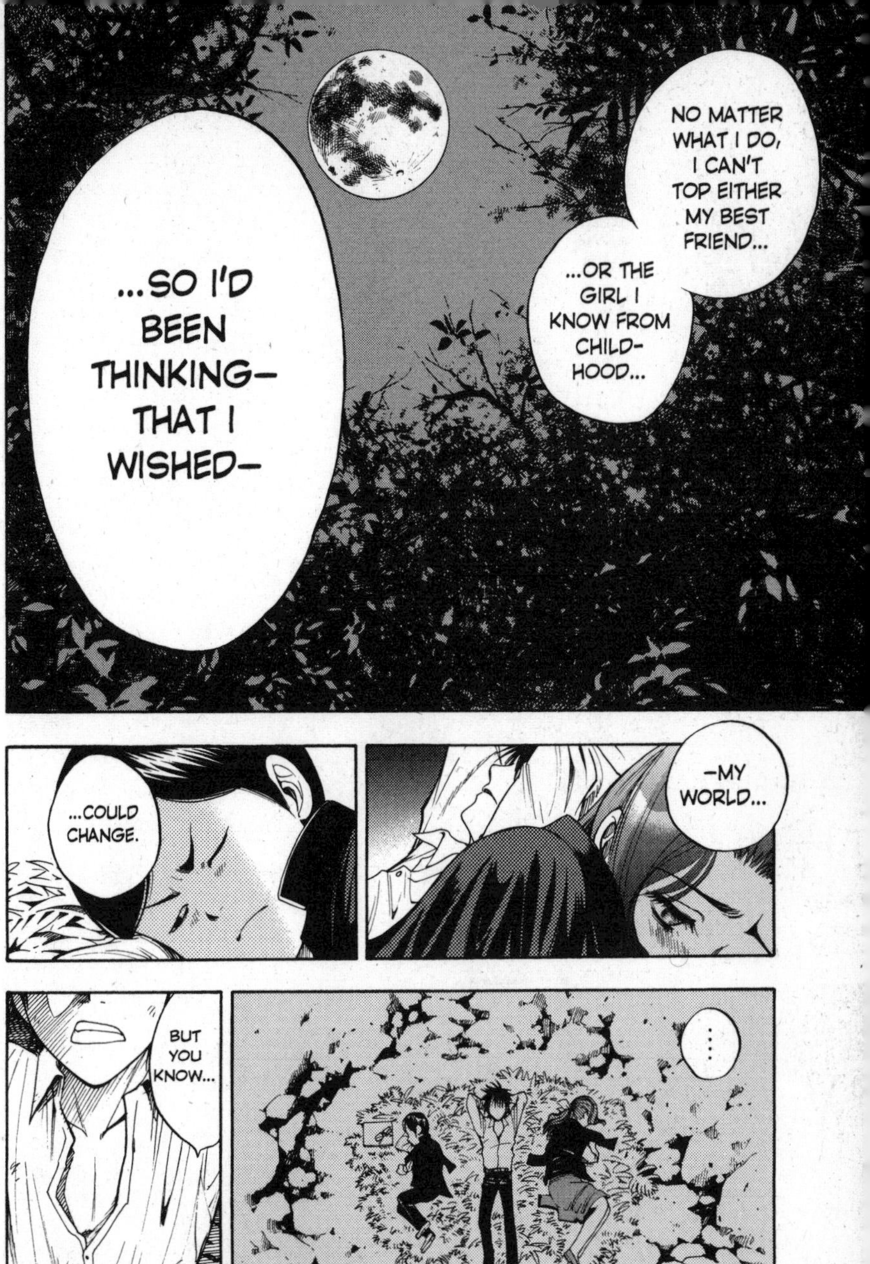
NO MATTER WHAT I DO, I CAN'T TOP EITHER MY BEST FRIEND...
...OR THE GIRL I KNOW FROM CHILD-HOOD...
...SO I'D BEEN THINKING—THAT I WISHED—
—MY WORLD...
...COULD CHANGE.
...
BUT YOU KNOW...

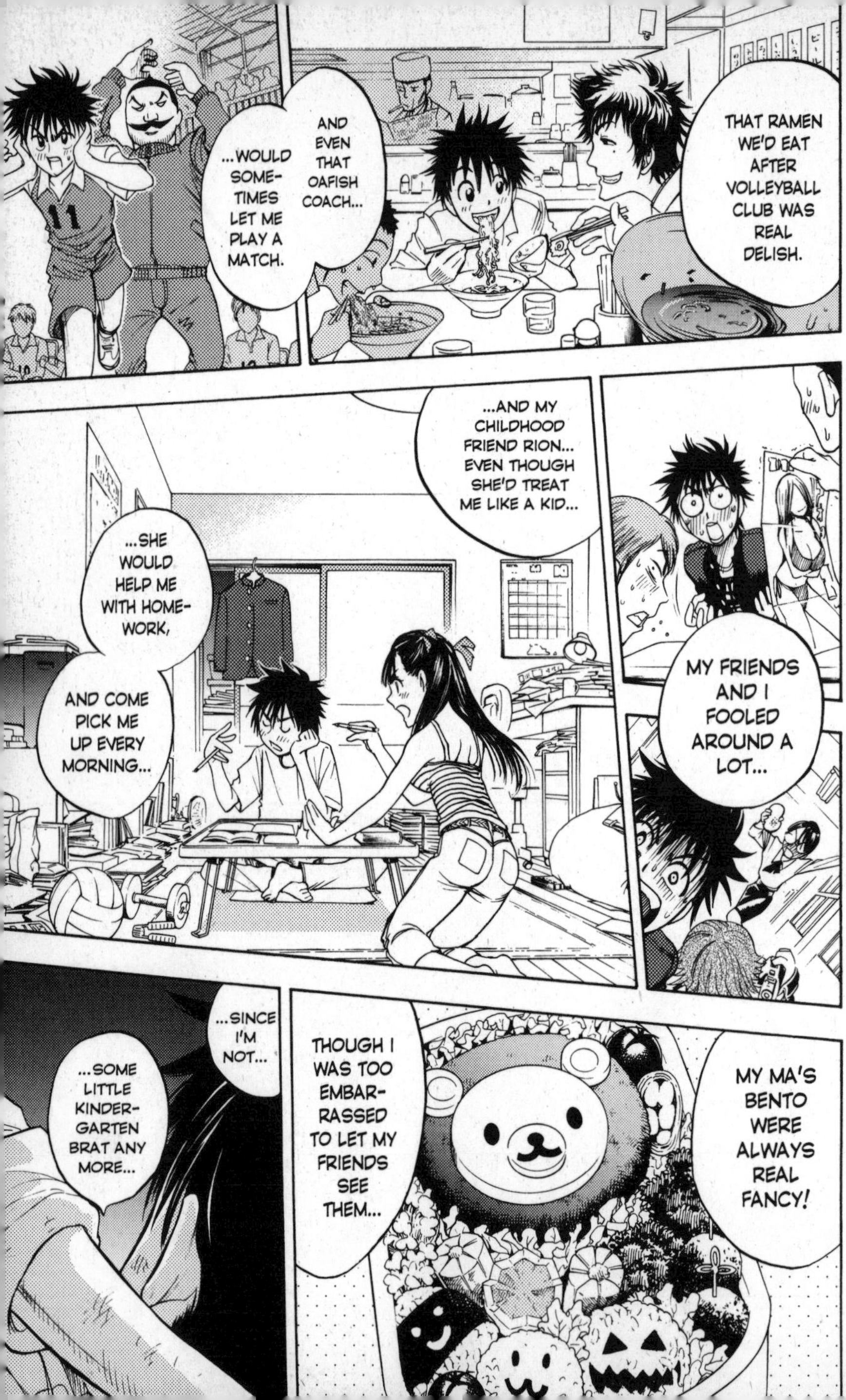
THAT RAMEN WE'D EAT AFTER VOLLEYBALL CLUB WAS REAL DELISH.
AND EVEN THAT OAFISH COACH...
...WOULD SOMETIMES LET ME PLAY A MATCH.
MY FRIENDS AND I FOOLED AROUND A LOT...
...AND MY CHILDHOOD FRIEND RION... EVEN THOUGH SHE'D TREAT ME LIKE A KID...
...SHE WOULD HELP ME WITH HOMEWORK,
AND COME PICK ME UP EVERY MORNING...
MY MA'S BENTO WERE ALWAYS REAL FANCY!
THOUGH I WAS TOO EMBARRASSED TO LET MY FRIENDS SEE THEM...
...SINCE I'M NOT...
...SOME LITTLE KINDERGARTEN BRAT ANY MORE...

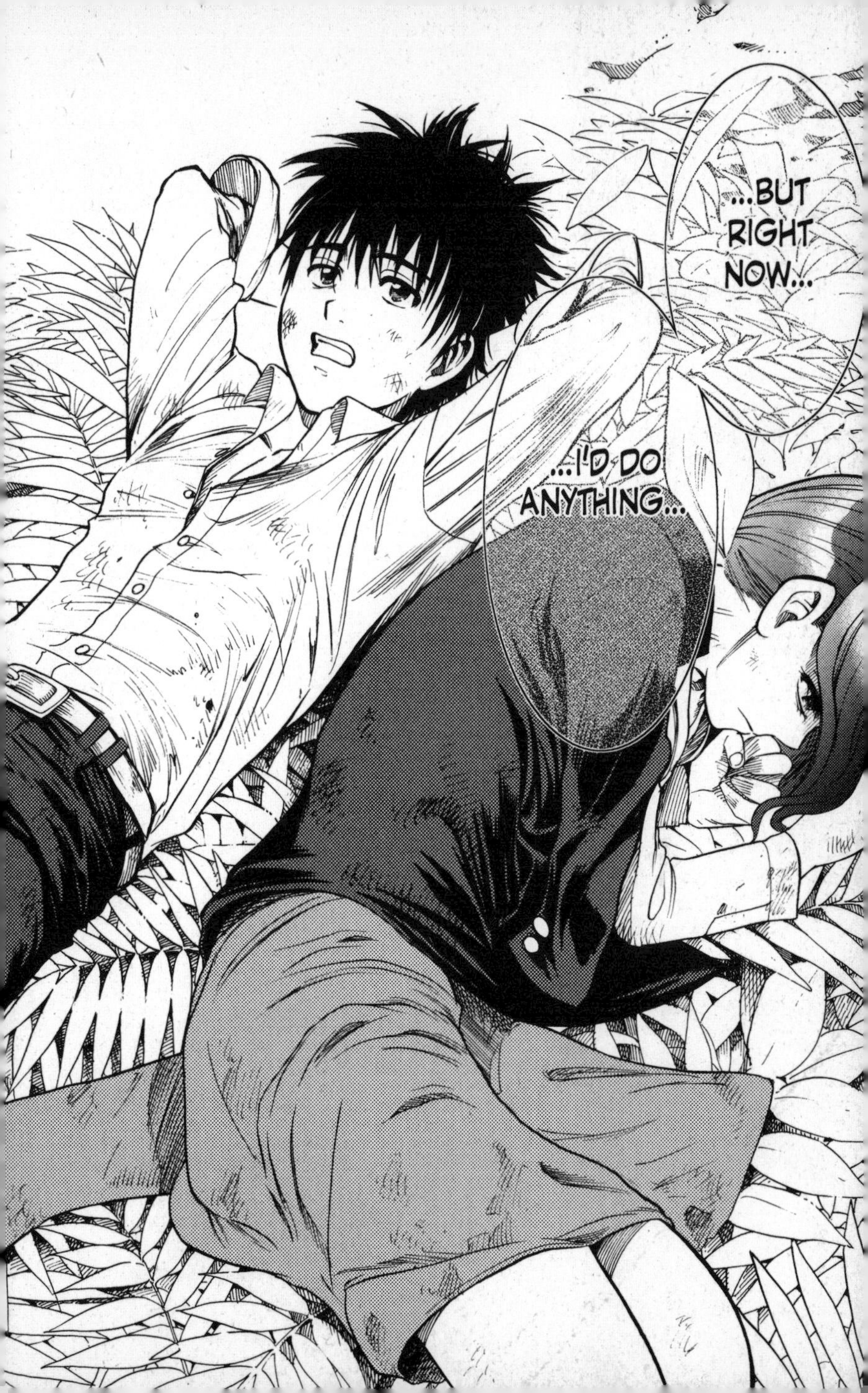
...BUT RIGHT NOW...
...I'D DO ANYTHING...

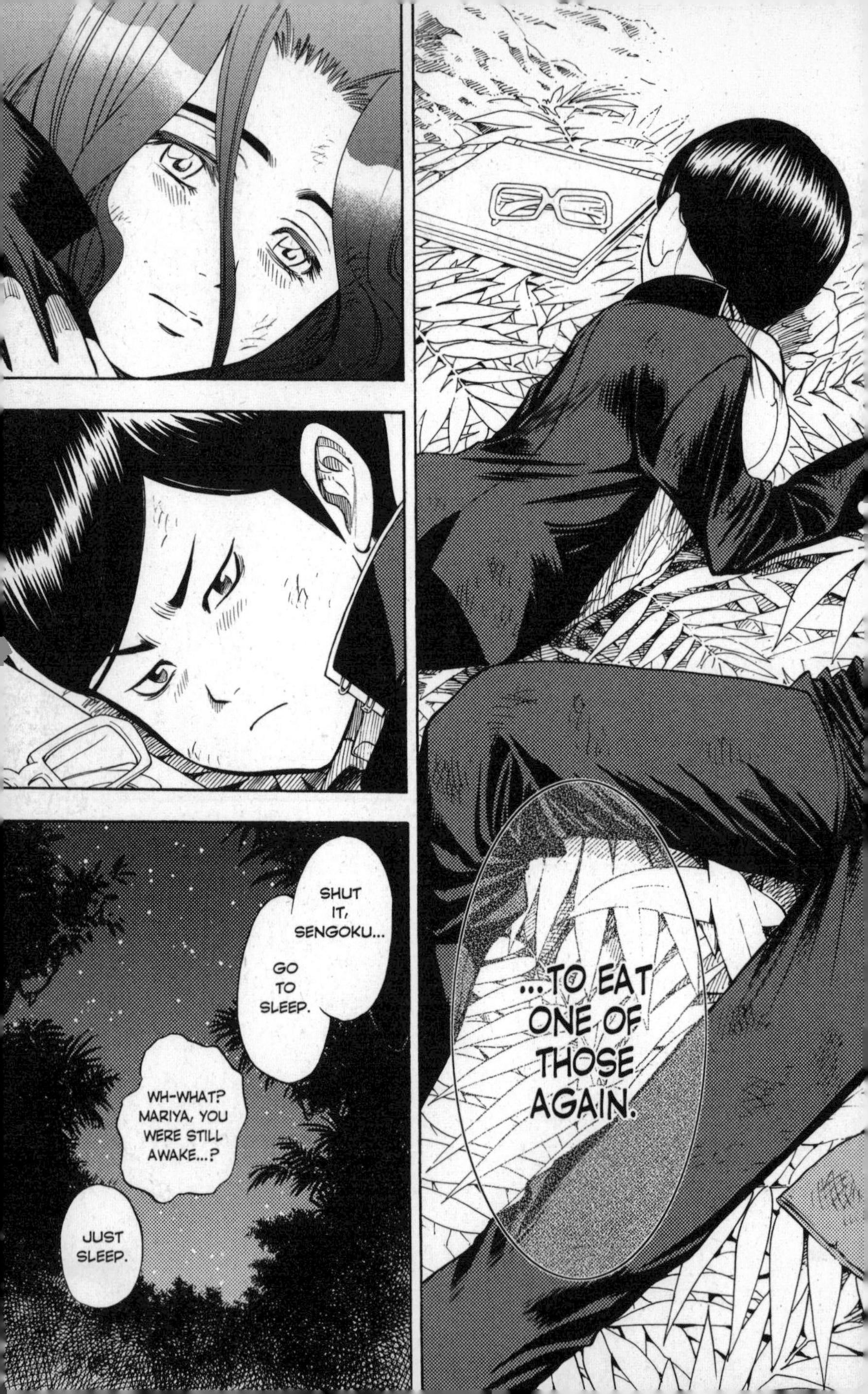
...TO EAT ONE OF THOSE AGAIN.
SHUT IT, SENGOKU...
GO TO SLEEP.
WH-WHAT? MARIYA, YOU WERE STILL AWAKE...?
JUST SLEEP.

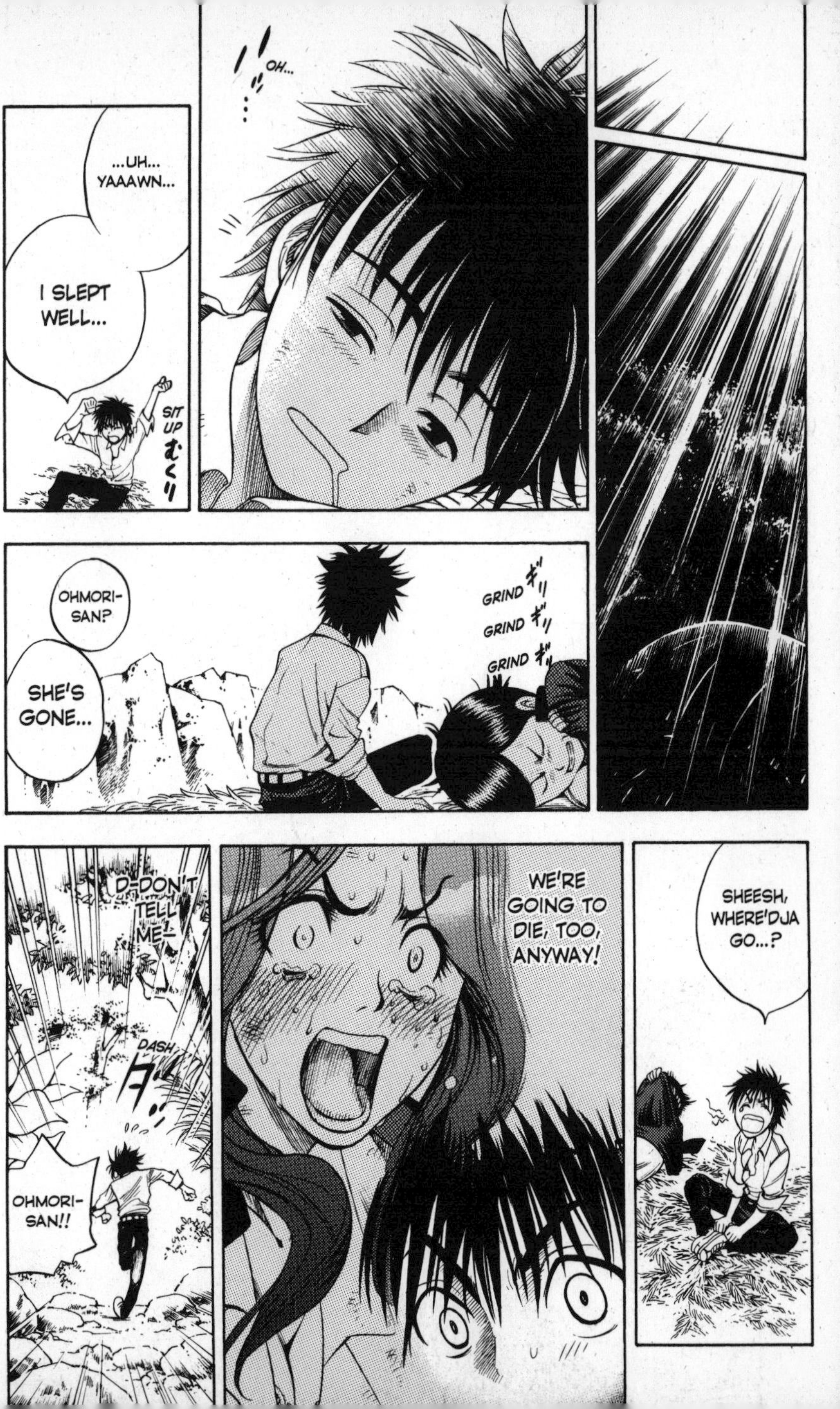
OH...
...UH... YAAAWN...
I SLEPT WELL...
SIT UP むくり
GRIND ギリ
GRIND ギリ
GRIND ギリ
OHMORI-SAN?
SHE'S GONE...
SHEESH, WHERE'DJA GO...?
WE'RE GOING TO DIE, TOO, ANYWAY!
D-DON'T TELL ME-
DASH
OHMORI-SAN!!

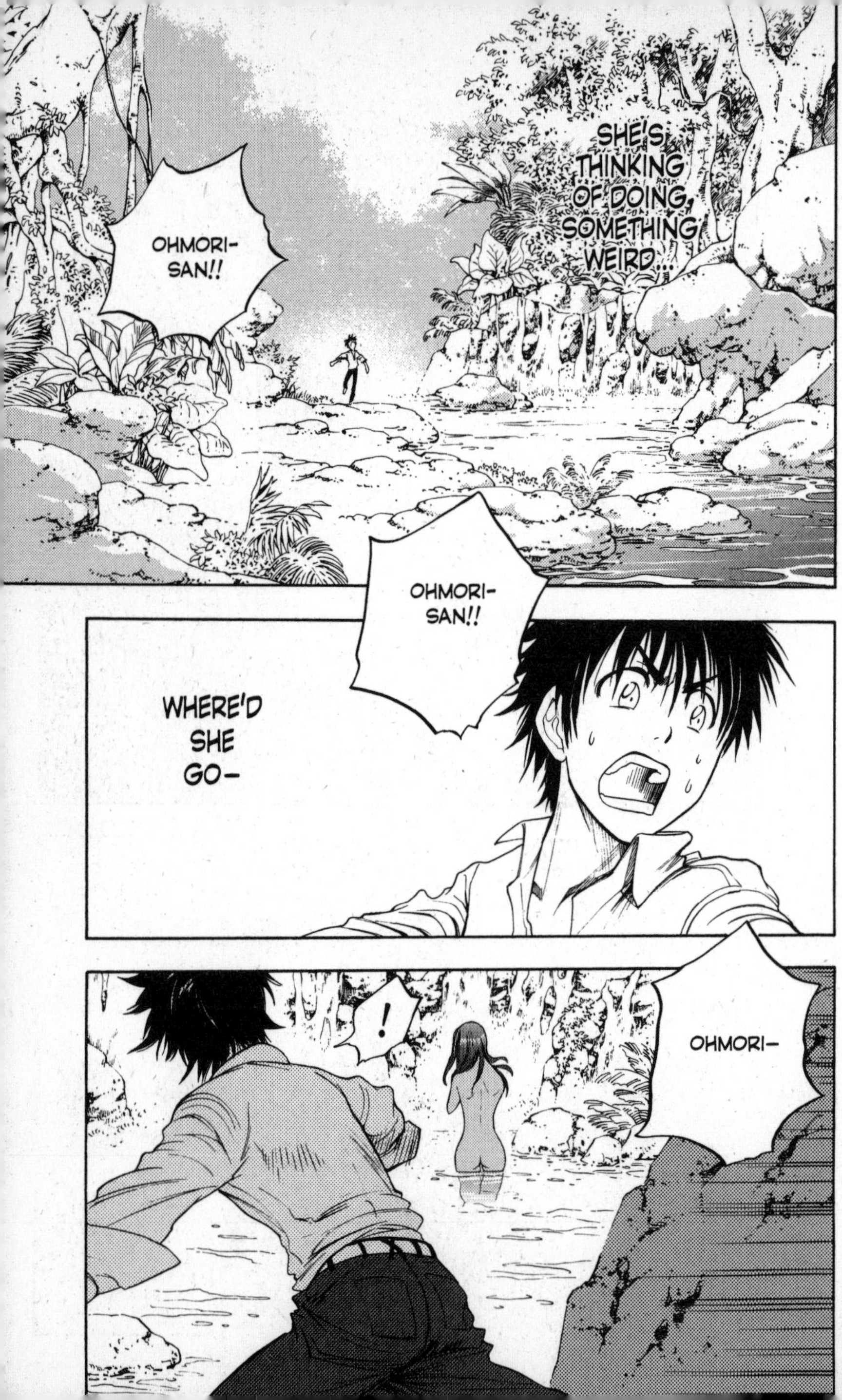
SHE'S THINKING OF DOING SOMETHING WEIRD...
OHMORI-SAN!!
OHMORI-SAN!!
WHERE'D SHE GO-
OHMORI-
!

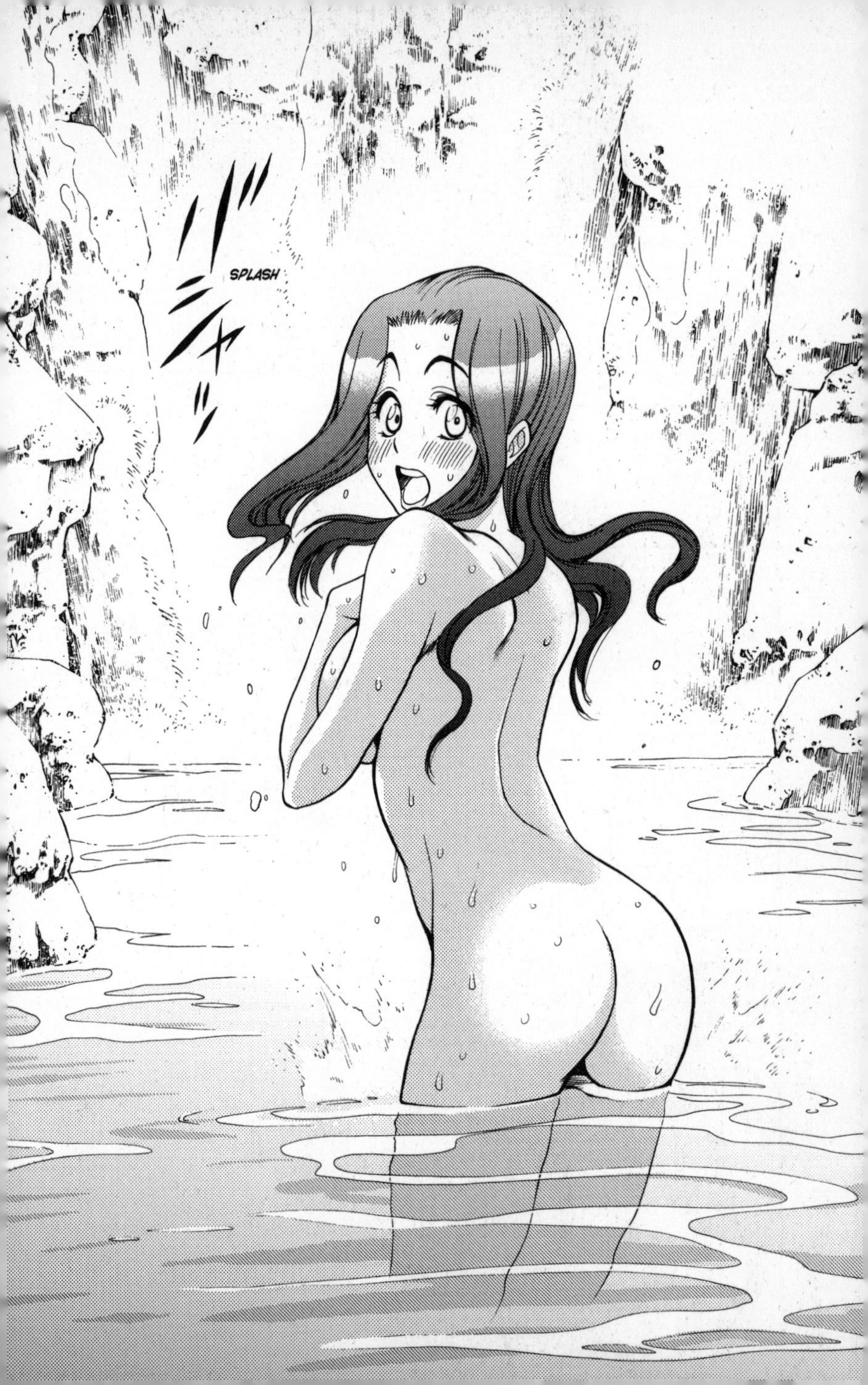
バシャッ
SPLASH

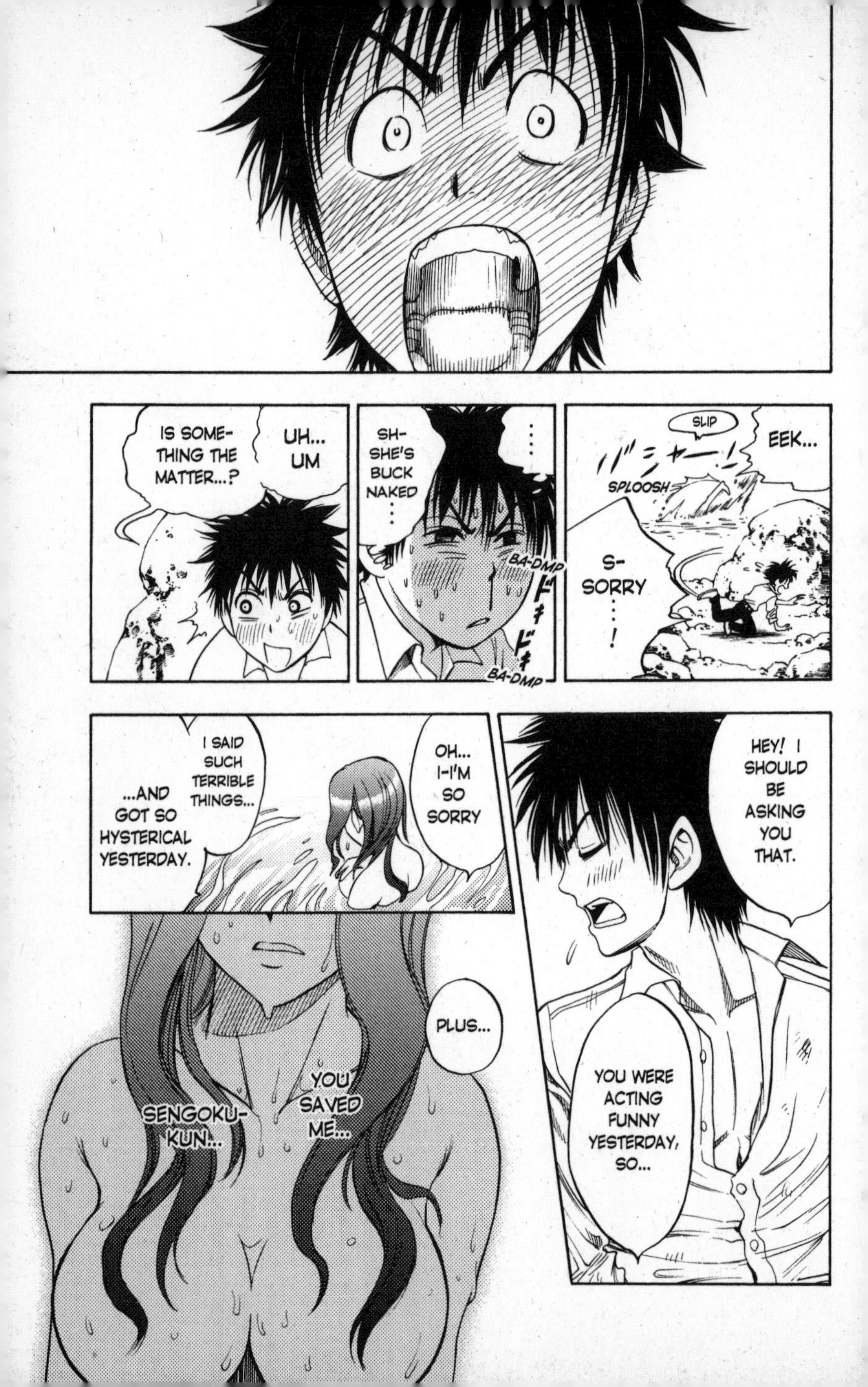

EEK...
SLIP
バシャー!
SPLOOSH
S-SORRY...!
...
SH-SHE'S BUCK NAKED...
BA-DMP
ドキドキ
BA-DMP
UH... UM
IS SOMETHING THE MATTER...?
HEY! I SHOULD BE ASKING YOU THAT.
YOU WERE ACTING FUNNY YESTERDAY, SO...
OH... I-I'M SO SORRY
I SAID SUCH TERRIBLE THINGS...
...AND GOT SO HYSTERICAL YESTERDAY.
PLUS...
YOU SAVED ME...
SENGOKU-KUN...

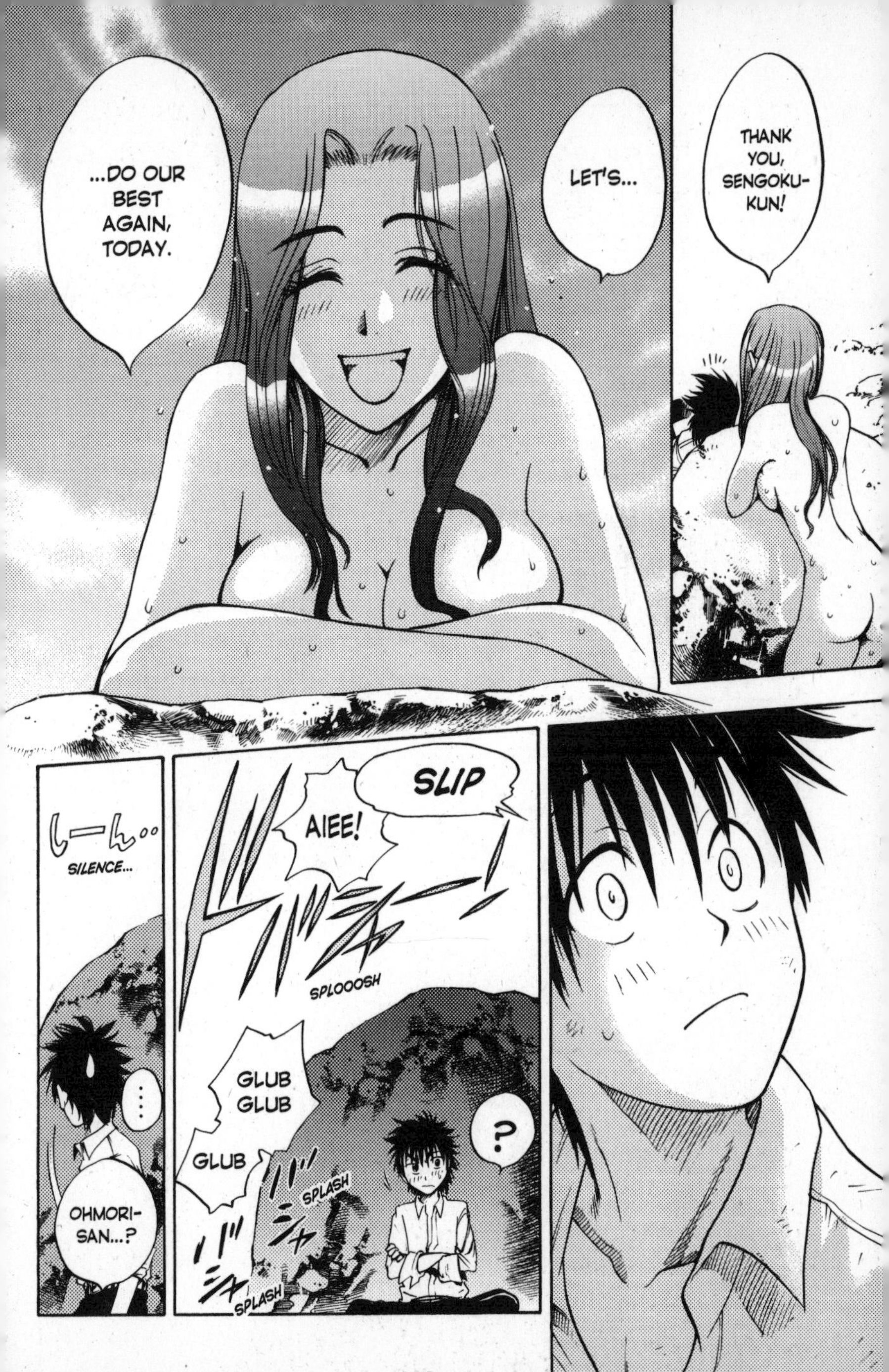
THANK YOU, SENGOKU-KUN!
LET'S...
...DO OUR BEST AGAIN, TODAY.
SLIP
AIEE!
SPLOOOSH
GLUB GLUB
?
GLUB
SPLASH
SPLASH
しーん。。
SILENCE...
...
OHMORI-SAN...?

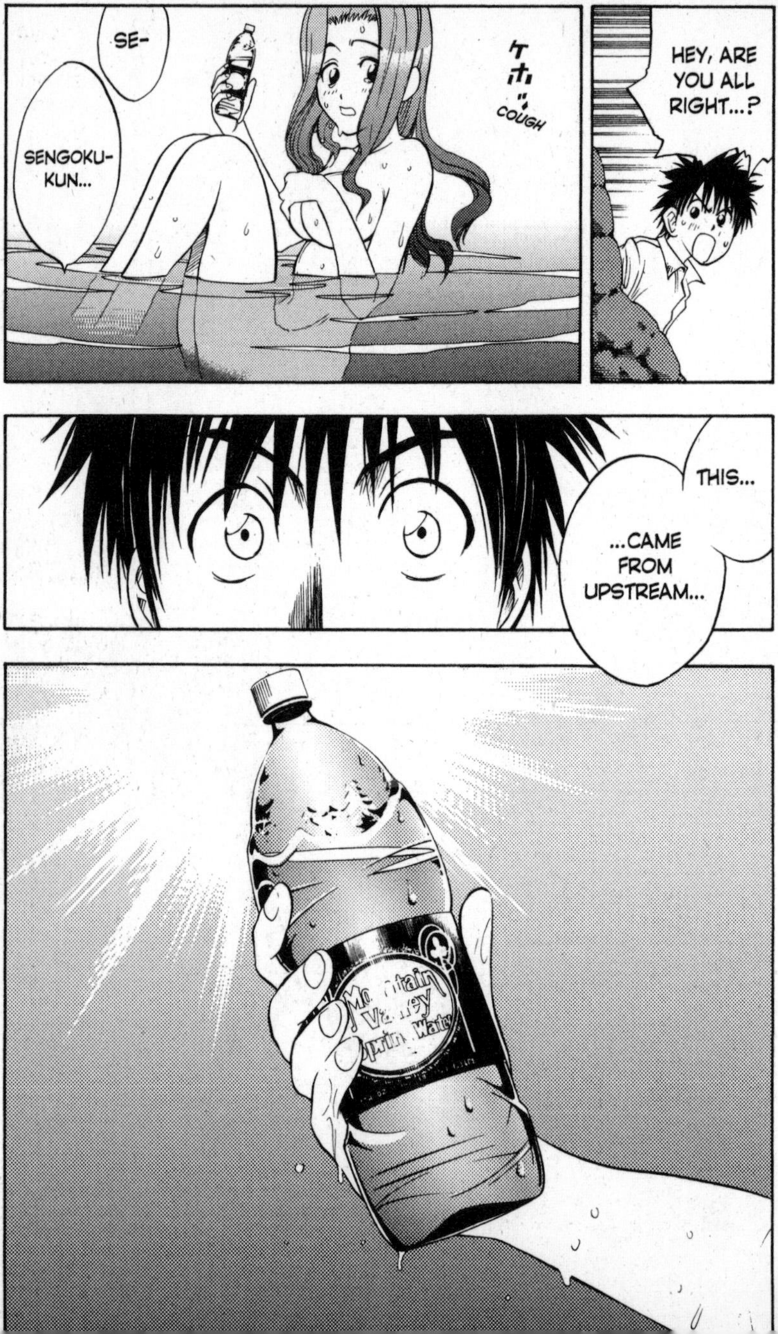
HEY, ARE YOU ALL RIGHT...?
ケホッ
COUGH
SE-
SENGOKU-KUN...
THIS...
...CAME FROM UPSTREAM...

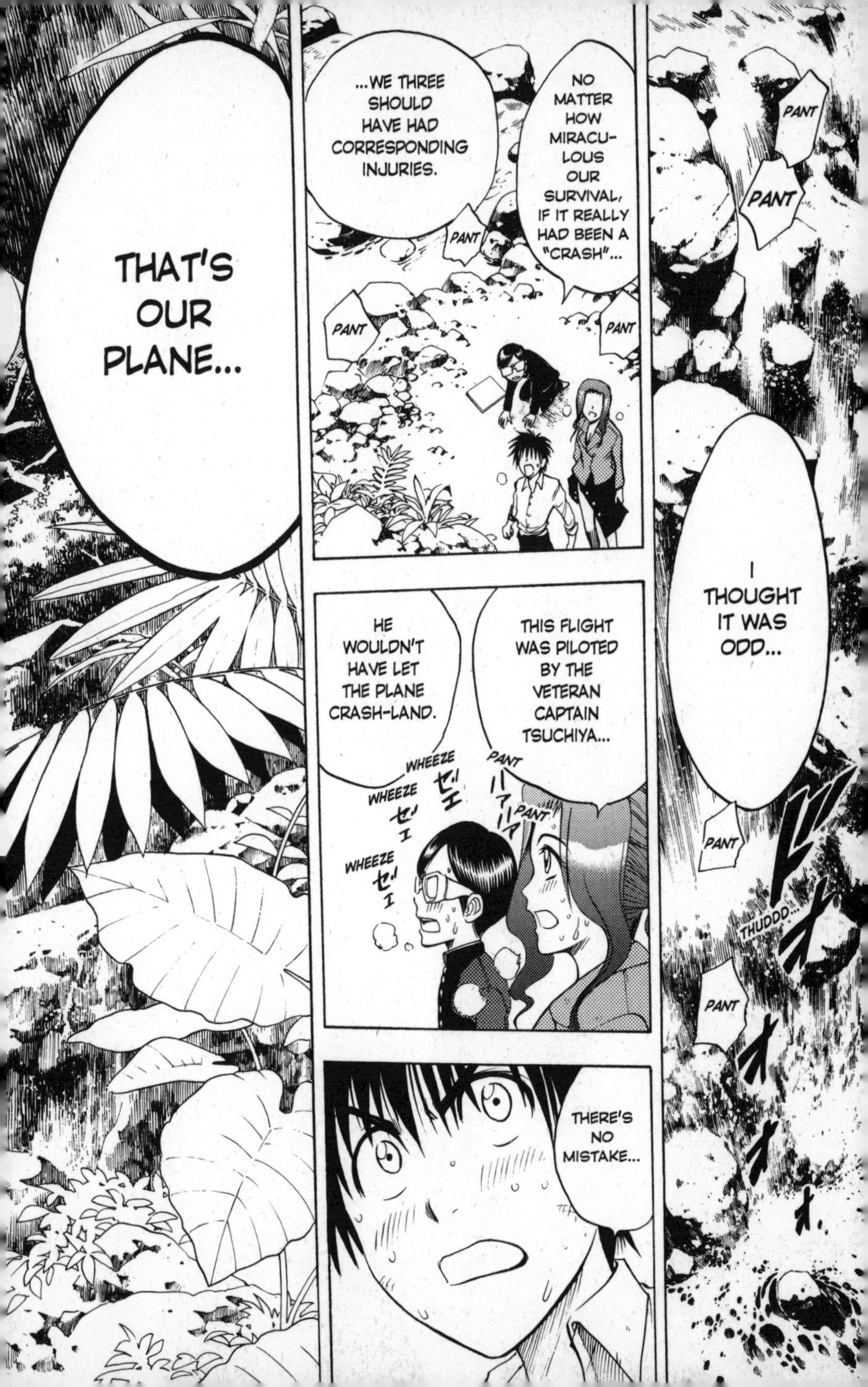
PANT
PANT
I THOUGHT IT WAS ODD...
PANT
THUDDD...
PANT
NO MATTER HOW MIRACULOUS OUR SURVIVAL, IF IT REALLY HAD BEEN A "CRASH"...
...WE THREE SHOULD HAVE HAD CORRESPONDING INJURIES.
PANT
PANT
PANT
THIS FLIGHT WAS PILOTED BY THE VETERAN CAPTAIN TSUCHIYA...
HE WOULDN'T HAVE LET THE PLANE CRASH-LAND.
PANT
PANT
WHEEZE
WHEEZE
WHEEZE
THERE'S NO MISTAKE...
THAT'S OUR PLANE...

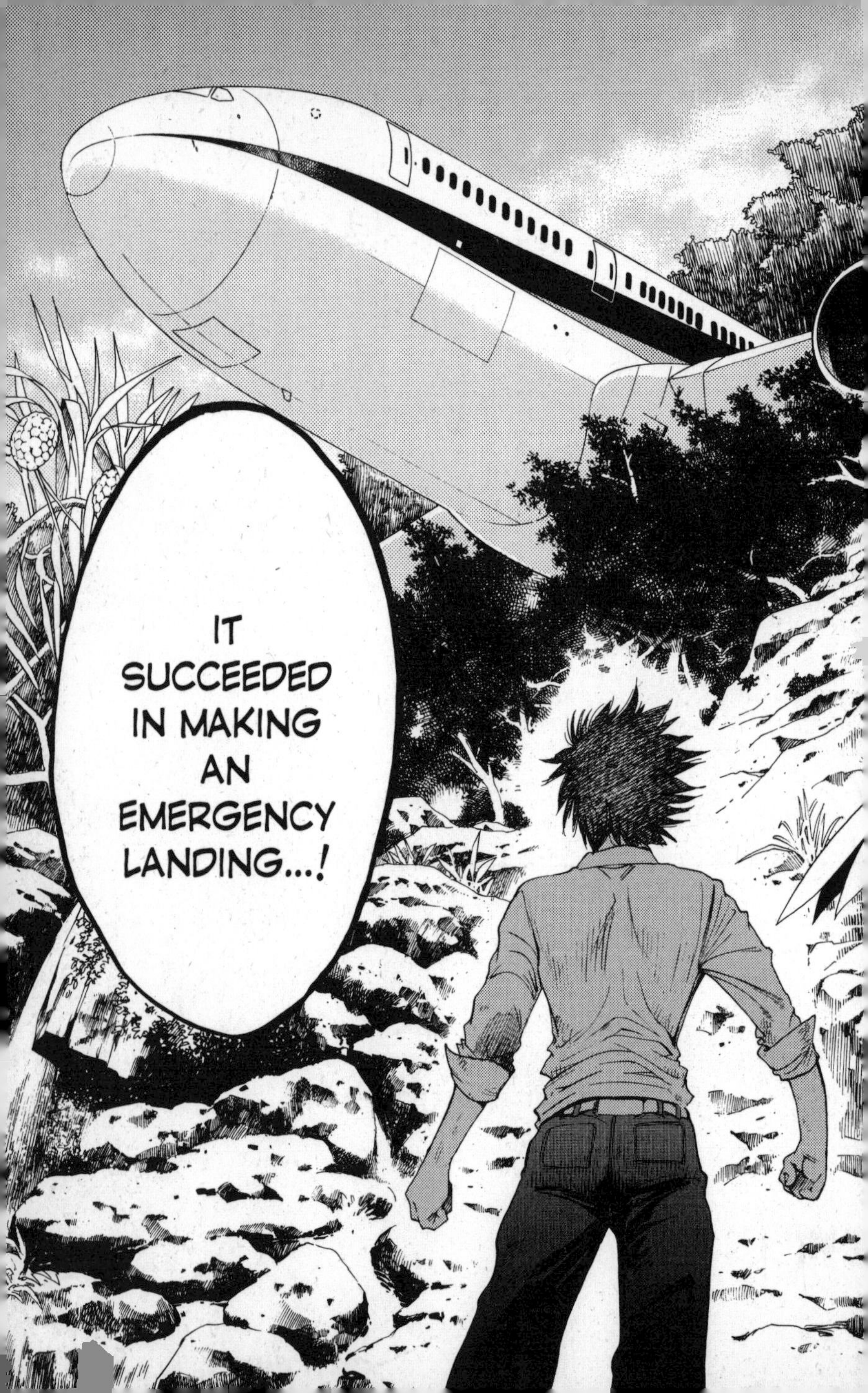
IT SUCCEEDED IN MAKING AN EMERGENCY LANDING...!

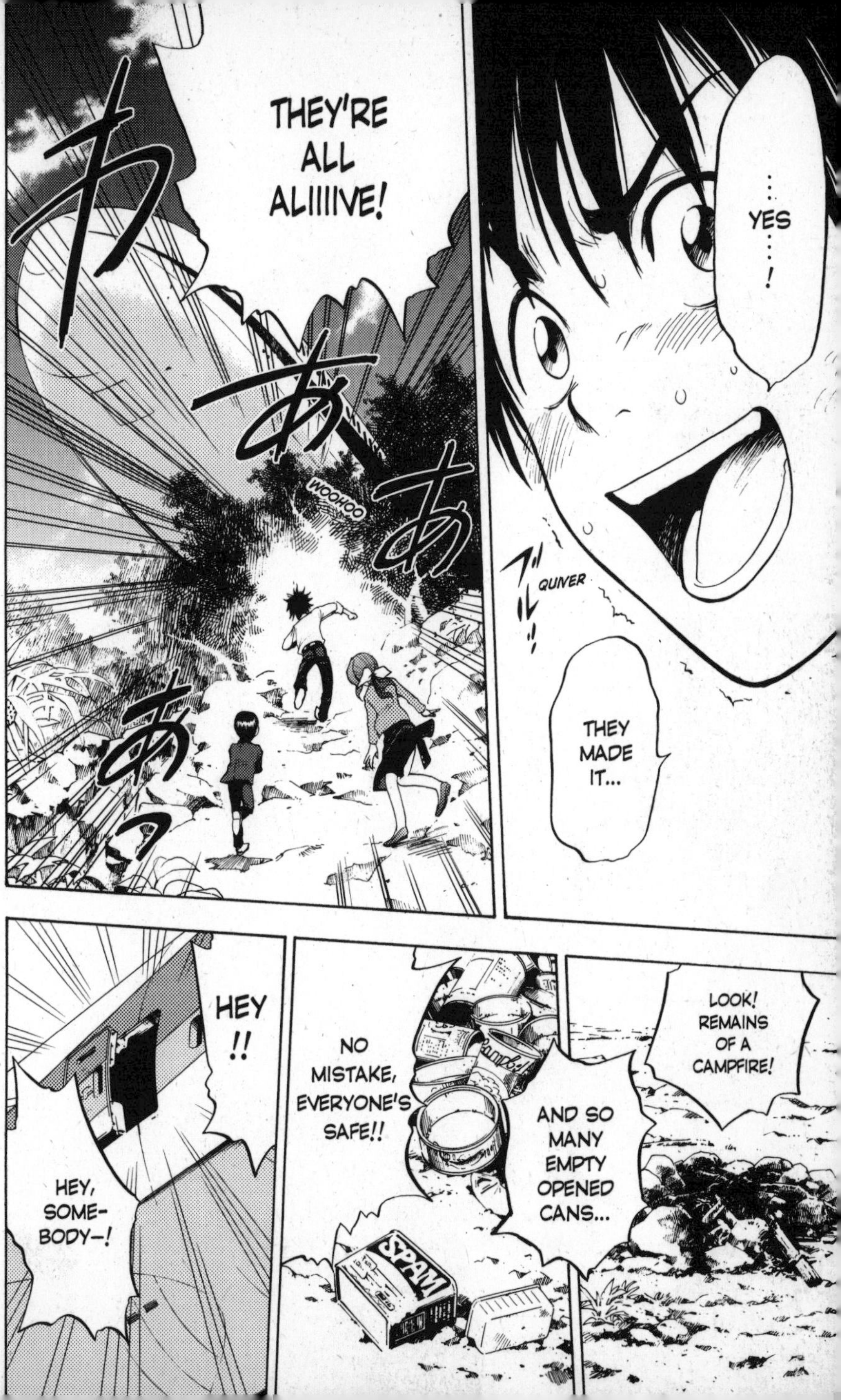
...YES...!
QUIVER
THEY MADE IT...
THEY'RE ALL ALIIIIVE!
わあああっ
WOOHOO
LOOK! REMAINS OF A CAMPFIRE!
AND SO MANY EMPTY OPENED CANS...
NO MISTAKE, EVERYONE'S SAFE!!
SPAM
HEY !!
HEY, SOME-BODY–!

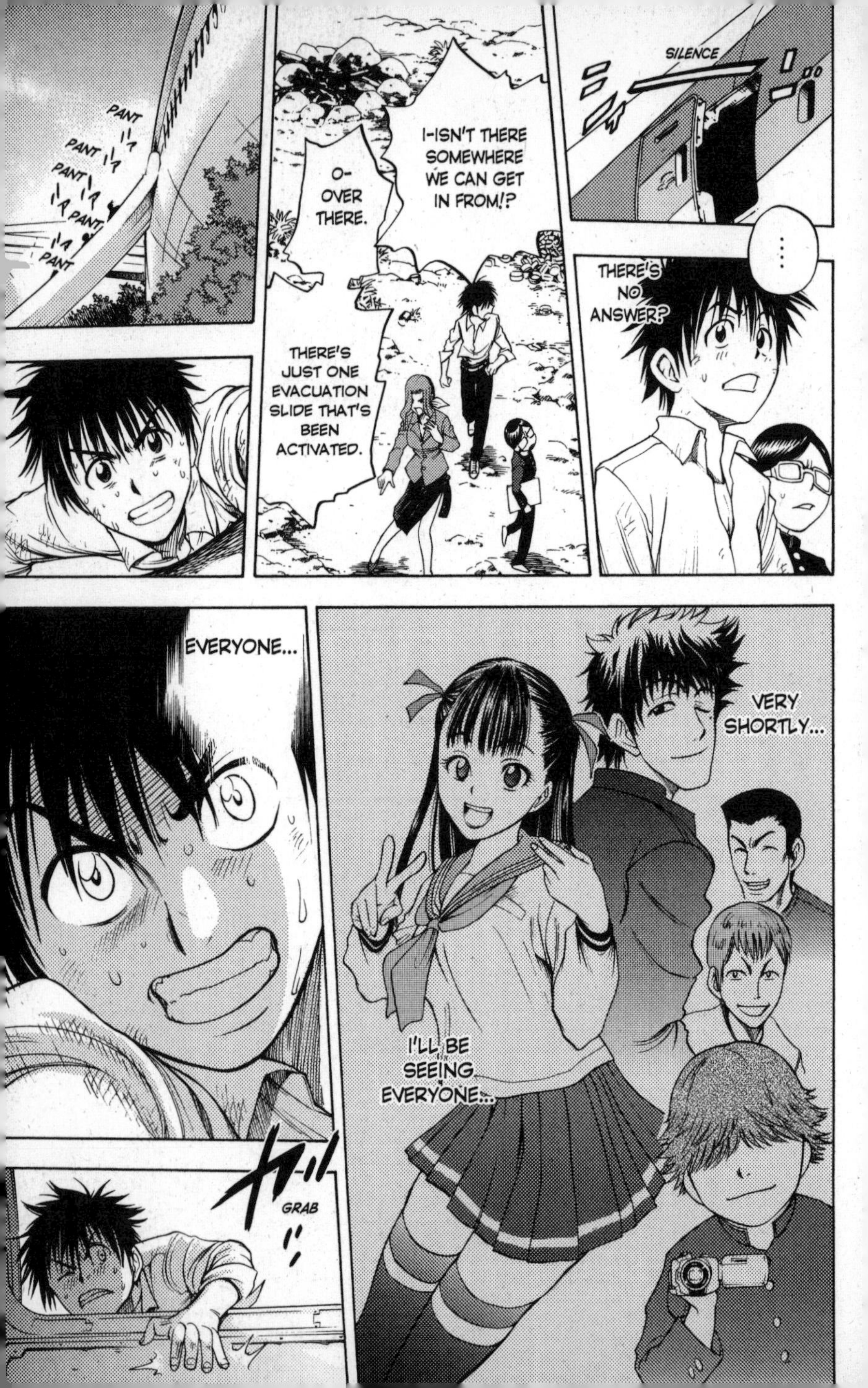
SILENCE
...
THERE'S NO ANSWER?
I-ISN'T THERE SOMEWHERE WE CAN GET IN FROM!?
O- OVER THERE.
THERE'S JUST ONE EVACUATION SLIDE THAT'S BEEN ACTIVATED.
PANT PANT PANT PANT PANT
VERY SHORTLY...
I'LL BE SEEING EVERYONE...
EVERYONE...
GRAB

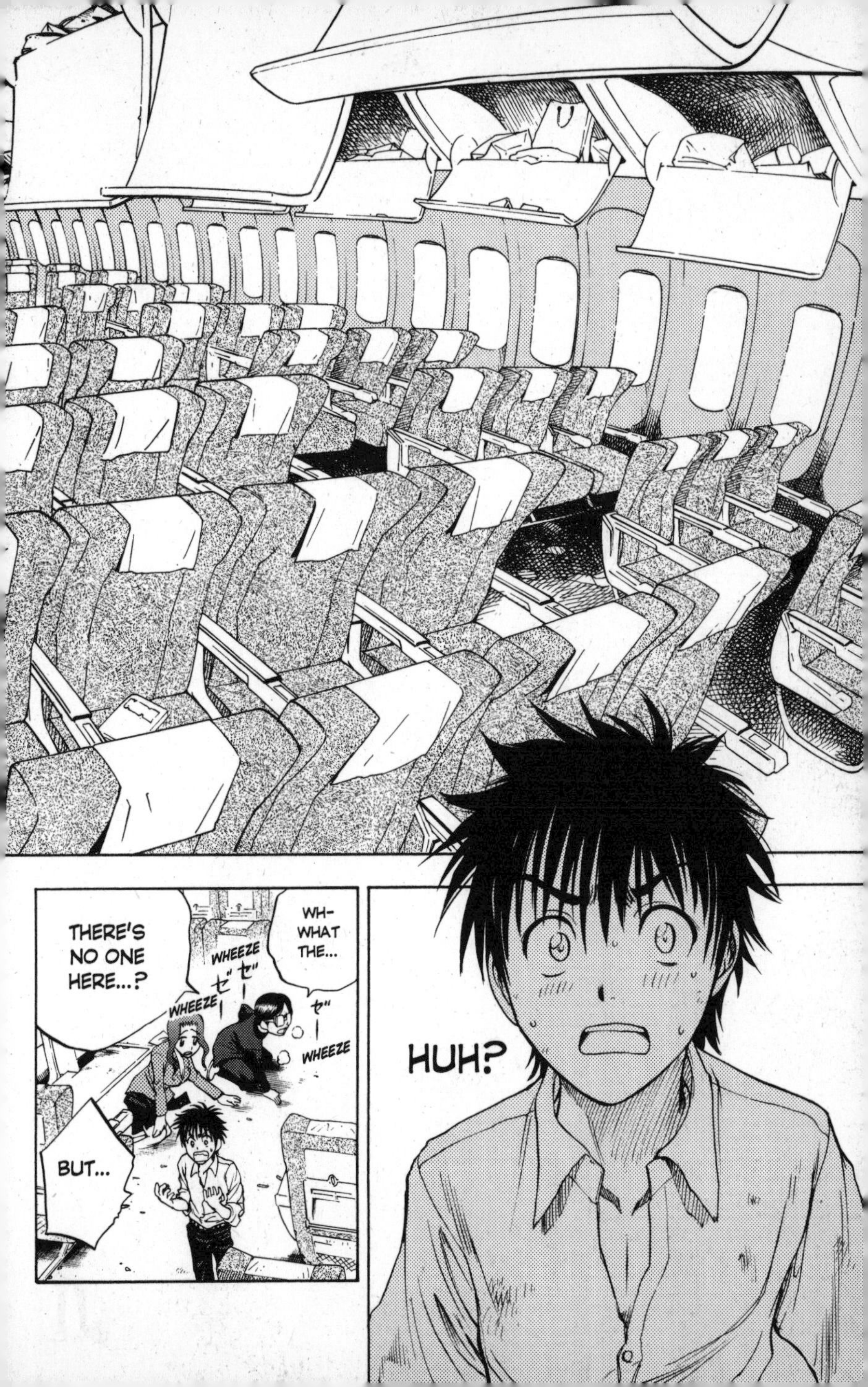
HUH?
WH- WHAT THE...
WHEEZE
ゼ ゼ
THERE'S NO ONE HERE...?
WHEEZE
ゼ ー
WHEEZE
BUT...

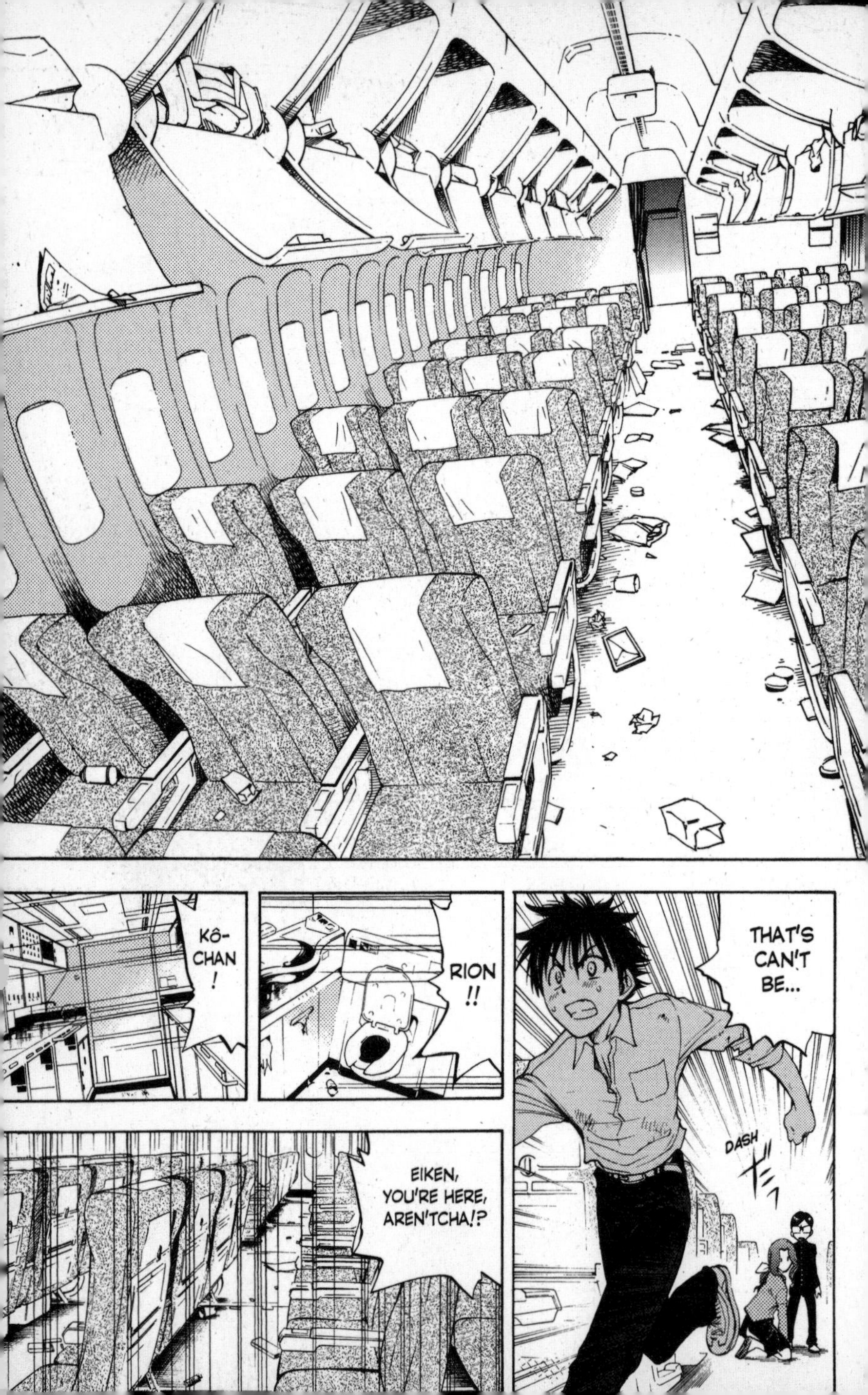
THAT'S CAN'T BE...
DASH
RION !!
KÔ-CHAN !
EIKEN, YOU'RE HERE, AREN'TCHA!?

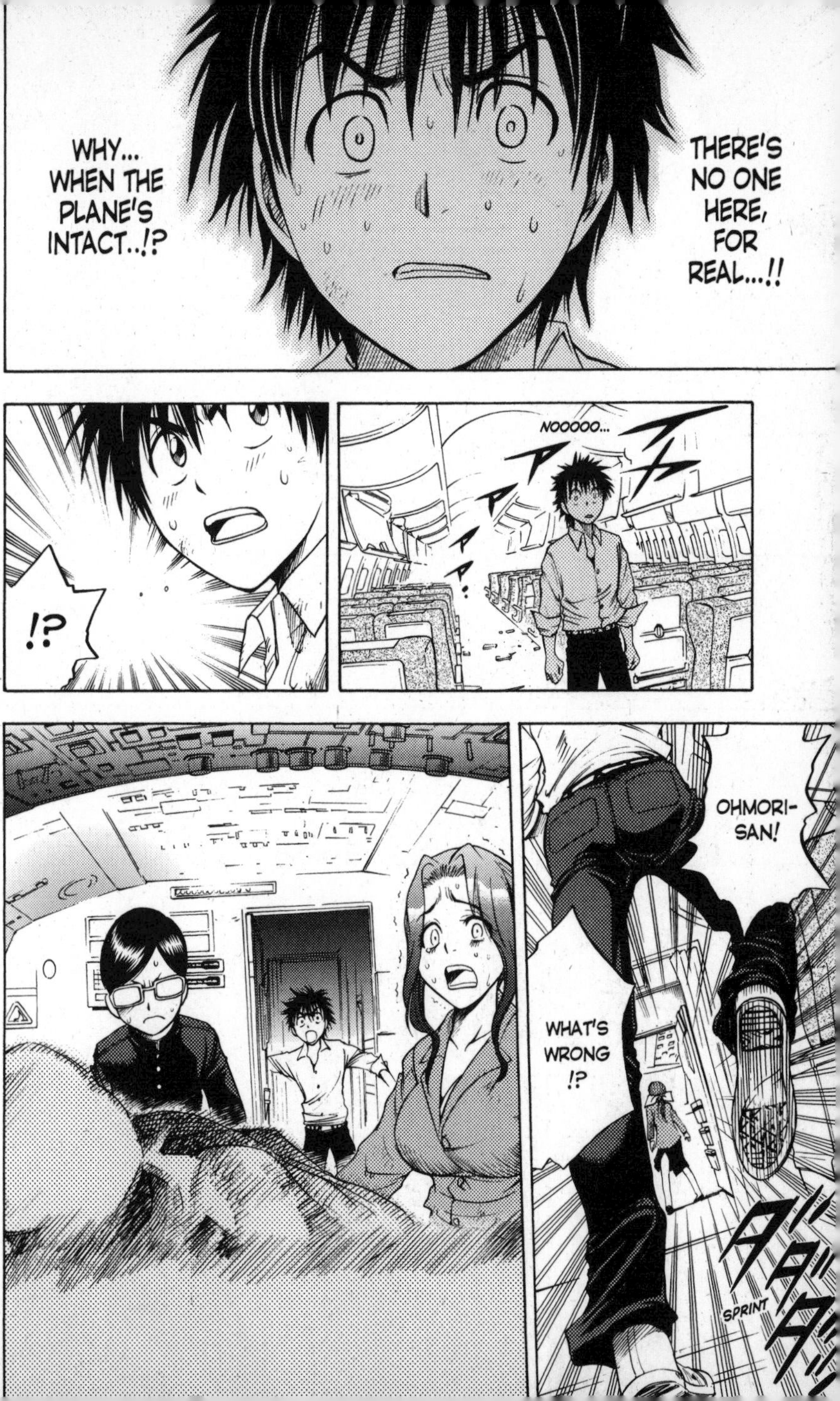
THERE'S NO ONE HERE, FOR REAL...!!
WHY... WHEN THE PLANE'S INTACT..!?
NOOOOO...
!?
OHMORI-SAN!
WHAT'S WRONG !?
SPRINT

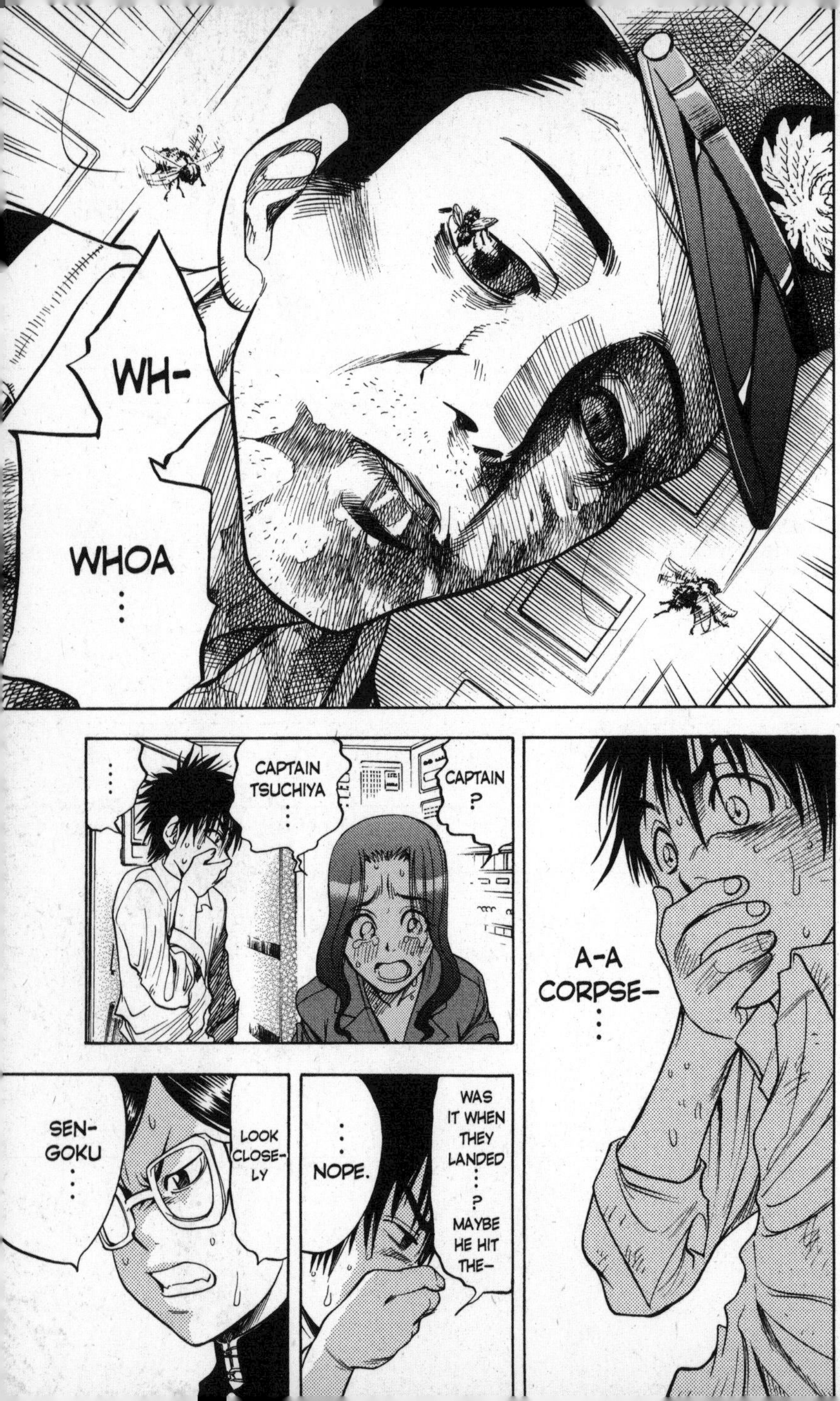

WH-
WHOA...
A-A CORPSE-...
CAPTAIN?
CAPTAIN TSUCHIYA...
...
WAS IT WHEN THEY LANDED...? MAYBE HE HIT THE-
...NOPE.
LOOK CLOSE-LY
SEN-GOKU...

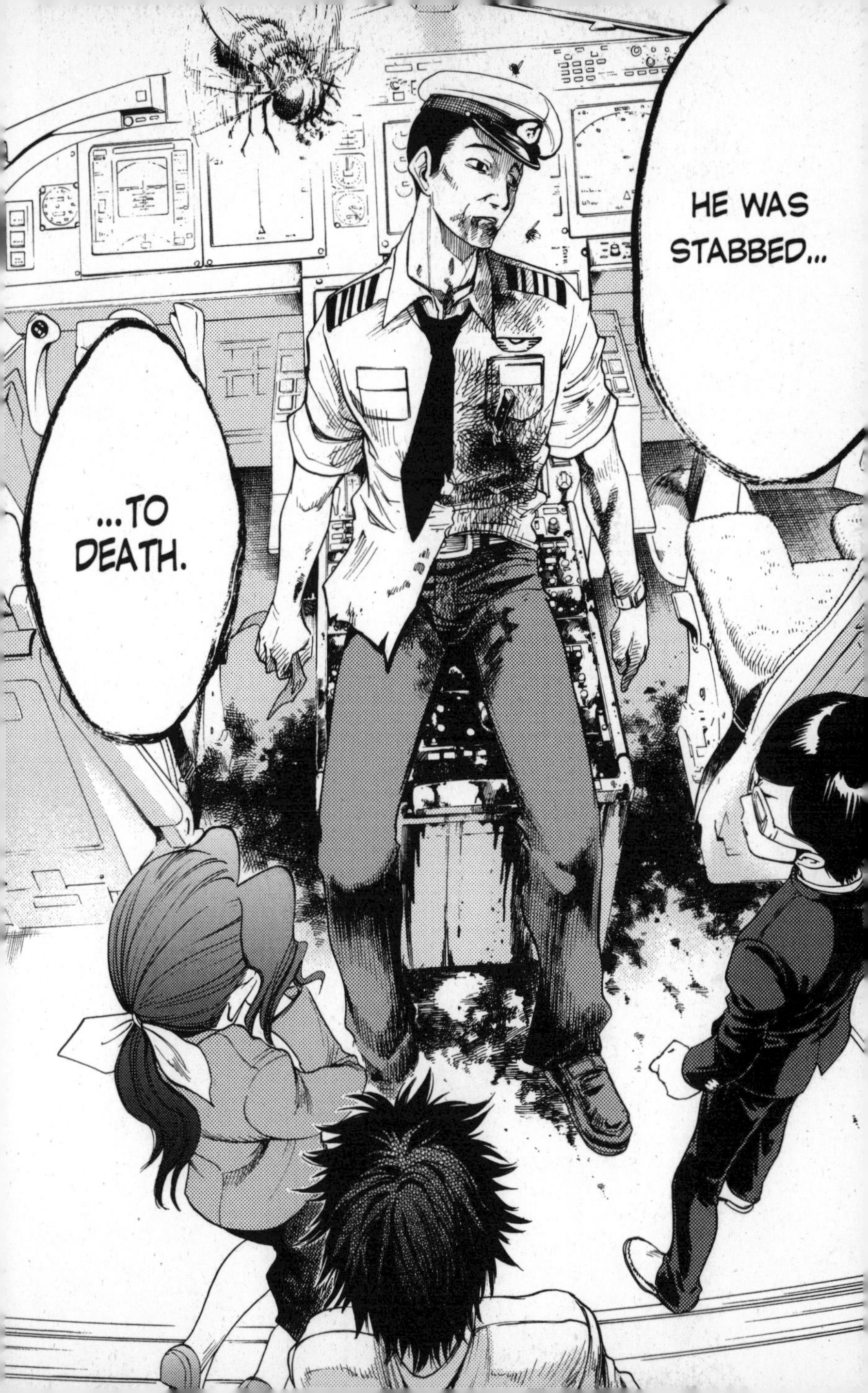
HE WAS STABBED...
...TO DEATH.

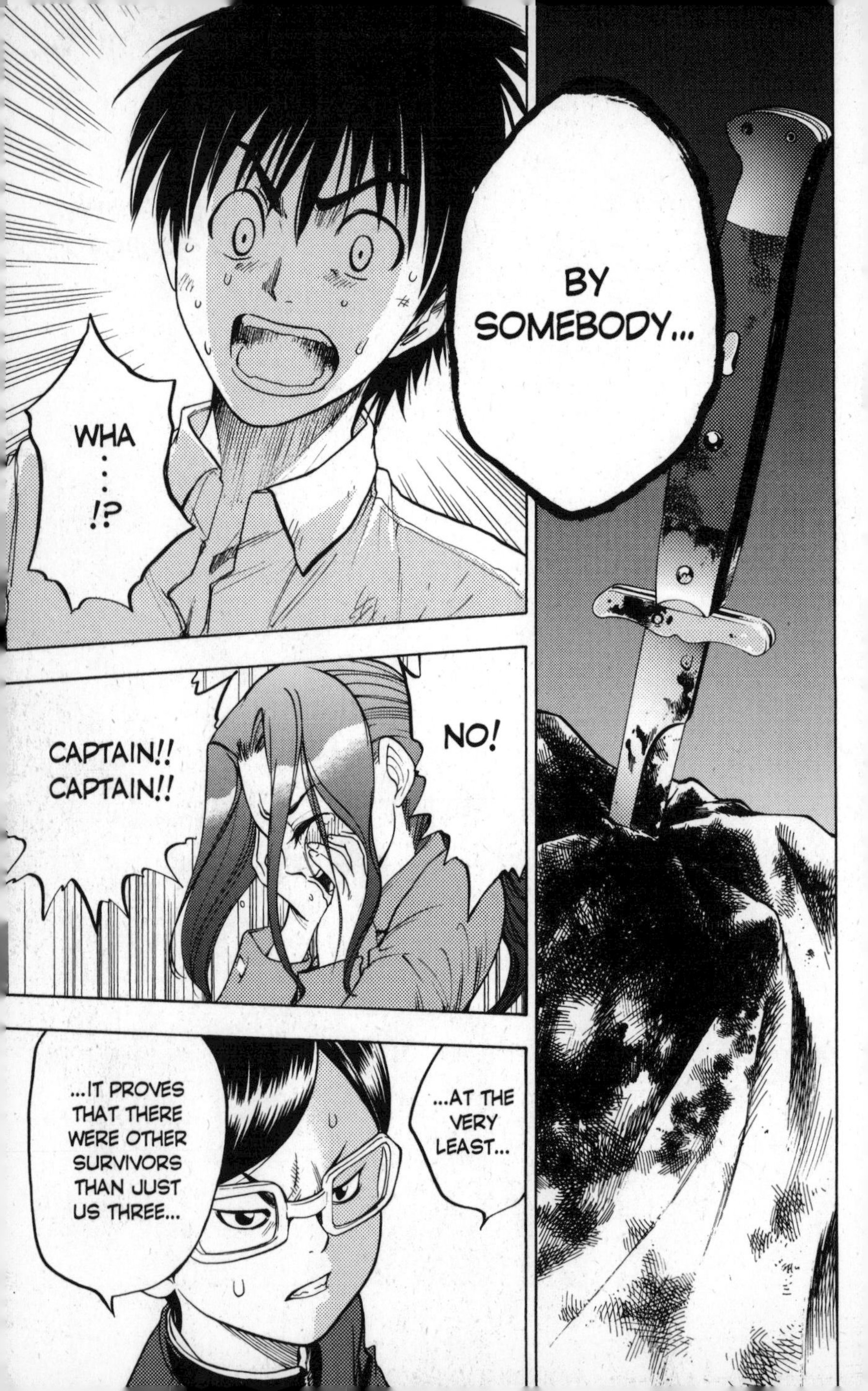
BY SOMEBODY...
WHA...!?
NO!
CAPTAIN!! CAPTAIN!!
...AT THE VERY LEAST...
...IT PROVES THAT THERE WERE OTHER SURVIVORS THAN JUST US THREE...

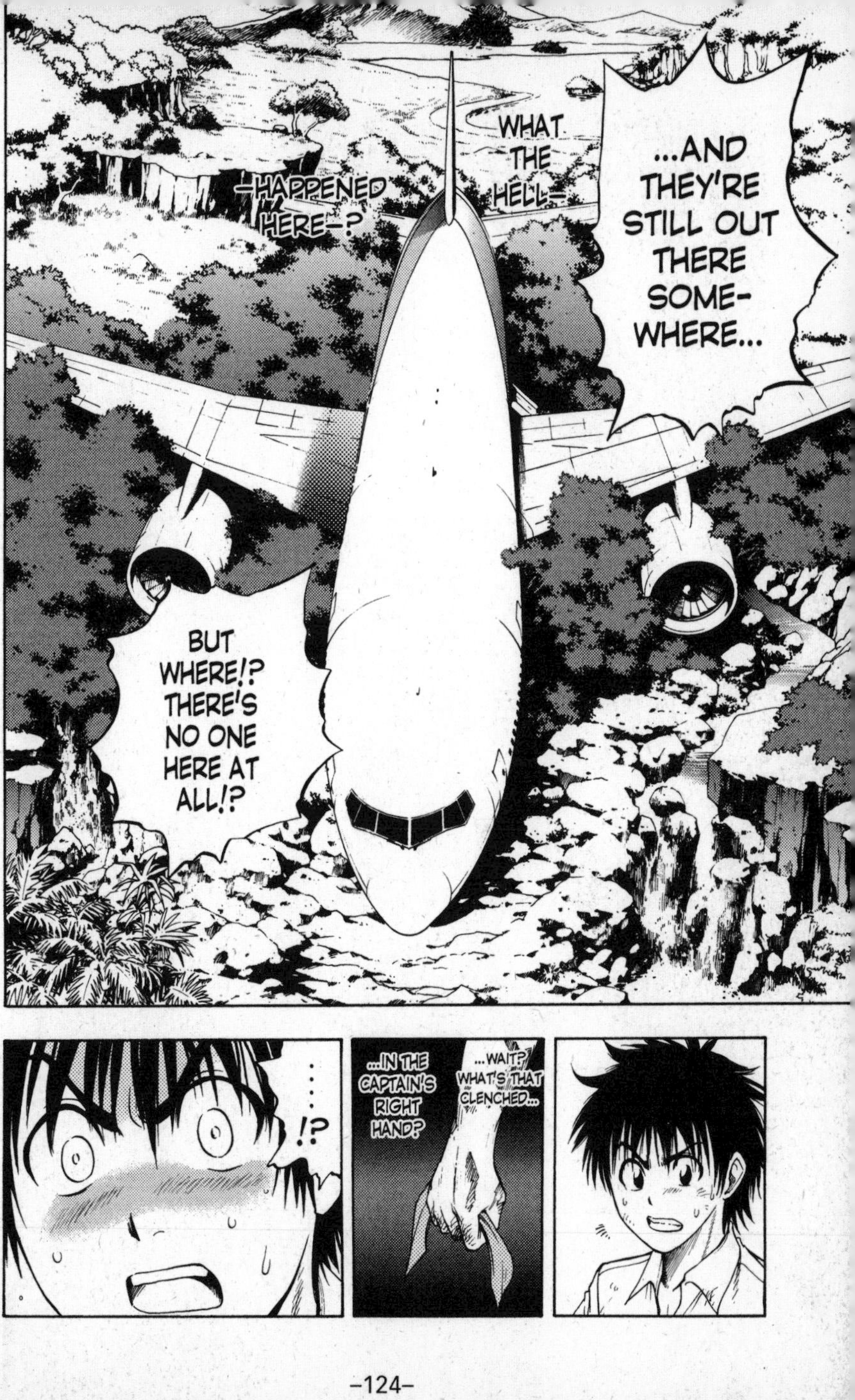
...AND THEY'RE STILL OUT THERE SOME-WHERE...
WHAT THE HELL—
—HAPPENED HERE—?
BUT WHERE!? THERE'S NO ONE HERE AT ALL!?
...WAIT? WHAT'S THAT CLENCHED...
...IN THE CAPTAIN'S RIGHT HAND?
......!?

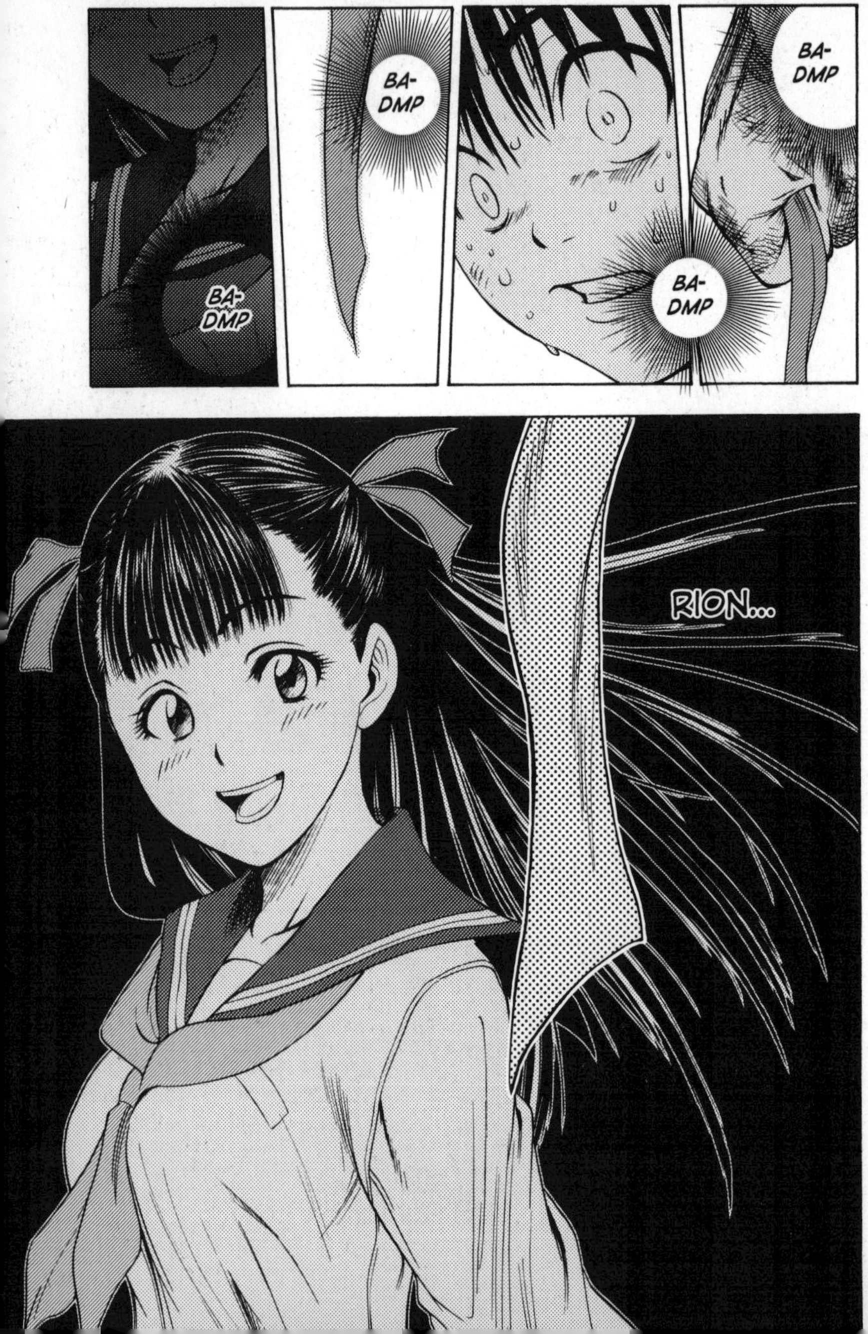
BA-DMP
BA-DMP
BA-DMP
BA-DMP
RION...

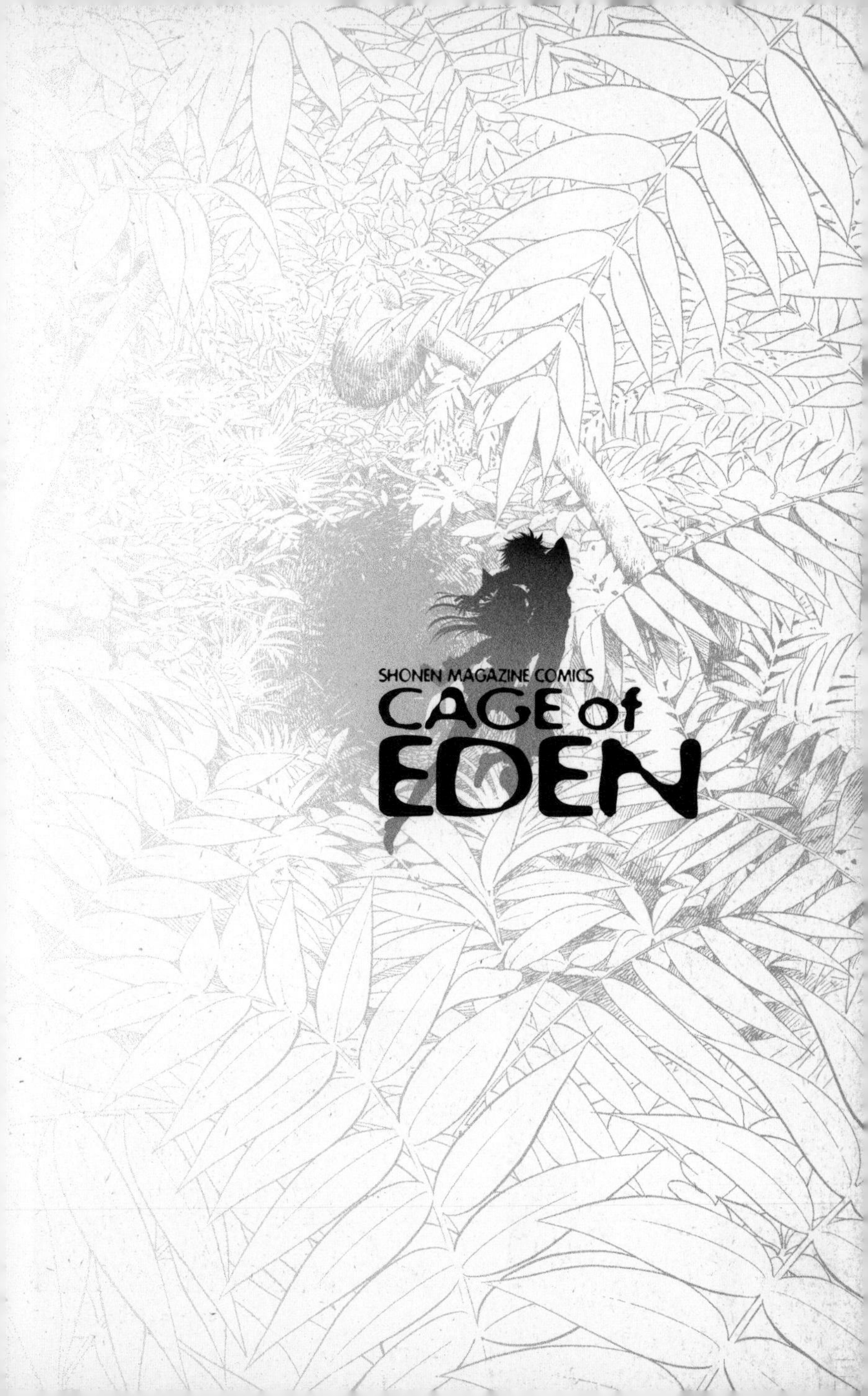
SHONEN MAGAZINE COMICS
CAGE of EDEN

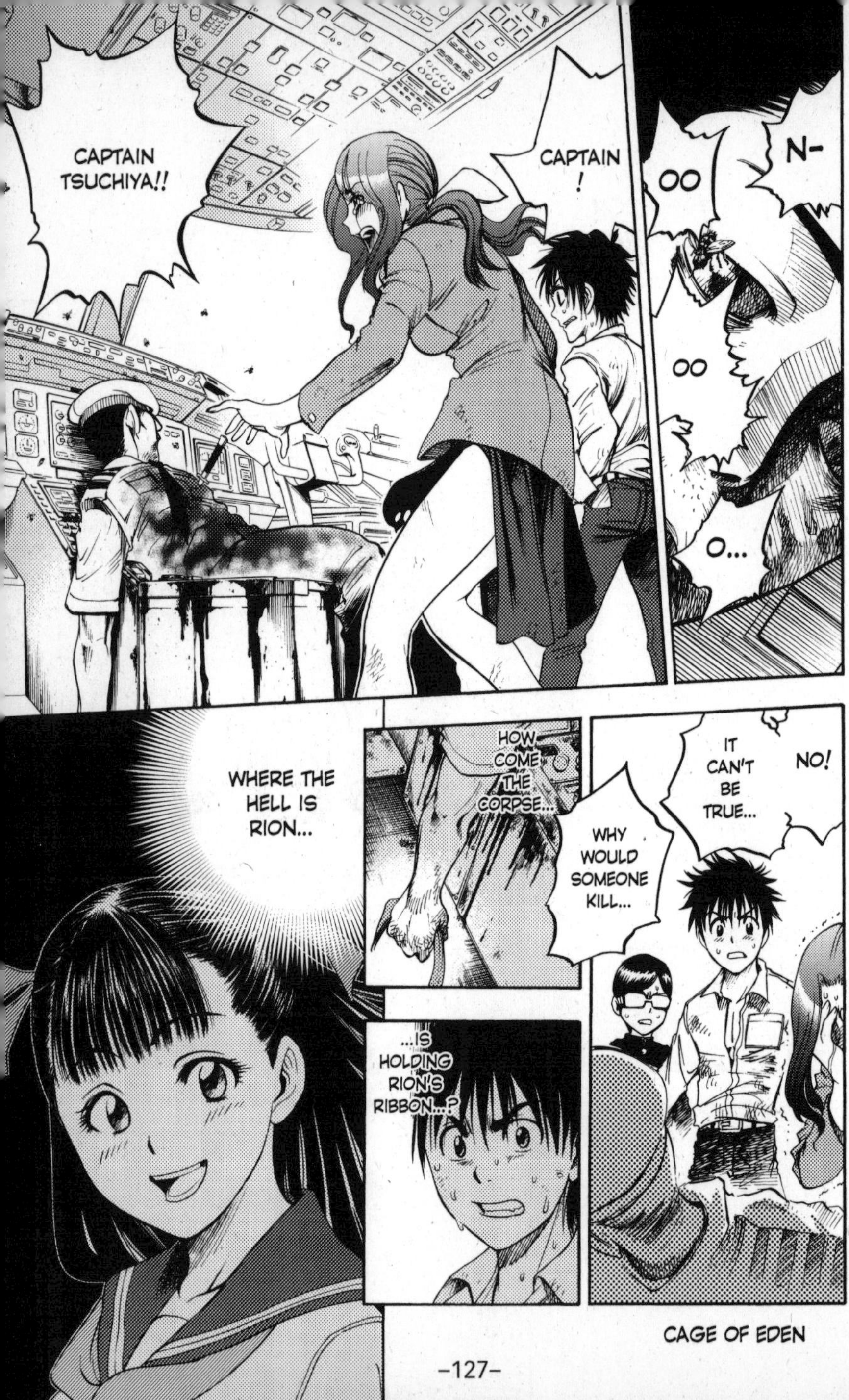
N-
OO
OO
O...
CAPTAIN!
CAPTAIN TSUCHIYA!!
NO!
IT CAN'T BE TRUE...
WHY WOULD SOMEONE KILL...
HOW COME THE CORPSE...
...IS HOLDING RION'S RIBBON...?
WHERE THE HELL IS RION...

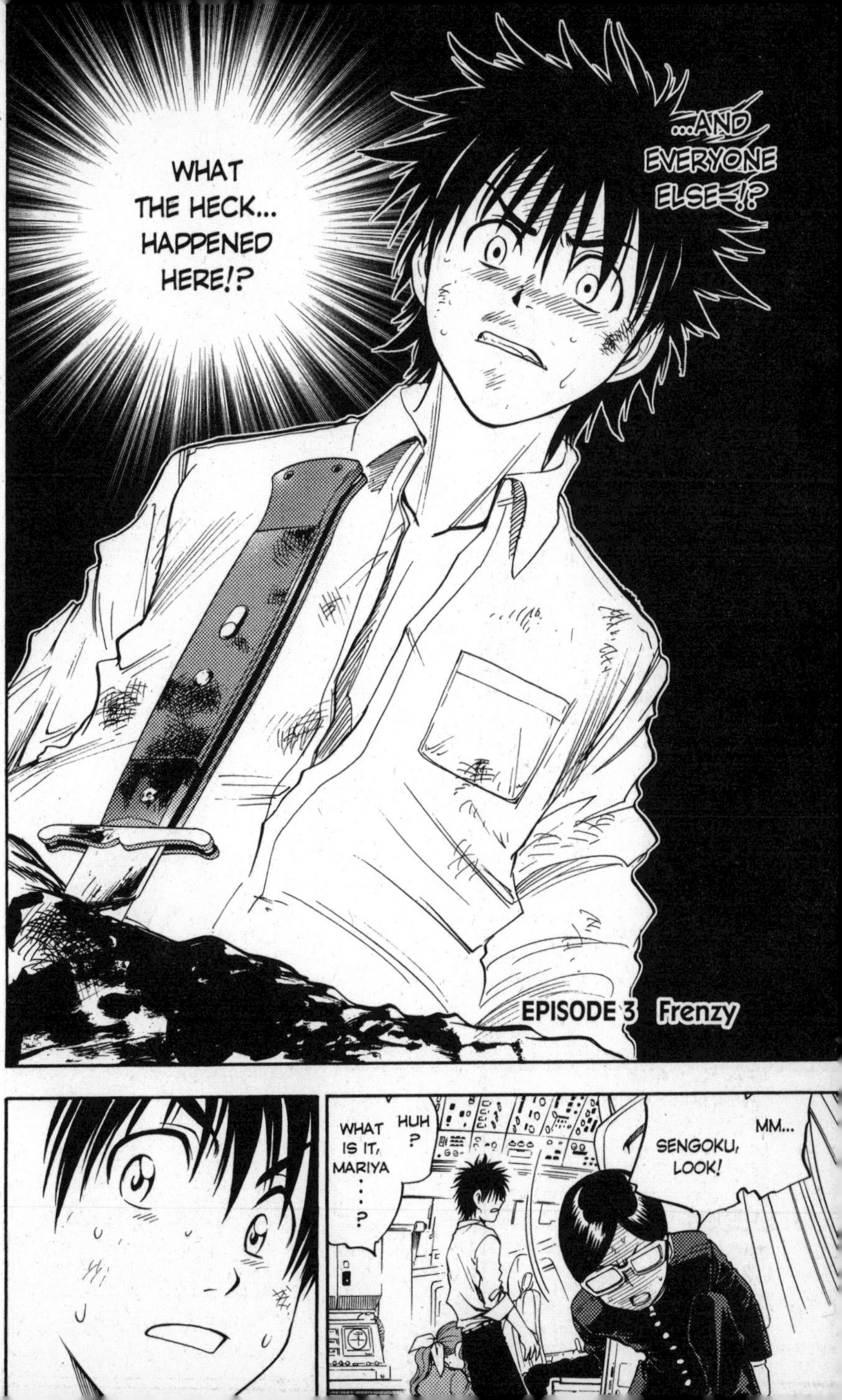
WHAT THE HECK... HAPPENED HERE!?
...AND EVERYONE ELSE—!?
EPISODE 3 Frenzy
MM...
SENGOKU, LOOK!
HUH?
WHAT IS IT, MARIYA...?

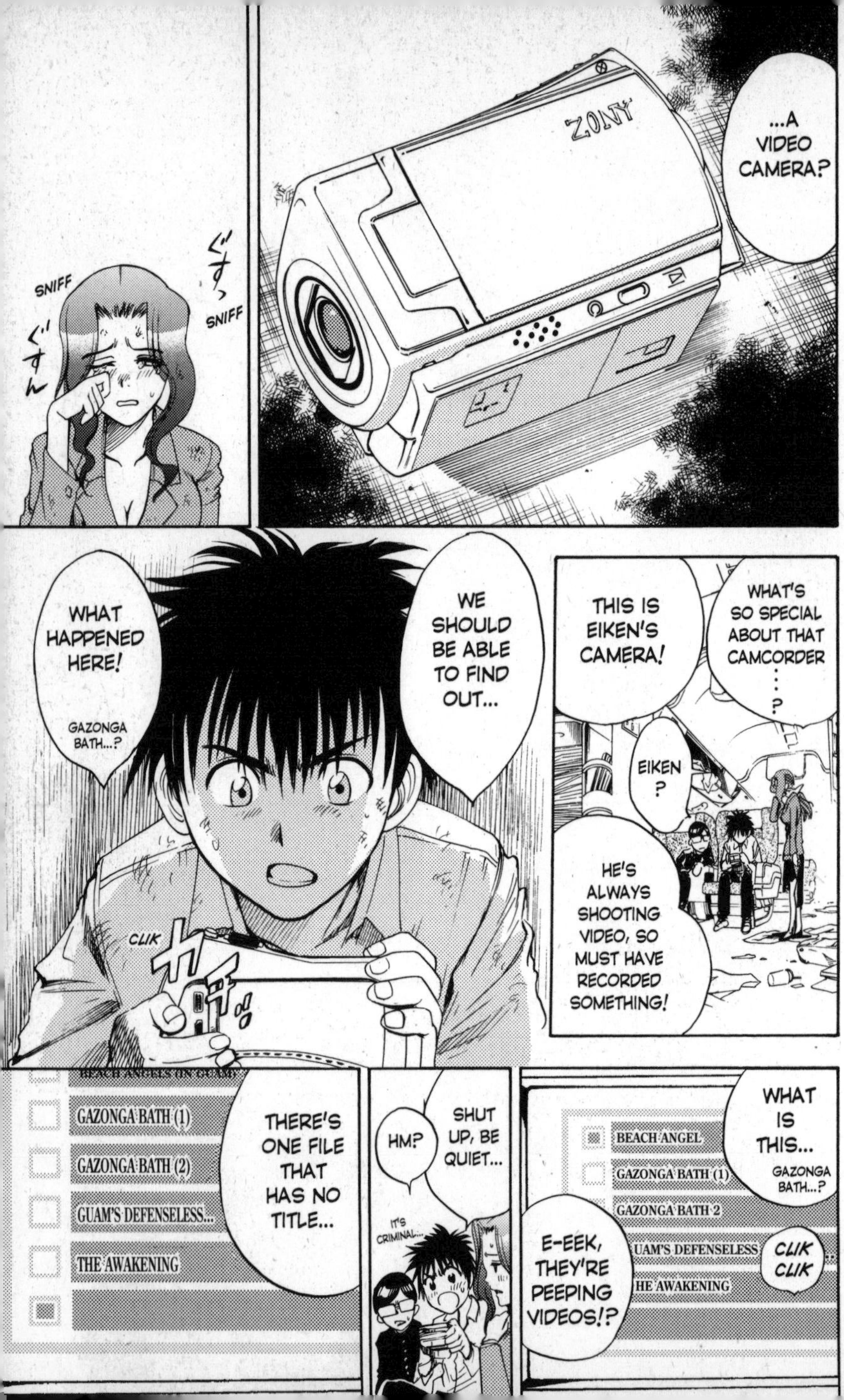
...A VIDEO CAMERA?
ZONY
ぐすっ
SNIFF
SNIFF
ぐすん
WHAT'S SO SPECIAL ABOUT THAT CAMCORDER...?
THIS IS EIKEN'S CAMERA!
EIKEN?
HE'S ALWAYS SHOOTING VIDEO, SO MUST HAVE RECORDED SOMETHING!
WE SHOULD BE ABLE TO FIND OUT...
WHAT HAPPENED HERE!
GAZONGA BATH...?
CLIK
WHAT IS THIS...
GAZONGA BATH...?
BEACH ANGEL
GAZONGA BATH (1)
GAZONGA BATH 2
UAM'S DEFENSELESS
HE AWAKENING
CLIK CLIK
E-EEK, THEY'RE PEEPING VIDEOS!?
SHUT UP, BE QUIET...
HM?
IT'S CRIMINAL...
THERE'S ONE FILE THAT HAS NO TITLE...
BEACH ANGELS (IN GUAM)
GAZONGA BATH (1)
GAZONGA BATH (2)
GUAM'S DEFENSELESS...
THE AWAKENING

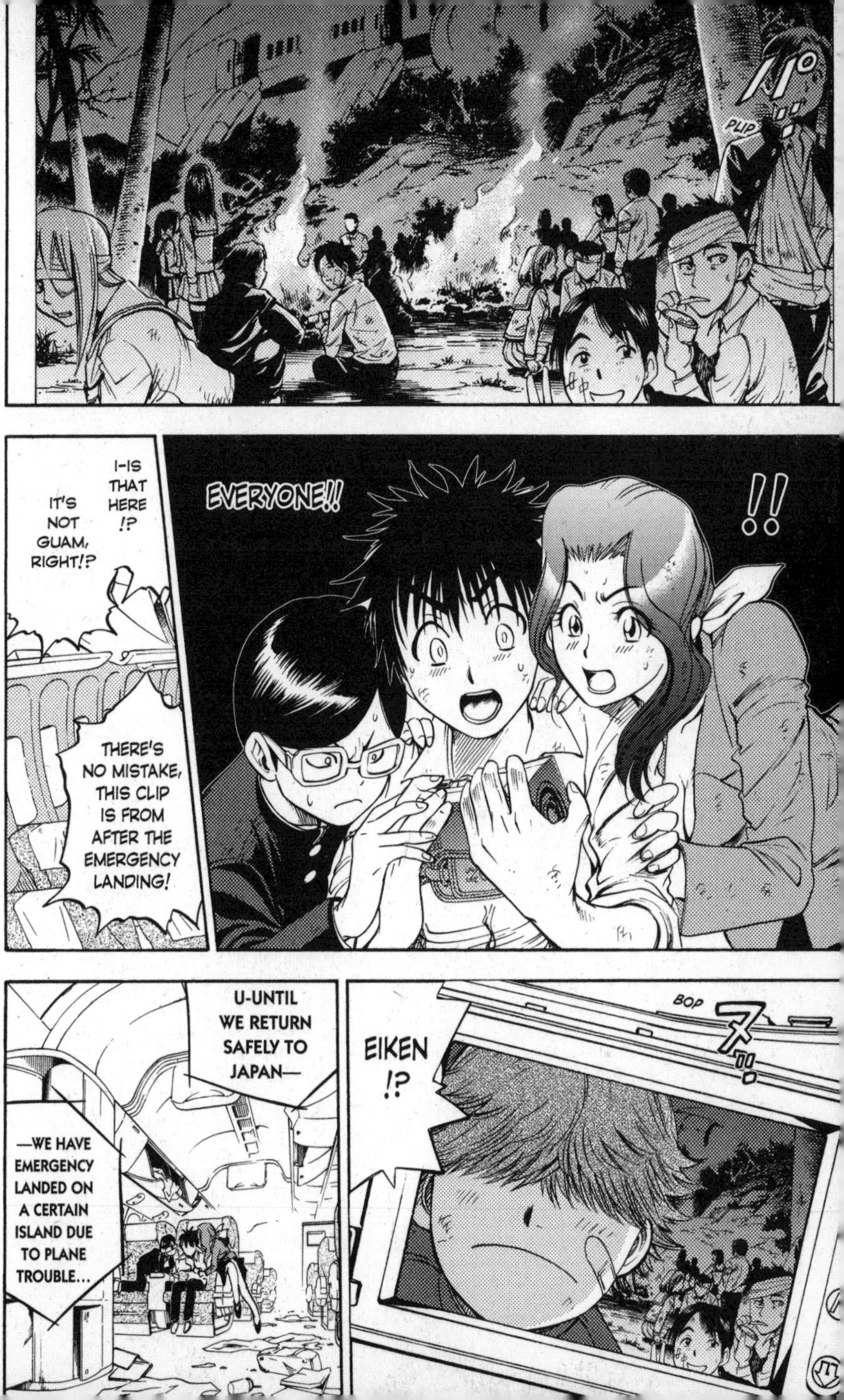
PLIP
!!
EVERYONE!!
I-IS THAT HERE !?
IT'S NOT GUAM, RIGHT!?
THERE'S NO MISTAKE, THIS CLIP IS FROM AFTER THE EMERGENCY LANDING!
BOP
EIKEN !?
U-UNTIL WE RETURN SAFELY TO JAPAN—
—WE HAVE EMERGENCY LANDED ON A CERTAIN ISLAND DUE TO PLANE TROUBLE...

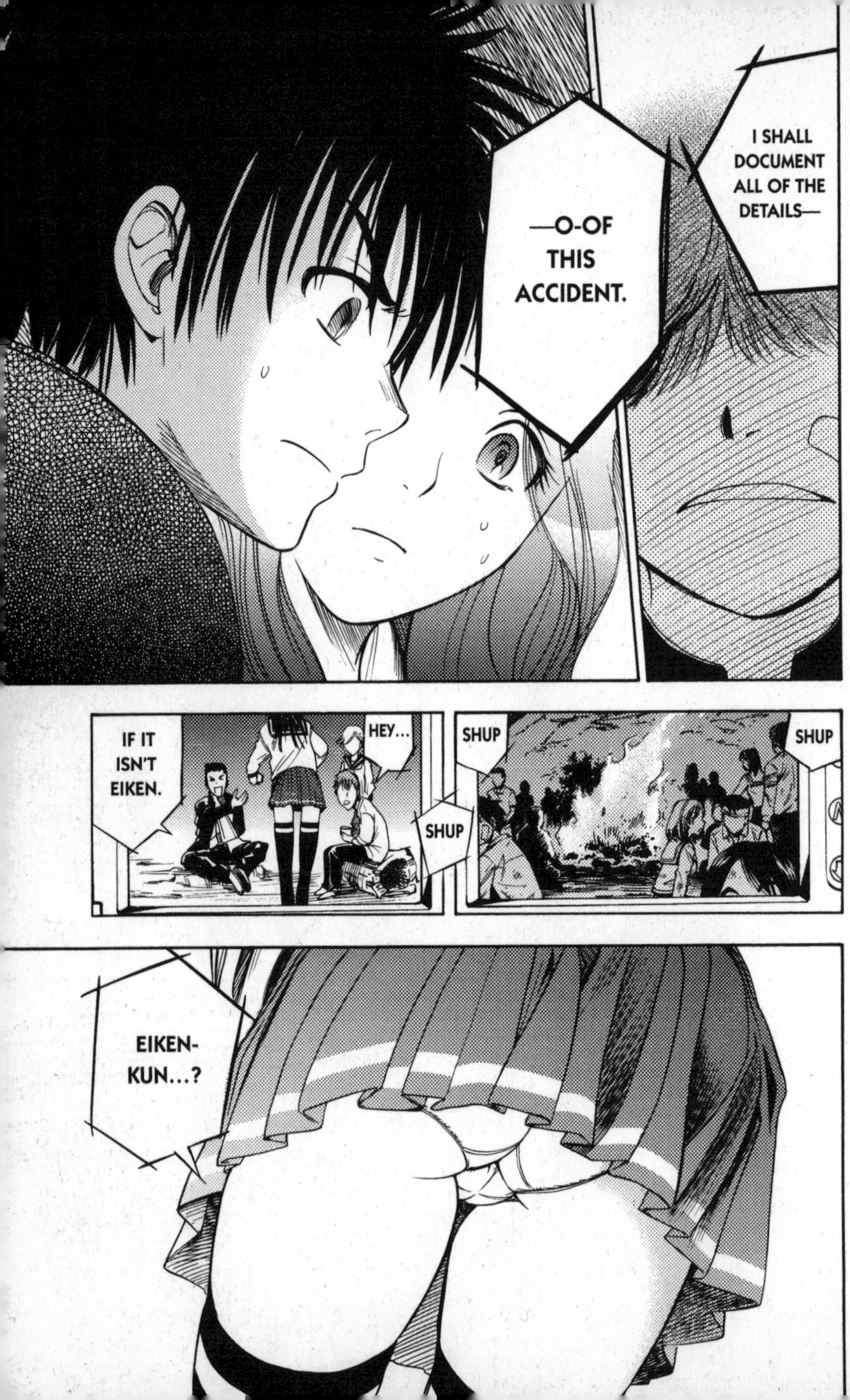
I SHALL DOCUMENT ALL OF THE DETAILS—
—O-OF THIS ACCIDENT.
SHUP
SHUP
HEY...
SHUP
IF IT ISN'T EIKEN.
EIKEN-KUN...?

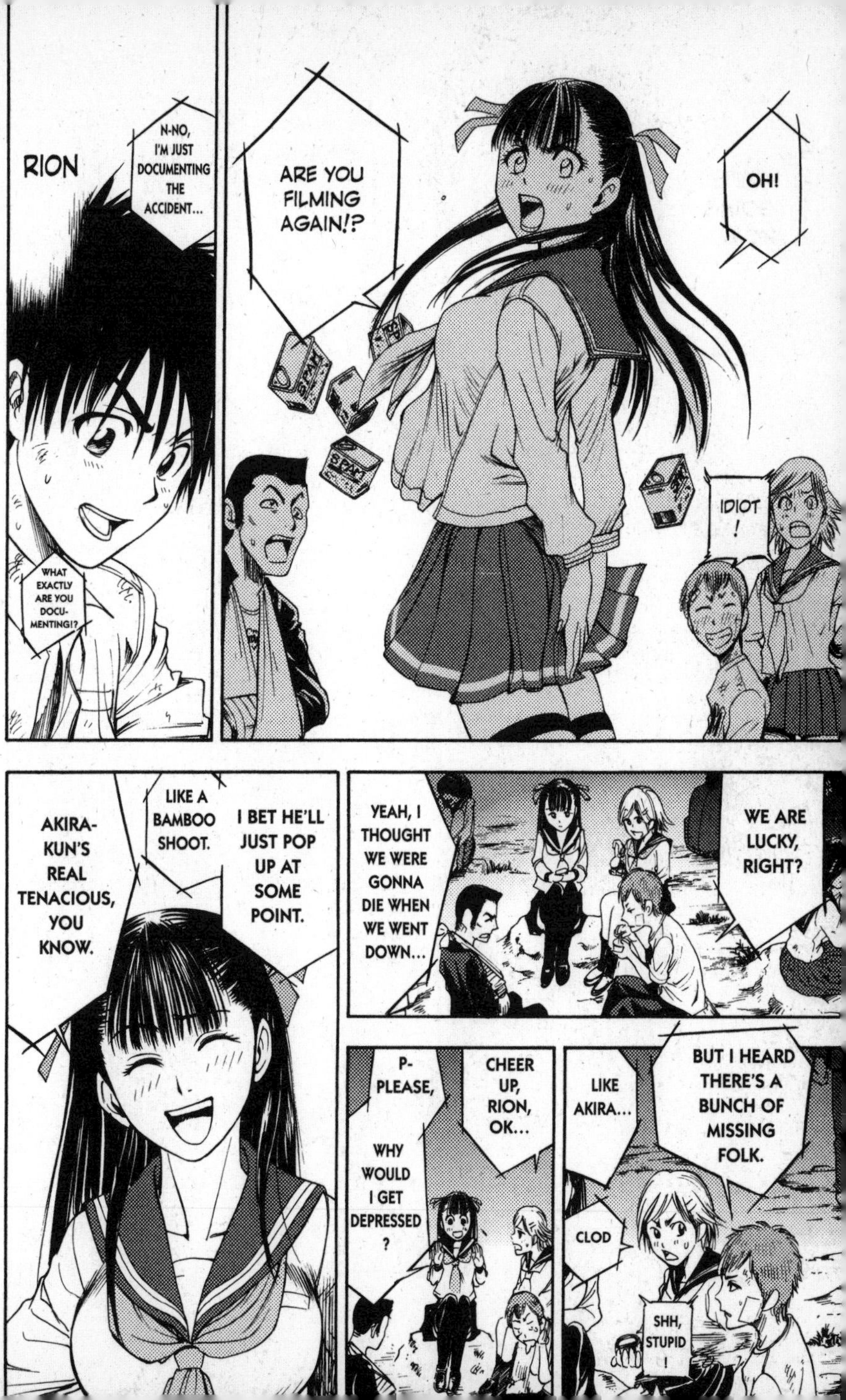
OH!
ARE YOU FILMING AGAIN!?
IDIOT!
N-NO, I'M JUST DOCUMENTING THE ACCIDENT...
RION
WHAT EXACTLY ARE YOU DOCU-MENTING!?
WE ARE LUCKY, RIGHT?
YEAH, I THOUGHT WE WERE GONNA DIE WHEN WE WENT DOWN...
BUT I HEARD THERE'S A BUNCH OF MISSING FOLK.
LIKE AKIRA...
CLOD
SHH, STUPID!
CHEER UP, RION, OK...
P-PLEASE,
WHY WOULD I GET DEPRESSED?
I BET HE'LL JUST POP UP AT SOME POINT.
LIKE A BAMBOO SHOOT.
AKIRA-KUN'S REAL TENACIOUS, YOU KNOW.

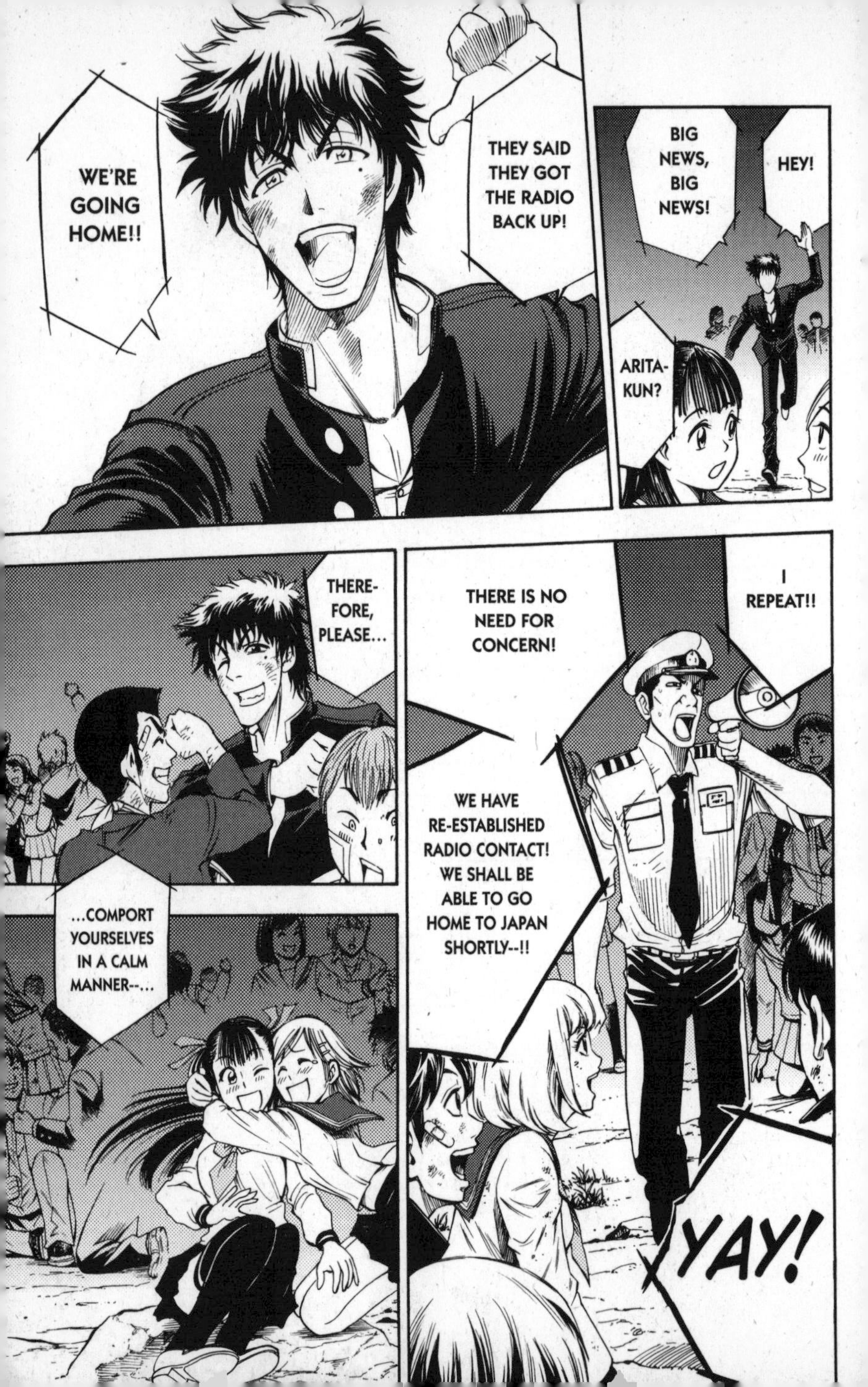
HEY!
BIG NEWS, BIG NEWS!
ARITA-KUN?
THEY SAID THEY GOT THE RADIO BACK UP!
WE'RE GOING HOME!!
I REPEAT!!
THERE IS NO NEED FOR CONCERN!
WE HAVE RE-ESTABLISHED RADIO CONTACT! WE SHALL BE ABLE TO GO HOME TO JAPAN SHORTLY--!!
YAY!
THERE-FORE, PLEASE...
...COMPORT YOURSELVES IN A CALM MANNER--...

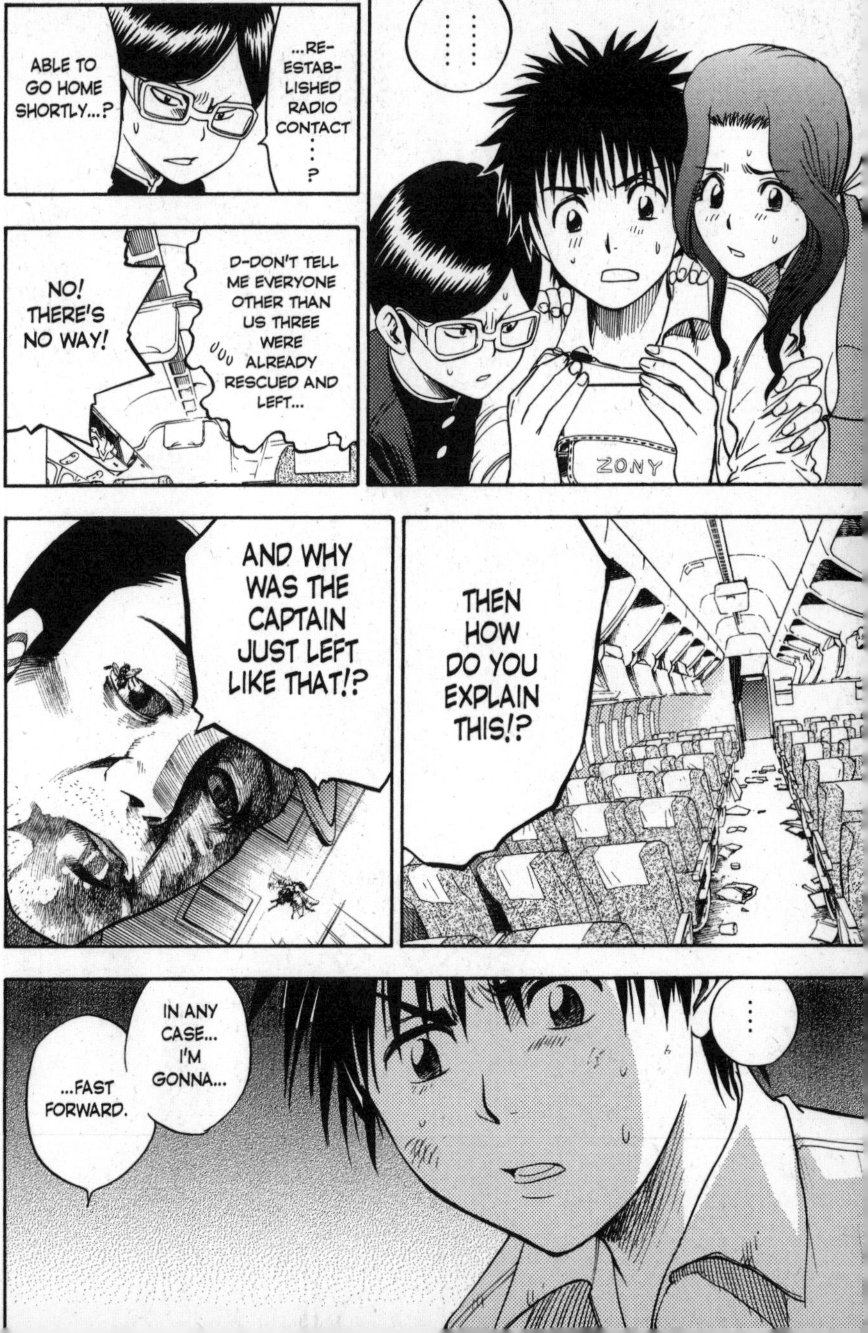
......
ZONY
...RE-ESTABLISHED RADIO CONTACT...?
ABLE TO GO HOME SHORTLY...?
D-DON'T TELL ME EVERYONE OTHER THAN US THREE WERE ALREADY RESCUED AND LEFT...
NO! THERE'S NO WAY!
THEN HOW DO YOU EXPLAIN THIS!?
AND WHY WAS THE CAPTAIN JUST LEFT LIKE THAT!?
....
IN ANY CASE... I'M GONNA...
...FAST FORWARD.

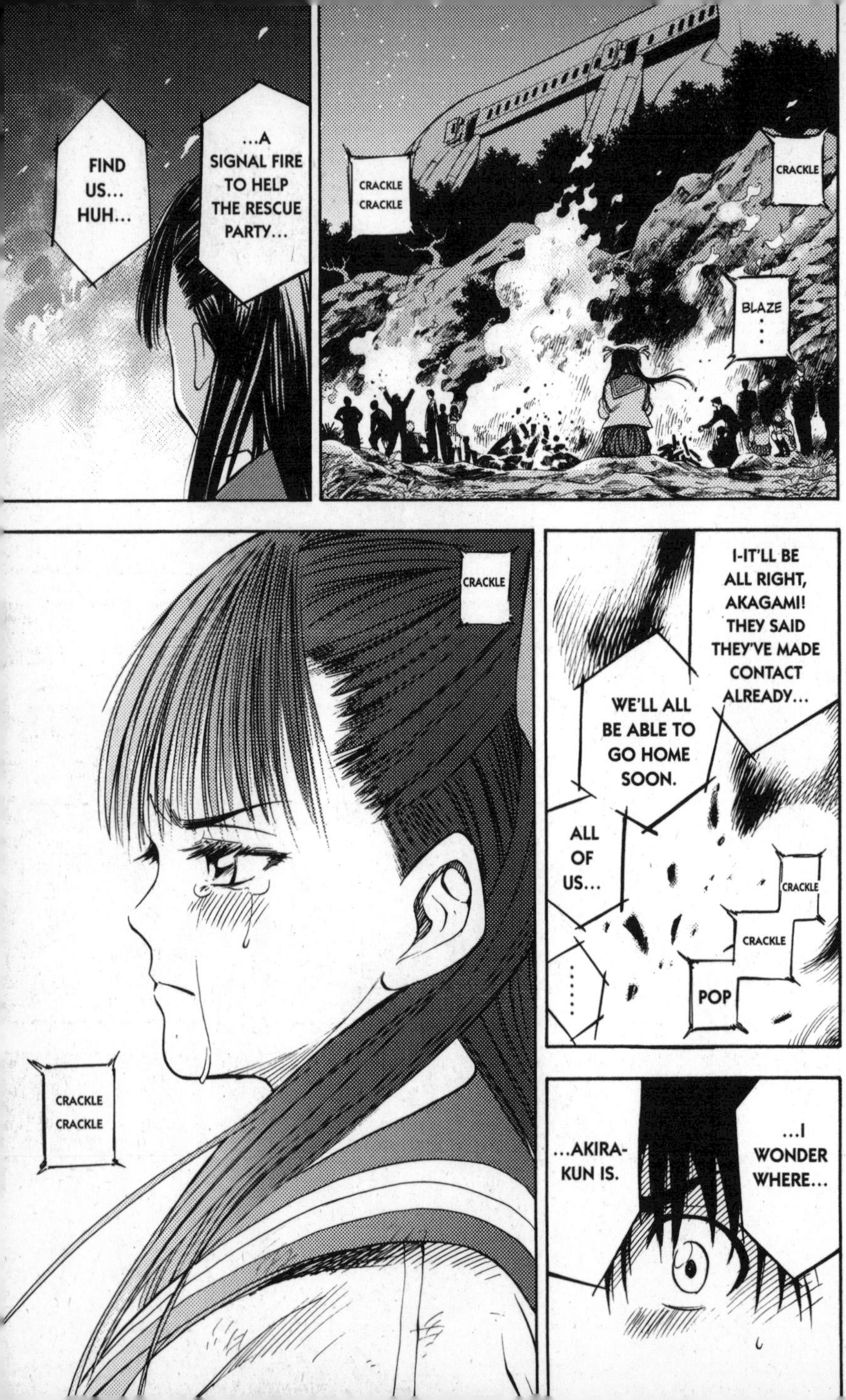
CRACKLE
BLAZE . . .
CRACKLE CRACKLE
...A SIGNAL FIRE TO HELP THE RESCUE PARTY...
FIND US... HUH...
I-IT'LL BE ALL RIGHT, AKAGAMI! THEY SAID THEY'VE MADE CONTACT ALREADY...
WE'LL ALL BE ABLE TO GO HOME SOON.
ALL OF US...
......
CRACKLE
CRACKLE
POP
...I WONDER WHERE...
...AKIRA-KUN IS.
CRACKLE
CRACKLE CRACKLE

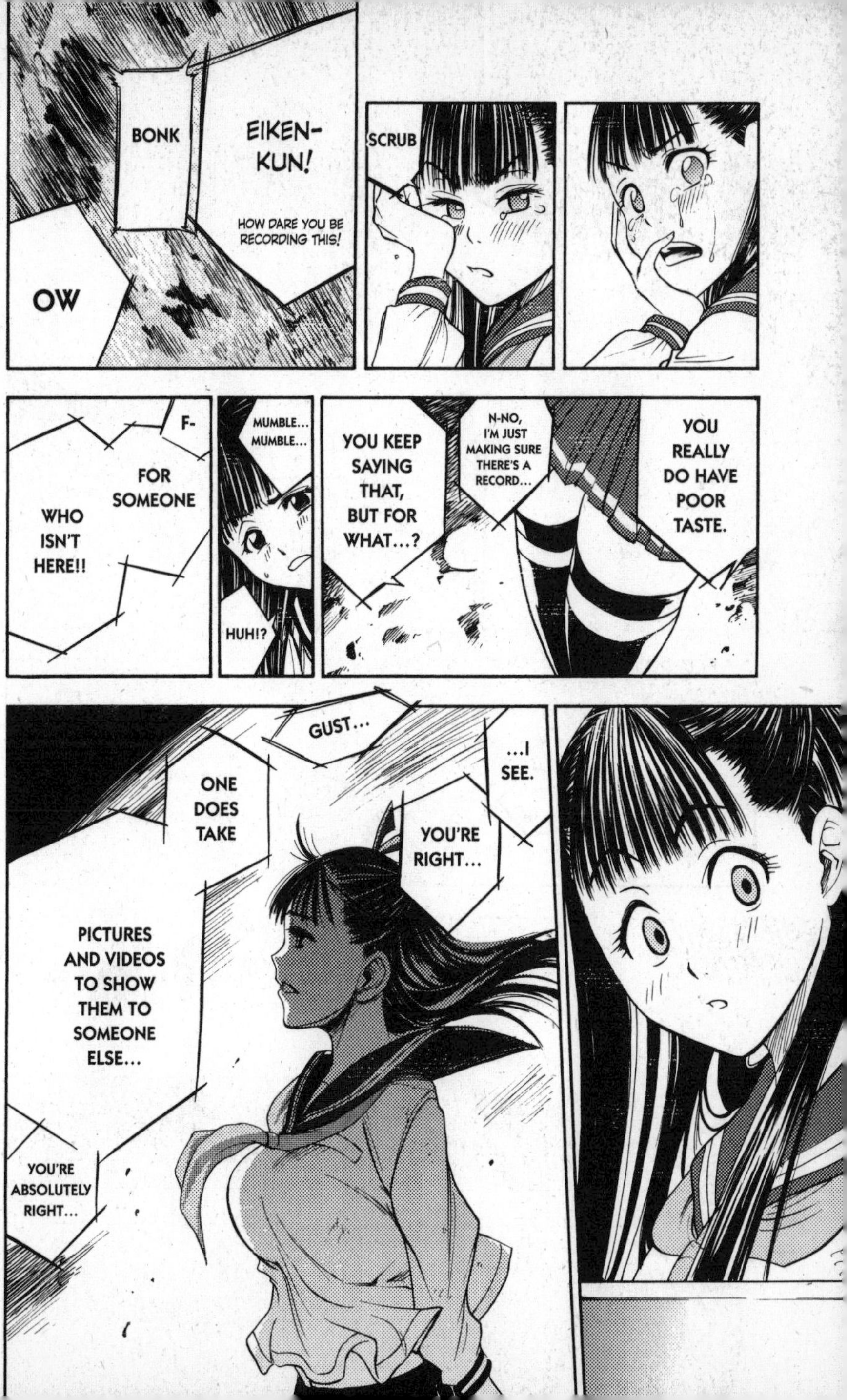
SCRUB
EIKEN-KUN!
BONK
HOW DARE YOU BE RECORDING THIS!
OW
YOU REALLY DO HAVE POOR TASTE.
N-NO, I'M JUST MAKING SURE THERE'S A RECORD...
YOU KEEP SAYING THAT, BUT FOR WHAT...?
MUMBLE... MUMBLE...
HUH!?
F-
FOR SOMEONE
WHO ISN'T HERE!!
GUST...
...I SEE.
YOU'RE RIGHT...
ONE DOES TAKE
PICTURES AND VIDEOS TO SHOW THEM TO SOMEONE ELSE...
YOU'RE ABSOLUTELY RIGHT...

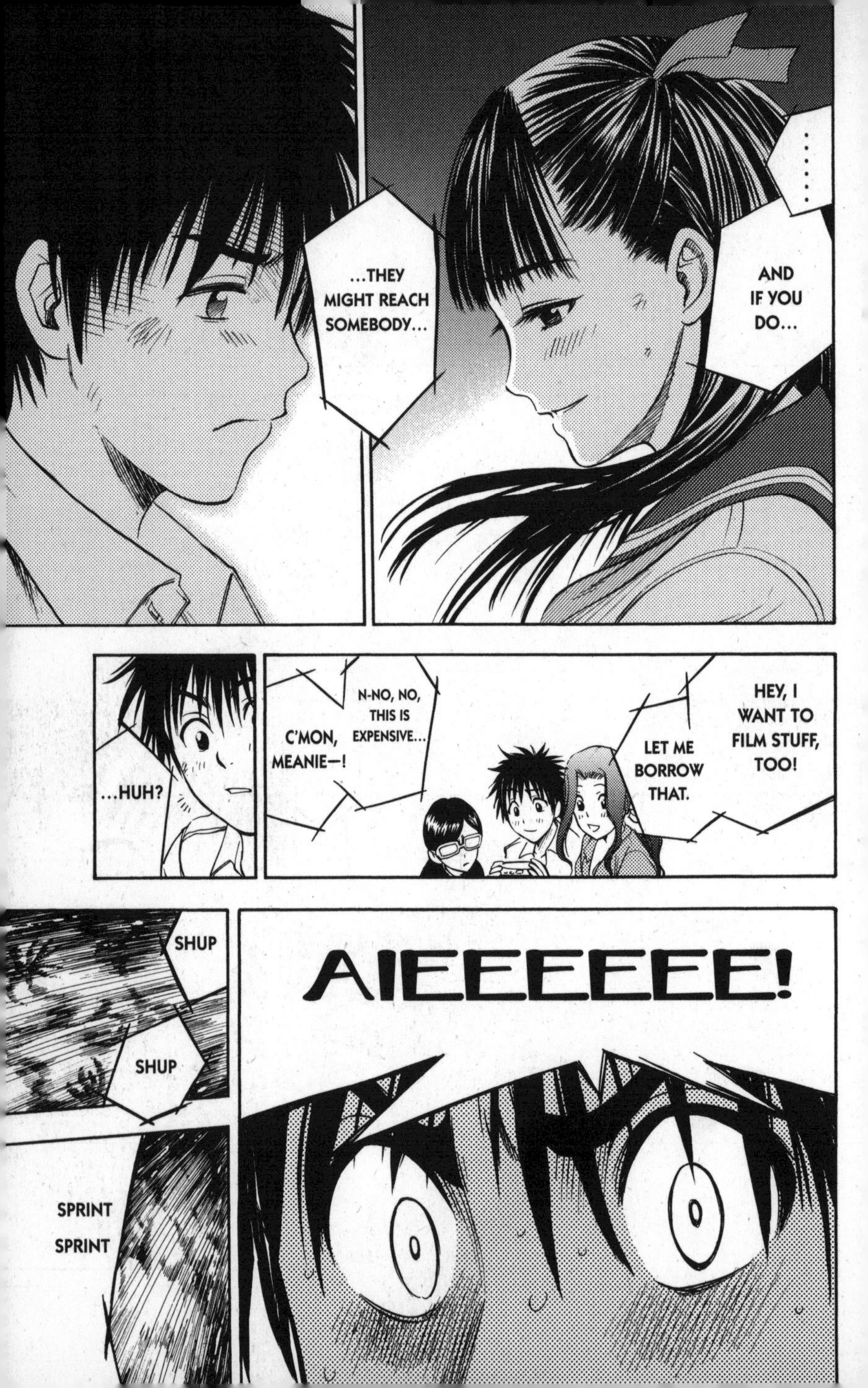
……
AND IF YOU DO…
…THEY MIGHT REACH SOMEBODY…
HEY, I WANT TO FILM STUFF, TOO!
LET ME BORROW THAT.
N-NO, NO, THIS IS EXPENSIVE…
C'MON, MEANIE—!
…HUH?
AIEEEEEEE!
SHUP
SHUP
SPRINT
SPRINT

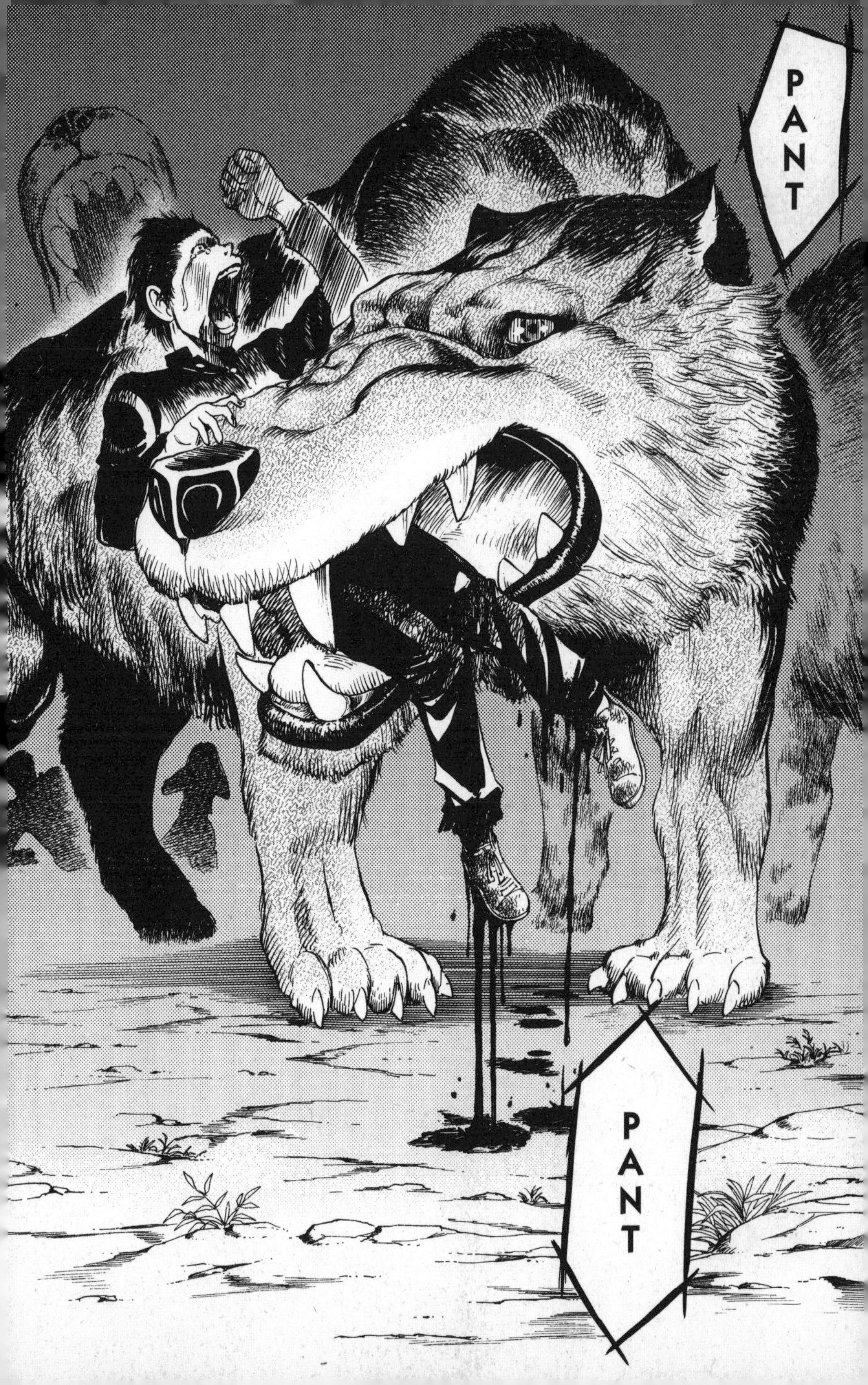
PANT
PANT

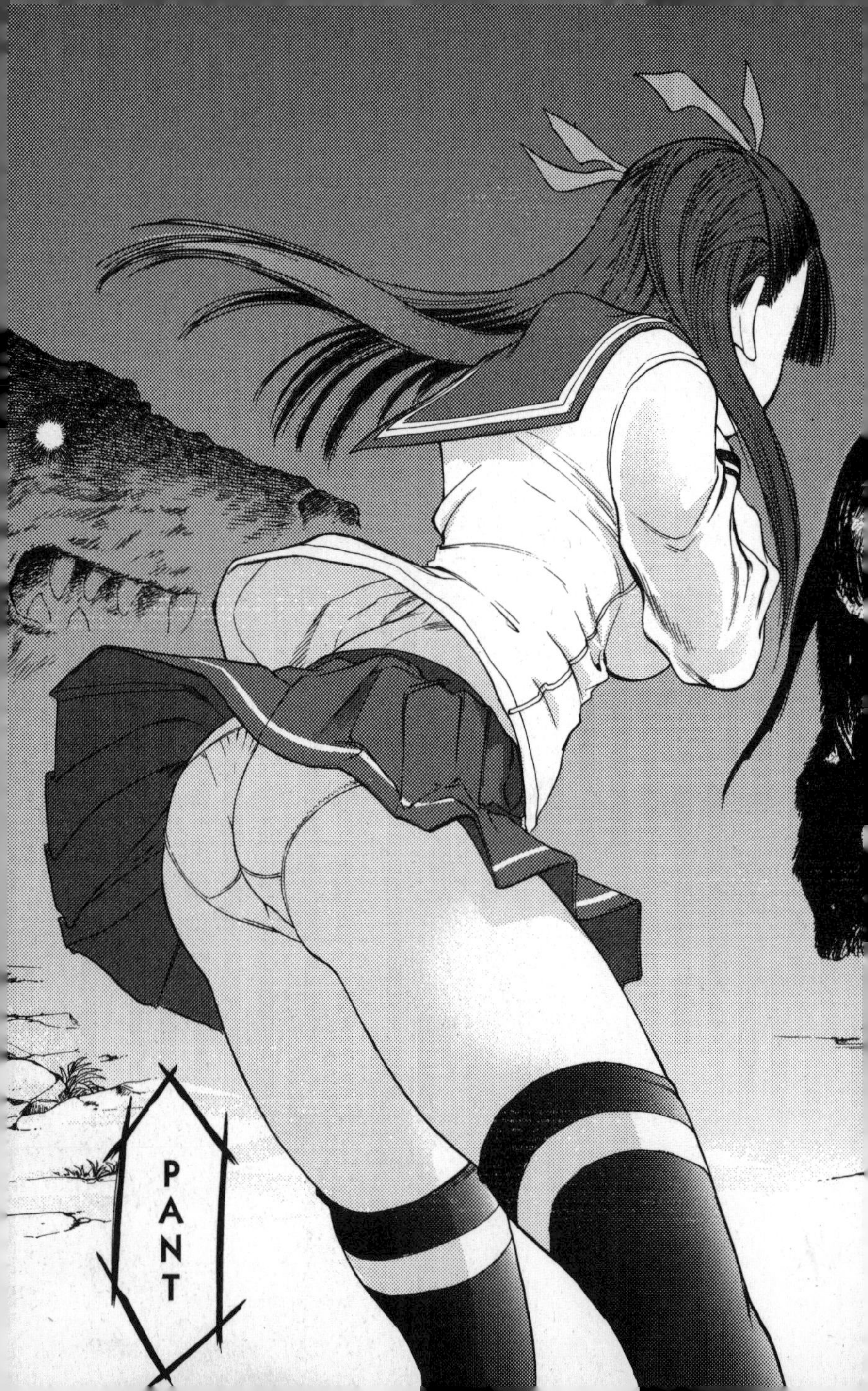
PANT

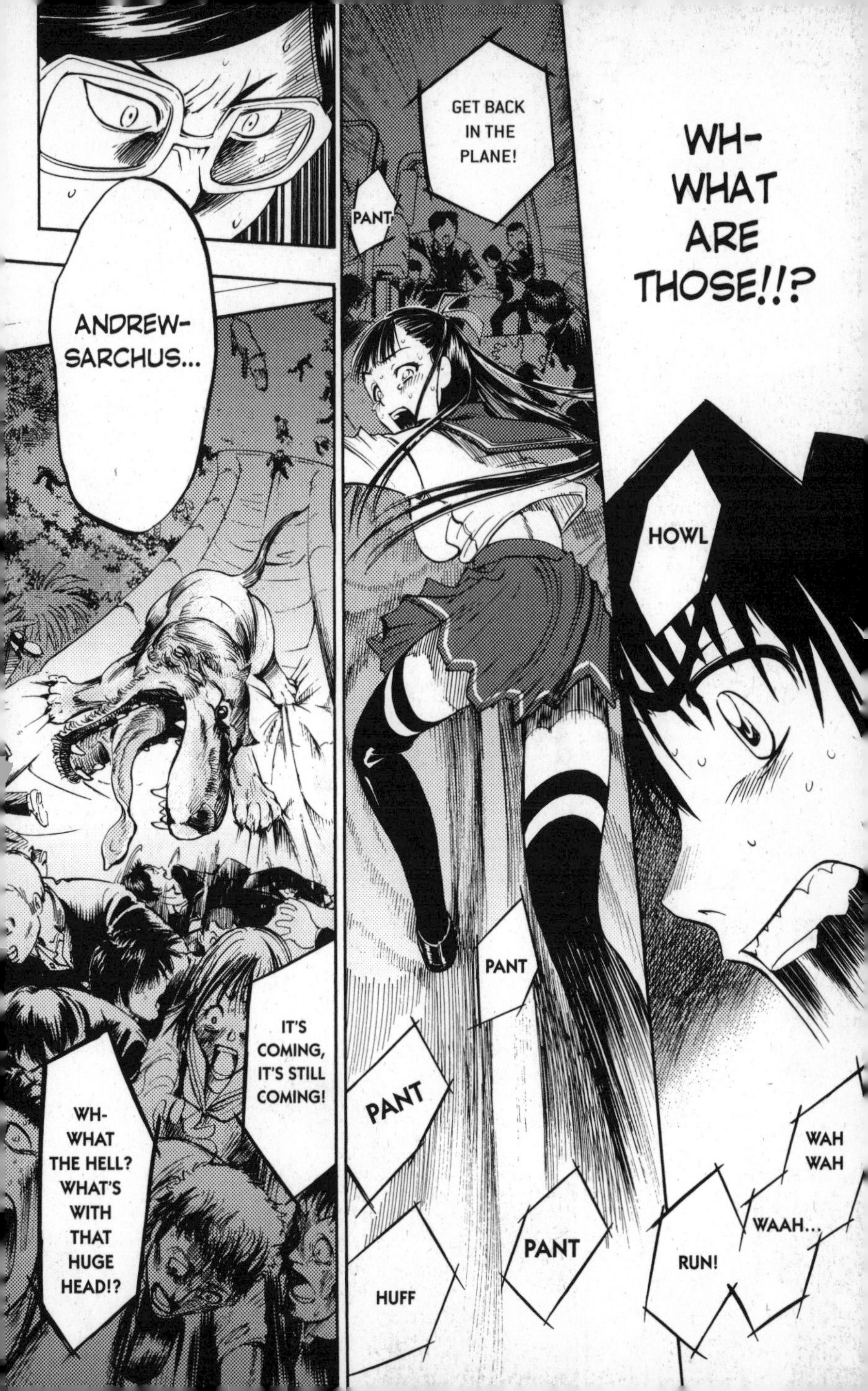
WH- WHAT ARE THOSE!!?
HOWL
WAH WAH
WAAH...
RUN!
GET BACK IN THE PLANE!
PANT
PANT
PANT
PANT
HUFF
ANDREW-SARCHUS...
IT'S COMING, IT'S STILL COMING!
WH- WHAT THE HELL? WHAT'S WITH THAT HUGE HEAD!?

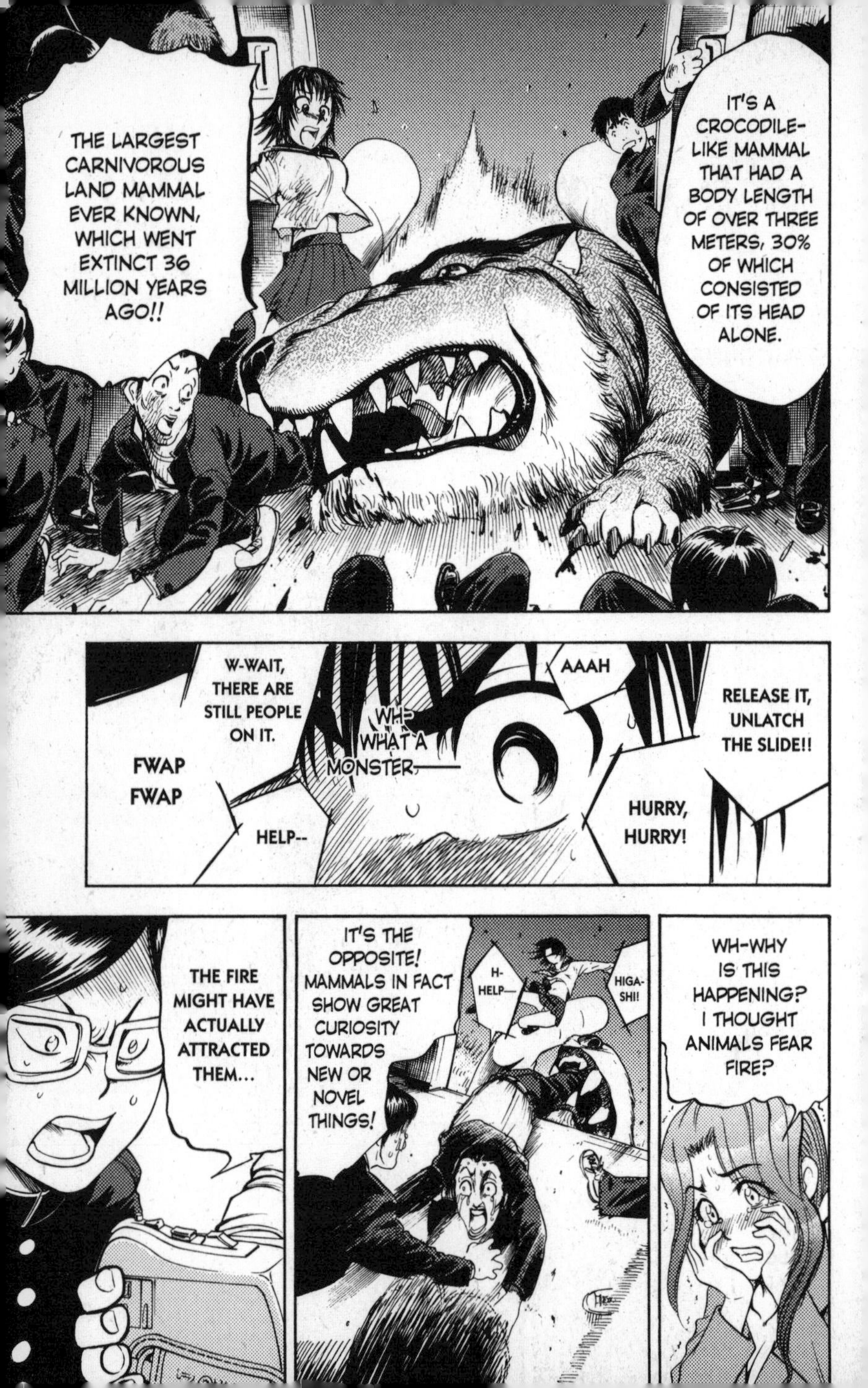
IT'S A CROCODILE-LIKE MAMMAL THAT HAD A BODY LENGTH OF OVER THREE METERS, 30% OF WHICH CONSISTED OF ITS HEAD ALONE.
THE LARGEST CARNIVOROUS LAND MAMMAL EVER KNOWN, WHICH WENT EXTINCT 36 MILLION YEARS AGO!!
RELEASE IT, UNLATCH THE SLIDE!!
AAAH
HURRY, HURRY!
WH- WHAT A MONSTER—
W-WAIT, THERE ARE STILL PEOPLE ON IT.
FWAP FWAP
HELP--
WH-WHY IS THIS HAPPENING? I THOUGHT ANIMALS FEAR FIRE?
HIGA-SHI!
H-HELP—
IT'S THE OPPOSITE! MAMMALS IN FACT SHOW GREAT CURIOSITY TOWARDS NEW OR NOVEL THINGS!
THE FIRE MIGHT HAVE ACTUALLY ATTRACTED THEM...

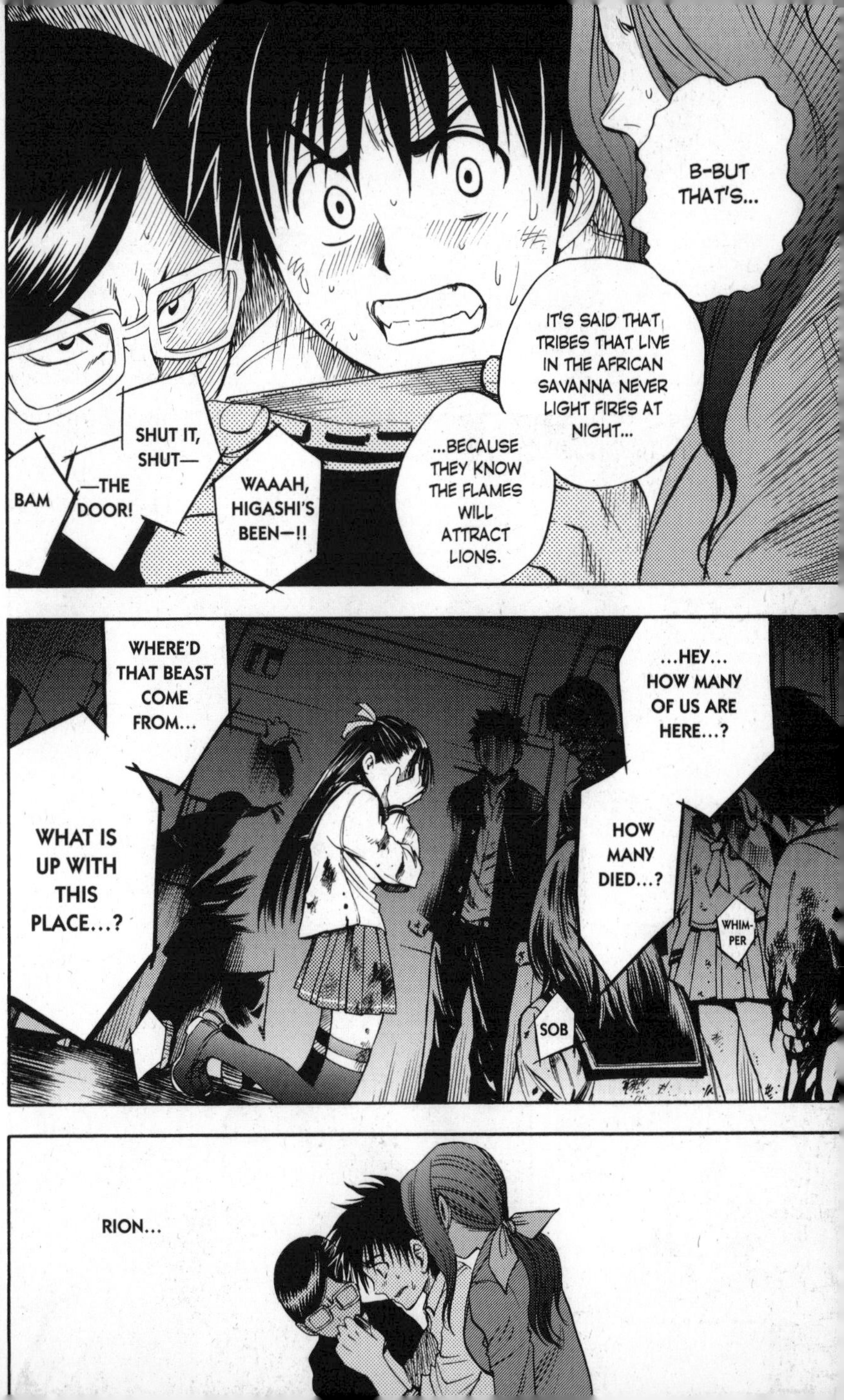
B-BUT THAT'S...
IT'S SAID THAT TRIBES THAT LIVE IN THE AFRICAN SAVANNA NEVER LIGHT FIRES AT NIGHT...
...BECAUSE THEY KNOW THE FLAMES WILL ATTRACT LIONS.
WAAAH, HIGASHI'S BEEN—!!
SHUT IT, SHUT—
—THE DOOR!
BAM
...HEY... HOW MANY OF US ARE HERE...?
WHIMPER
HOW MANY DIED...?
SOB
WHERE'D THAT BEAST COME FROM...
WHAT IS UP WITH THIS PLACE...?
RION...

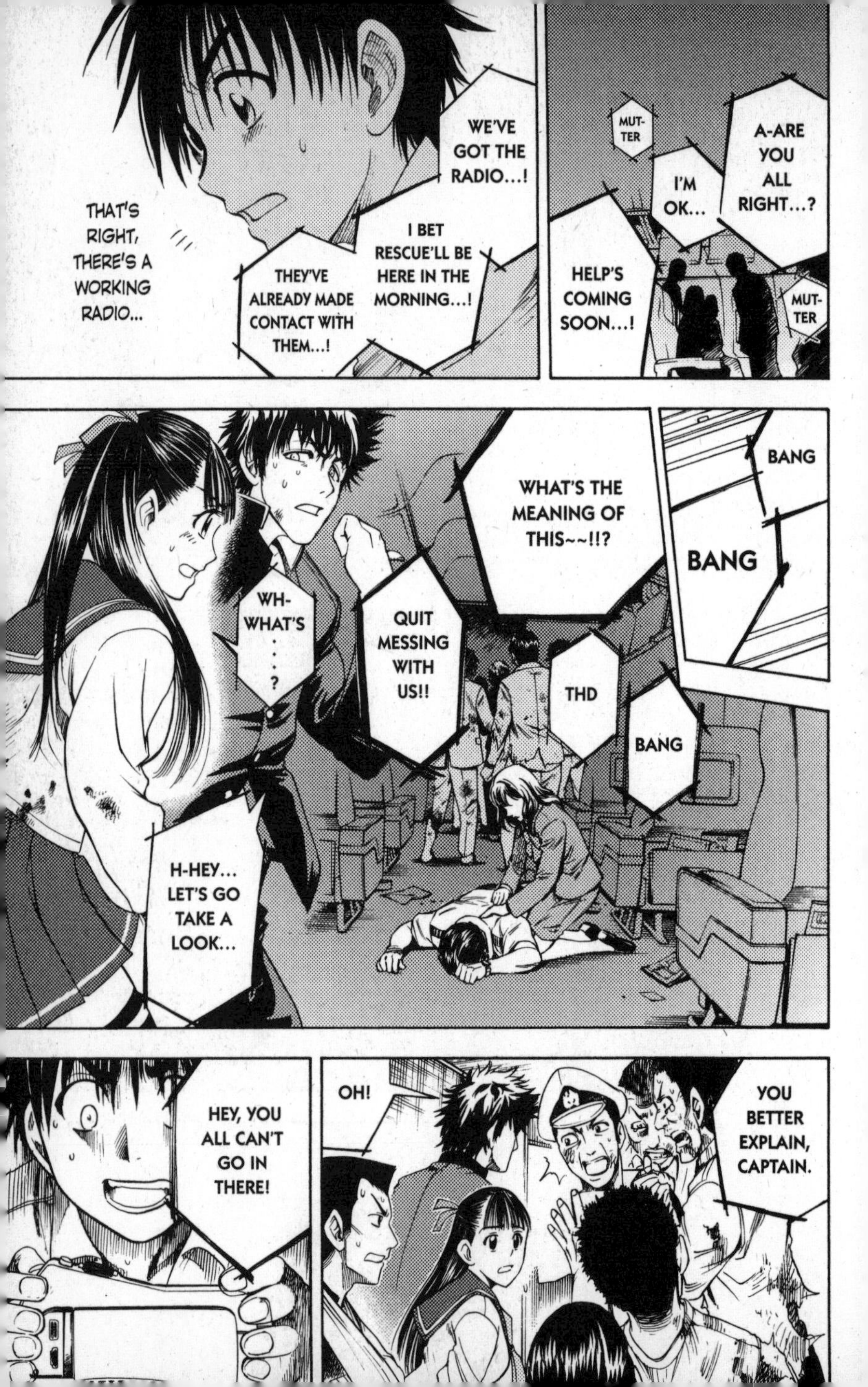
A-ARE YOU ALL RIGHT...?
MUT-TER
I'M OK...
MUT-TER
HELP'S COMING SOON...!
WE'VE GOT THE RADIO...!
I BET RESCUE'LL BE HERE IN THE MORNING...!
THEY'VE ALREADY MADE CONTACT WITH THEM...!
THAT'S RIGHT, THERE'S A WORKING RADIO...
BANG
BANG
WHAT'S THE MEANING OF THIS~~!!?
THD
BANG
QUIT MESSING WITH US!!
WH-WHAT'S...?
H-HEY... LET'S GO TAKE A LOOK...
YOU BETTER EXPLAIN, CAPTAIN.
OH!
HEY, YOU ALL CAN'T GO IN THERE!

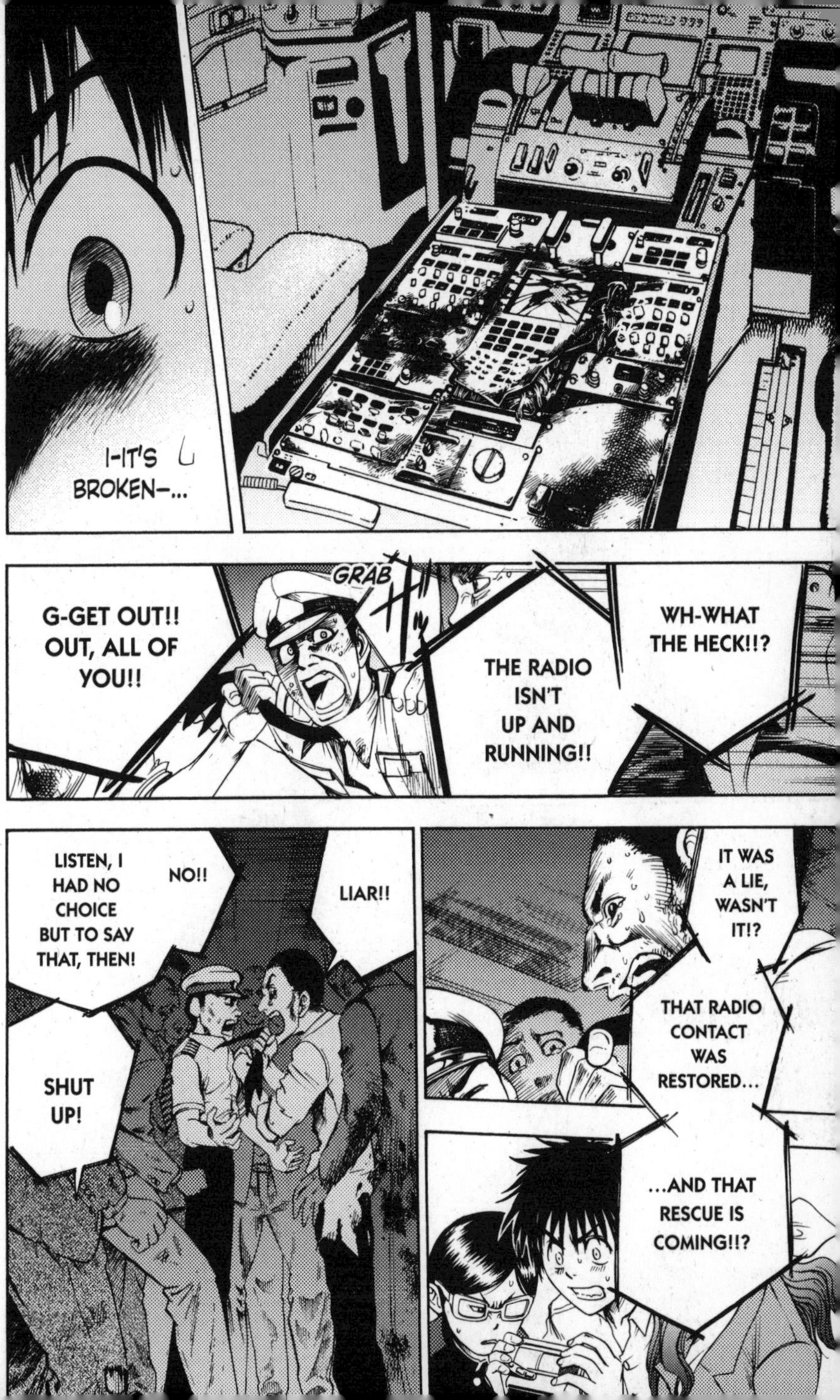
I-IT'S BROKEN–...
WH-WHAT THE HECK!!?
THE RADIO ISN'T UP AND RUNNING!!
GRAB
G-GET OUT!! OUT, ALL OF YOU!!
IT WAS A LIE, WASN'T IT!?
THAT RADIO CONTACT WAS RESTORED...
...AND THAT RESCUE IS COMING!!?
LIAR!!
NO!!
LISTEN, I HAD NO CHOICE BUT TO SAY THAT, THEN!
SHUT UP!

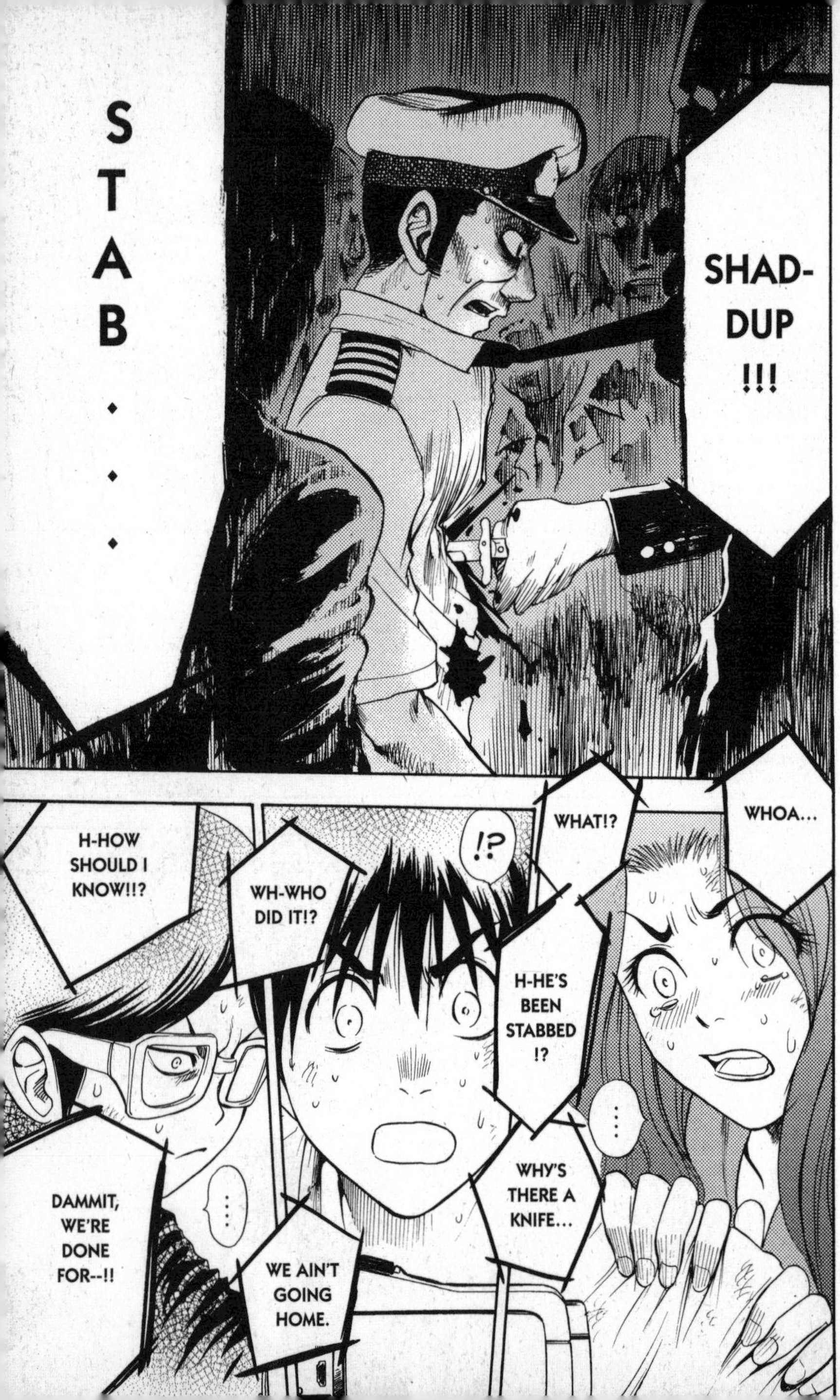
SHAD-DUP!!!
STAB...
WHOA...
WHAT!?
!?
H-HE'S BEEN STABBED!?
WH-WHO DID IT!?
H-HOW SHOULD I KNOW!!?
...
WHY'S THERE A KNIFE...
...
WE AIN'T GOING HOME.
DAMMIT, WE'RE DONE FOR--!!

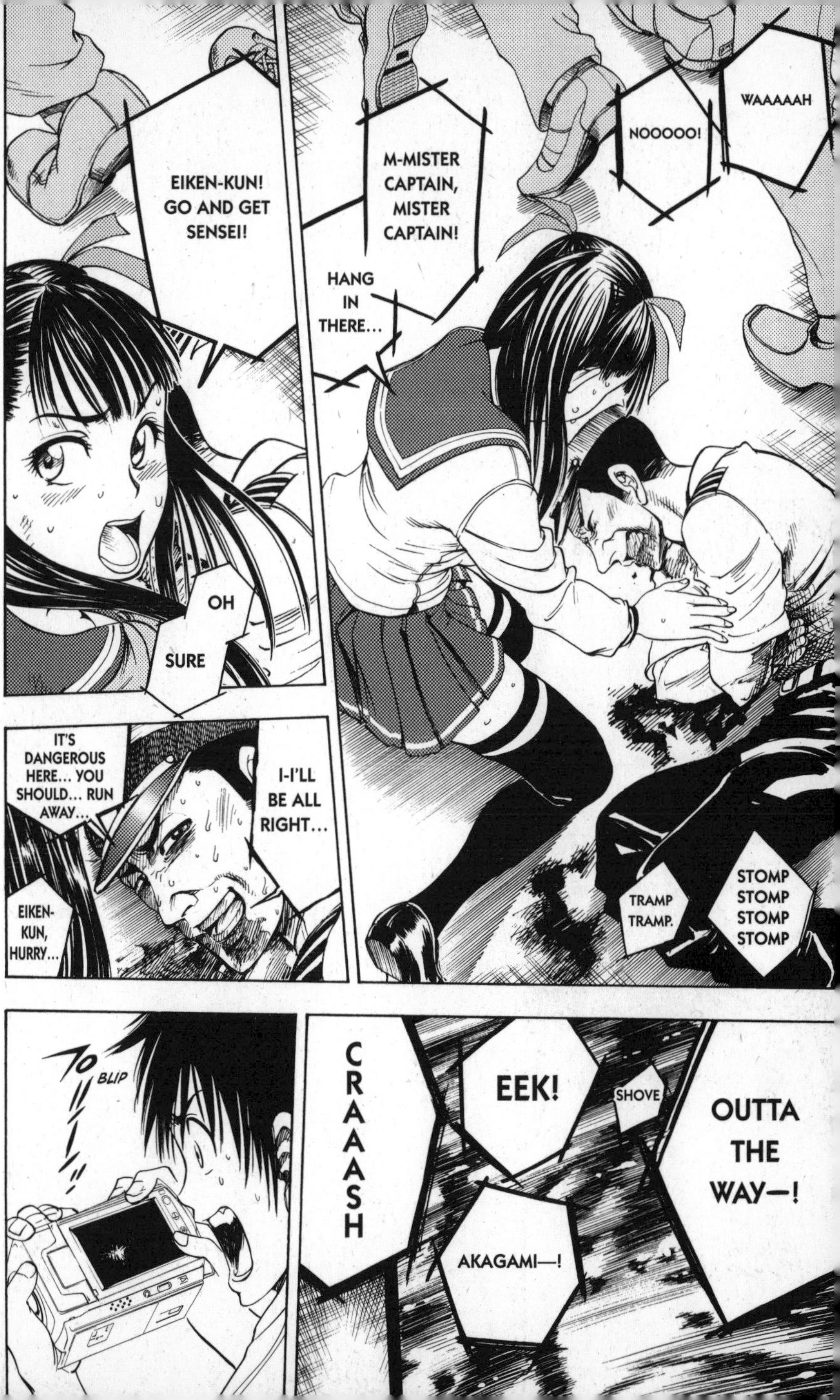
WAAAAAH
NOOOOO!
M-MISTER CAPTAIN, MISTER CAPTAIN!
HANG IN THERE…
STOMP STOMP STOMP STOMP
TRAMP TRAMP.
EIKEN-KUN! GO AND GET SENSEI!
OH
SURE
I-I'LL BE ALL RIGHT…
IT'S DANGEROUS HERE… YOU SHOULD… RUN AWAY…
EIKEN-KUN, HURRY…
OUTTA THE WAY—!
SHOVE
EEK!
CRAAASH
AKAGAMI—!
BLIP

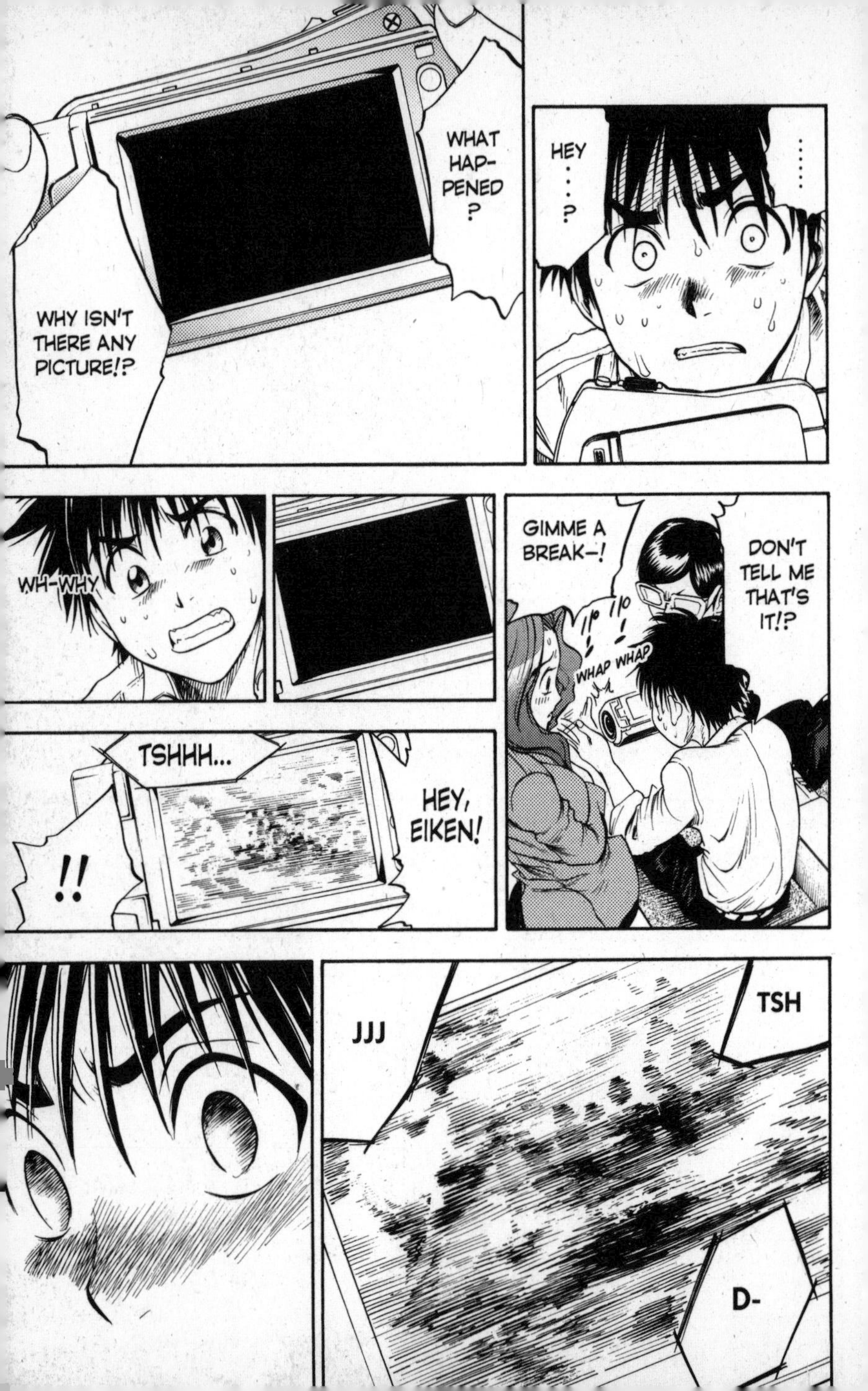
......
HEY...?
WHAT HAP-PENED?
WHY ISN'T THERE ANY PICTURE!?
DON'T TELL ME THAT'S IT!?
GIMME A BREAK-!
WHAP WHAP
WH-WHY
HEY, EIKEN!
TSHHH...
!!
TSH
JJJ
D-

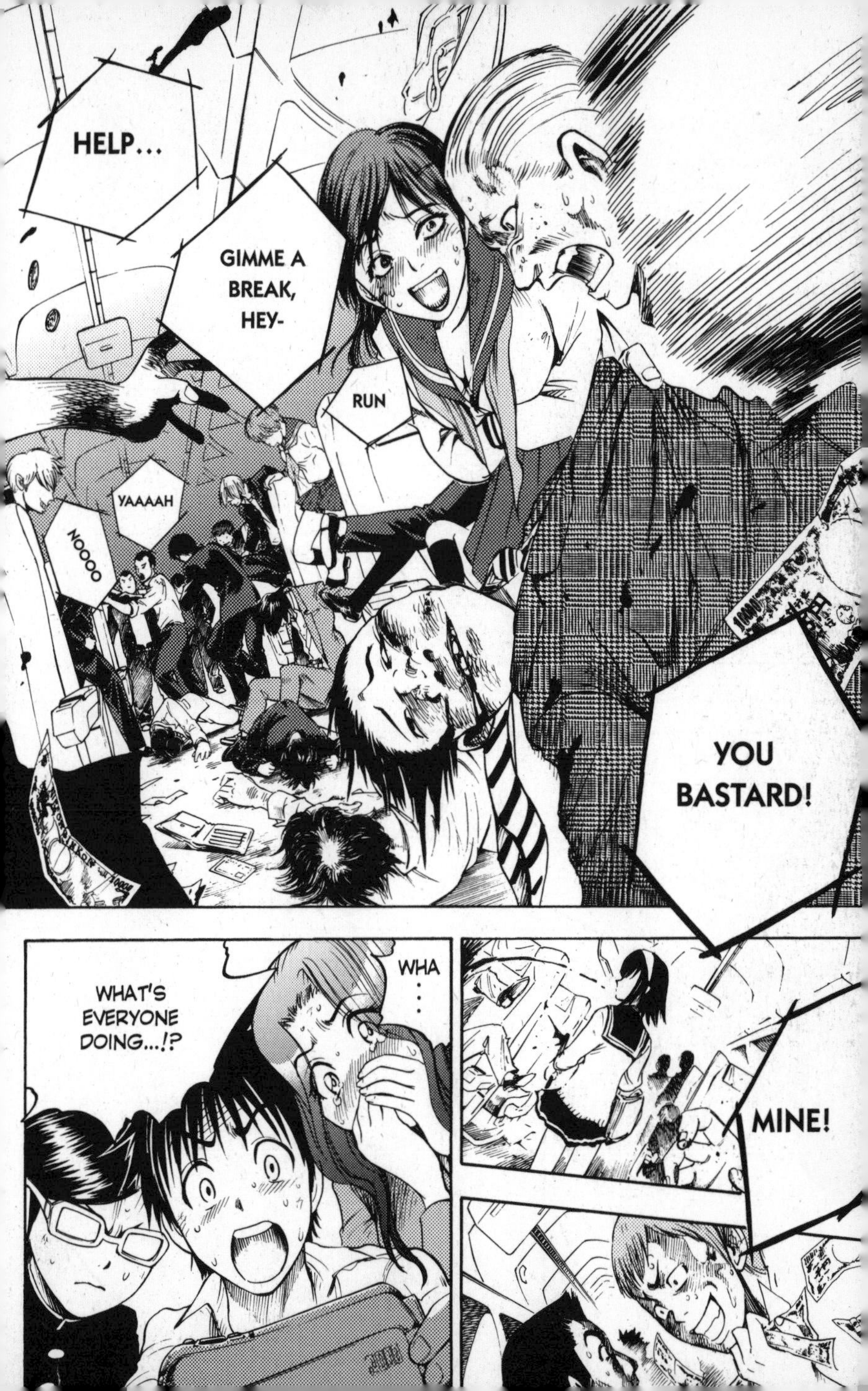
HELP...
GIMME A BREAK, HEY-
RUN
YAAAAH
NOOOO
YOU BASTARD!
MINE!
WHA...
WHAT'S EVERYONE DOING...!?

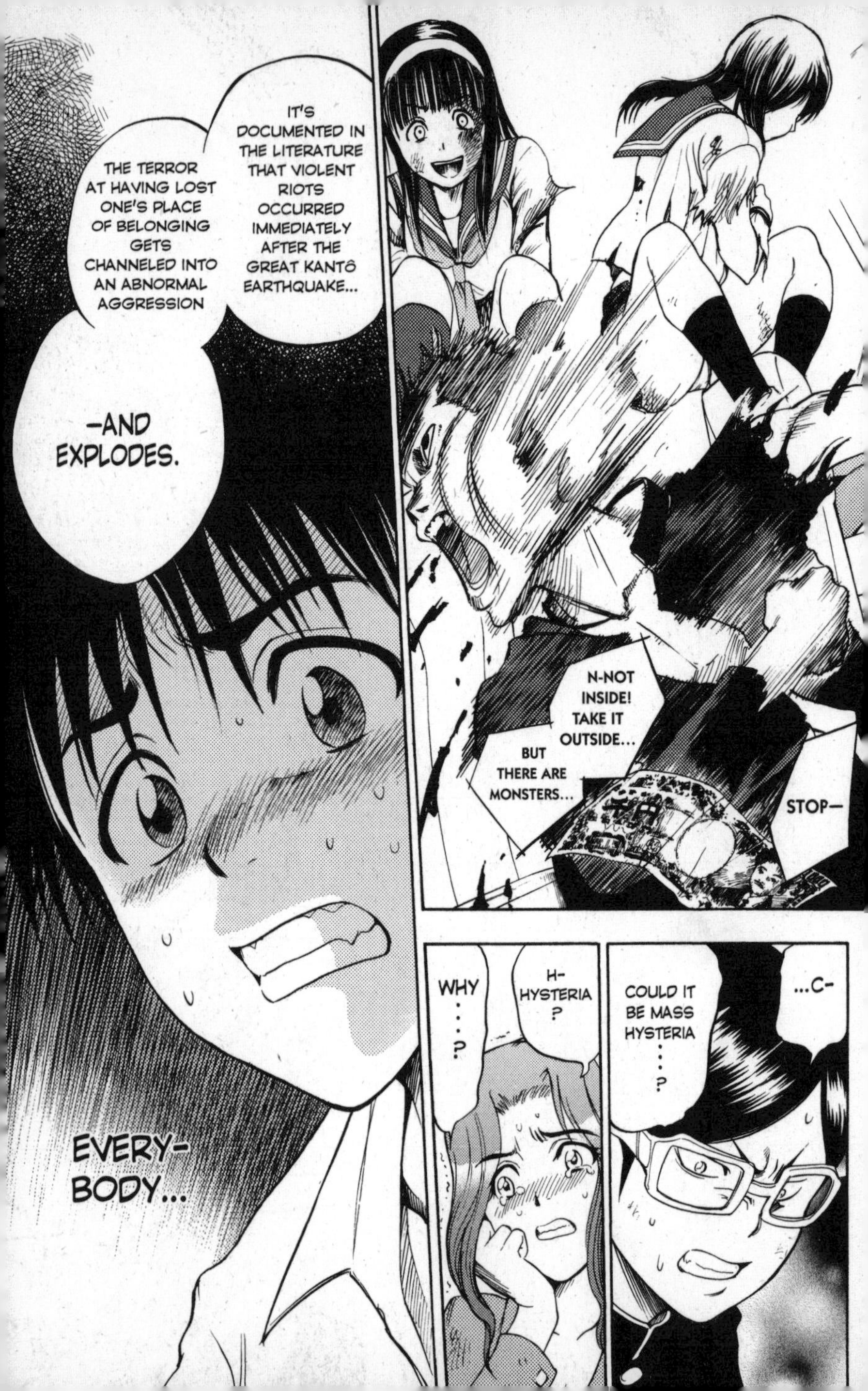
N-NOT INSIDE! TAKE IT OUTSIDE...
BUT THERE ARE MONSTERS...
STOP—
...C-
COULD IT BE MASS HYSTERIA...?
H-HYSTERIA?
WHY...?
IT'S DOCUMENTED IN THE LITERATURE THAT VIOLENT RIOTS OCCURRED IMMEDIATELY AFTER THE GREAT KANTÔ EARTHQUAKE...
THE TERROR AT HAVING LOST ONE'S PLACE OF BELONGING GETS CHANNELED INTO AN ABNORMAL AGGRESSION
–AND EXPLODES.
EVERY-BODY...

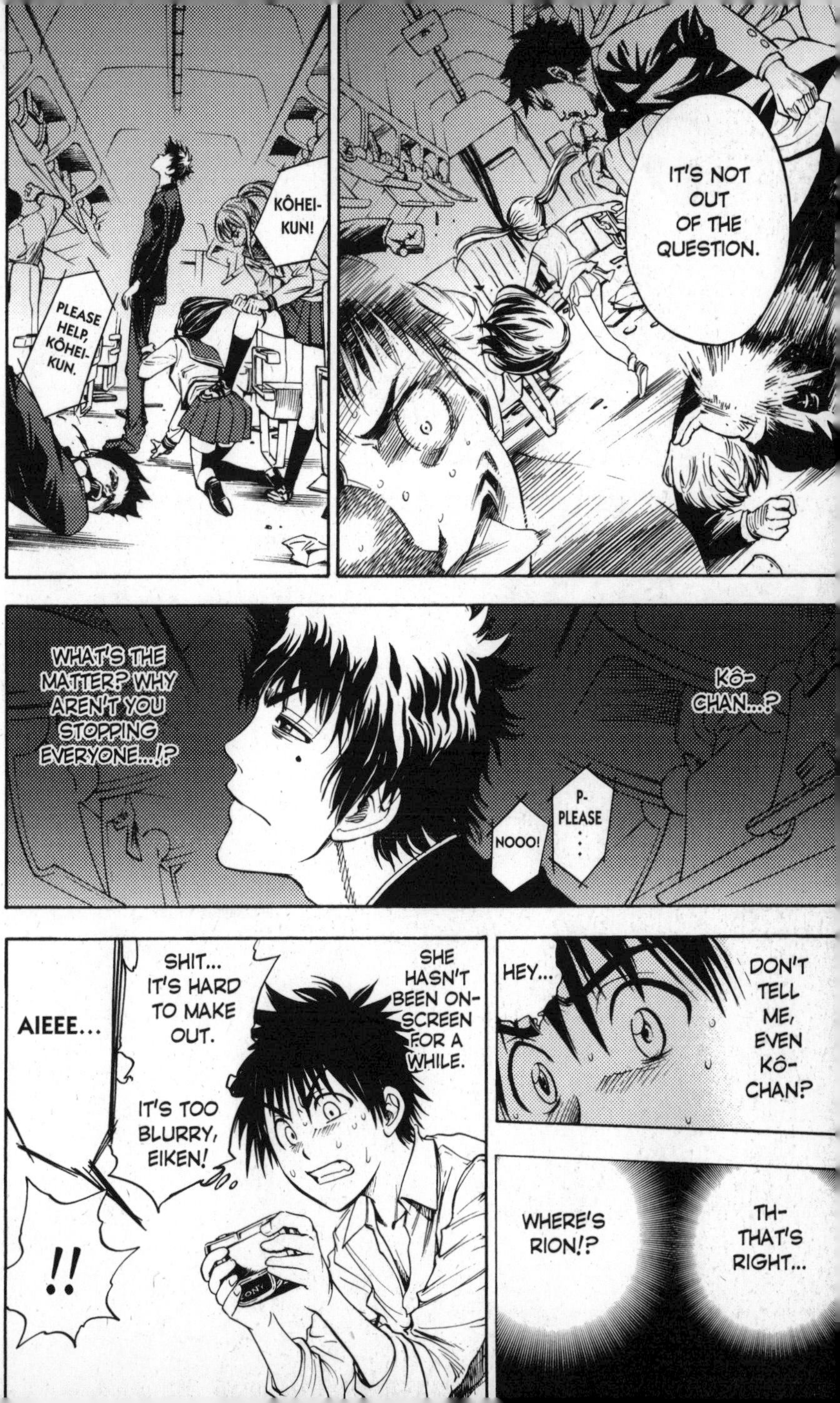
IT'S NOT OUT OF THE QUESTION.
KÔHEI-KUN!
PLEASE HELP, KÔHEI-KUN.
KÔ-CHAN...?
P-PLEASE...
NOOO!
WHAT'S THE MATTER? WHY AREN'T YOU STOPPING EVERYONE...!?
HEY...
DON'T TELL ME, EVEN KÔ-CHAN?
TH-THAT'S RIGHT...
WHERE'S RION!?
SHE HASN'T BEEN ON-SCREEN FOR A WHILE.
SHIT... IT'S HARD TO MAKE OUT.
AIEEE...
IT'S TOO BLURRY, EIKEN!
!!

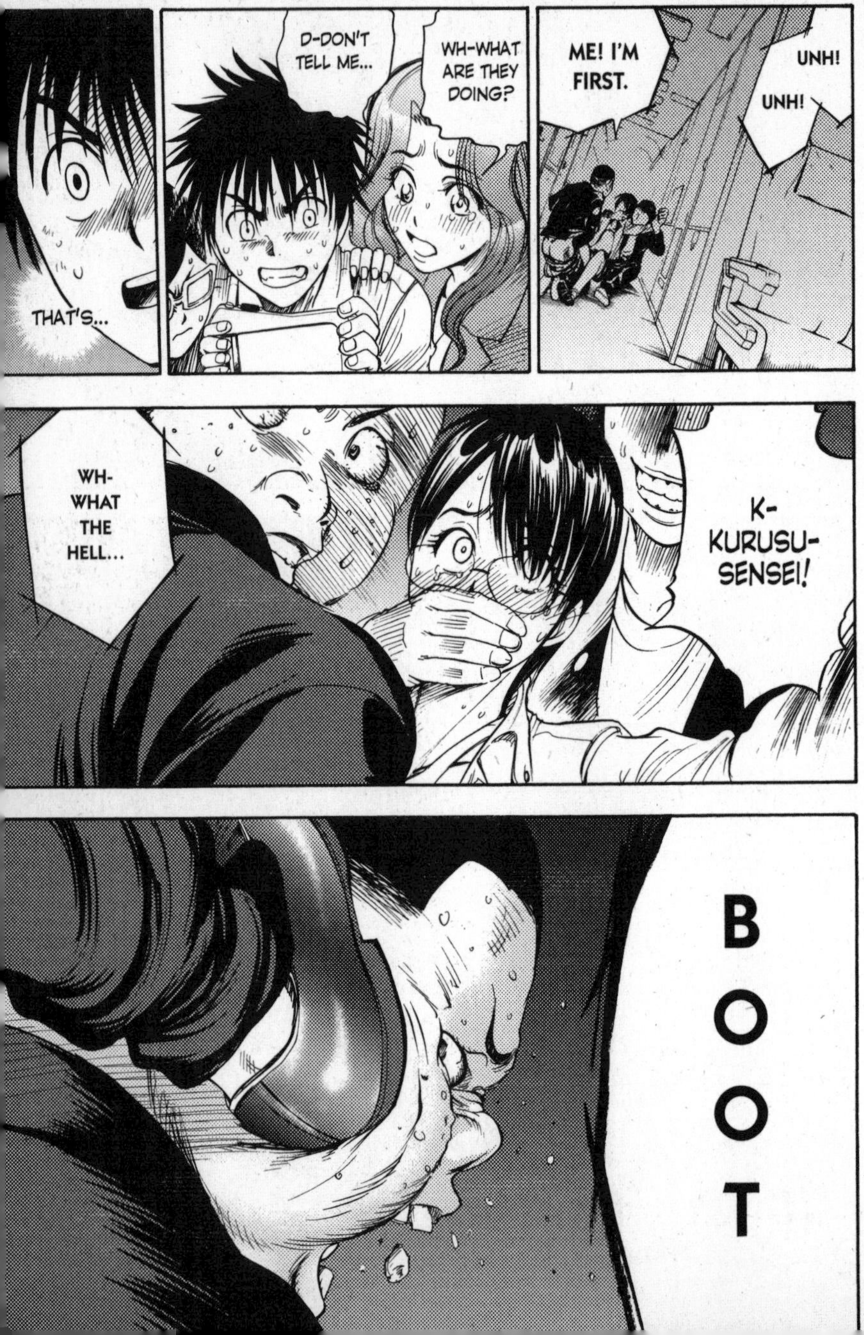
ME! I'M FIRST.
UNH!
UNH!
WH-WHAT ARE THEY DOING?
D-DON'T TELL ME...
THAT'S...
K-KURUSU-SENSEI!
WH-WHAT THE HELL...
BOOT

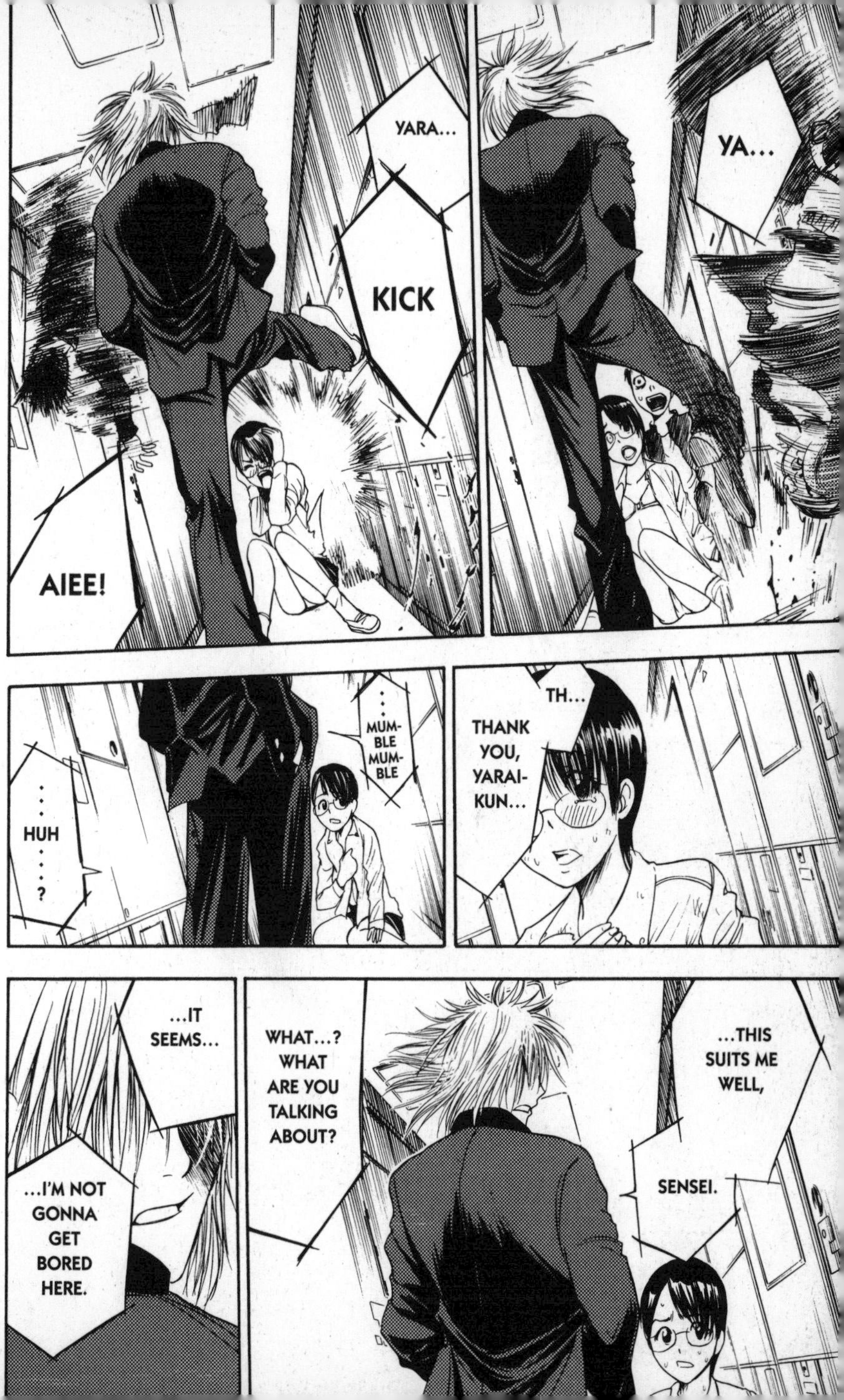
YA...
YARA...
KICK
AIEE!
TH...
THANK YOU, YARAI-KUN...
...MUMBLE MUMBLE
...HUH...?
...THIS SUITS ME WELL,
SENSEI.
WHAT...? WHAT ARE YOU TALKING ABOUT?
...IT SEEMS...
...I'M NOT GONNA GET BORED HERE.

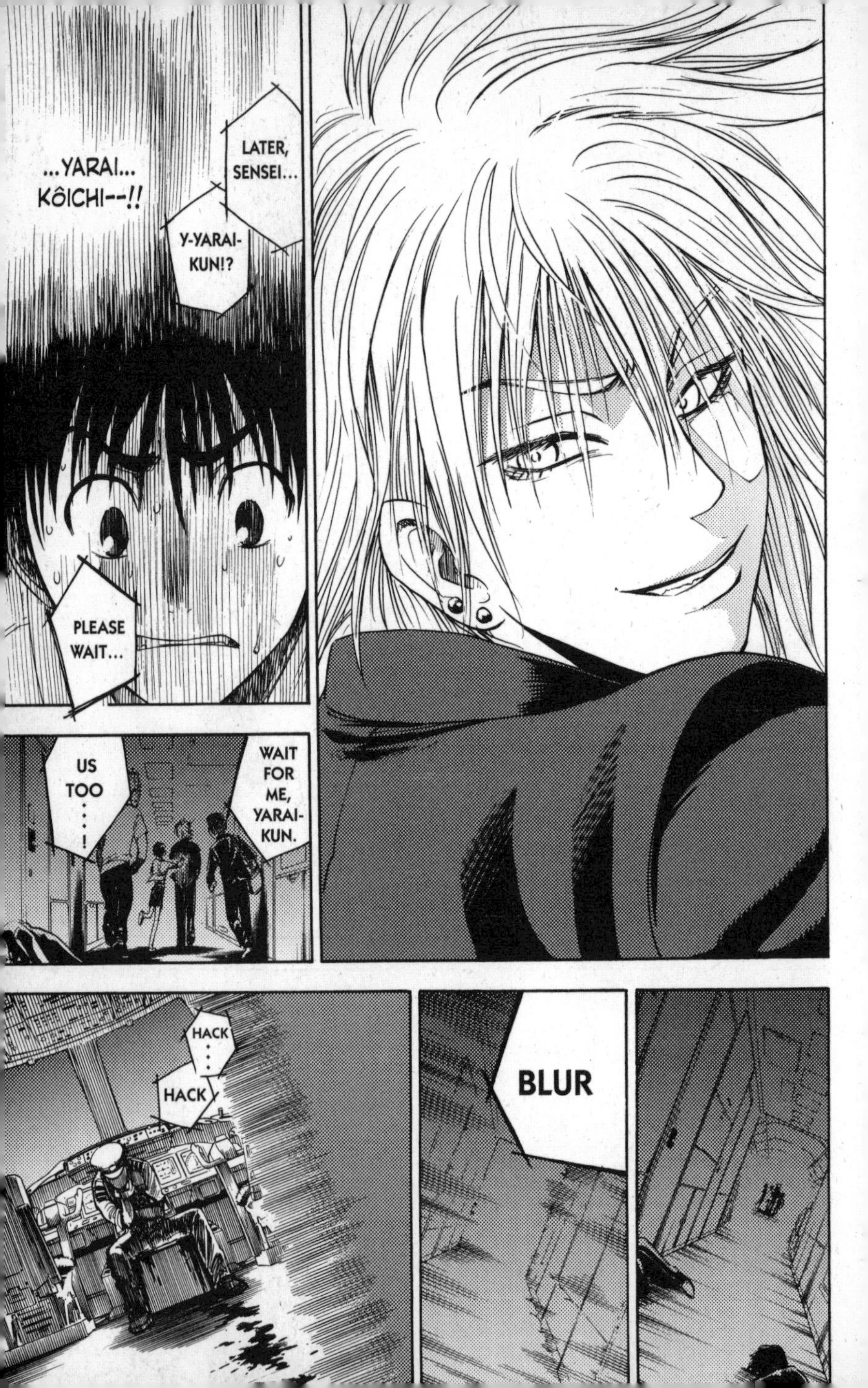

LATER, SENSEI...
Y-YARAI-KUN!?
...YARAI... KÔICHI--!!
PLEASE WAIT...
WAIT FOR ME, YARAI-KUN.
US TOO.....!
BLUR
HACK....
HACK

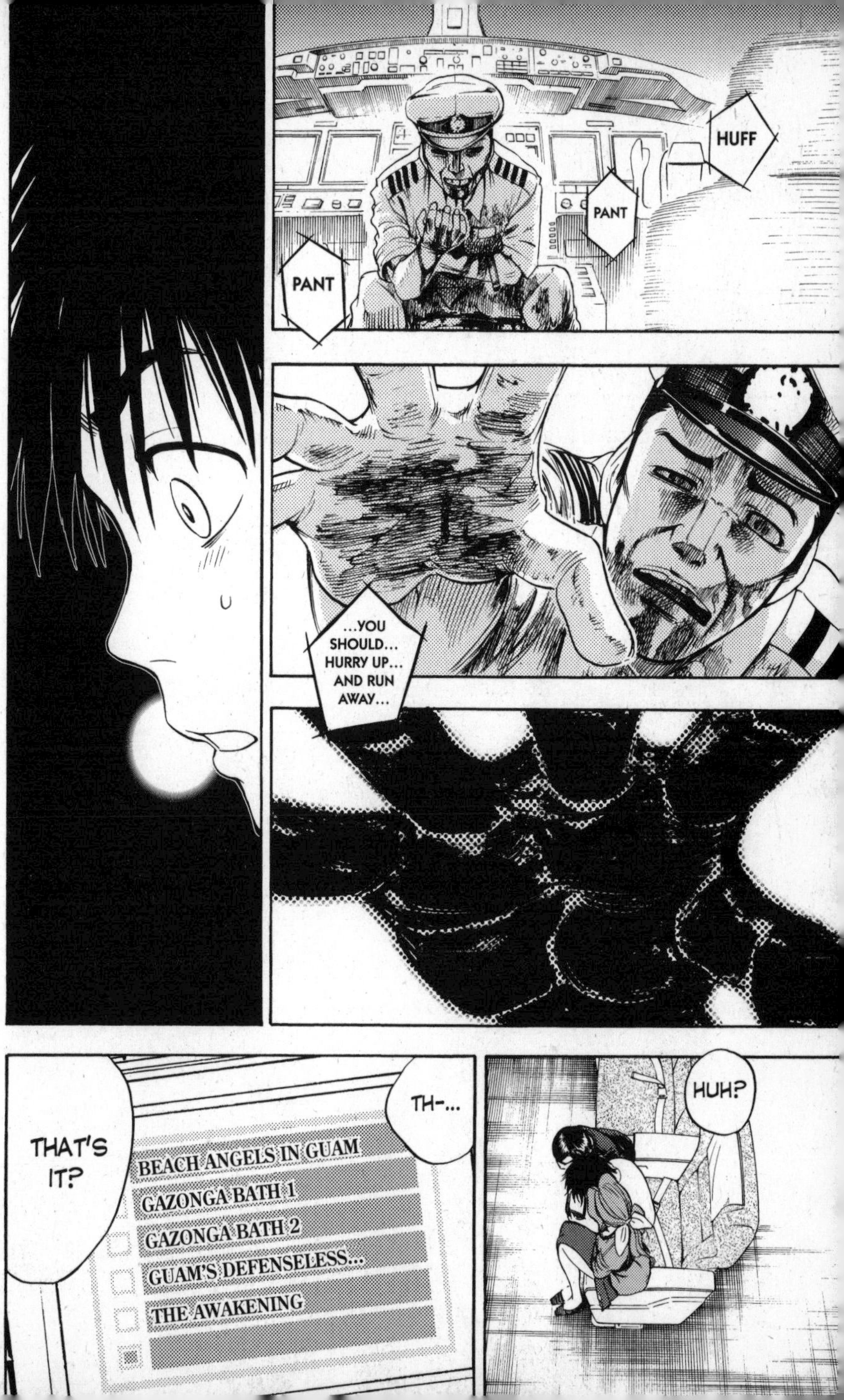
HUFF
PANT
PANT
...YOU SHOULD... HURRY UP... AND RUN AWAY...
HUH?
TH-...
THAT'S IT?
BEACH ANGELS IN GUAM
GAZONGA BATH 1
GAZONGA BATH 2
GUAM'S DEFENSELESS...
THE AWAKENING

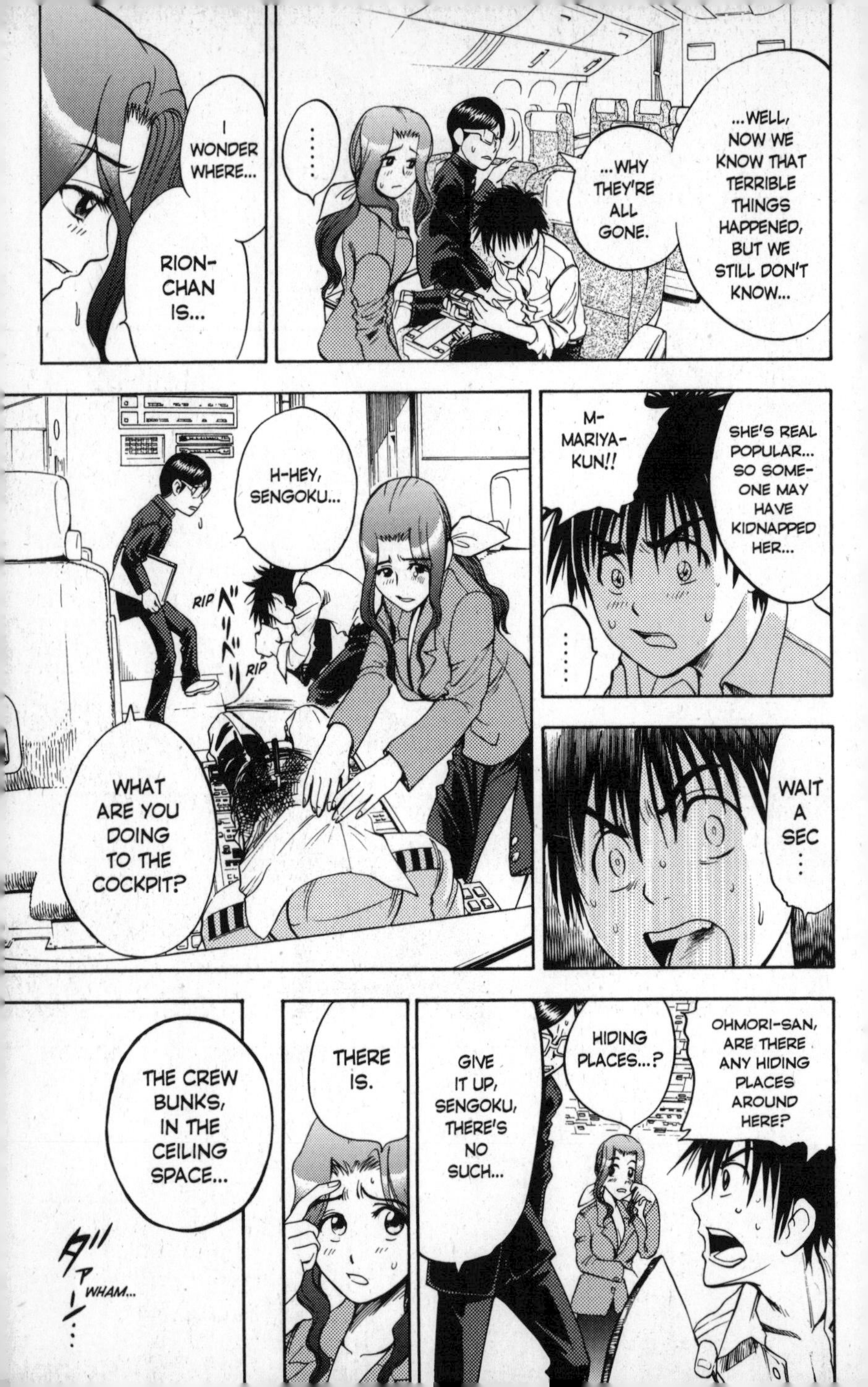
...WELL, NOW WE KNOW THAT TERRIBLE THINGS HAPPENED, BUT WE STILL DON'T KNOW...
...WHY THEY'RE ALL GONE.
......
I WONDER WHERE...
RION-CHAN IS...
SHE'S REAL POPULAR... SO SOME-ONE MAY HAVE KIDNAPPED HER...
M-MARIYA-KUN!!
......
WAIT A SEC...
H-HEY, SENGOKU...
RIP
RIP
WHAT ARE YOU DOING TO THE COCKPIT?
OHMORI-SAN, ARE THERE ANY HIDING PLACES AROUND HERE?
HIDING PLACES...?
GIVE IT UP, SENGOKU, THERE'S NO SUCH...
THERE IS.
THE CREW BUNKS, IN THE CEILING SPACE...
WHAM...

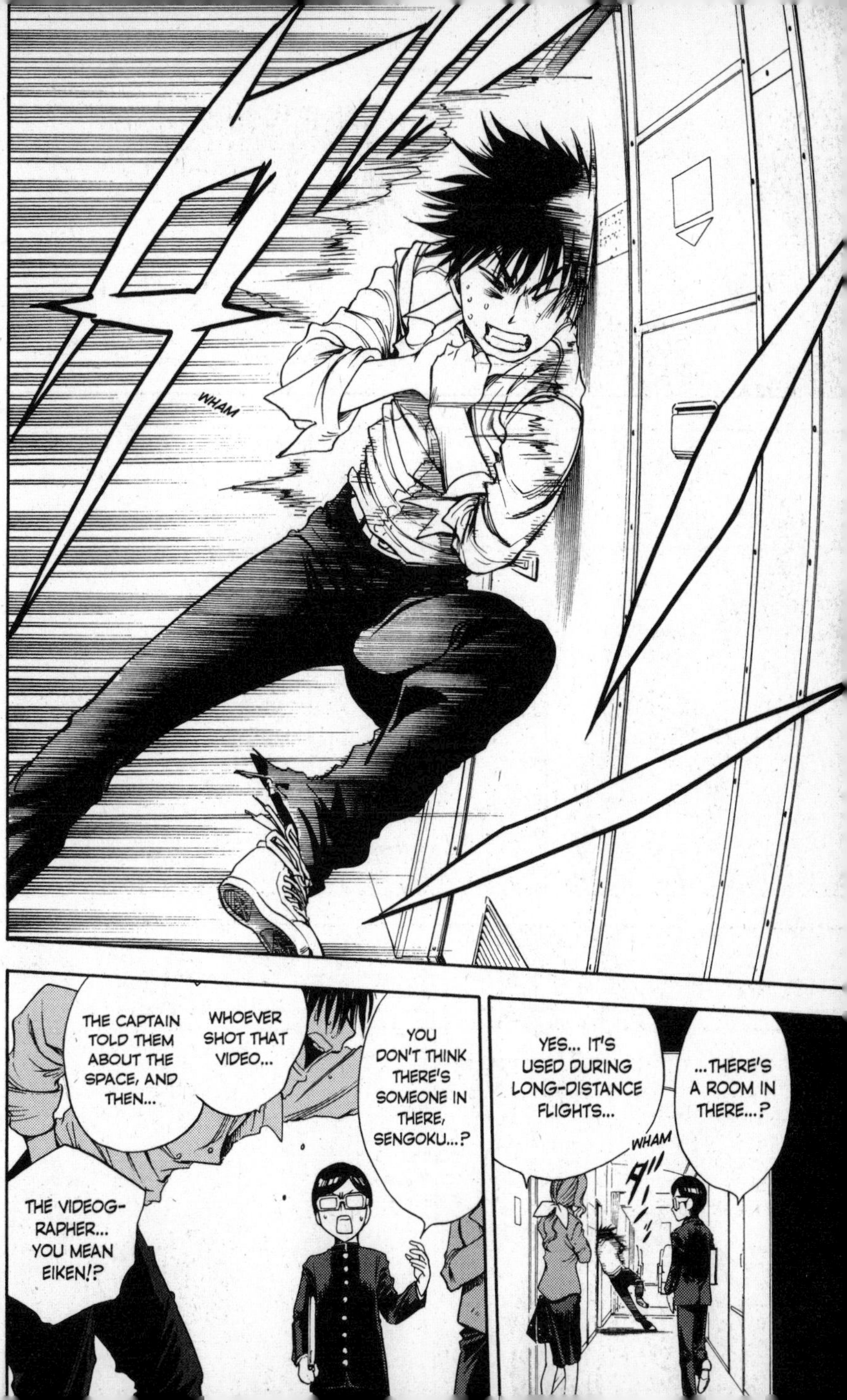
WHAM
...THERE'S A ROOM IN THERE...?
YES... IT'S USED DURING LONG-DISTANCE FLIGHTS...
WHAM
YOU DON'T THINK THERE'S SOMEONE IN THERE, SENGOKU...?
WHOEVER SHOT THAT VIDEO...
THE CAPTAIN TOLD THEM ABOUT THE SPACE, AND THEN...
THE VIDEOG-RAPHER... YOU MEAN EIKEN!?

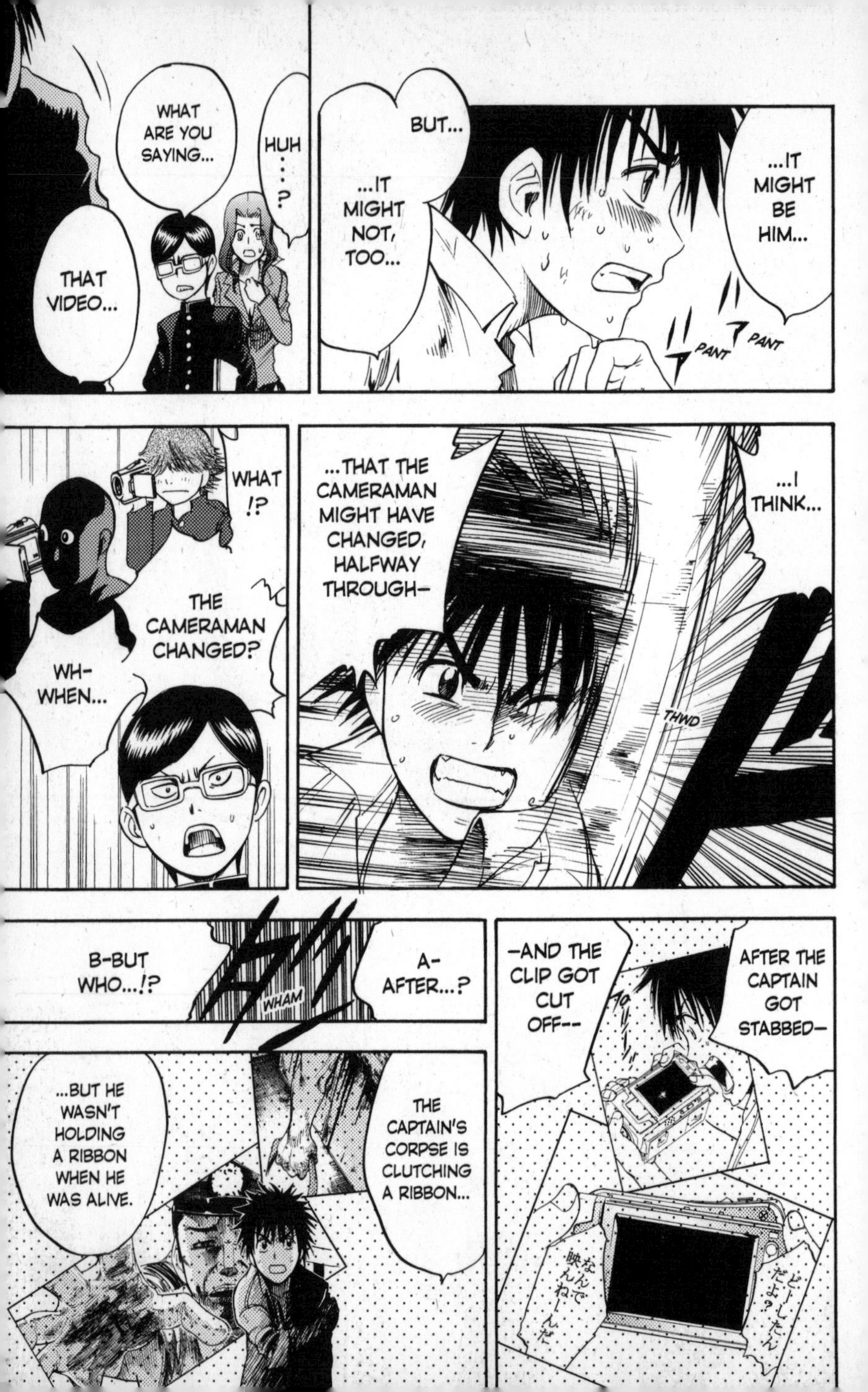
...IT MIGHT BE HIM...
BUT...
...IT MIGHT NOT, TOO...
PANT PANT
HUH...?
WHAT ARE YOU SAYING...
THAT VIDEO...
...I THINK...
...THAT THE CAMERAMAN MIGHT HAVE CHANGED, HALFWAY THROUGH-
THWD
WHAT !?
THE CAMERAMAN CHANGED?
WH- WHEN...
AFTER THE CAPTAIN GOT STABBED-
-AND THE CLIP GOT CUT OFF--
どーしたんだよ？
なんで映んねーんだ
A- AFTER...?
WHAM
B-BUT WHO...!?
THE CAPTAIN'S CORPSE IS CLUTCHING A RIBBON...
...BUT HE WASN'T HOLDING A RIBBON WHEN HE WAS ALIVE.

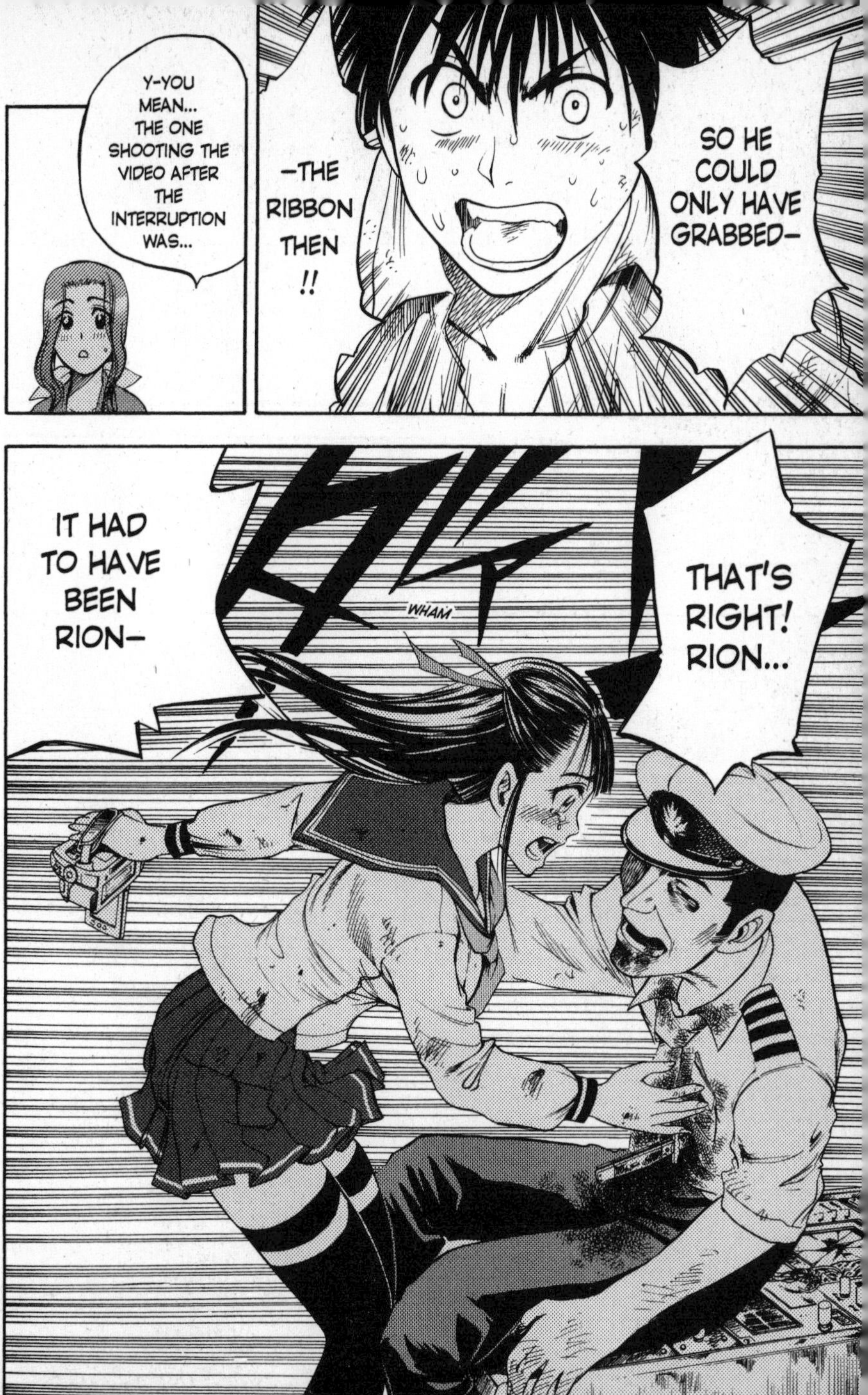
SO HE COULD ONLY HAVE GRABBED–
–THE RIBBON THEN !!
Y-YOU MEAN... THE ONE SHOOTING THE VIDEO AFTER THE INTERRUPTION WAS...
THAT'S RIGHT! RION...
WHAM
IT HAD TO HAVE BEEN RION–

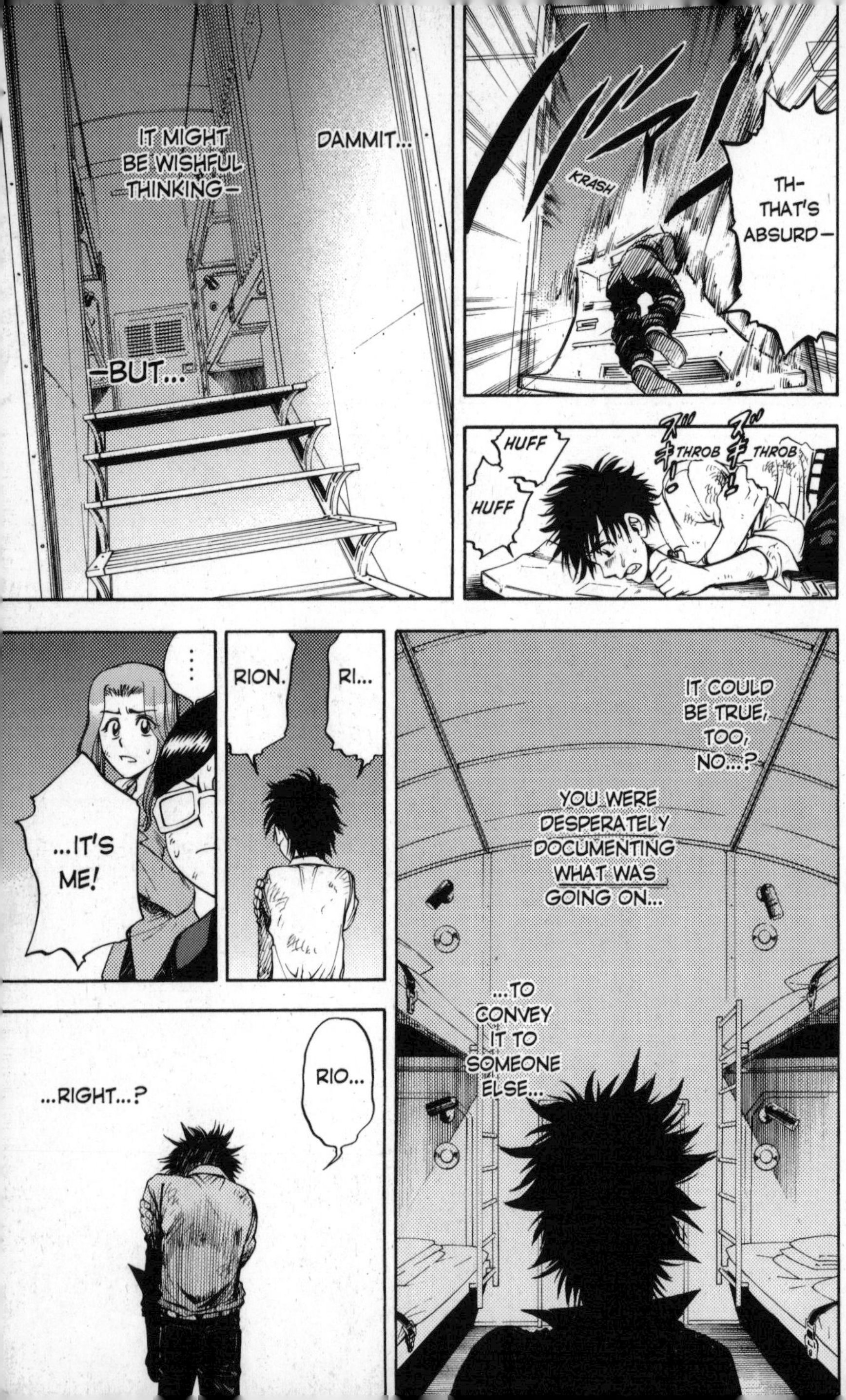
TH- THAT'S ABSURD—
KRASH
THROB THROB
HUFF HUFF
DAMMIT...
IT MIGHT BE WISHFUL THINKING—
—BUT...
IT COULD BE TRUE, TOO, NO...?
YOU WERE DESPERATELY DOCUMENTING WHAT WAS GOING ON...
...TO CONVEY IT TO SOMEONE ELSE...
RI...
RION.
....
...IT'S ME!
RIO...
...RIGHT...?

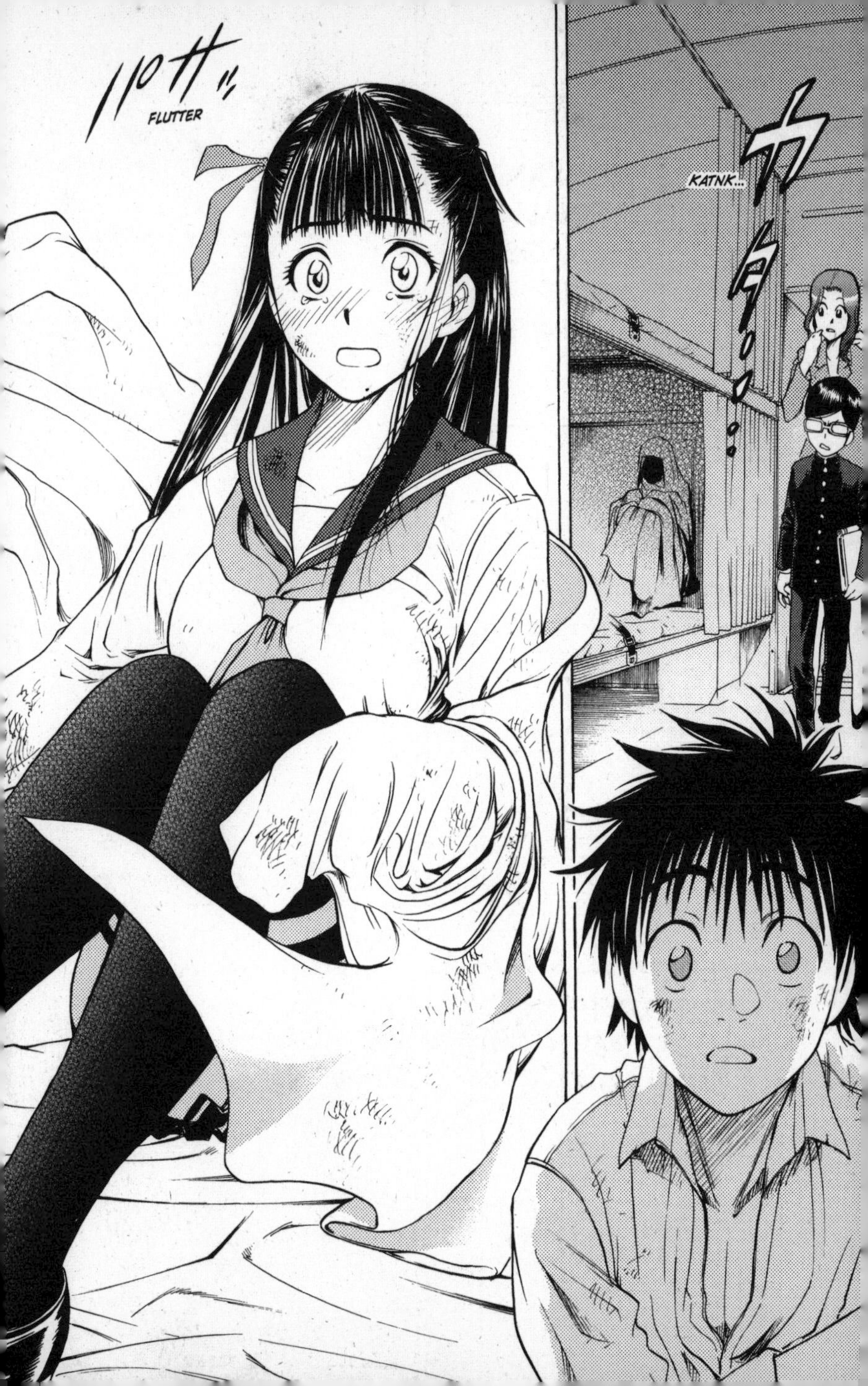
KATNK...
FLUTTER

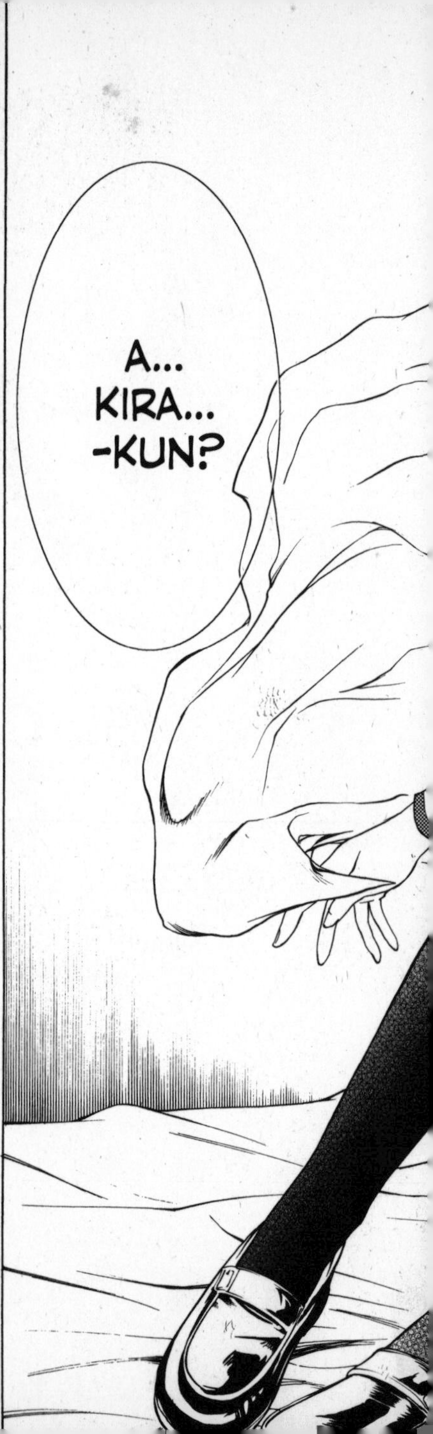
A... KIRA... -KUN?

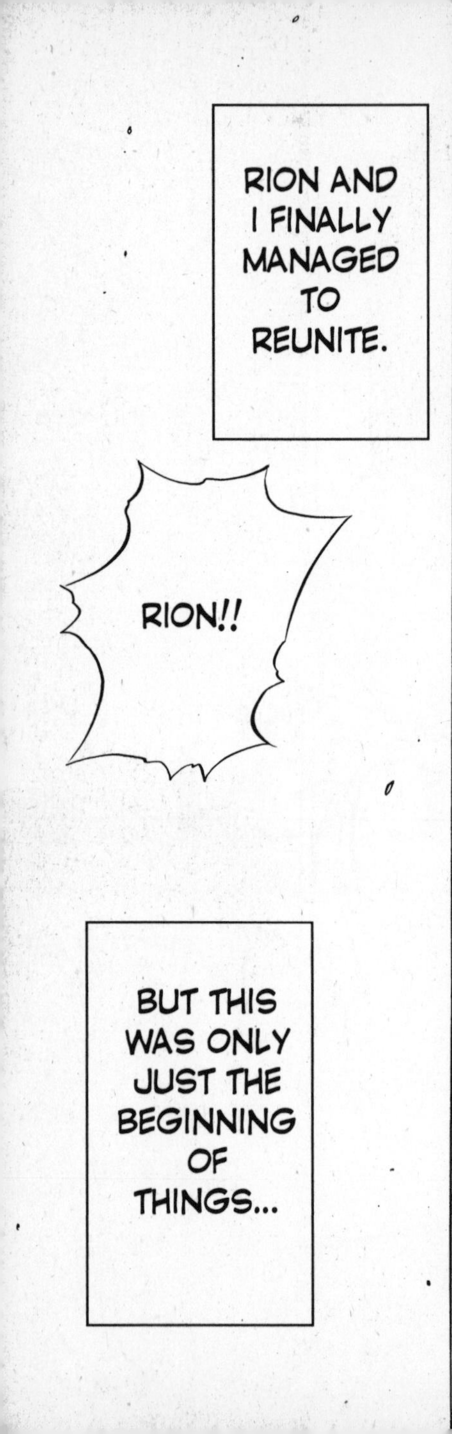
RION AND I FINALLY MANAGED TO REUNITE.
RION!!
BUT THIS WAS ONLY JUST THE BEGINNING OF THINGS...

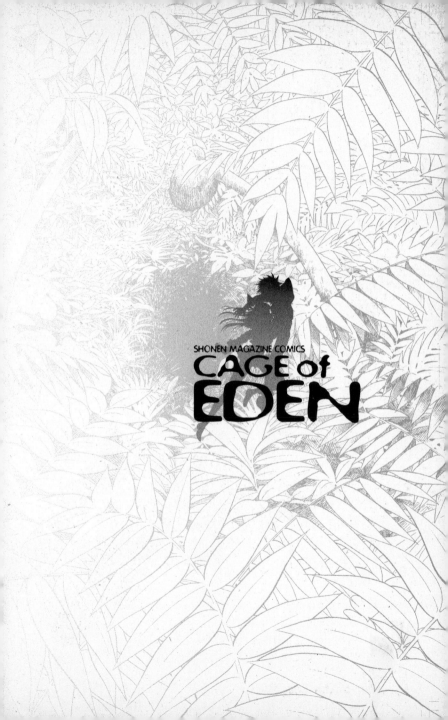

SHONEN MAGAZINE COMICS

CAGE of EDEN

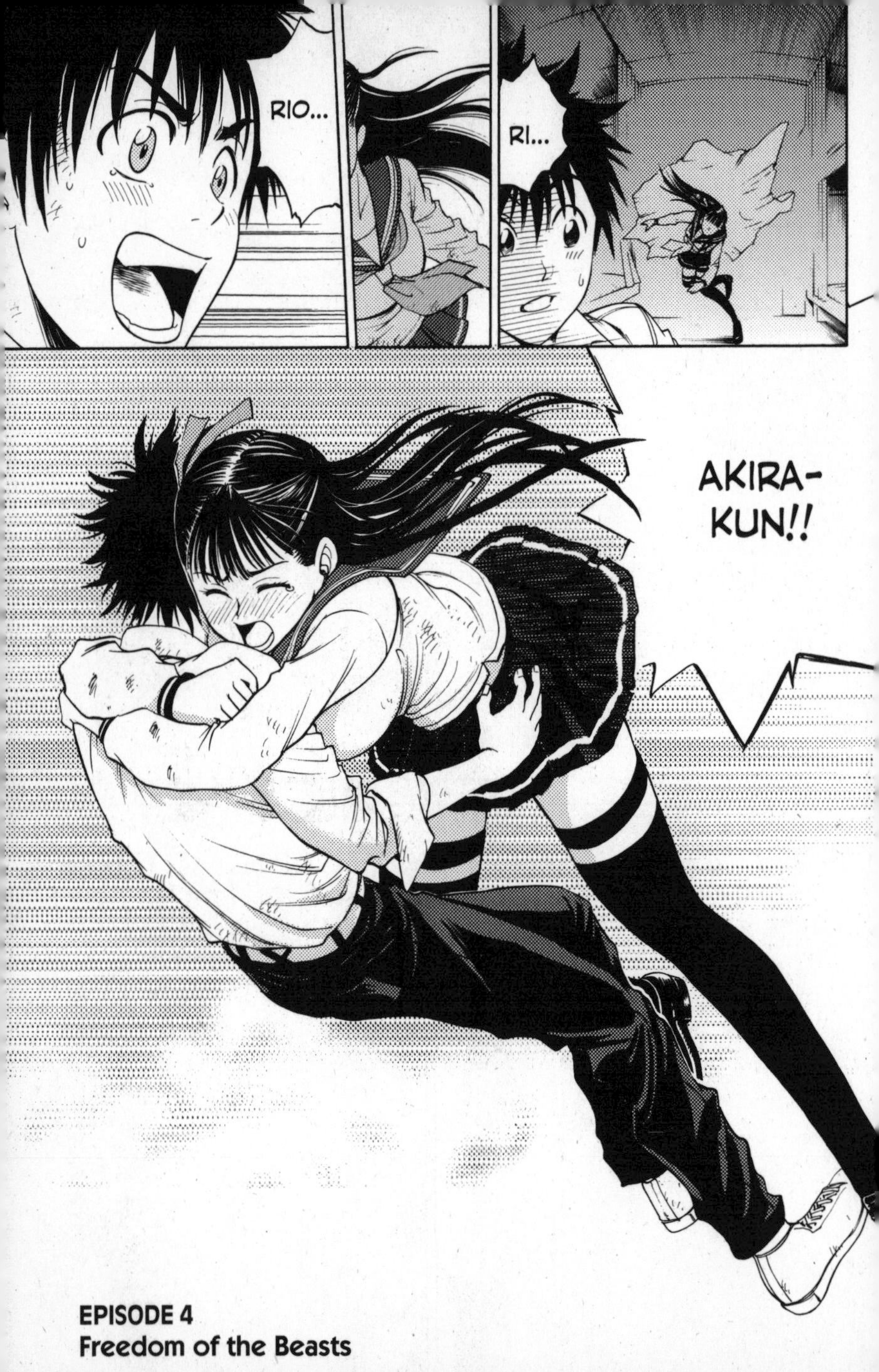
RI...
RIO...
AKIRA-KUN!!

EPISODE 4
Freedom of the Beasts

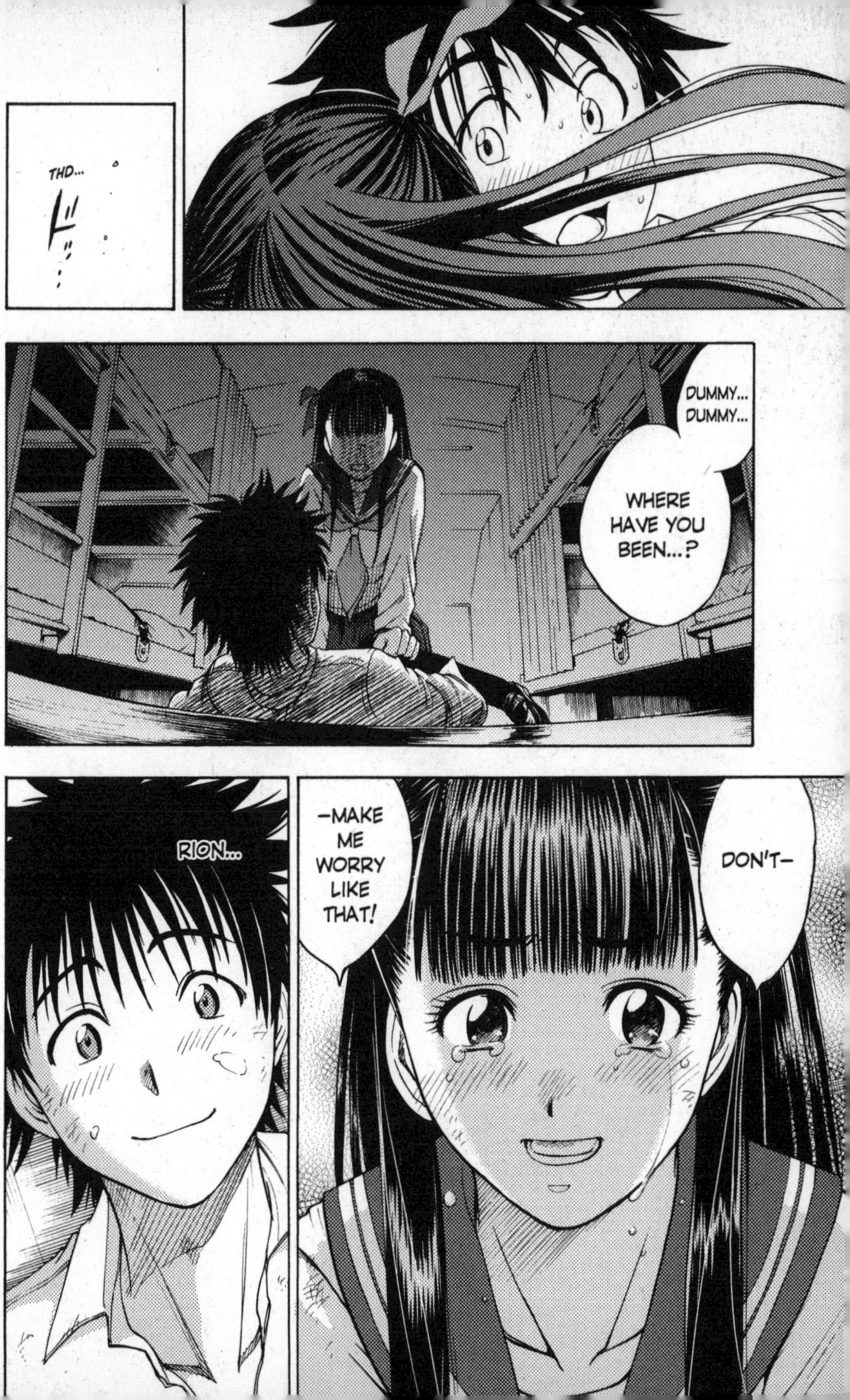
THD...
ドッ
DUMMY... DUMMY...
WHERE HAVE YOU BEEN...?
DON'T-
-MAKE ME WORRY LIKE THAT!
RION...

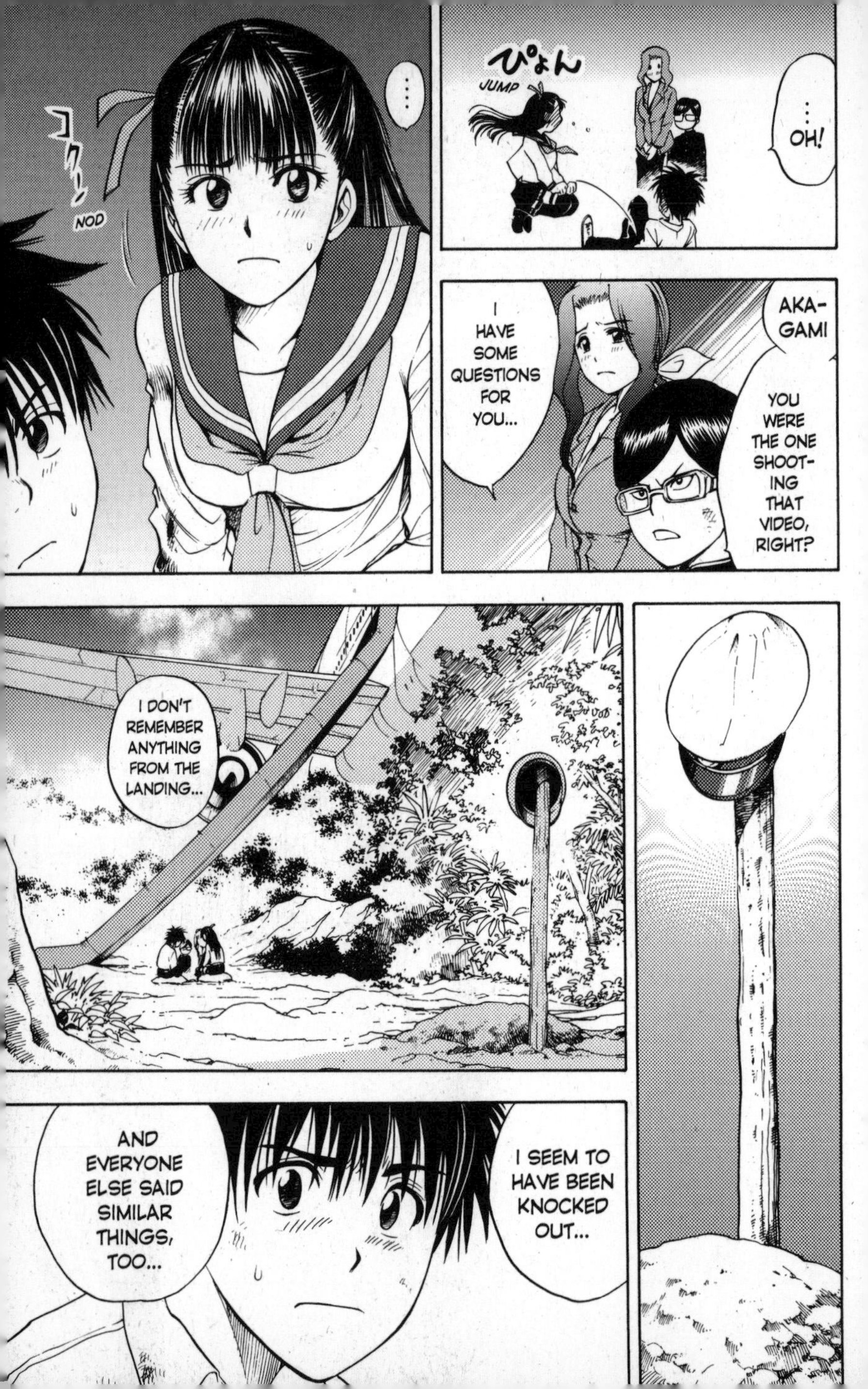

...OH!
ぴょん
JUMP
AKA-GAMI!
YOU WERE THE ONE SHOOTING THAT VIDEO, RIGHT?
I HAVE SOME QUESTIONS FOR YOU...
...
コクーン
NOD
I DON'T REMEMBER ANYTHING FROM THE LANDING...
I SEEM TO HAVE BEEN KNOCKED OUT...
AND EVERYONE ELSE SAID SIMILAR THINGS, TOO...

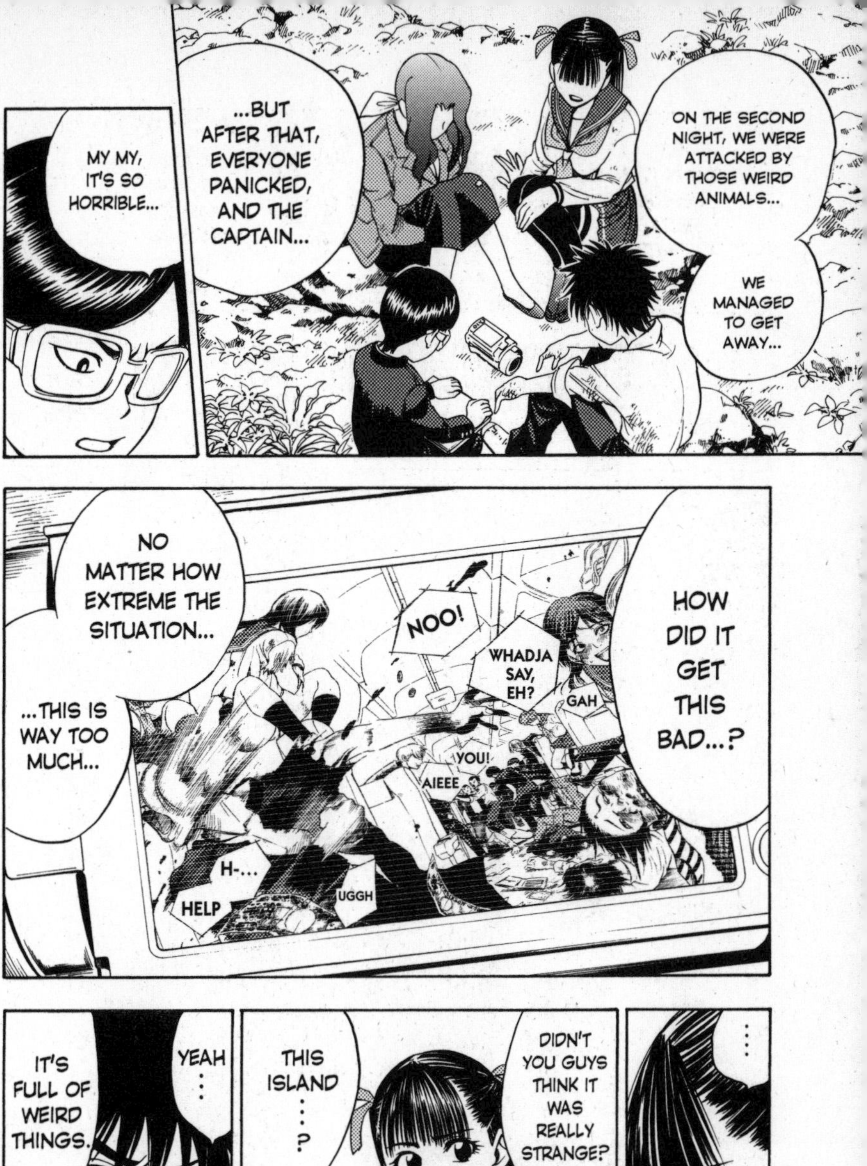
ON THE SECOND NIGHT, WE WERE ATTACKED BY THOSE WEIRD ANIMALS...
WE MANAGED TO GET AWAY...
...BUT AFTER THAT, EVERYONE PANICKED, AND THE CAPTAIN...
MY MY, IT'S SO HORRIBLE...
HOW DID IT GET THIS BAD...?
NOO!
WHADJA SAY, EH?
GAH
YOU!
AIEEE
UGGH
H-...
HELP
NO MATTER HOW EXTREME THE SITUATION...
...THIS IS WAY TOO MUCH...
...
DIDN'T YOU GUYS THINK IT WAS REALLY STRANGE?
THIS ISLAND...?
YEAH...
IT'S FULL OF WEIRD THINGS.

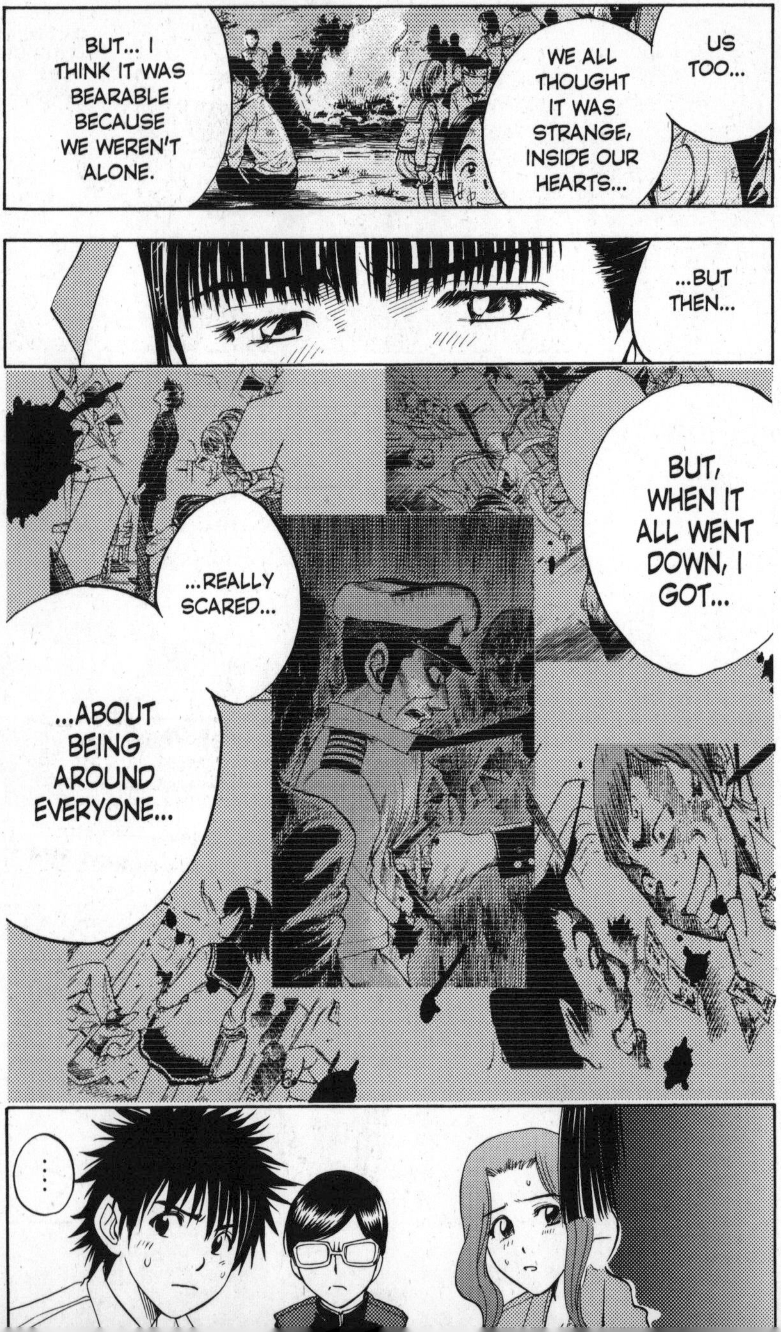
US TOO...
WE ALL THOUGHT IT WAS STRANGE, INSIDE OUR HEARTS...
BUT... I THINK IT WAS BEARABLE BECAUSE WE WEREN'T ALONE.
...BUT THEN...
BUT, WHEN IT ALL WENT DOWN, I GOT...
...REALLY SCARED...
...ABOUT BEING AROUND EVERYONE...
....

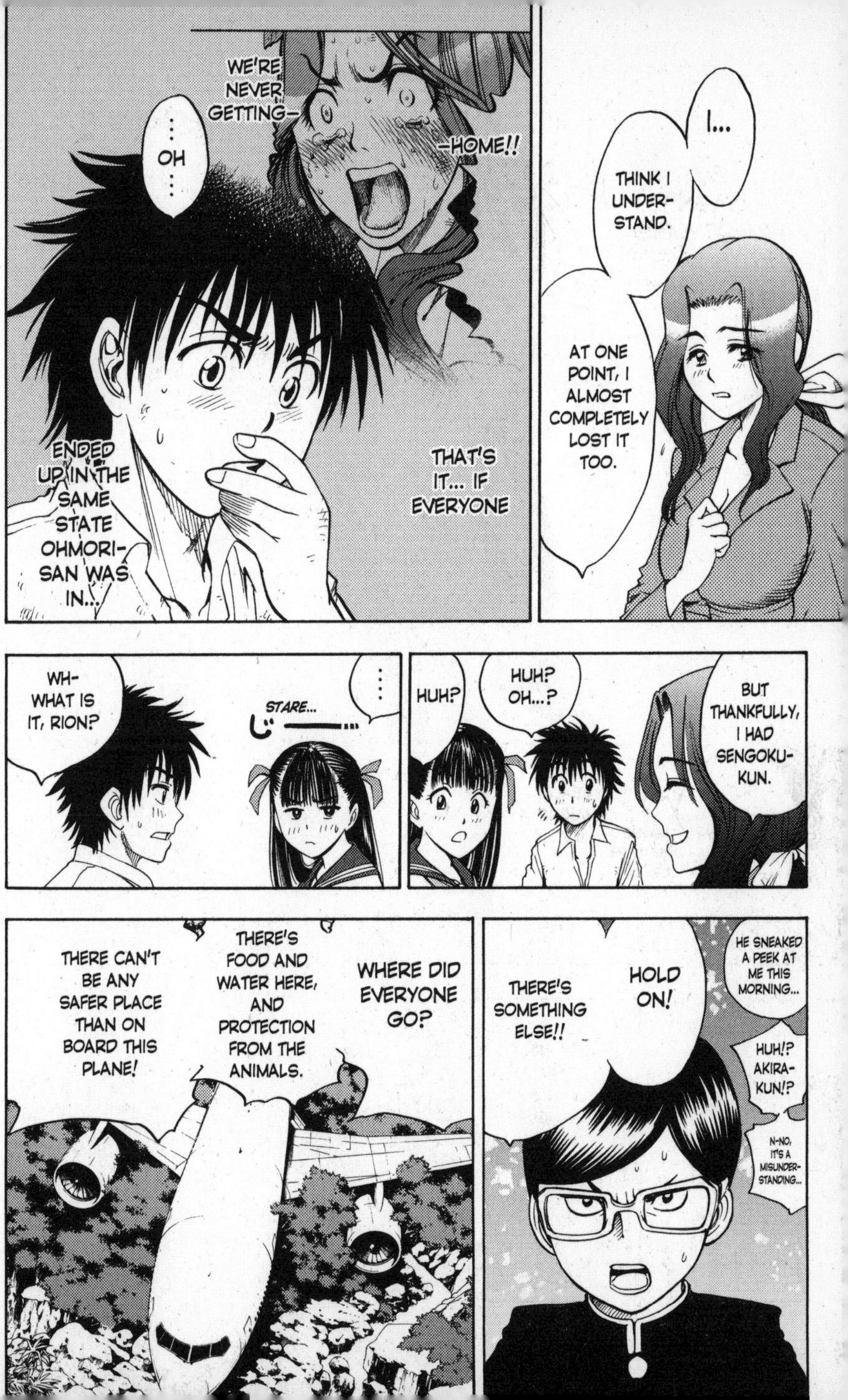
I...
THINK I UNDER-STAND.
AT ONE POINT, I ALMOST COMPLETELY LOST IT TOO.
THAT'S IT... IF EVERYONE
ENDED UP IN THE SAME STATE OHMORI-SAN WAS IN...
WE'RE NEVER GETTING-
-HOME!!
...OH...
BUT THANKFULLY, I HAD SENGOKU-KUN.
HUH? OH...?
HUH?
....
STARE...
じーー…
WH-WHAT IS IT, RION?
HE SNEAKED A PEEK AT ME THIS MORNING...
HUH!? AKIRA-KUN!?
N-NO, IT'S A MISUNDER-STANDING...
HOLD ON!
THERE'S SOMETHING ELSE!!
WHERE DID EVERYONE GO?
THERE'S FOOD AND WATER HERE, AND PROTECTION FROM THE ANIMALS.
THERE CAN'T BE ANY SAFER PLACE THAN ON BOARD THIS PLANE!

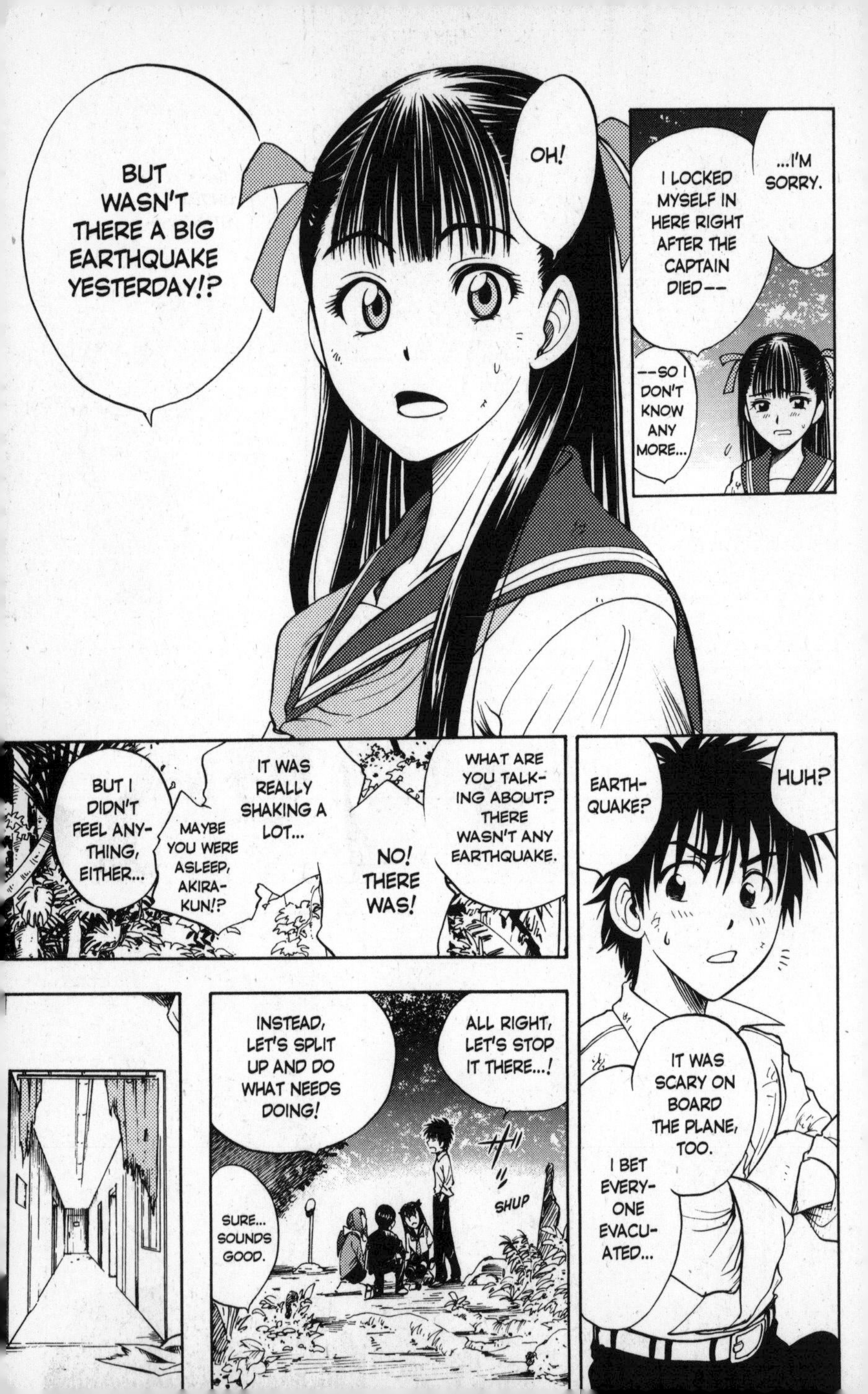
...I'M SORRY.
I LOCKED MYSELF IN HERE RIGHT AFTER THE CAPTAIN DIED--
--SO I DON'T KNOW ANY MORE...
OH!
BUT WASN'T THERE A BIG EARTHQUAKE YESTERDAY!?
HUH?
EARTH-QUAKE?
IT WAS SCARY ON BOARD THE PLANE, TOO.
I BET EVERY-ONE EVACU-ATED...
WHAT ARE YOU TALK-ING ABOUT? THERE WASN'T ANY EARTHQUAKE.
NO! THERE WAS!
IT WAS REALLY SHAKING A LOT...
MAYBE YOU WERE ASLEEP, AKIRA-KUN!?
BUT I DIDN'T FEEL ANY-THING, EITHER...
ALL RIGHT, LET'S STOP IT THERE...!
INSTEAD, LET'S SPLIT UP AND DO WHAT NEEDS DOING!
SHUP
SURE... SOUNDS GOOD.

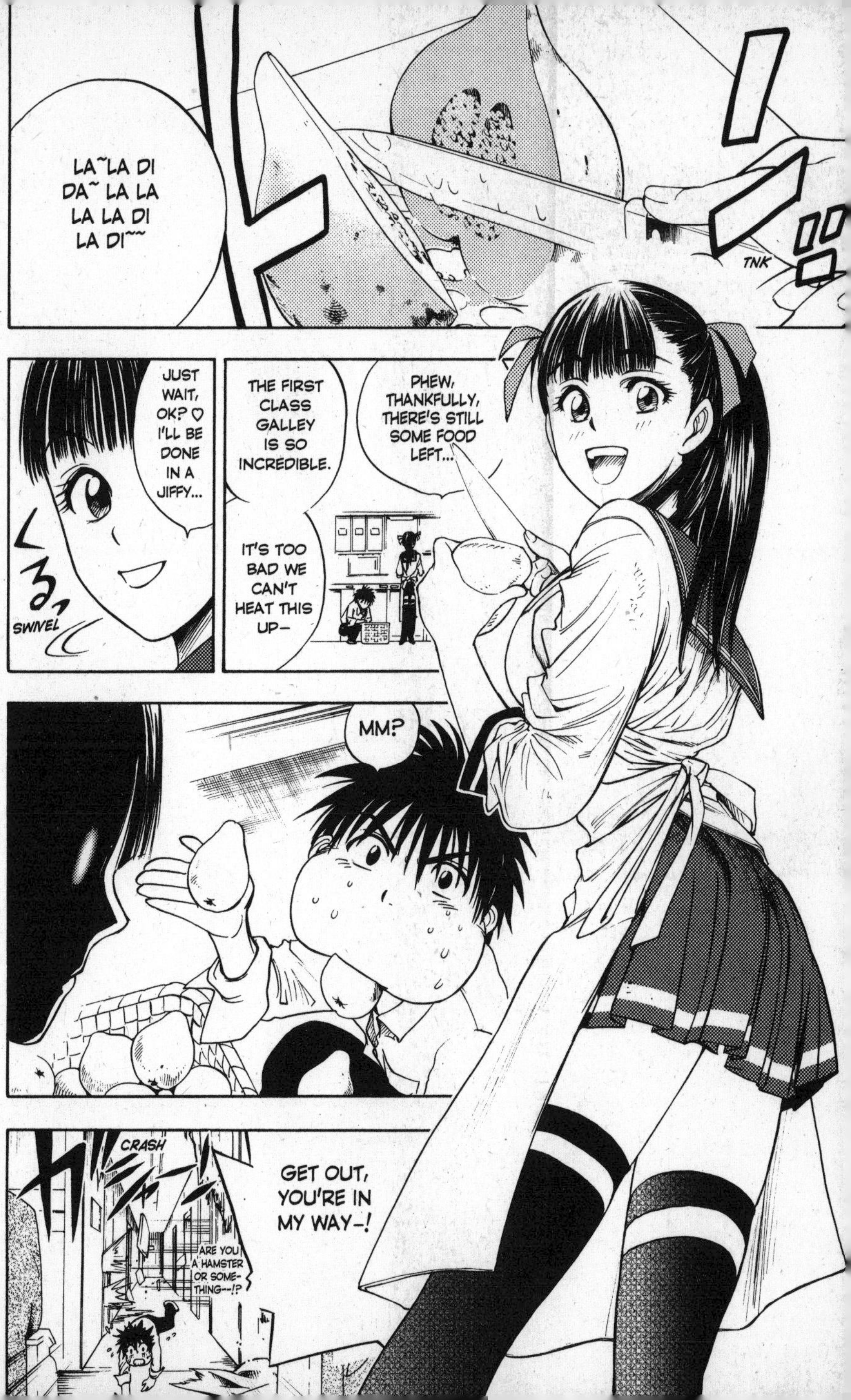

TNK
LA~LA DI DA~ LA LA LA LA DI LA DI~~
PHEW, THANKFULLY, THERE'S STILL SOME FOOD LEFT...
THE FIRST CLASS GALLEY IS SO INCREDIBLE.
IT'S TOO BAD WE CAN'T HEAT THIS UP–
JUST WAIT, OK? ♡ I'LL BE DONE IN A JIFFY...
SWIVEL
MM?
GET OUT, YOU'RE IN MY WAY–!
CRASH
ARE YOU A HAMSTER OR SOME-THING--!?

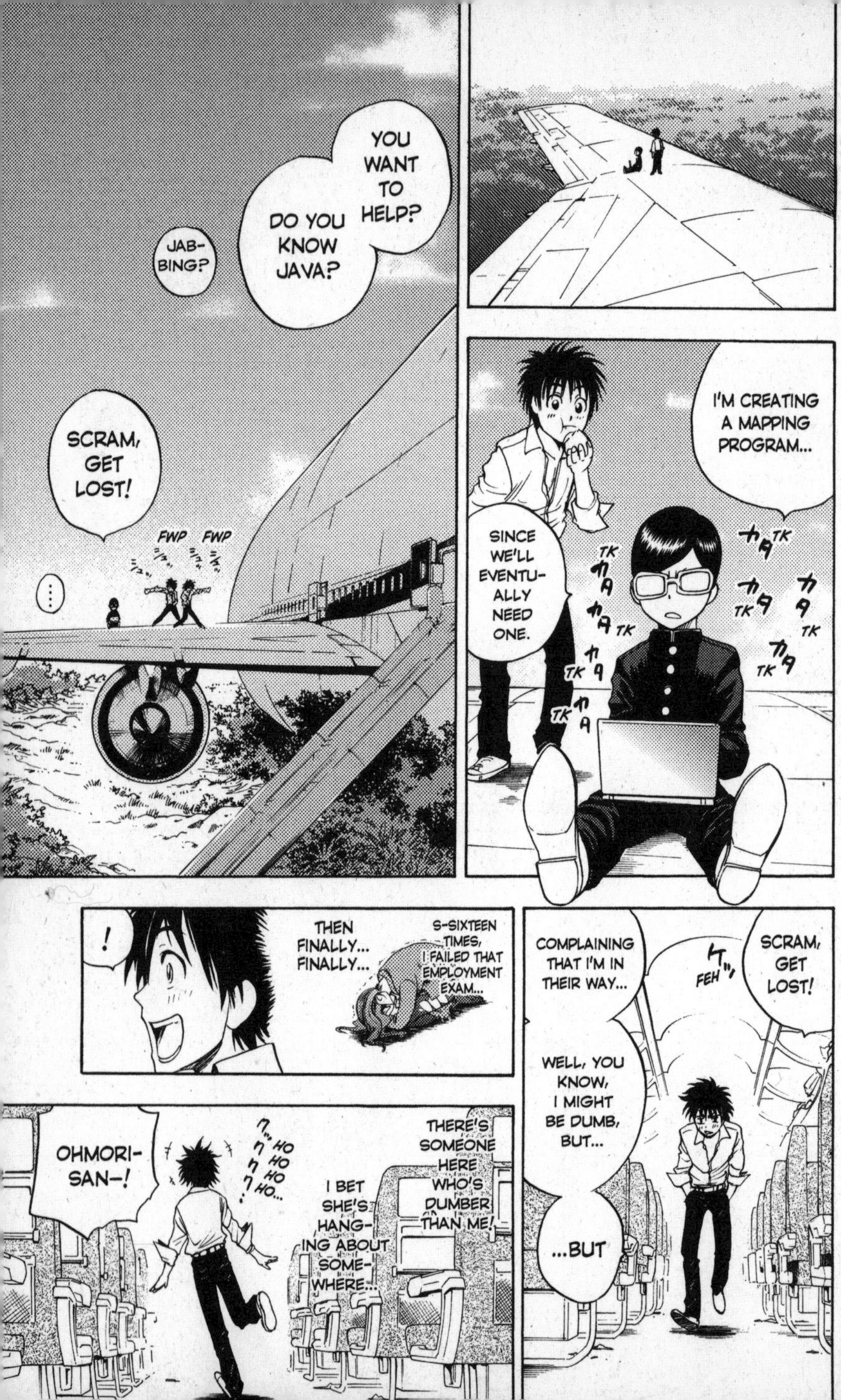
I'M CREATING A MAPPING PROGRAM...
TK TK TK TK TK TK TK TK TK
SINCE WE'LL EVENTU-ALLY NEED ONE.
YOU WANT TO HELP?
DO YOU KNOW JAVA?
JAB-BING?
SCRAM, GET LOST!
FWP FWP
...
SCRAM, GET LOST!
FEH
COMPLAINING THAT I'M IN THEIR WAY...
WELL, YOU KNOW, I MIGHT BE DUMB, BUT...
...BUT
S-SIXTEEN TIMES, I FAILED THAT EMPLOYMENT EXAM...
THEN FINALLY... FINALLY...
!
THERE'S SOMEONE HERE WHO'S DUMBER THAN ME!
I BET SHE'S HANG-ING ABOUT SOME-WHERE...
HO HO HO HO...
OHMORI-SAN-!

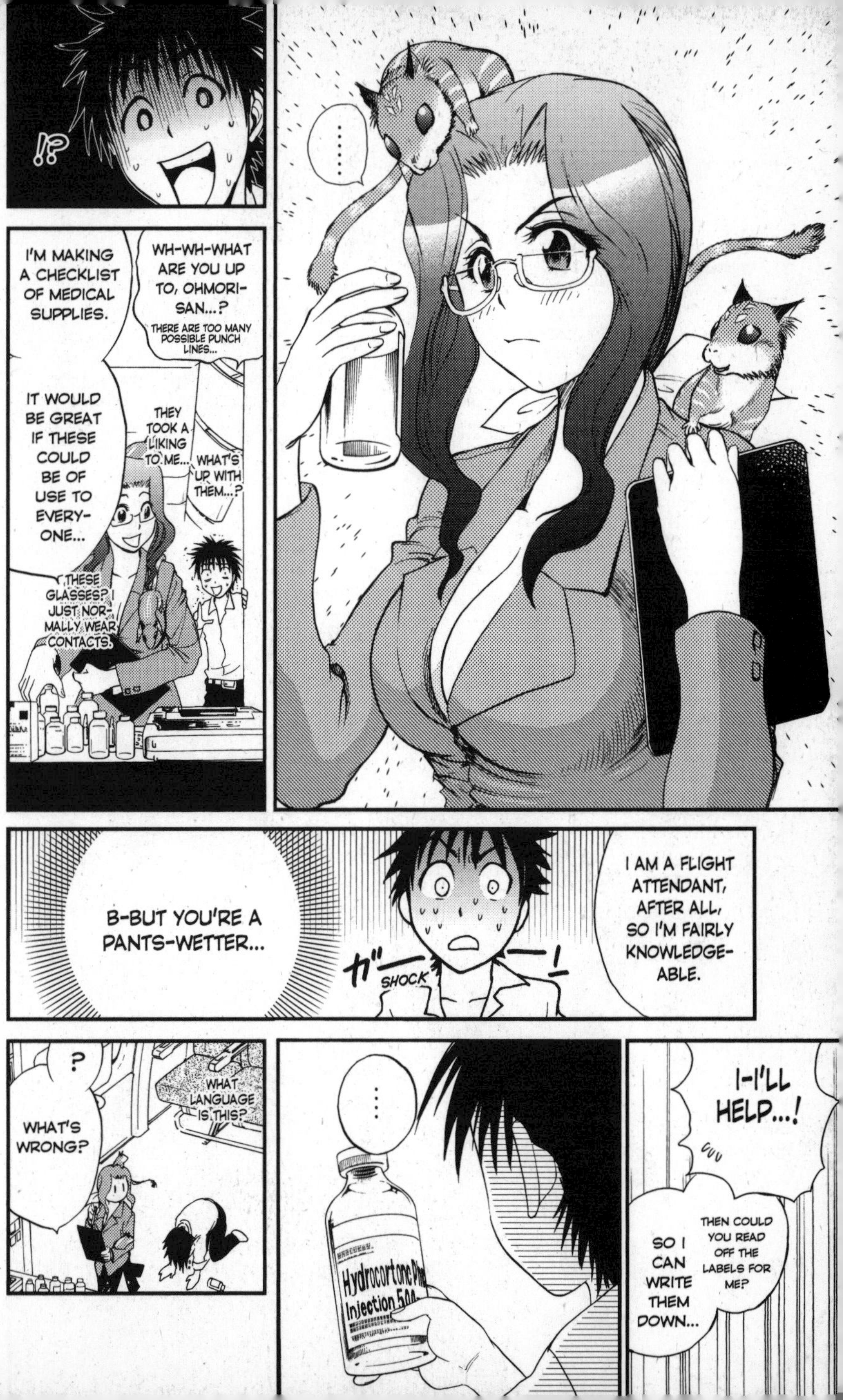
......
!?
WH-WH-WHAT ARE YOU UP TO, OHMORI-SAN...?
THERE ARE TOO MANY POSSIBLE PUNCH LINES...
I'M MAKING A CHECKLIST OF MEDICAL SUPPLIES.
WHAT'S UP WITH THEM...?
THEY TOOK A LIKING TO ME...
IT WOULD BE GREAT IF THESE COULD BE OF USE TO EVERY-ONE...
THESE GLASSES? I JUST NOR-MALLY WEAR CONTACTS.
I AM A FLIGHT ATTENDANT, AFTER ALL, SO I'M FAIRLY KNOWLEDGE-ABLE.
SHOCK
B-BUT YOU'RE A PANTS-WETTER...
I-I'LL HELP...!
THEN COULD YOU READ OFF THE LABELS FOR ME?
SO I CAN WRITE THEM DOWN...
....
Hydrocortone
Injection
?
WHAT LANGUAGE IS THIS?
WHAT'S WRONG?

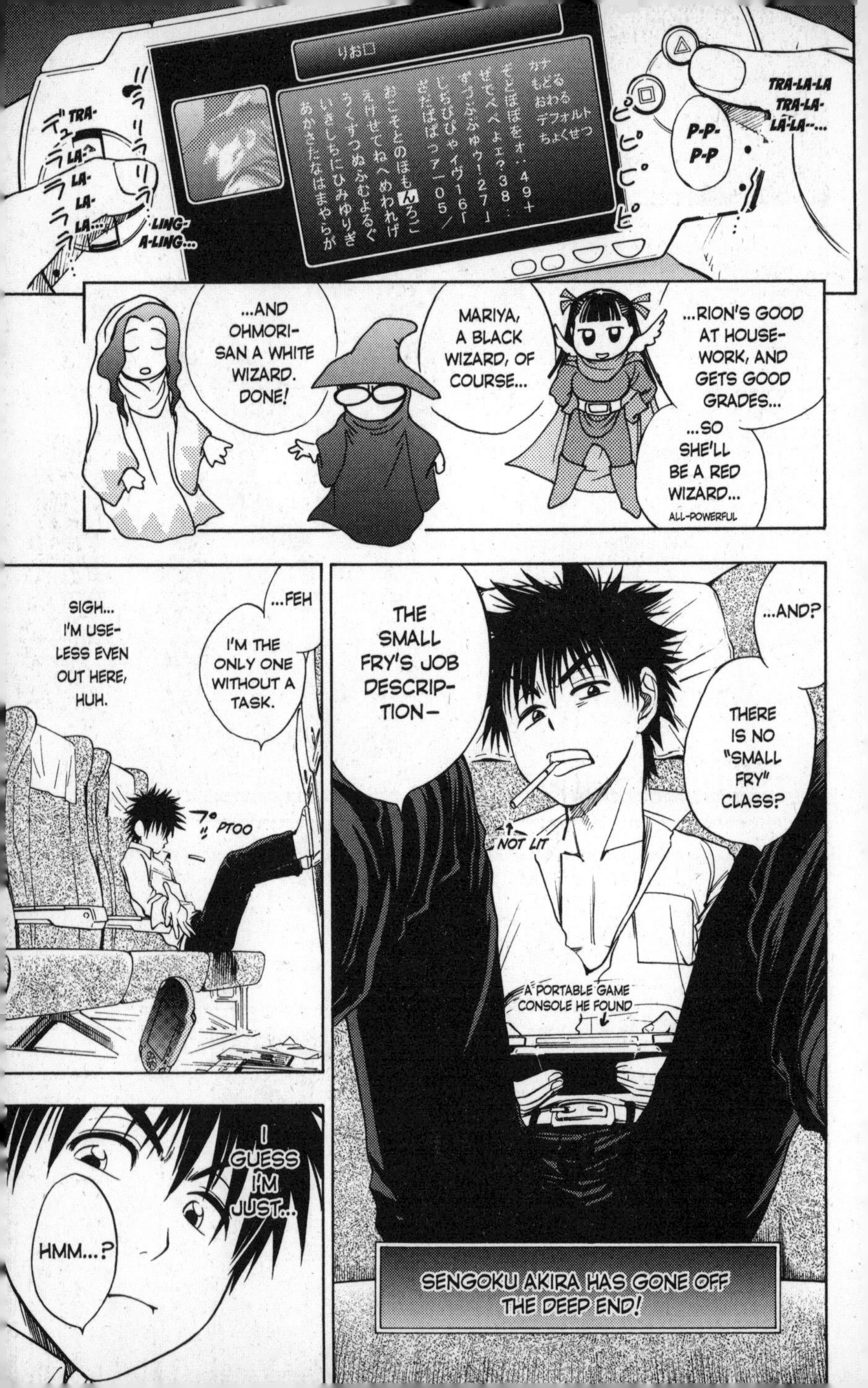
TRA-LA-LA TRA-LA-LA-LA--...
P-P-P-P
ピピピピ
カナ もどる おわる デフォルト ちょくせつ
LING-A-LING...
TRA-LA-LA-LA...
...RION'S GOOD AT HOUSE-WORK, AND GETS GOOD GRADES...
...SO SHE'LL BE A RED WIZARD...
ALL-POWERFUL
MARIYA, A BLACK WIZARD, OF COURSE...
...AND OHMORI-SAN A WHITE WIZARD. DONE!
...AND?
THERE IS NO "SMALL FRY" CLASS?
THE SMALL FRY'S JOB DESCRIPTION—
NOT LIT
A PORTABLE GAME CONSOLE HE FOUND
SENGOKU AKIRA HAS GONE OFF THE DEEP END!
...FEH
I'M THE ONLY ONE WITHOUT A TASK.
SIGH... I'M USE-LESS EVEN OUT HERE, HUH.
PTOO
I GUESS I'M JUST...
HMM...?

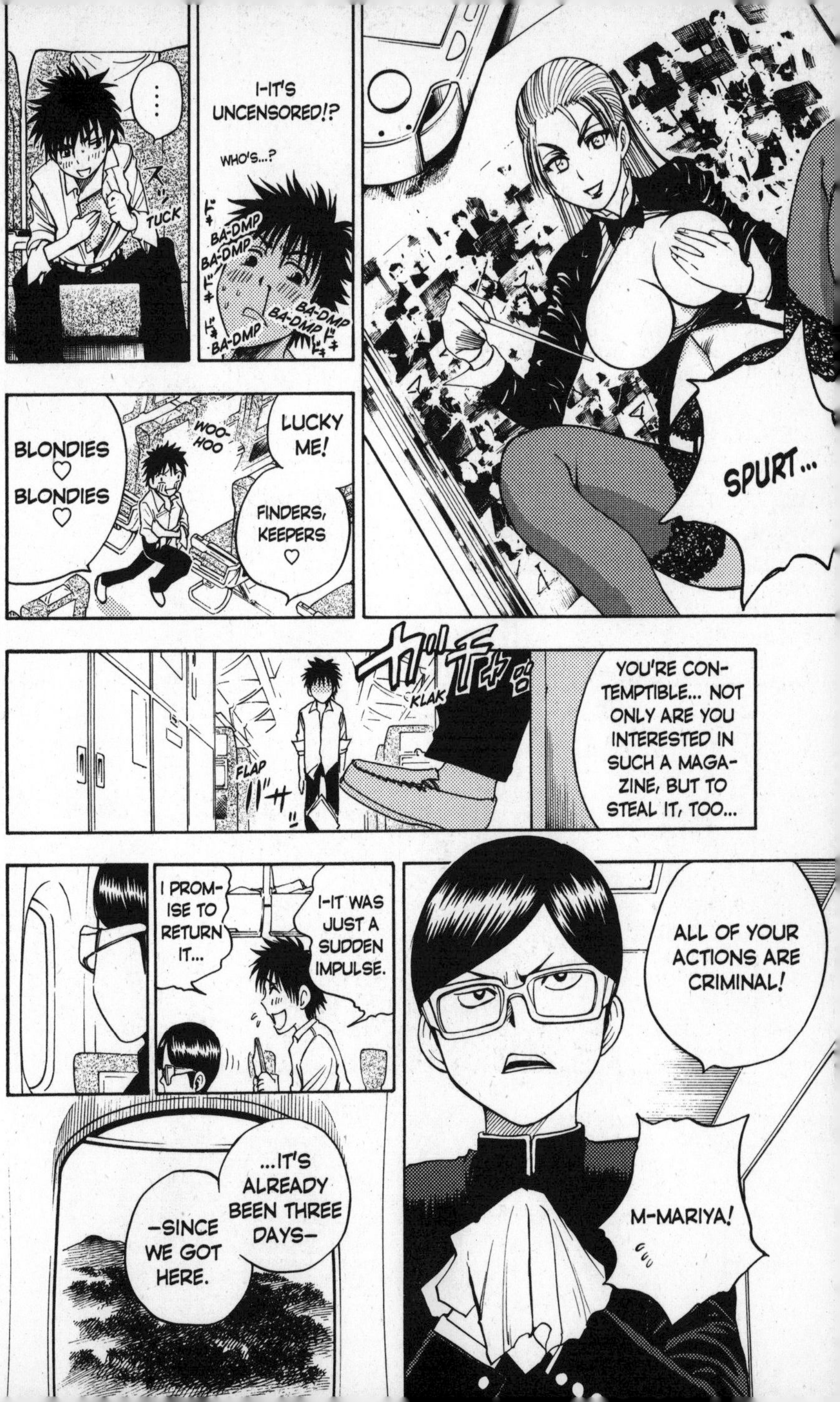
SPURT...
I-IT'S UNCENSORED!?
WHO'S...?
BA-DMP
BA-DMP
BA-DMP
BA-DMP
BA-DMP
...
TUCK
LUCKY ME!
FINDERS, KEEPERS ♡
WOO-HOO
BLONDIES ♡ BLONDIES ♡
YOU'RE CONTEMPTIBLE... NOT ONLY ARE YOU INTERESTED IN SUCH A MAGAZINE, BUT TO STEAL IT, TOO...
KLAK
FLAP
ALL OF YOUR ACTIONS ARE CRIMINAL!
M-MARIYA!
I-IT WAS JUST A SUDDEN IMPULSE.
I PROMISE TO RETURN IT...
...IT'S ALREADY BEEN THREE DAYS—
—SINCE WE GOT HERE.

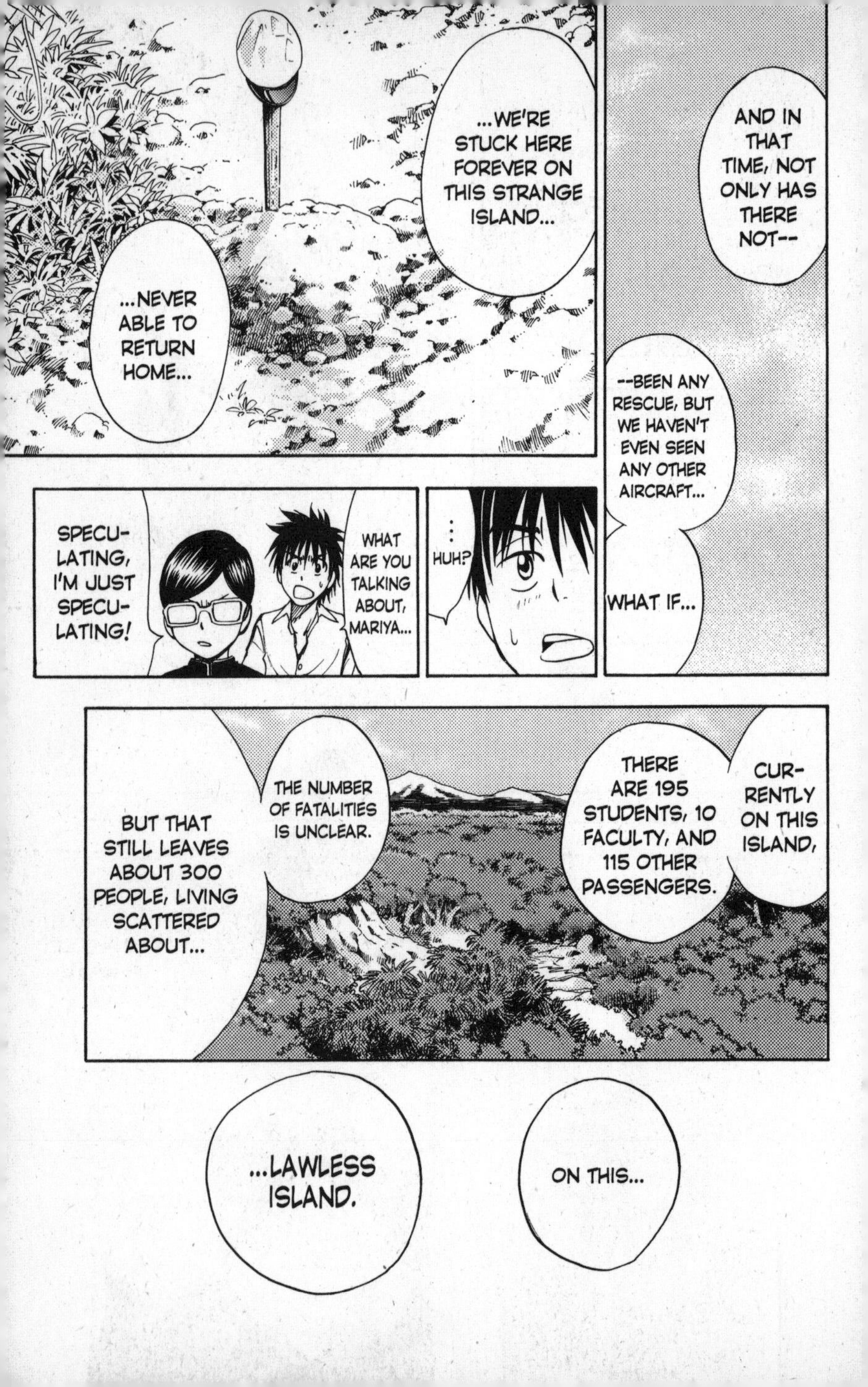
AND IN THAT TIME, NOT ONLY HAS THERE NOT--
--BEEN ANY RESCUE, BUT WE HAVEN'T EVEN SEEN ANY OTHER AIRCRAFT...
WHAT IF...
...WE'RE STUCK HERE FOREVER ON THIS STRANGE ISLAND...
...NEVER ABLE TO RETURN HOME...
...
HUH?
WHAT ARE YOU TALKING ABOUT, MARIYA...
SPECU-LATING, I'M JUST SPECU-LATING!
CUR-RENTLY ON THIS ISLAND,
THERE ARE 195 STUDENTS, 10 FACULTY, AND 115 OTHER PASSENGERS.
THE NUMBER OF FATALITIES IS UNCLEAR.
BUT THAT STILL LEAVES ABOUT 300 PEOPLE, LIVING SCATTERED ABOUT...
ON THIS...
...LAWLESS ISLAND.

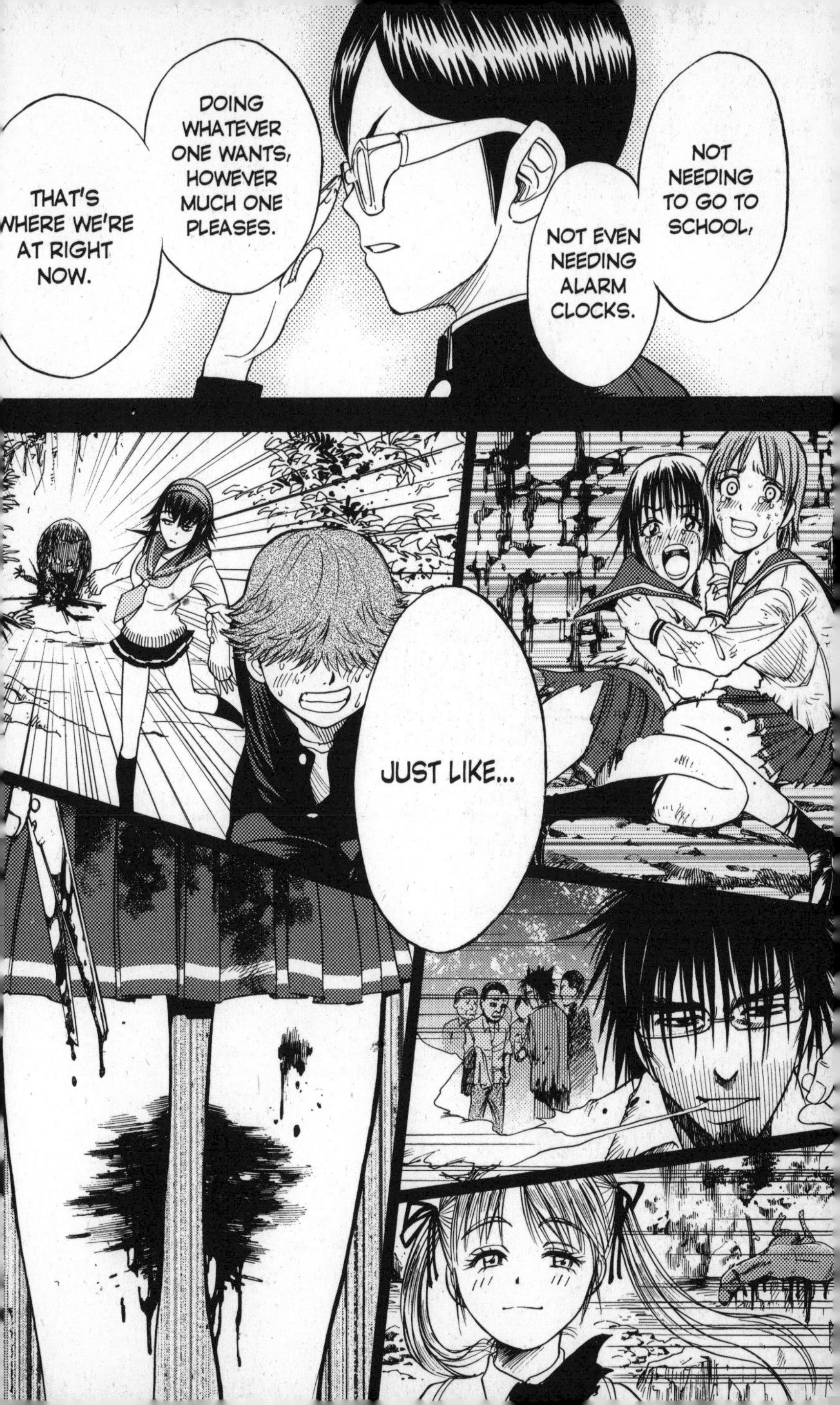
NOT NEEDING TO GO TO SCHOOL,
NOT EVEN NEEDING ALARM CLOCKS.
DOING WHATEVER ONE WANTS, HOWEVER MUCH ONE PLEASES.
THAT'S WHERE WE'RE AT RIGHT NOW.
JUST LIKE...

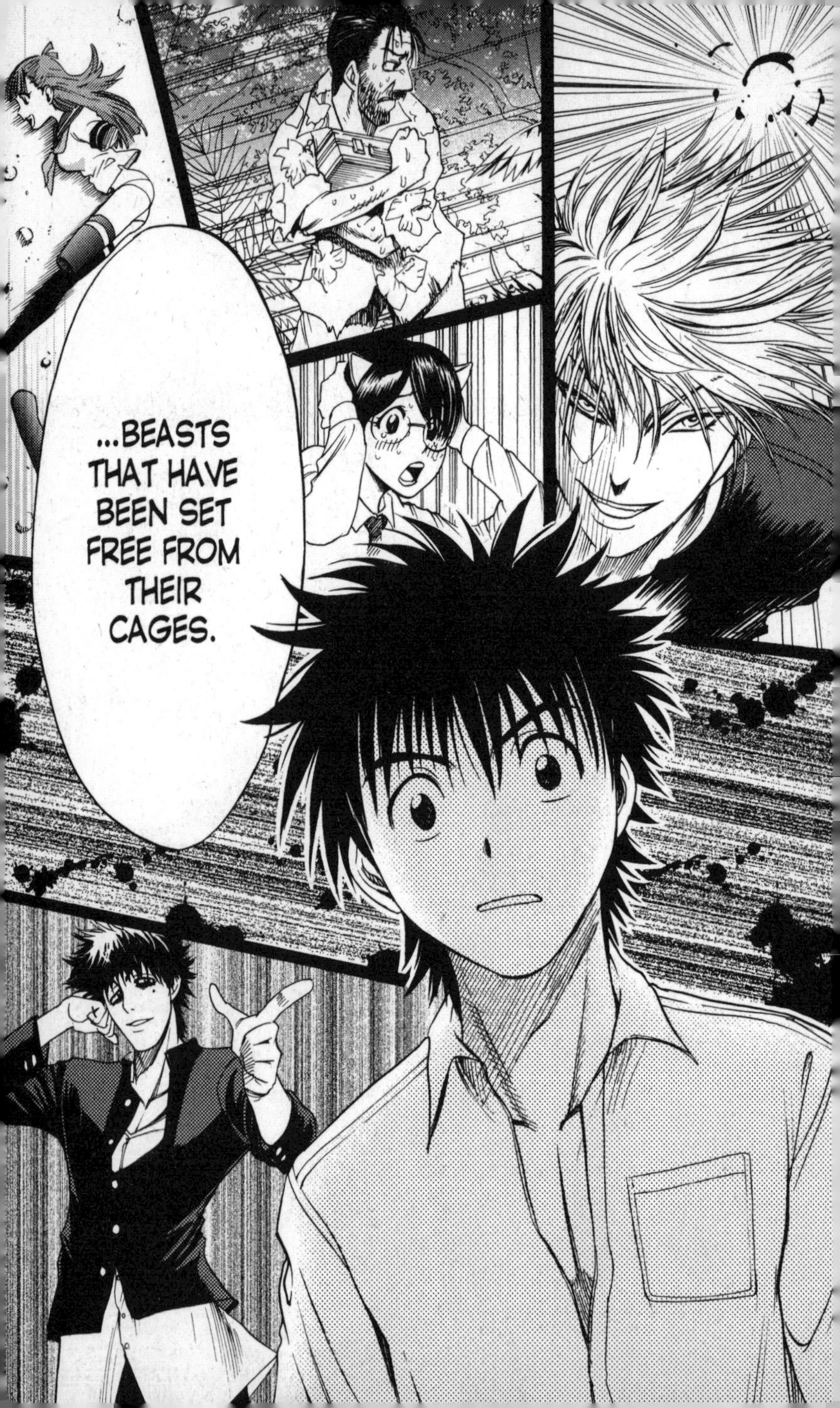
...BEASTS THAT HAVE BEEN SET FREE FROM THEIR CAGES.

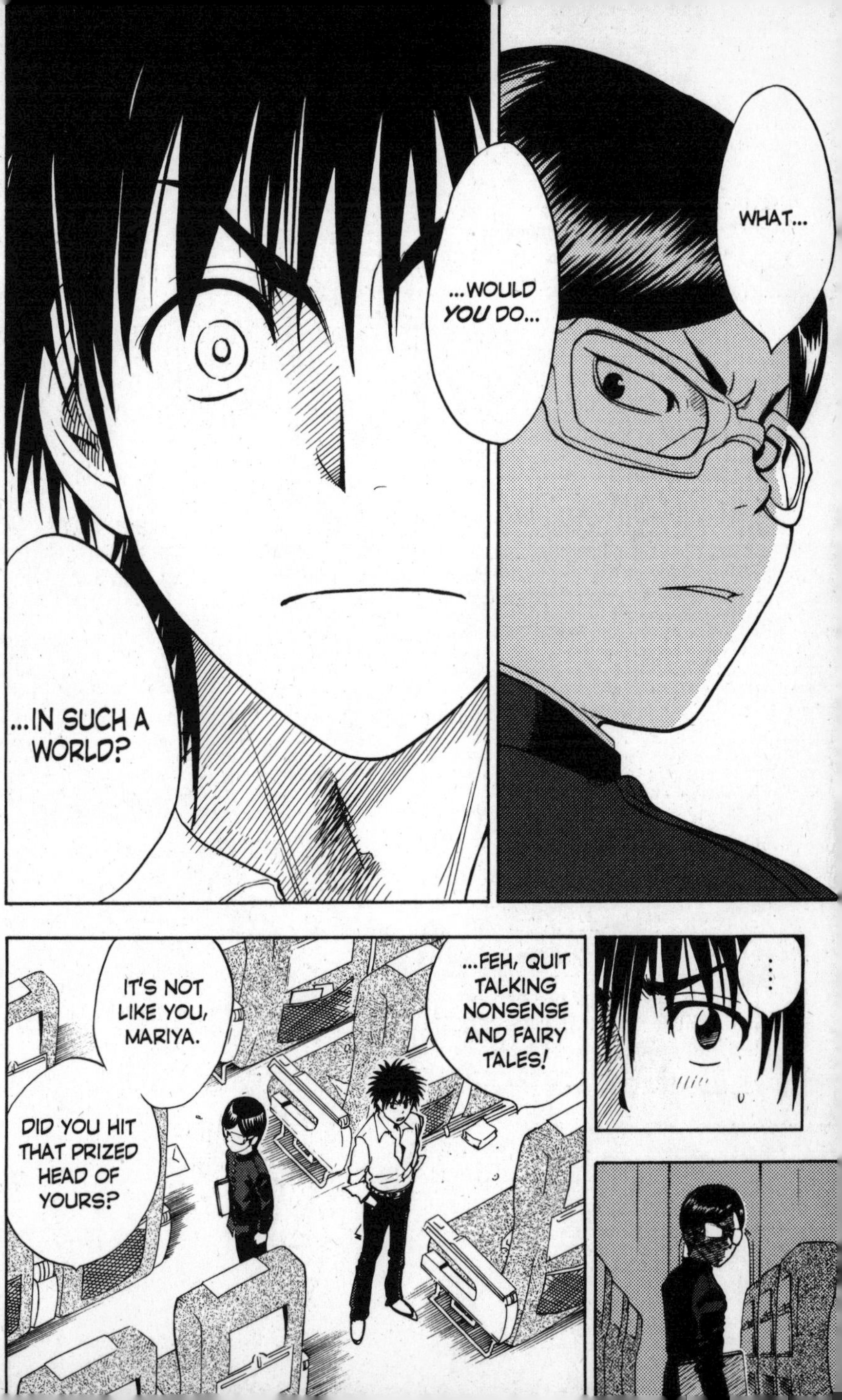
WHAT...
...WOULD *YOU* DO...
...IN SUCH A WORLD?
....
...FEH, QUIT TALKING NONSENSE AND FAIRY TALES!
IT'S NOT LIKE YOU, MARIYA.
DID YOU HIT THAT PRIZED HEAD OF YOURS?

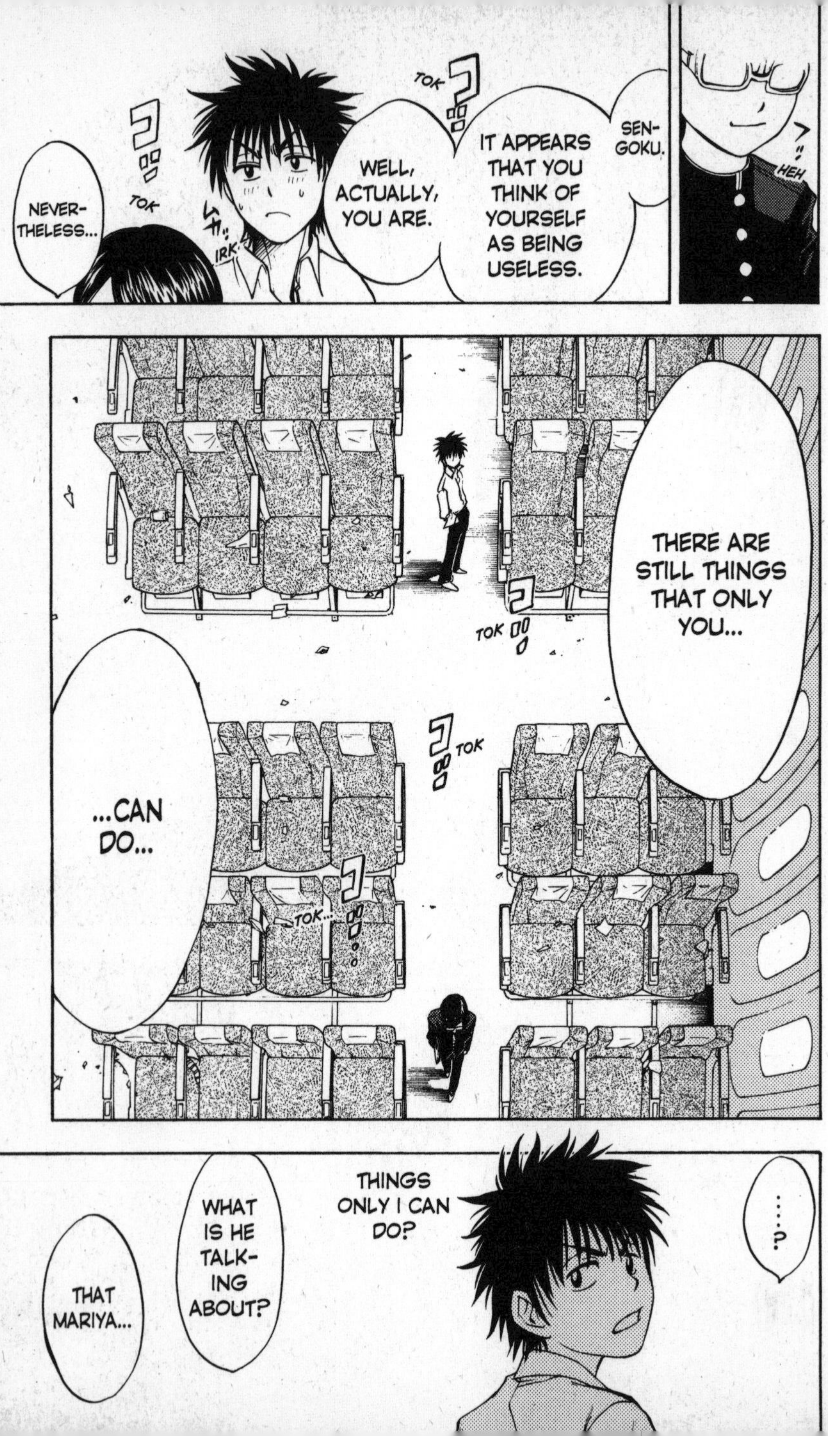
SEN-GOKU.
HEH
IT APPEARS THAT YOU THINK OF YOURSELF AS BEING USELESS.
TOK
WELL, ACTUALLY, YOU ARE.
IRK
TOK
NEVER-THELESS...
THERE ARE STILL THINGS THAT ONLY YOU...
TOK
TOK
...CAN DO...
TOK...
...?
THINGS ONLY I CAN DO?
WHAT IS HE TALK-ING ABOUT?
THAT MARIYA...

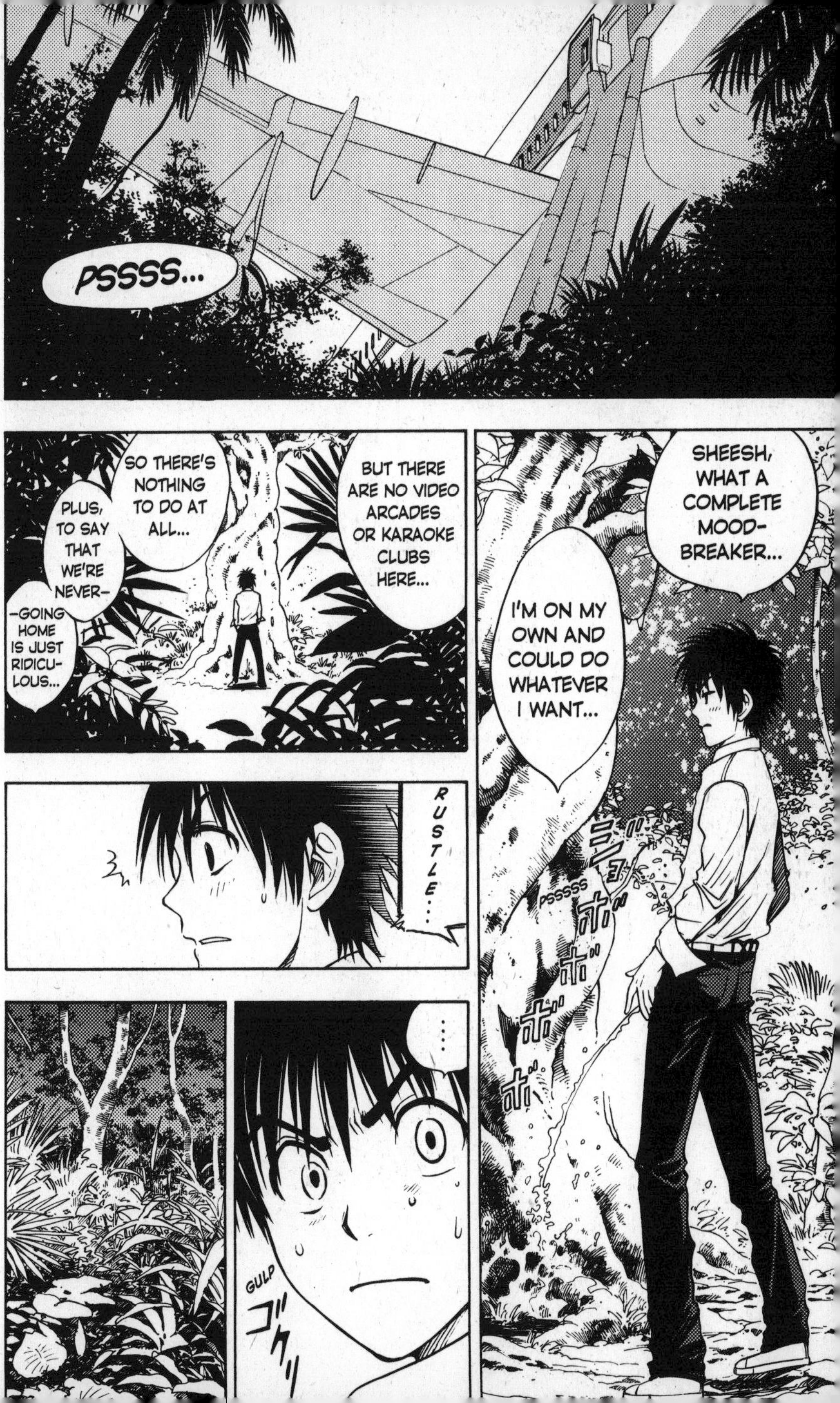
PSSSS...
SHEESH, WHAT A COMPLETE MOOD-BREAKER...
I'M ON MY OWN AND COULD DO WHATEVER I WANT...
PSSSSS
BUT THERE ARE NO VIDEO ARCADES OR KARAOKE CLUBS HERE...
SO THERE'S NOTHING TO DO AT ALL...
PLUS, TO SAY THAT WE'RE NEVER-
-GOING HOME IS JUST RIDICULOUS...
RUSTLE...
....
GULP

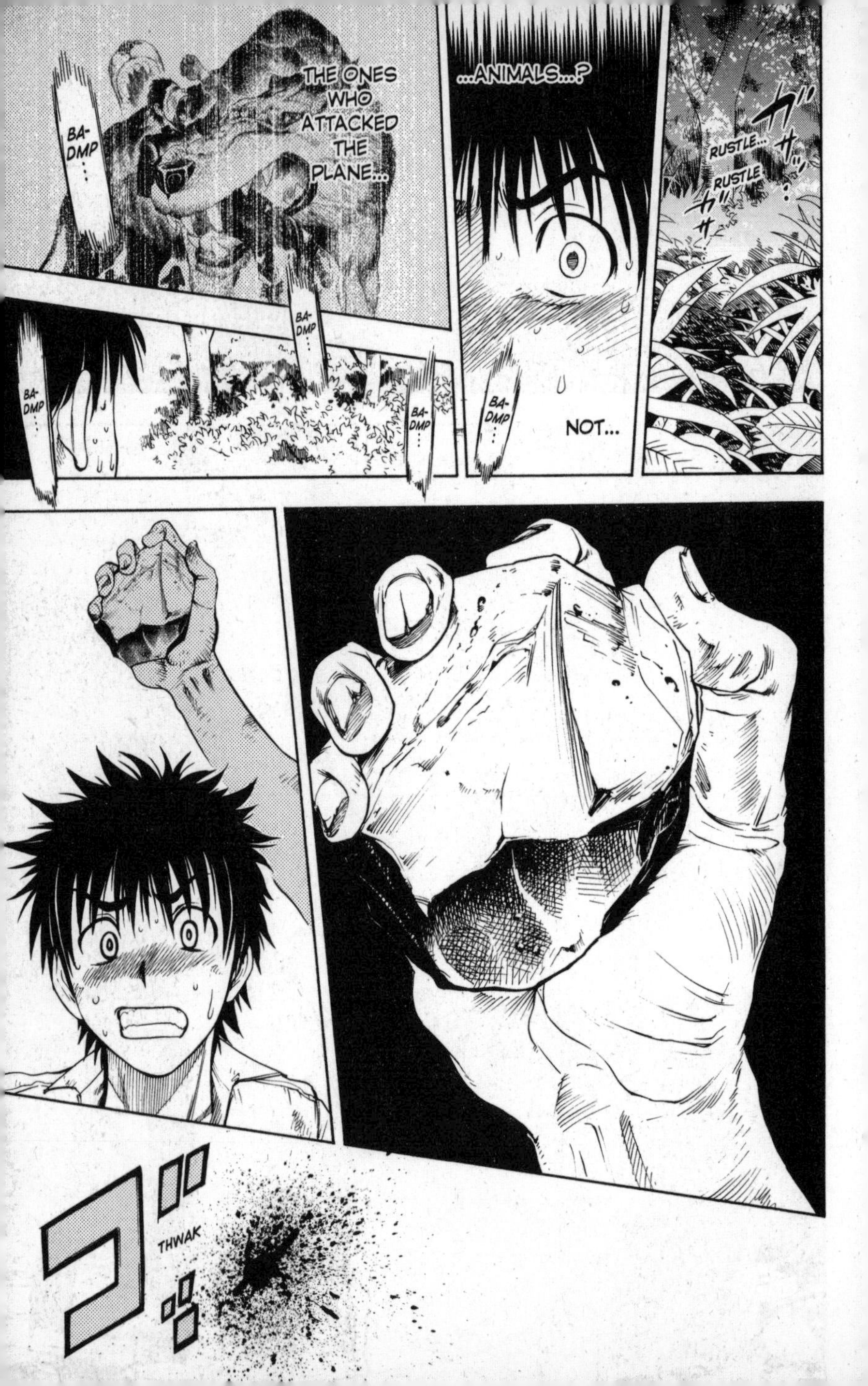
RUSTLE... RUSTLE
...ANIMALS...?
BA-DMP...
NOT...
THE ONES WHO ATTACKED THE PLANE...
BA-DMP...
BA-DMP...
BA-DMP...
BA-DMP...
THWAK

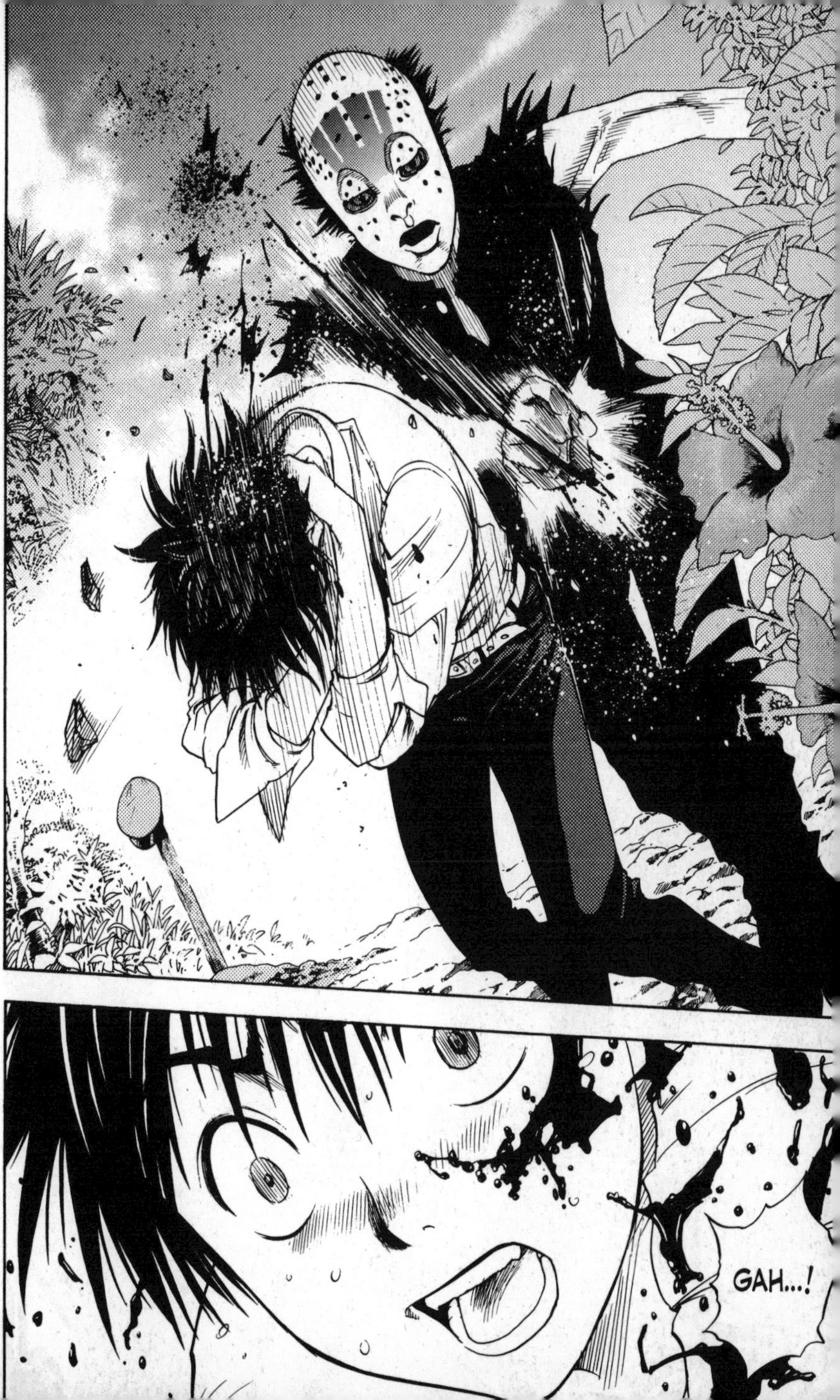
GAH...!

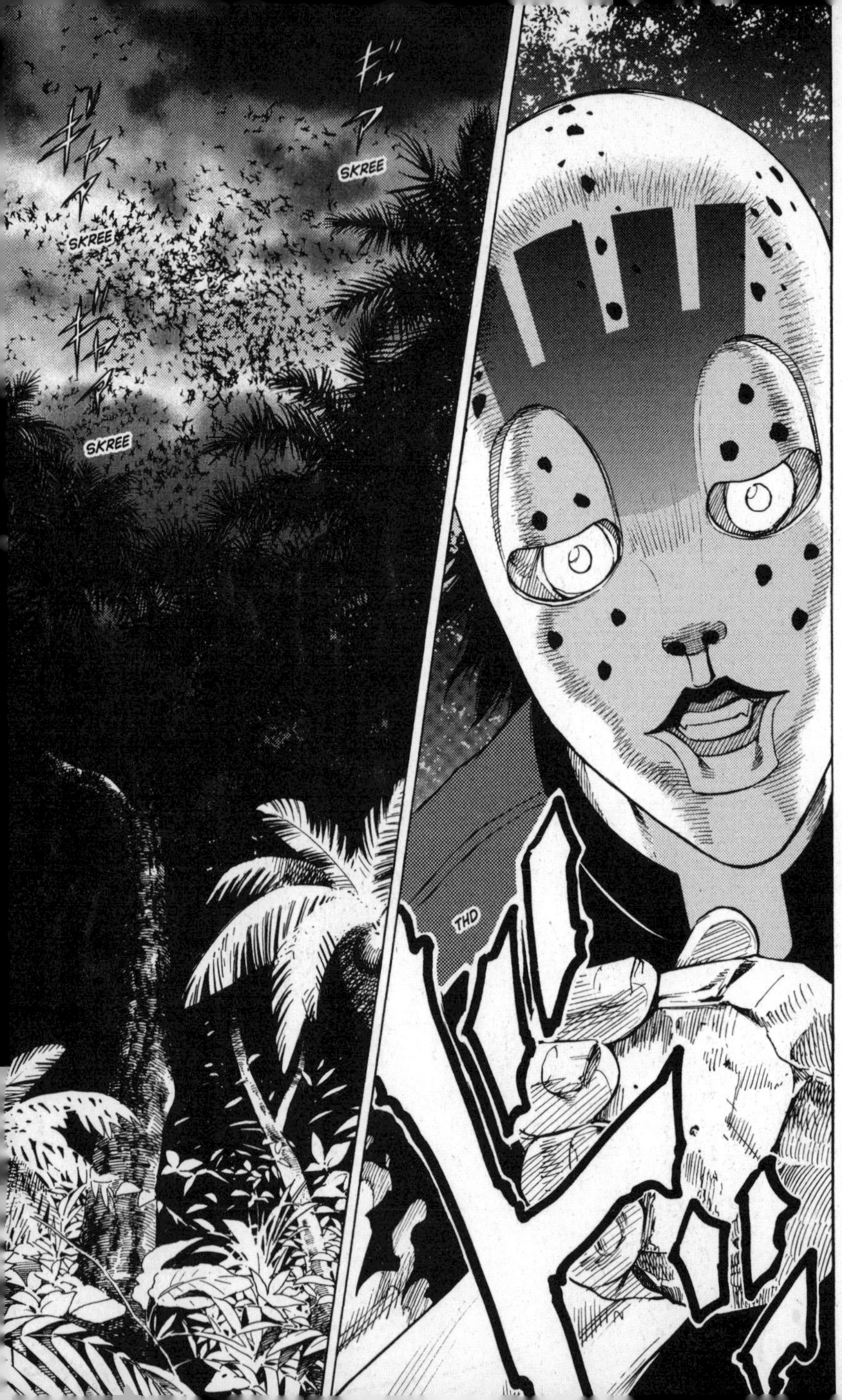
THD
SKREE
SKREE
SKREE

To be continued...

AKAGAMI RION

Born May 27
Gemini
15 years old
155cm tall
Blood type O
BWH: 90•56•88
Extracirricular Activity:
Gymnastics Club
Family members: father, mother
Likes: cleaning one's ears, bathing
Dislikes: caterpillars, eels

SENGOKU AKIRA

Born November 2
Scorpio
14 years old
151cm tall
Body weight 50kg
Blood type A
Extracirricular Activity:
Volleyball Club
Family members: mother
Likes: fried chicken, porn videos
Dislikes: bathing

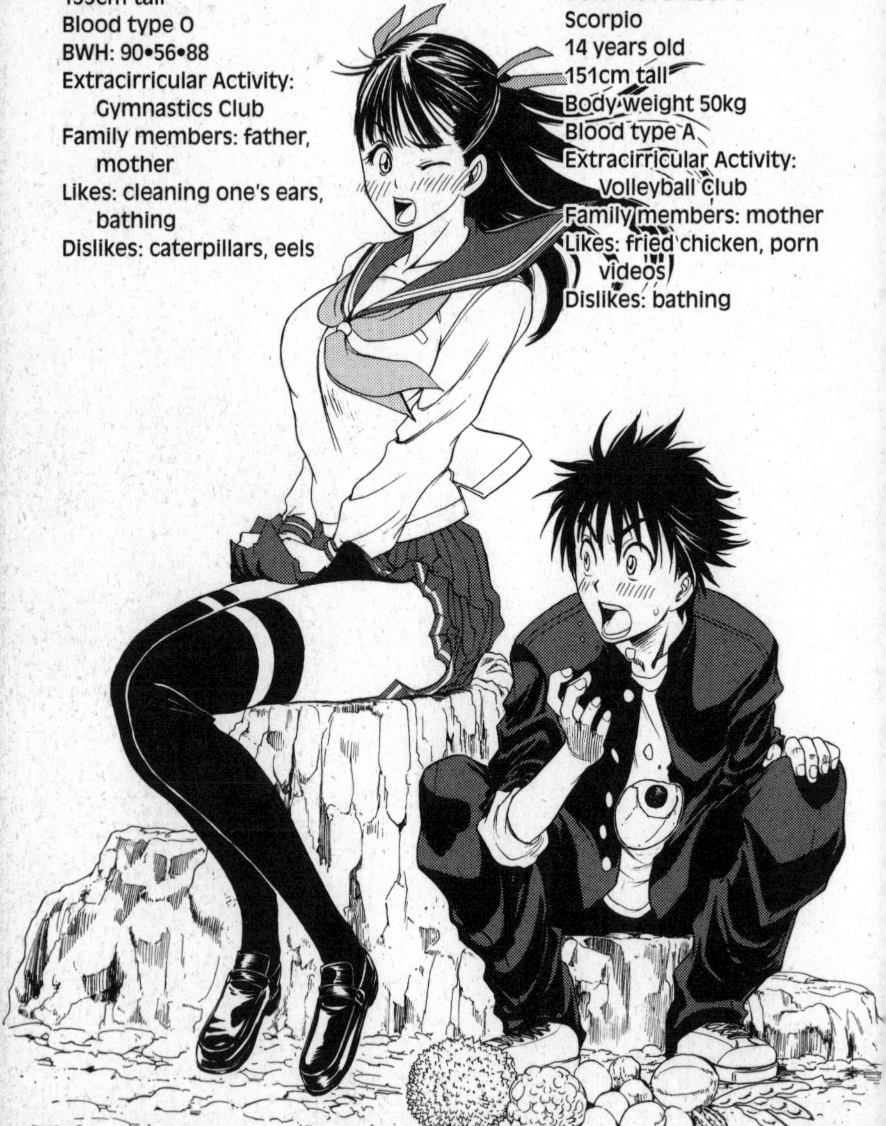

ENCYCLOPEDIA of EXTINCT ANIMALS

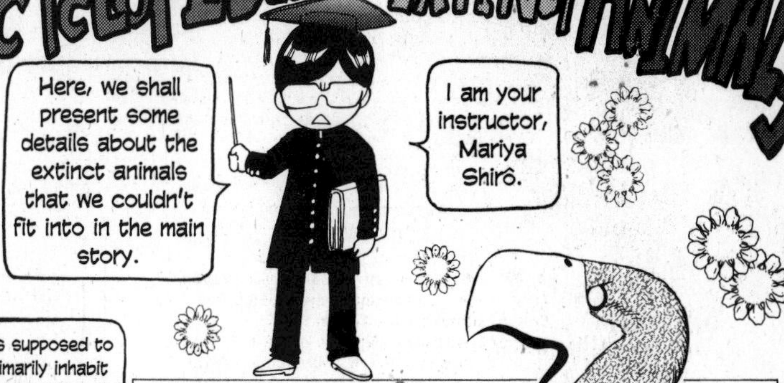
I am your instructor, Mariya Shirô.
Here, we shall present some details about the extinct animals that we couldn't fit into in the main story.

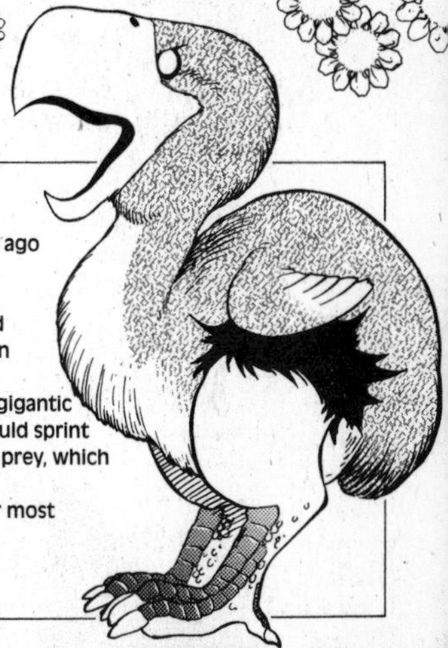

DIATRYMA

Scientific name: Diatryma
Period of existence: 57~50 million years ago
Distribution: North America, Europe
Size: 2.15~2.5m tall

A type of giant bird species that thrived immediately following the extinction of dinosaurs.

Its wings were vestigial. It possessed a gigantic head and hook-shaped beak, and could sprint at speeds of 70km per hour after its prey, which it would kick to death.

To the mammals of its time, it was their most fearsome enemy.

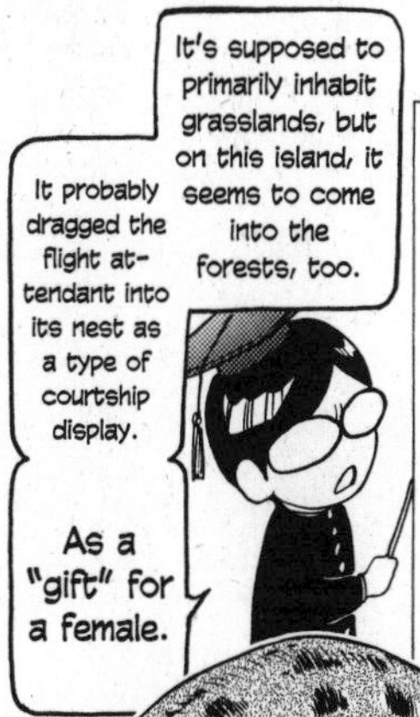
It's supposed to primarily inhabit grasslands, but on this island, it seems to come into the forests, too.
It probably dragged the flight at-tendant into its nest as a type of courtship display.
As a "gift" for a female.

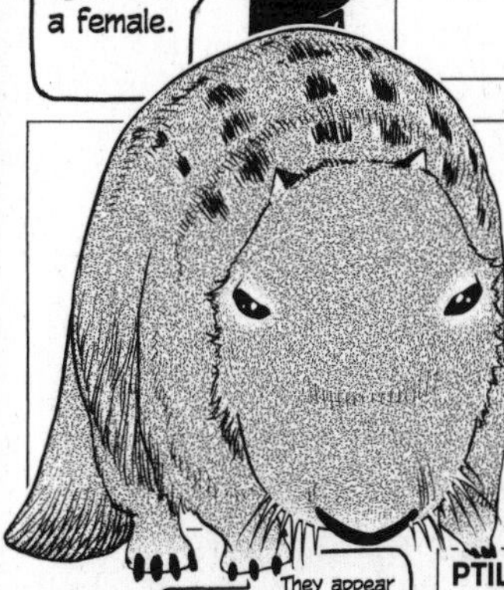

EUMEGAMYS

Scientific name: Eumegamys
Period of existence: 11~2 million years ago
Distribution: South America
Size: Skull length roughly 50cm

The largest rodent to have ever existed.

It was about the size of a modern hippopotamus, and thought to have been at least partially aquatic, but its full ecology is not known.

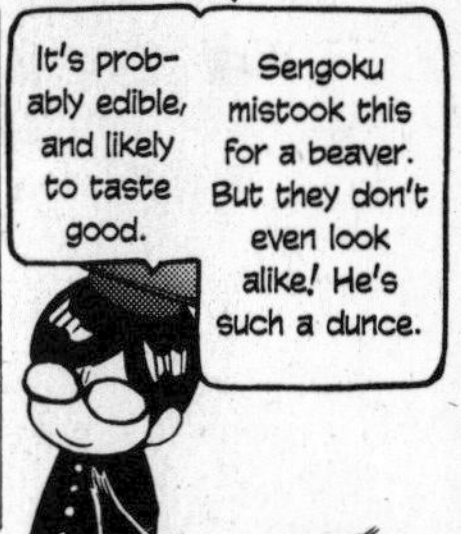
Sengoku mistook this for a beaver. But they don't even look alike! He's such a dunce.
It's prob-ably edible, and likely to taste good.

PTILODUS

Scientific name: Ptilodus
Period of existence: 65~55 million years ago
Distribution: North America, Europe
Size: head and body length 15~20cm

A Multituberculata species that survived the Cretaceous Period.

Arboreal, it possessed a long tail that could wrap around branches and fingers that could grip objects. It is postulated to have been a squirrel-like creature.

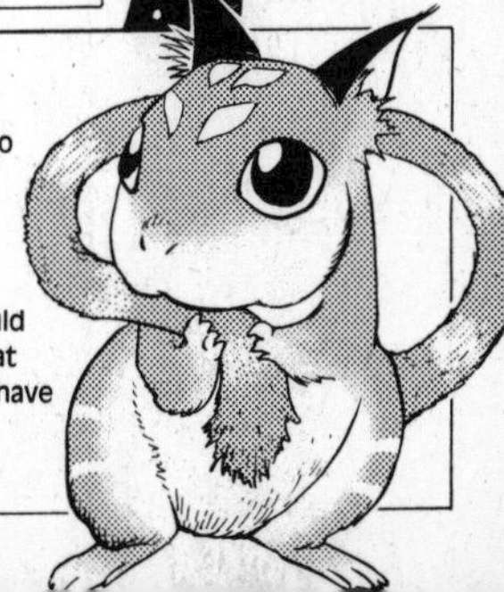

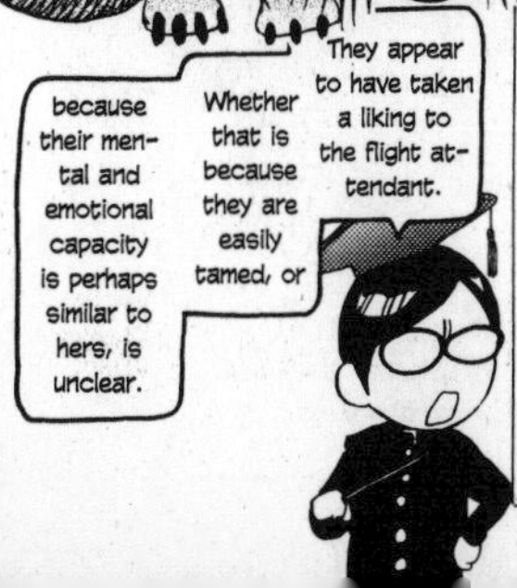
They appear to have taken a liking to the flight at-tendant.
Whether that is because they are easily tamed, or
because their men-tal and emotional capacity is perhaps similar to hers, is unclear.

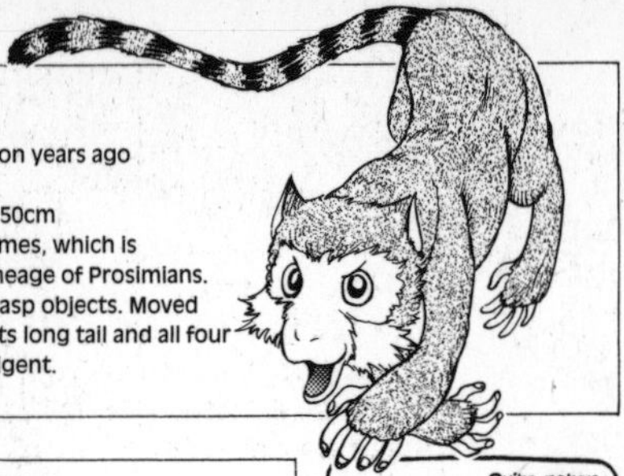

NOTHARCTUS

Scientific name: Notharctus
Period of existence: 50~47 million years ago
Distribution: North America
Size: head and body length 40~50cm
Belongs to Infraorder Adapiformes, which is considered the ancestral lineage of Prosimians. Was arboreal and able to grasp objects. Moved very sharply, fully utilizing its long tail and all four limbs, and was highly intelligent.

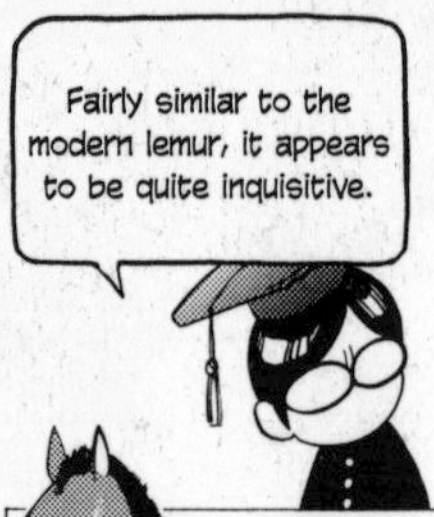
Fairly similar to the modern lemur, it appears to be quite inquisitive.

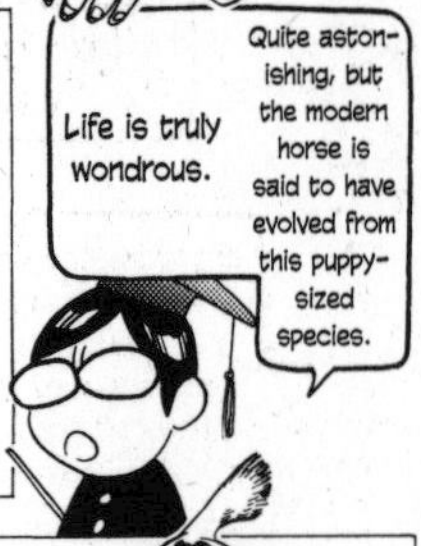
Quite astonishing, but the modern horse is said to have evolved from this puppy-sized species.
Life is truly wondrous.

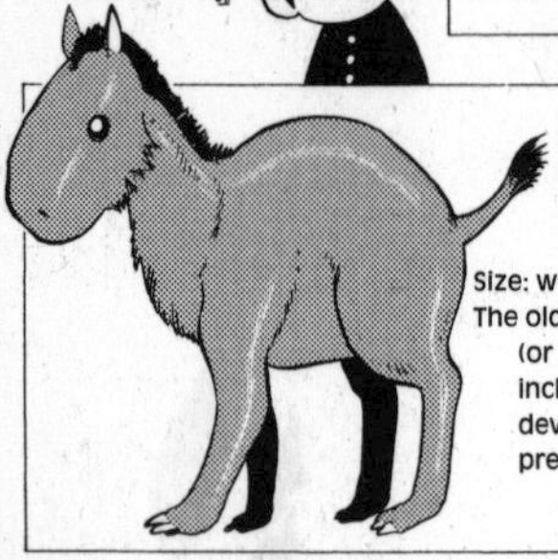

HYRACOTHERIUM

Scientific name: Hyracotherium
Period of existence: 55~35 million years ago
Distribution: North America, Europe
Size: withers height 20~30cm
The oldest known horse, also known as Eohippus (or "Dawn Horse"). Inhabited forests, and its diet included tender tree leaves. It possessed highly developed hindquarters, and when attacked by predators, was able to escape at high speeds.

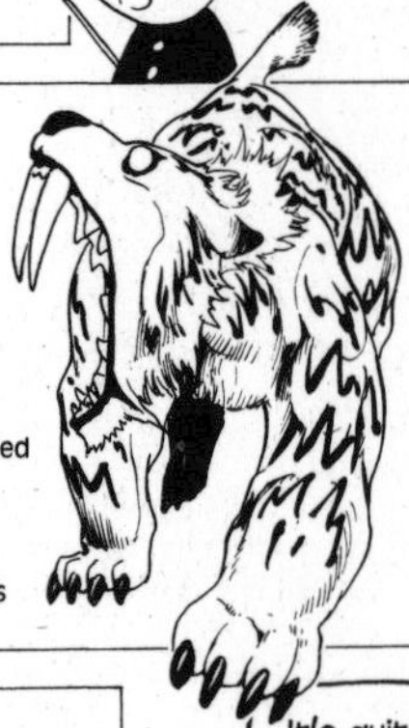

SMILODON

Scientific name: Smilodon
Period of existence: 2 million~10 thousand years ago
Distribution: North and South America
Size: full body length roughly 2m, shoulder height roughly 1m
A carnivorous felid that was about the same size as a modern tiger. The edges of its 25cm-long fangs were serrated, and it could open its jaws up to 120 degrees wide. It is thought to have been slow-footed and thus hunted by ambush. After pouncing on its prey and pressing it down, it would pierce its prey with its fangs and either inflict a mortal wound or cause death by exsanguinations. There are theories that they may have traveled in groups.

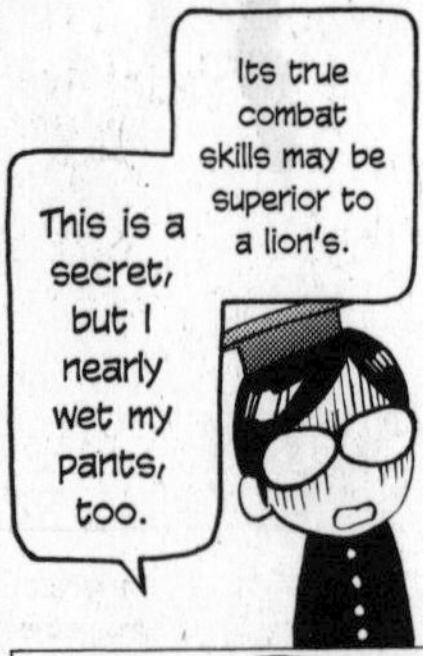
Its true combat skills may be superior to a lion's.
This is a secret, but I nearly wet my pants, too.

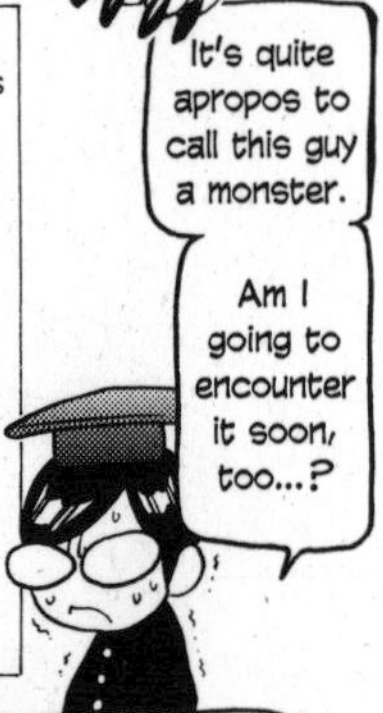
It's quite apropos to call this guy a monster.
Am I going to encounter it soon, too...?

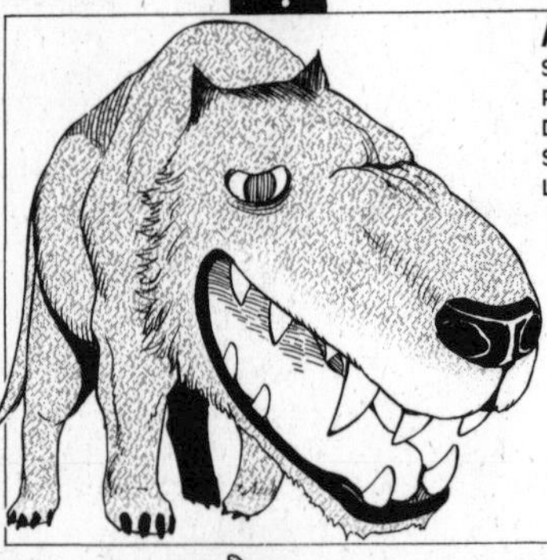

ANDREWSARCHUS

Scientific name: Andrewsarchus mongoliensis
Period of existence: 45~36 million years ago
Distribution: Asia
Size: full length 5.5m
Largest terrestrial carnivorous mammal ever known. Possessed gigantic canine teeth and powerful molars that could even pulverize bones, with which it chewed its prey in its mighty jaws. Given its size, it probably was not able to swiftly chase after its prey. There are various theories that it may have been a carrion eater, or omnivorous, but since only a single skull fossil has been excavated, much is still unknown about it.

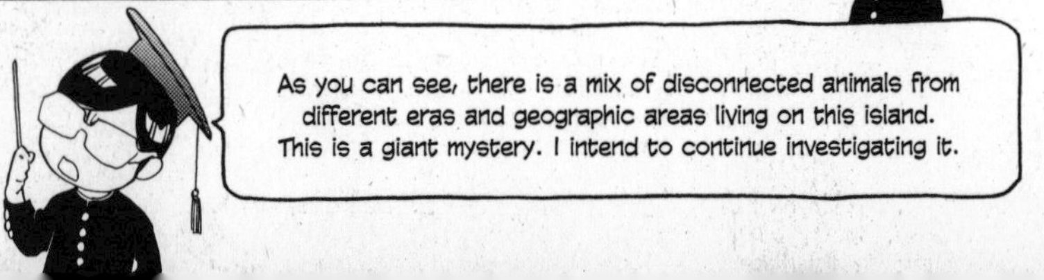
As you can see, there is a mix of disconnected animals from different eras and geographic areas living on this island. This is a giant mystery. I intend to continue investigating it.

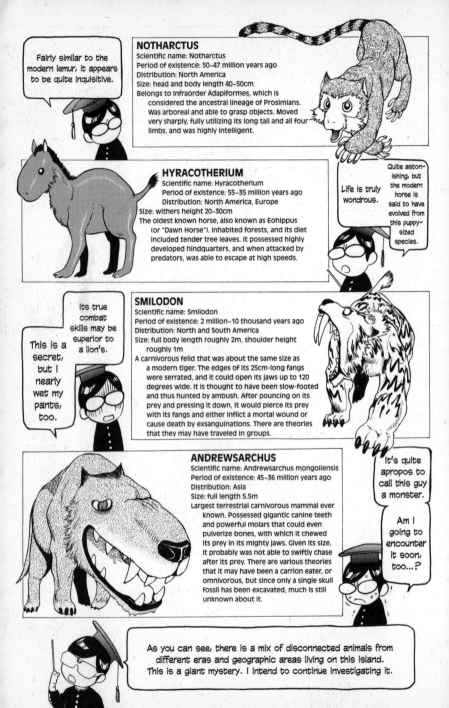

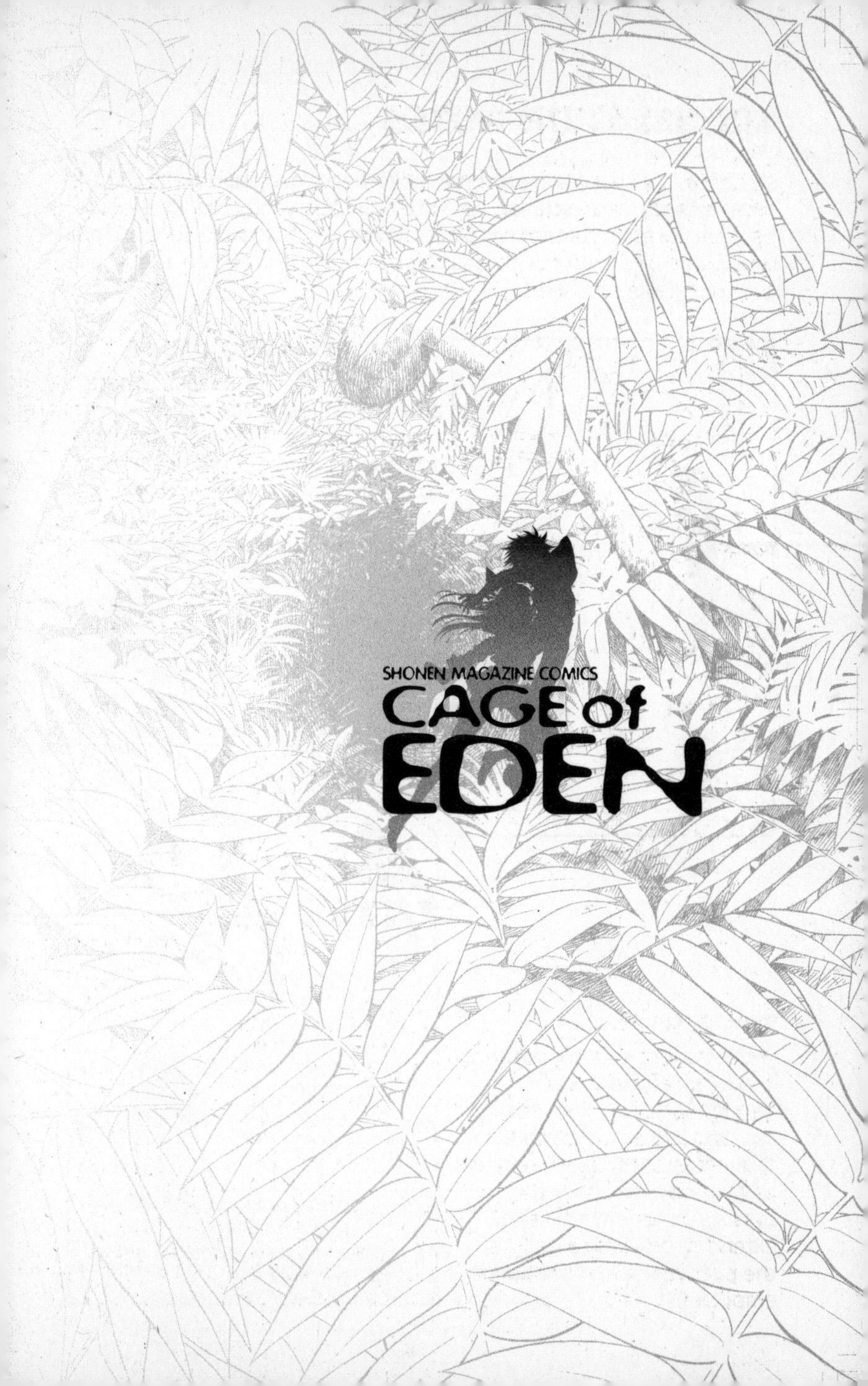
SHONEN MAGAZINE COMICS
CAGE of EDEN

TRANSLATION NOTES

Japanese is a tricky language for most Westerners, and translation is often more art than science. For your edification and reading pleasure, here are notes on some of the places where we could have gone in a different direction with our translation of the work, or where a Japanese cultural reference is used.

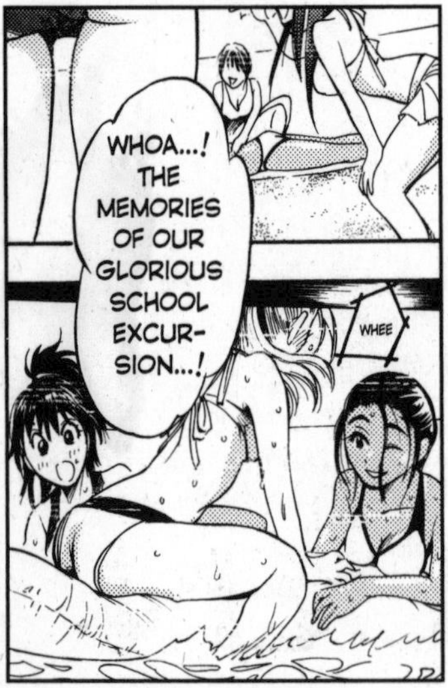
WHEE
WHOA...! THE MEMORIES OF OUR GLORIOUS SCHOOL EXCUR-SION...!

School excursion, page 9

A common practice in Japan, where an entire school grade travels together, with teachers as escorts and guardians, during semester or summer breaks. Originally meant as educational experiences and to widen the horizon of those who could not afford to travel much, it is now seen more as opportunities to forge stronger social bonds and foster camaraderie.

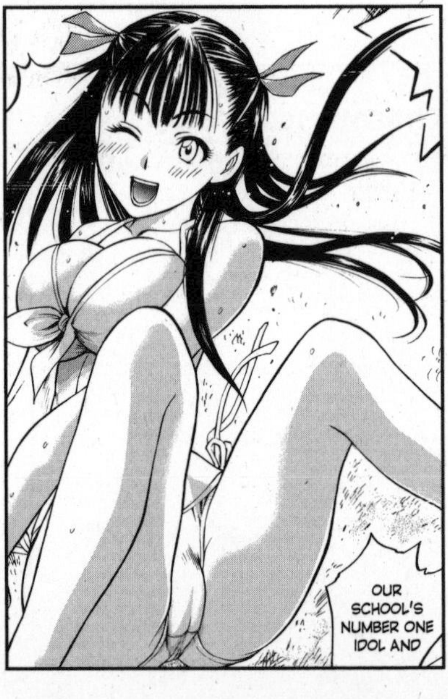
OUR SCHOOL'S NUMBER ONE IDOL AND

Idol, page 11

While most commonly referring to young female media personalities, such as J-pop artists, actresses, and models (but occasionally also foreigners and young male stars), this Japanese phenomenon can extend to civilians as well, i.e. the prettiest student or junior employee.

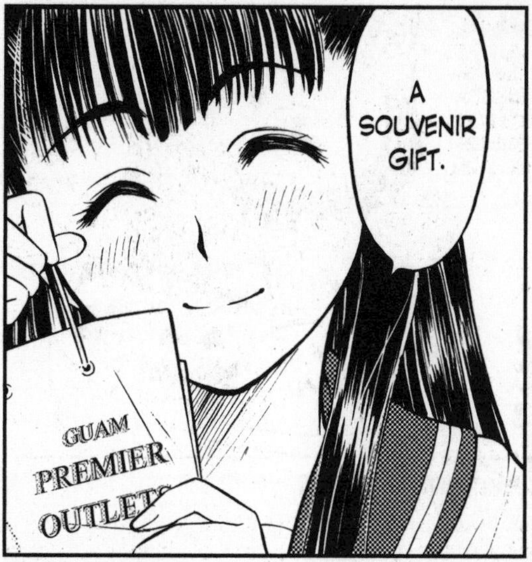
A SOUVENIR GIFT.
GUAM PREMIER OUTLETS

Souvenir gift, page 14

It is customary in Japan, for those who are traveling, to buy and bring small gifts home for good friends, family, and if of working age, one's co-workers and associates.

Chocobo, page 50

A large, usually flightless bird-like creature character from the Final Fantasy video game series.

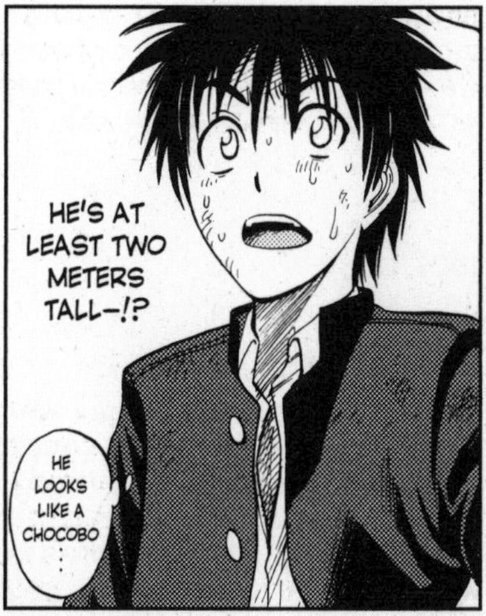
HE'S AT LEAST TWO METERS TALL–!?
HE LOOKS LIKE A CHOCOBO...

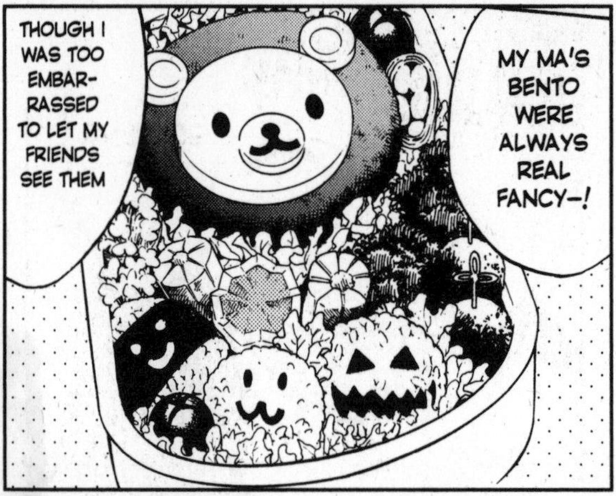
MY MA'S BENTO WERE ALWAYS REAL FANCY–!
THOUGH I WAS TOO EMBAR-RASSED TO LET MY FRIENDS SEE THEM

Bento (Obento), page 105

Boxed meals prepared for students or spouses by a family member (most commonly the mother/wife or sister/daughter). It can also refer to pre-prepared boxed meals available for purchase at train stations, supermarkets, and delis.

Great Kantô Earthquake, page 149

A devastating earthquake of Richter scale magnitude 7.9, that struck the region encompassing Tokyo on September 1, 1923. It combined with a strong typhoon that also struck the area around the same time, resulting in over 100,000 deaths.

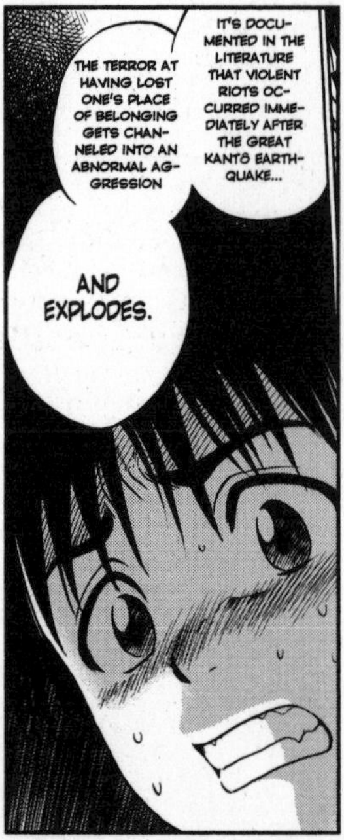
IT'S DOCU-MENTED IN THE LITERATURE THAT VIOLENT RIOTS OC-CURRED IMME-DIATELY AFTER THE GREAT KANTÔ EARTH-QUAKE...
THE TERROR AT HAVING LOST ONE'S PLACE OF BELONGING GETS CHAN-NELED INTO AN ABNORMAL AG-GRESSION
AND EXPLODES.

BWH (3 Sizes), page 185

An abbreviation for bust, waist, and hip, and denotes each respective circumference measurement. Originally intended for the purpose of aiding seamstresses to make or fit clothes, it is currently also used by women in their personal ads or profiles to describe their proportions to the viewer.

Preview of

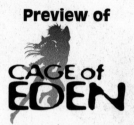

CAGE of EDEN

We're pleased to present you a preview from *Cage of Eden* 2. Please check our website www.kodanshacomics.com to see when this volume will be available in English. For now you'll have to make do with Japanese!

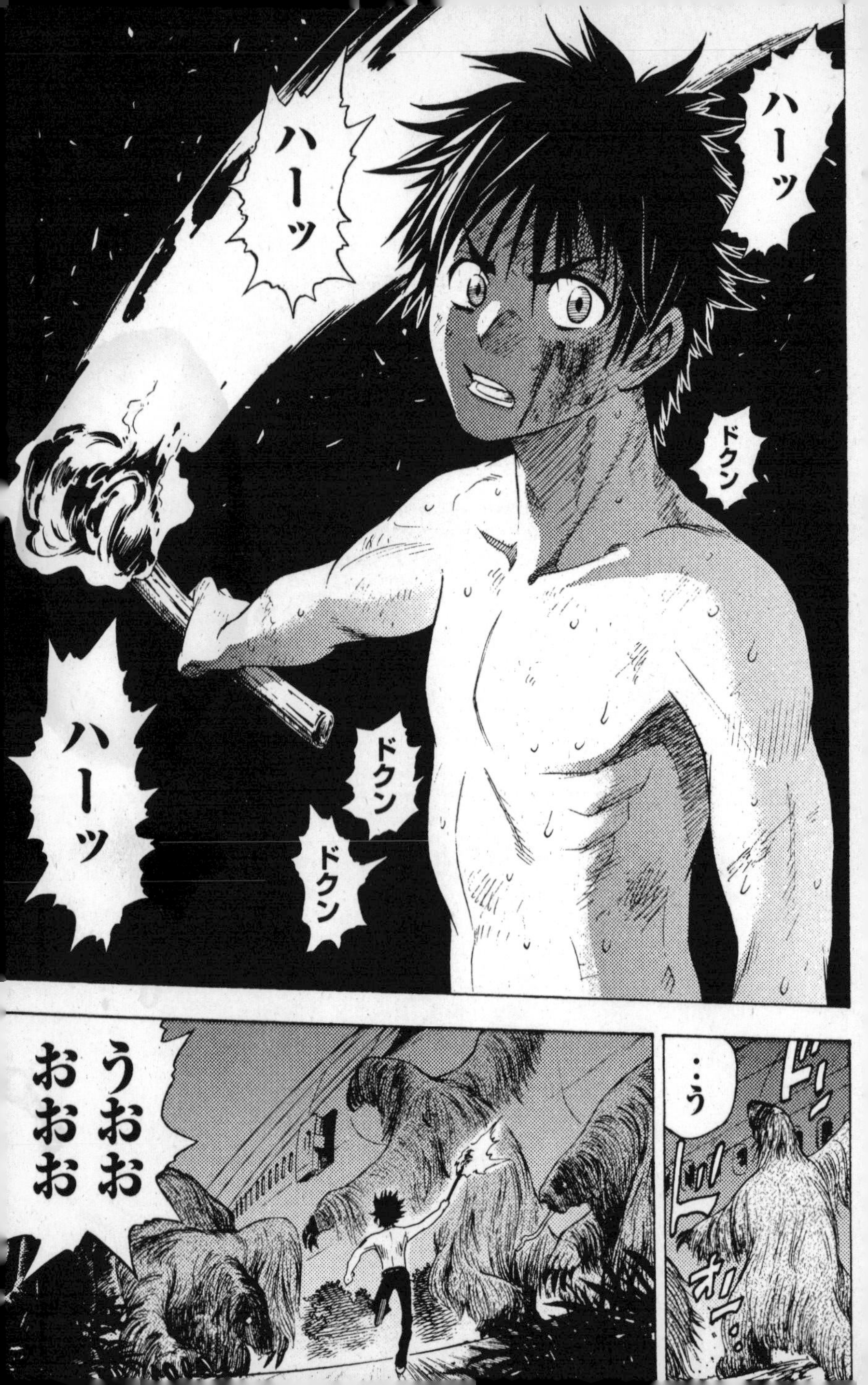
ハーッ
ハーッ
ドクン
ドクン
ドクン
ハーッ
…う
ドードーオー。。
うおおおおお

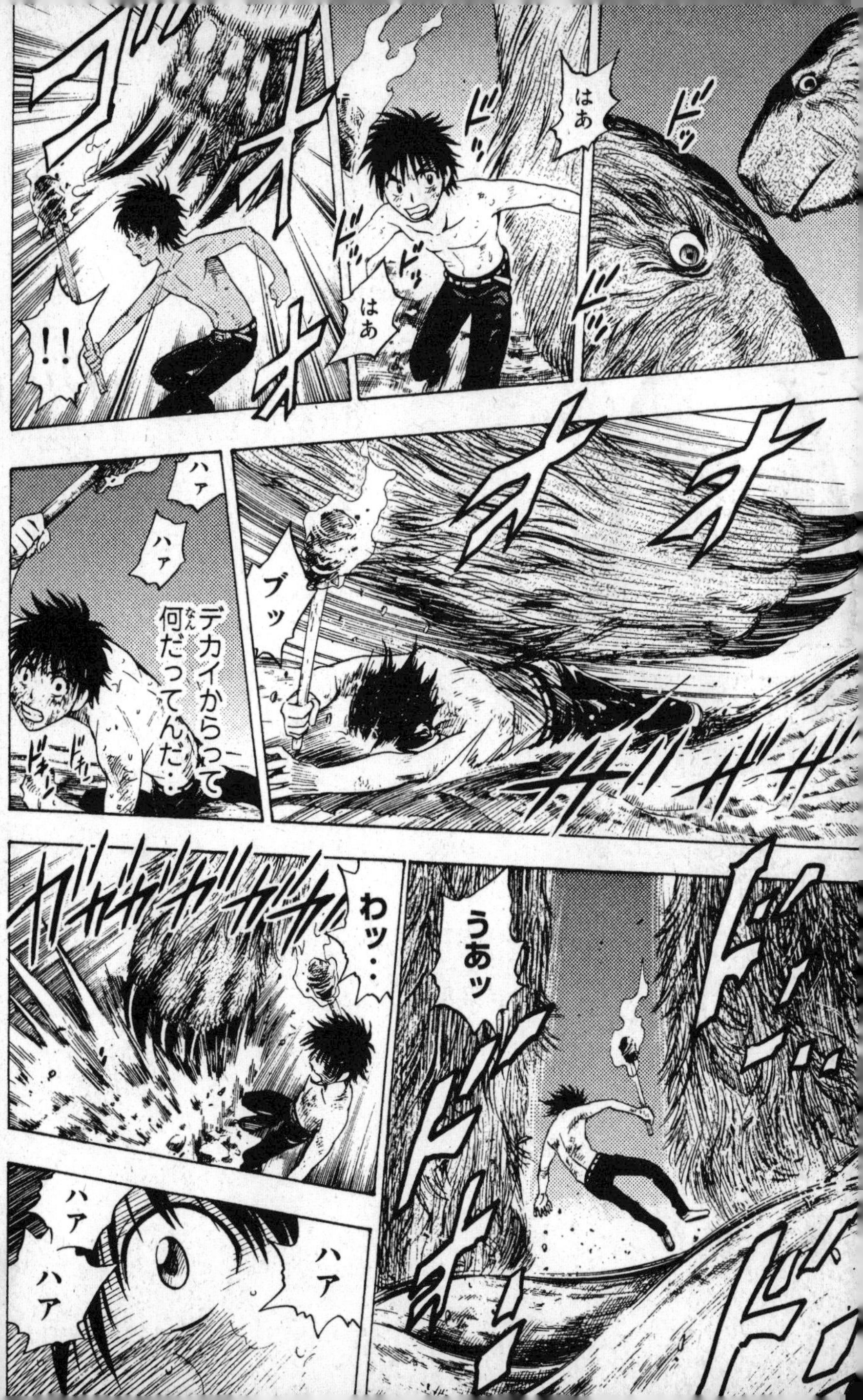
ドッ
はあ
ドッ
はあ
ゴオオオ
!!
オオオ
ブッ
ザザザ
ハァ
ハァ
デカイからって何だってんだ・・
うあッ
わッ・・
ハァ
ハァ
ハァ
ハァ

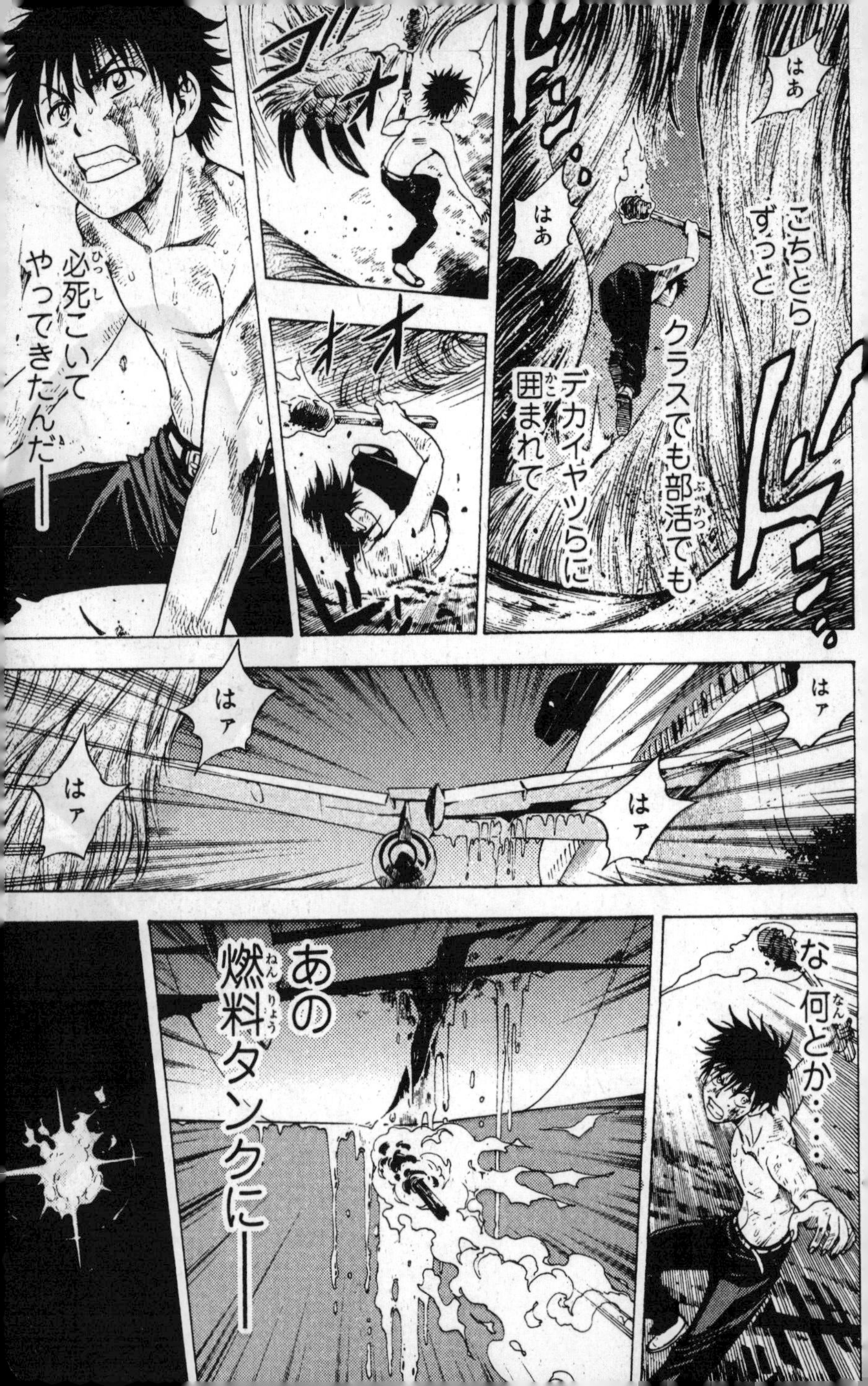

はあ
こちとらずっと
クラスでも部活でも
デカイヤツらに囲まれて
はあ
ゴオ
オオ
必死こいてやってきたんだー
はァ
はァ
はァ
はァ
な 何とか……
あの燃料タンクにー

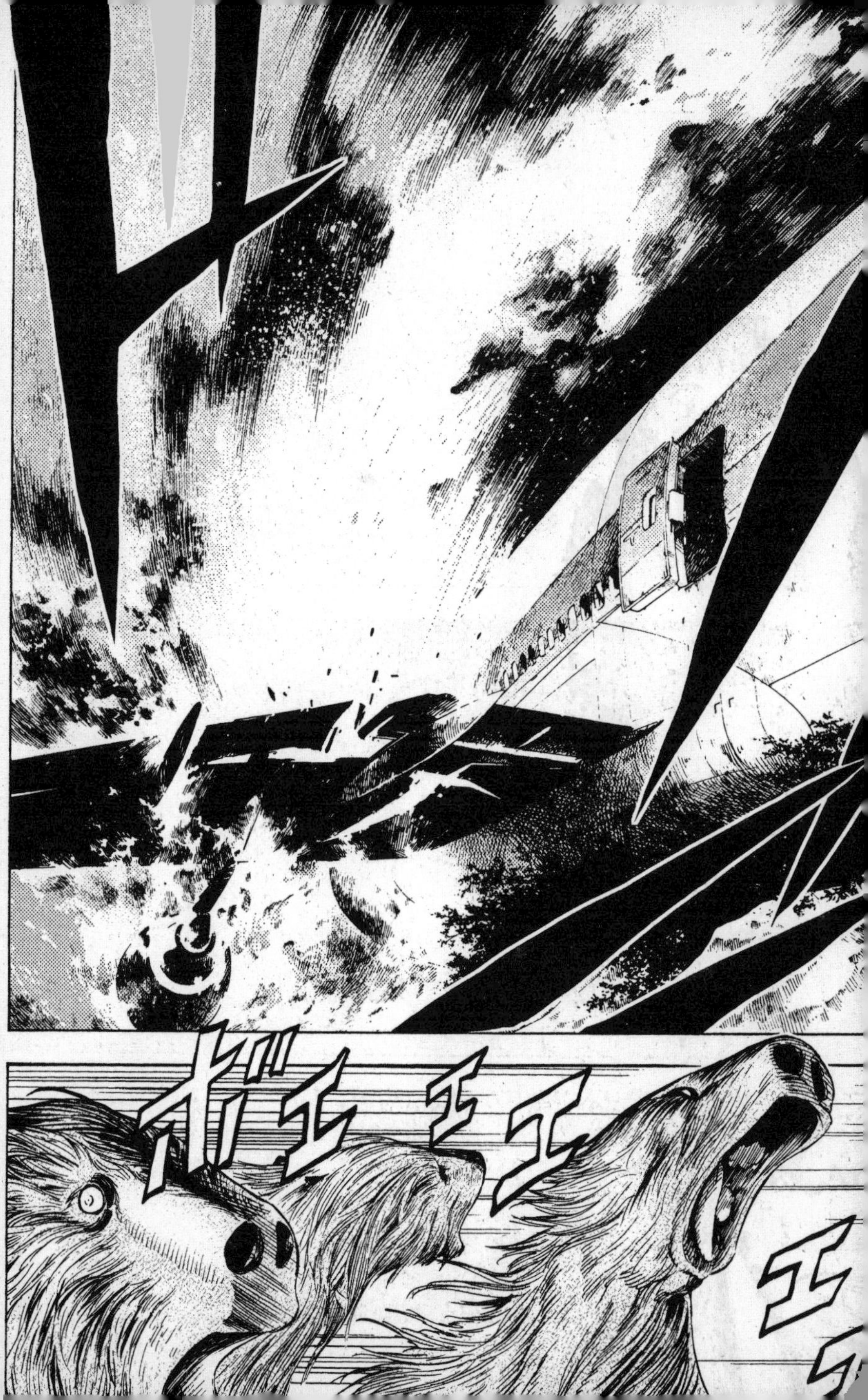
オ゛エエエエ

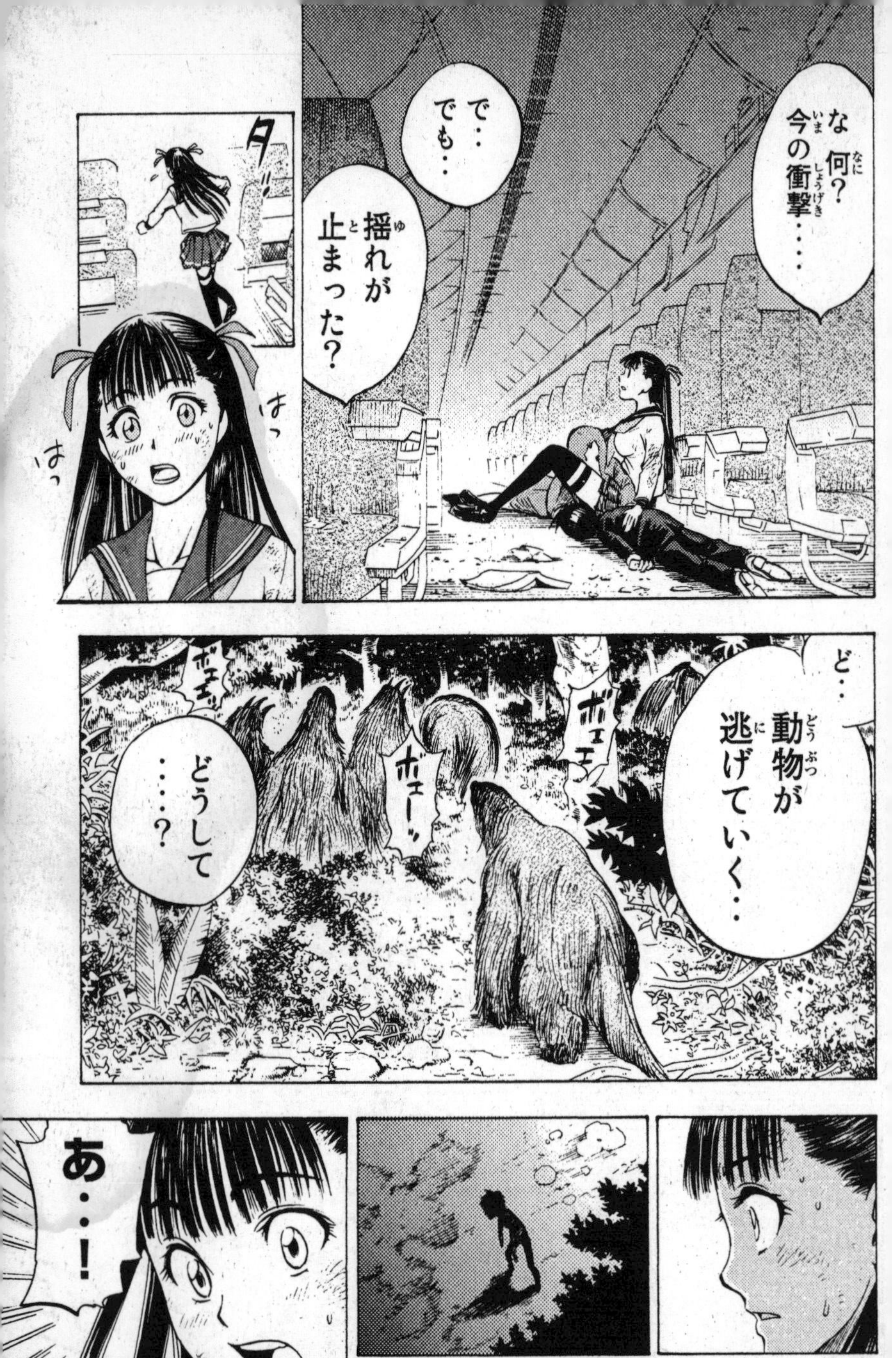

な何？今の衝撃・・・・
で・・でも・・・
揺れが止まった？
タ
はっ
はっ
ど・・動物が逃げていく・・
ボェ
ボェー
ボェ
どうして・・・？
あ・・・！

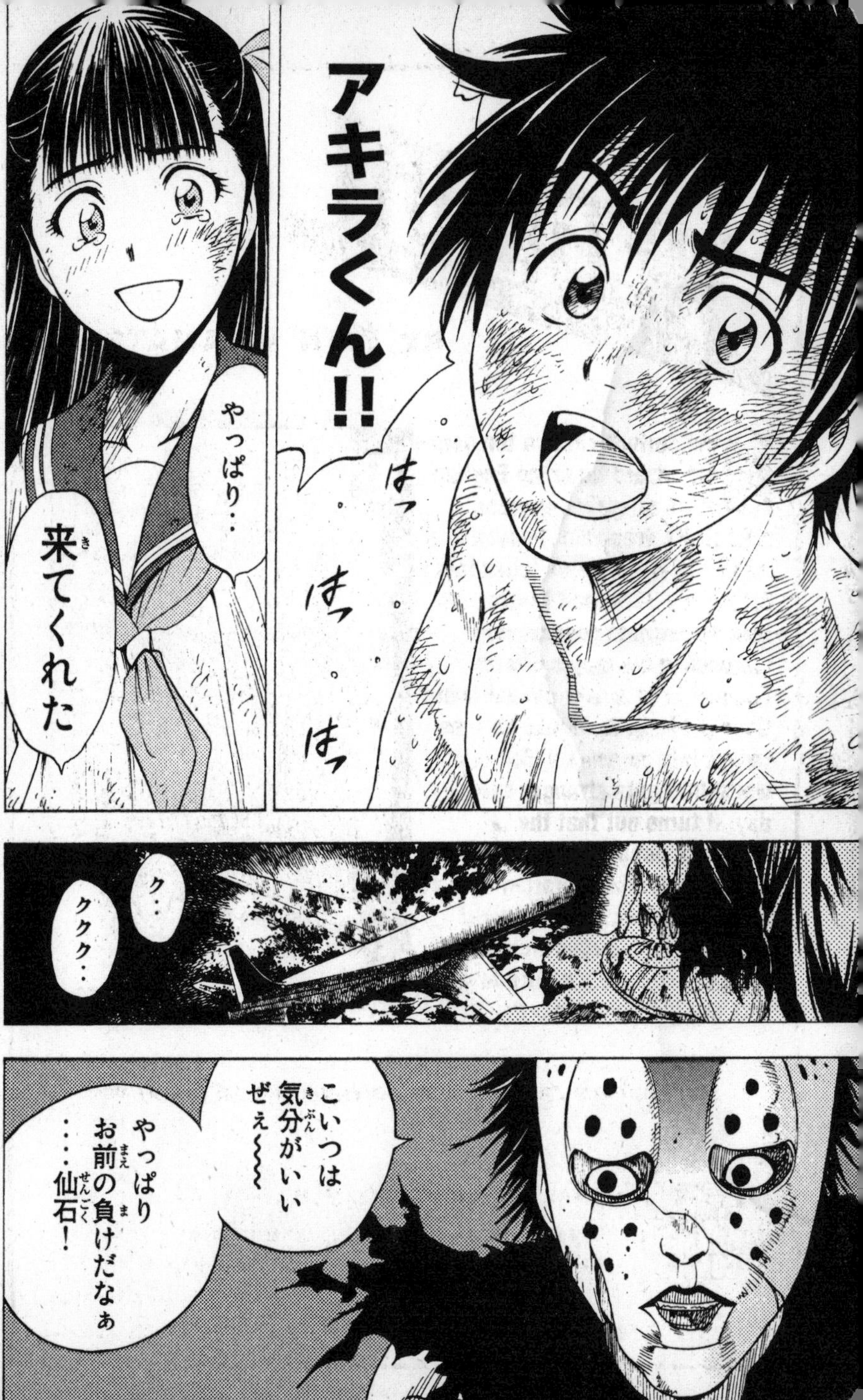
アキラくん!!
はっ
はっ
はっ
やっぱり・・
来てくれた
ク・・
ククク・・
こいつは気分がいいぜぇ〜〜〜
やっぱりお前の負けだなぁ・・・・仙石!

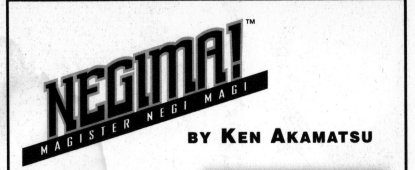

NEGIMA!™

MAGISTER NEGI MAGI

BY KEN AKAMATSU

Negi Springfield is a ten-year-old wizard teaching English at an all-girls Japanese school. He dreams of becoming a master wizard like his legendary father, the Thousand Master. At first his biggest concern was concealing his magic powers, because if he's ever caught using them publicly, he thinks he'll be turned into an ermine! But in a world that gets stranger every day, it turns out that the strangest people of all are Negi's students! From a librarian with a magic book to a centuries-old vampire, from a robot to a ninja, Negi will risk his own life to protect the girls in his care!

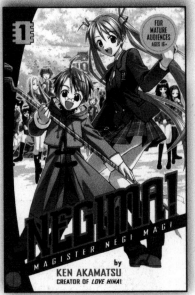

Ages: 16+

Special extras in each volume! Read them all!

VISIT WWW.KODANSHACOMICS.COM TO:
• View release date calendars for upcoming volumes
• Find out the latest about new Kodansha Comics series

Negima © 2004 Ken Akamatsu / KODANSHA LTD. All rights reserved.

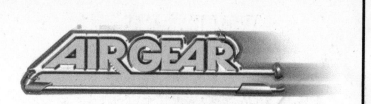

BY OH!GREAT

Itsuki Minami needs no introduction—everybody's heard of the "Babyface" of the Eastside. He's the strongest kid at Higashi Junior High School, easy on the eyes but dangerously tough when he needs to be. Plus, Itsuki lives with the mysterious and sexy Noyamano sisters. Life's never dull, but it becomes downright dangerous when Itsuki leads his school to victory over vindictive Westside punks with gangster connections. Now he stands to lose his school, his friends, and everything he cares about. But in his darkest hour, the Noyamano girls give him an amazing gift, one that just might help him save his school: a pair of Air Trecks. These high-tech skates are more than just supercool. They'll enable Itsuki to execute the wildest, most aggressive moves ever seen—and introduce him to a thrilling and terrifying new world.

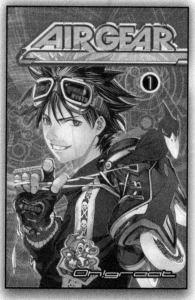

Ages: 16+

Special extras in each volume! Read them all!

KODANSHA COMICS

VISIT WWW.KODANSHACOMICS.COM TO:
• View release date calendars for upcoming volumes
• Find out the latest about new Kodansha Comics series

Air Gear © 2003 Oh!great / KODANSHA LTD. All rights reserved.

FROM HIRO MASHIMA, CREATOR OF **RAVE MASTER**

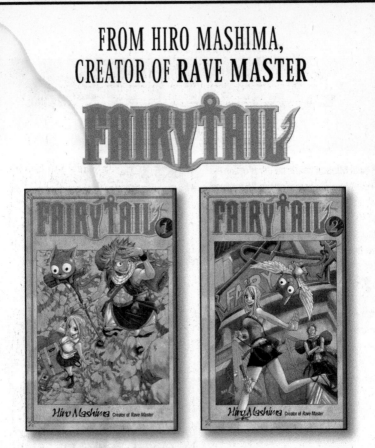

Lucy has always dreamed of joining the Fairy Tail, a club for the most powerful sorcerers in the land. But once she becomes a member, the fun really starts!

Special extras in each volume! Read them all!

RATING T AGES 13+

VISIT WWW.KODANSHACOMICS.COM TO:
- View release date calendars for upcoming volumes
- Find out the latest about new Kodansha Comics series

Fairy Tail © 2006 Hiro Mashima / KODANSHA LTD. All rights reserved.

TOMARE!

[STOP!]

You are going the wrong way!

Manga is a completely different type of reading experience.

To start at the *beginning*, go to the *end*!

That's right! Authentic manga is read the traditional Japanese way—from right to left, exactly the *opposite* of how American books are read. It's easy to follow: Just go to the other end of the book, and read each page—and each panel—from the right side to the left side, starting at the top right. Now you're experiencing manga as it was meant to be.